P9-DGE-246

175
D

THE
HOUSEWARES
STORY

A HISTORY OF THE AMERICAN HOUSEWARES INDUSTRY

Earl Lifshey

THE HOUSEWARES STORY

National Housewares Manufacturers Association | Chicago

Copyright © 1973 by the National Housewares Manufacturers Association

All rights reserved. This book or parts thereof must not
be reproduced without permission from the publisher:
National Housewares Manufacturers Association,
1130 Merchandise Mart, Chicago, Illinois 60654

Library of Congress Catalog Card Number: 72-92666

Printed in the United States of America

Contents

Preface

The publication of *The Housewares Story* is one of the proudest accomplishments of the National Housewares Manufacturers Association in its thirty-four years of service to the American Housewares Industry.

We're sure this lively and comprehensive history of a fascinating business will prove to be of great interest to all members of the industry, veterans and newcomers alike; we hope further that this important "first" will enrich their understanding of the industry and make them even more proud to be a part of the amazing conglomerate called Housewares.

It was in 1968 that the industry leaders then serving as NHMA Directors determined the time had come for "someone" to chronicle the American economic miracle that is Housewares; that someone should write the story of this lusty, sprawling giant that has grown at ever-increasing speed in the years since World War II, reaching an annual retail volume of $15 billion in 1972. They felt it was time that someone weave into words the narrative of an industry whose thousands of manufacturing plants stretch from coast to coast, and whose myriad products are found in every room in every home in the United States. No small job!

The principal question confronting the Board of Directors was *who* that someone should be. But, of course, the answer was obvious to all: Earl Lifshey, a man whose experience, background and talent eminently qualified him to take on this major production!

Fortunately for the Housewares Industry, Earl promptly accepted the commission of this exciting undertaking. He immediately began one of the most thorough and painstaking research tasks ever attempted. Earl's natural curiosity about anything and everything took over, his journalistic intuition came into full play, and he was off on what he later described as the most stimulating challenge of his almost half-century career of editorial and merchandising endeavors in the Housewares Industry.

No one but those closest to him during these past four years can fully appreciate Earl's dedication to the detective work necessary to unearth the people, the facts and the figures about an industry whose roots literally go back to the first man who cooked a piece of raw meat with a crudely improvised utensil. And no one will ever know the number of hours, nor the amount of intense effort, Earl poured into producing this sweeping history of a many-faceted industry.

The Housewares Story is of course dedicated to the thousands of men and women who make up the Housewares Industry, to those former and present manufacturers, representatives, buyers, trade press editors and others who contributed so much to this book. Without their help this thorough and comprehensive story could not have been written.

The National Housewares Manufacturers Association is proud to have played the initial role in the conception of this history of the American Housewares Industry. We hope you will share our pride and take pleasure in the intriguing historical saga that Earl Lifshey has woven in *The Housewares Story.*

Dolph Zapfel
Managing Director
National Housewares Manufacturers Association

8

With Thanks and Appreciation

I would like to thank Dolph Zapfel, managing director, and the Board of Directors of the National Housewares Manufacturers Association for inviting me to undertake this challenging assignment, and particularly for the complete editorial freedom that I had. At no time was that freedom proscribed or hampered. For the author, nothing is more important.

Such freedom carries with it complete responsibility for the book and that responsibility is, of course, mine. If, despite very diligent efforts to prevent errors, there happen to be certain errors of omission or commission, the blame is entirely mine also. However, the reader should remember that this is primarily the history of housewares, not an encyclopedia of housewares. Even in a volume of this size, the limitations of space were enormous and, for me, often almost heartbreaking.

Even if one had been able to keep a record of the hundreds of people, both in and outside the housewares industry who provided invaluable assistance of one kind or another during the four years this book was emerging, it would obviously be impractical to list them all here. Yet without their generous help and counsel, this book could never have been compiled. I want each of them to know that I shall always be most appreciative for all they did.

Special thanks and recognition go to Harcourt Brace Jovanovich, publishers of *Housewares Magazine,* formerly *House Furnishing Review.* Dating back to 1894, this pioneer trade publication provided a major source of information about the industry. The publishers have graciously permitted extensive quotations from its pages for which I am deeply grateful. And to the John Crerar Library, Chicago, for making its almost complete files of that publication so freely available, goes sincere thanks, too.

The staff of the Fort Lauderdale, Florida, public library, on which I have called repeatedly for research assistance, has not only responded very helpfully but most graciously. I am deeply indebted for all they have done.

I want to extend my particular personal thanks to James Ward and Kathleen Ineman of The Lakeside Press for the extremely helpful, encouraging assistance and guidance they provided in the final editing and design of this material. Their comprehension and understanding of the many and often difficult problems that were encountered and their skill in helping to find a happy solution went far to lighten my burden.

Finally, I am especially grateful to Susie for her understanding and untiring patience in being a "typewriter widow" during the years her husband was so engrossed in writing *The Housewares Story.*

E.L.
Fort Lauderdale, Florida 1972

9

Introduction

The artifacts of a culture, historians and archaeologists tell us, offer the most revealing evidence about what the people were like and how they lived.

The things they used in their homes have, of course, invariably been a major source of such evidence. And if some day archaeologists were dependent solely upon those artifacts we call "housewares" for information about Americans, they would tell a fascinating story.

The history of the American housewares industry reflects the development of this nation's universally admired, often envied, highest-in-the-world standard of living. What more eloquent evidence can one hope to find that illustrates how the lives—and the living, even the thinking—of a people have changed over the years than such a simple thing as a can opener, for example. Once it was a little household tool that cost ten cents—but in place of that, Americans insisted upon an electric machine that opens their cans effortlessly. A machine that costs at least one hundred times as much!

The story of American housewares is the history of an industry whose products, because of their extreme diversity, reveal clearly and comprehensively the fabulous progress of technology and manufacturing processes over the years.

It is a history that embraces the story of the countless remarkable new materials that continue to be developed every day. This book tells the detailed story of the American housewares industry. It is a dynamic industry, producing hundreds of thousands of products that, to a far greater extent in this country than anywhere else, make life's daily housekeeping chores easier, less time-consuming, and more pleasant.

It may come as a surprise to some people that America's great housewares industry, according to the best estimates, accounted for almost $15 billion in retail sales in 1972. Yet it really is not an industry at all! Nowhere in the pages of the absorbing *Standard Industrial Classification Manual,* which lists and officially numbers almost every industry in this country, will you find "housewares."

But the omission isn't due to an error on the part of the Office of Statistical Standard, United States Government Bureau of the Budget, which compiles and publishes the manual. It is merely a formal indication that, technically at least, housewares fails to qualify officially as an industry because of its great diversity of somewhat unrelated products. With all due deference to the SIC, however, the housewares business has deservedly earned recognition as an industry in its own right.

Its record of growth and accomplishment is tremendously impressive. Never has the industry been more dynamic than it is now; never has its wide and deep feeling of self-confidence been more justified. But it is a feeling sharply tempered by an acute awareness that success never arrives without including in its baggage new demands and increased responsibilities.

The housewares business is not merely unique; it is something of a phenomenon. Basically, it is a conglomeration of several hundred thousand of the most diverse and seemingly unrelated consumer products—coffee makers and pruning shears, garbage pails and oven thermometers, floor mops and picnic grills, shower curtains and...you name it!

To complicate this complexity even more, the production of this merchandise is spread among thousands of manufacturers of all types and sizes, in scores of different officially listed industries located practically everywhere in these fifty United States.

This industry, by its very nature, is something special. Its diversity endows the housewares business with a degree of strength and stamina it would not otherwise enjoy—an economic characteristic of vital importance. The confluence of so many different fields of activity, the centralized focus of such marketing and merchandising activity for such a wide range of products, provides a built-in dynamism and internal drive few other industries can match. None can surpass it.

Yet that diversity has its drawbacks and weaknesses. For one example, getting really representative, thoroughly dependable industrywide statistics is an extremely difficult if not impossible task. Some progress has been made but there is still a long, hard road ahead in this area.

Of course it is not until these thousands of different items are assembled and displayed for sale in retail stores that, collectively, they finally assume their public identity as housewares. And it is that all-inclusive word, housewares, by which the nation's homemakers have come to know and to want the innumerable practical and pretty products that, literally, are gathered from all corners of the earth by this industry.

It was the emergence of the department store in the latter half of the past century that spawned the housewares department as we have come to know it. The conditions and economics of those days encouraged the expansion of housewares departments. Some of the great department stores, many of which have long since passed into the pages of history, had housewares departments of enormous size, owing less to the extensive assortment of items than to the practice of maintaining large stocks of goods on the selling floor. Such refinements as cost accounting and the pressure for getting maximum sales per square foot did not come until much later.

Departments of such magnitude, it must be remembered, marked great progress for house furnishing goods. For years before then (and to tell the truth, a great many times since), such merchandise

12

was considered by most merchants as something of a necessary evil, to be tolerated, but certainly never promoted.

Flashback to Sunday, October 9, 1881, when *The New York Times's* retail advertising was concentrated on one page. What does the reader see? Not one advertisement for house furnishings.

"Silks and Velvets…Millinery and Trimmings…Genuine Alexandre Kid Gloves…Ribbons and Laces and Fine French Flowers… Black Satin Merveilleux and Black Cashmere…Hats and Bonnets …and a Full Line of Mourning Goods…." But not a line, not a word about house furnishings—even in the advertisement of a store called R. H. Macy and Company.

Those were the days when feather dusters, coal scuttles, and wash boilers, along with sad irons and a few similar, equally utilitarian and unglamorous items that composed the entire house furnishing goods stock were invariably to be found down in the basement, all but hidden under the stairs.

Today the housewares industry has grown to a size and sophistication that no one in 1881 could possibly have imagined. Today the average large department store housewares department carries an assortment of from twenty-five thousand to thirty thousand items, if not more. No one who has ever browsed through such a department can fail to be impressed by the seemingly unlimited, almost bewildering array of products on sale.

There is, it seems, virtually no task inside, outside, or, for that matter, anywhere else around the home for which someone, somewhere, in the long, long aisles of the housewares industry has not developed a device of some sort by which, he hopes, the task in question will be made painless or even a pleasure. For the housewares industry, the "affluent society" is no mere phrase or convenient label. Make that better mousetrap—or better anything else that will take the irk out of housework— and the American homemaker is usually ready, willing, and able to add it to the never ending collection of equipment that challenges the chores of Home, Sweet Home.

It should not be denied even by the industry's staunchest supporters that there are times when the enthusiastic commercial urge of such creative ingenuity generates a speed that leaves practicality far behind. Fortunately that does not occur very often. But it *does* occur, and then the eager purchaser discovers that using an entrancing new gadget or gimmick proves to be far more bother than the original chore it was created to simplify!

However, the magic touch of a Prince Charming called "Merchandising" has transformed a once homely Cinderella business into one whose products now radiate beauty of form and color. Fashion has become an integral and important part of housewares. No longer is it sufficient for competitive survival that a product be practical and well made. Those qualities are now taken for granted (unfortunately, sometimes lucklessly), and in this new era of consumer protection all products had better be all of that.

Bloomingdale's poster announces a sale on "a new art form"—housewares.

But just that is no longer enough. Now a housewares product must be beautifully designed and styled in just the right fashion colors. Today's color isn't just color per se; it must be in style.

In a relatively short time fashion has come a long way in the housewares industry. But how far it has come was neatly pinpointed in 1969 when Bloomingdale's, New York, which has one of the finest housewares departments in the country, announced its fall housewares sale with a colorful poster of striking geometric design and only these few words: *"Housewares—A New Art Form...Sixth Floor."*

In the dim past, ironmongery, as household utensils were then known, found its way to the consumer in simple, direct ways. There was, for example, the smithy (who often made at least part of it); the general merchandise or hardware merchant; the Yankee tin peddler; the jobbers; and then the mail-order newcomers.

It is in relatively recent times, as products proliferated, that their distribution has also proliferated so amazingly. In the words of Jimmy Durante, "Everybody wants to get into the act"; and from what one now sees around the marketplace, almost everybody in the retail business sells housewares.

Some of the earliest to be attracted were the so-called drug stores. The discount stores, of course, cut their eyeteeth on electric housewares back in the postdepression era when such merchandise still carried a list price and those "stores" were often nothing more than a small room in an obscure corner of an upper floor in some big city office building. "But," it was whispered by those in the know, "they can get it for you wholesale!"

Then there were the house-to-house operators; the jewelry stores with their "dollar down and fifty cents a week plan"; the furniture stores, who also loved these "account openers"; the variety stores, which even when they were merely "five and tens," leaned heavily on housewares. Then came the supermarkets with their rack jobbers; the auto supply stores; and gas and oil stations, not to overlook the premium and trading stamp fields, in which modern housewares now play a major role. One is prompted to ask, "Is there no end to it?" The answer is undoubtedly no.

It is no exaggeration to add that all this would be impossible if it were not for the National Housewares Expositions, which the National Housewares Manufacturers Association holds for the industry semiannually on a nonprofit basis. Nothing reflects the growth of the industry more dramatically than this show—the largest individual trade exposition held under one roof anywhere in the entire world.

The show provides a huge funnel of distribution through which a never ending array of housewares products from thousands of worldwide sources, large and small, flows for the personal inspection and buying convenience of housewares merchants who come from all over the world.

The show accomplishes all this at a low cost and with an efficiency unsurpassed. The value of it to the industry is inestimable.

Beat the Big One

HEART ATTACK

One American dies every 48 seconds from Heart Attack. 660,000 every year. back. Here's what you can do to **One—HEART ATTACK.**

know the symptoms?

ual warnings are:

- Prolonged, heavy pressure or squeezing pain in the *center* of the chest, behind the breastbone.
- Pain may spread to the shoulder, arm, neck or jaw.
- Pain or discomfort is often accompanied by sweating.
- Nausea, vomiting and shortness of breath may also occur.

Half of all Heart Attack deaths occur before the victim gets to the hospital.

Thank you
for your contribution to the
HEART FUND
Signed _Carol Tracker_
Heart Fund Volunteer Date 2/25/23

s industry that in its ranks ging from the big corpora- ls to the small, individual es. Sometimes these firms erchandise; but often some d that they are well repre- art, the manufacturers of dium-size companies.

possible for even a very small newcomer can main- an thrive and grow in the narketplace is something v much intrinsic merit the ent and money there is to and ingenuity can go very get.

vity in the industry toward seemed the most logical of small manufacturers of ogether in some sort of a very slow in coming, but mergers, a notable num- e in housewares in recent

has such a unique and main so relatively cohe- and function collectively

the housewares industry assumes its identity with ustry's semiannual trade ness" and industry cohe-

And that semiannual show—What makes *it* possible? For that the industry itself must get all the credit. Beginning soon after the turn of the century, the house furnishing goods industry engaged in twenty-five years of trial-and-error seeking to find itself—looking for some way to achieve self-recognition, if not survival as an industry. Looking for self-fulfillment perhaps. In any case, it was immature, confused, and awkward. But the country was growing and so was the industry.

In 1927 much of the frustration came to an end. The National House Furnishing Manufacturers Association (later the NHMA) was organized. The following January it staged its first industry-sponsored, nonprofit trade show—and the housewares business was on the way to finding itself.

There were a great many difficulties. For a time the friction between rival associations threatened to destroy all the hard-earned progress and set the industry back many years. Finally, goodwill and wisdom prevailed.

There is no known record of anyone having made a particularly ringing speech around that time calling for "industry leadership," or warning in so many eloquent words that the survival and salvation of the housewares business depended upon the willingness and ability of all those different kinds of manufacturers to concentrate on their common purpose—rather than to divide and die over their differences. What is of paramount importance is that the housewares industry has demonstrated the kind of leadership and self-discipline of which any industry could be justifiably proud.

And even more to this industry's credit, it was not a one-man show. As different companies were called upon to contribute the time and counsel of their top executives to plan the policies and guide the course of the NHMA, there was always a prompt response and wholehearted cooperation. It is a salutary situation when the members of a highly competitive industry consistently manage to give such an account of themselves, and the record of their dedicated services speaks for itself.

Here, then, is a report of that record. It starts at the very beginning—because it is only when we look back to see where we once were that we can fully appreciate just how far we have come. It is a report based upon the diligent and conscientious efforts of scores of extremely helpful people, both within and outside the industry.

Most regrettably, however, as the housewares people themselves can appreciate and understand better than anyone else, it is impossible, even in a book as large as this, for such a report to be as complete from every standpoint as one would want it to be. Maybe—but only maybe—that could have been done fifty years ago, but not today. All of which again speaks eloquently for the industry's gigantic growth.

The general guidelines that have governed the selection and presentation of material in this report have been an evaluation of its basic contribution to the "state of the art" of housewares. In some instances, despite intensive research, little or no factual information is any longer available. In other areas the enormous amount of information and material available created difficult problems of elimination and selection.

Even though there have been unavoidable and certainly unintentional omissions—as well as, no doubt, a share of equally unintentional errors of commission—it is hoped that the housewares story as related here will provide a judicious and accurate account of America's great housewares industry.

16

THE
HOUSEWARES
STORY

in the beginning

The beginning…just when was it? When you go back far enough the most appropriate place to start the history of housewares is with the first culinary item of all: the stick—the simple wooden skewer—on which prehistoric man hung his meat while it cooked. Or, to be precise, while it broiled.

If the skewer lacked certain efficiencies in performance and refinements in design, at least the cost was right. It even had the very modern advantage of being disposable after use.

Cooking food—and later, preparing and storing it—have always been matters of the most vital necessity for man; his very life depends on it. Thus food and the implements and utensils he devised for it, have shared a unique relationship right from the beginning.

Down through the ages, mostly by accident, man has left a record of that relationship. All over the world, too, archaeologists have long been engaged in sifting and sorting out the most significant and important visible evidence they discover.

In the great museums of many countries where these ancient housewares are now on view, they tell a fascinating, though silently eloquent, story of how our forebears once went about the business of keeping house, such as it was, with the kind of things which today we would call housewares…things they used for preparing and cooking food, for eating and drinking, for cleaning and washing. As one looks at these pieces of the past, it requires little imagination to visualize them in actual use. How very far we have come since then.

For the kitchen or the counting house? In any case, a weighing vessel was a luxury item in bronze. From Pompeii, Italy.

Courtesy Field Museum of Natural History, Chicago.

Dating from the seventh to the second century, B.C., tombs of the Etruscans, an ancient people of Italy, have yielded a variety of household articles of such surprising modernity that they would cause little comment if reproduced today. This saucepan of bronze was made for a very discriminating clientele! From Pompeii, Italy.

Courtesy Field Museum of Natural History, Chicago.

Shallow pans for frying were already distinguished from the deeper saucepans. Bronze, with elegantly decorated handles. From Pompeii, Italy.

Courtesy Field Museum of Natural History, Chicago.

Until recent times, kettles were large, all purpose boiling pots, like this Etruscan model. Bronze. From Pompeii, Italy.

Courtesy Field Museum of Natural History, Chicago.

Found wherever ancient stone age man has lived, from 500,000 B.C. to Neolithic times (10,000 B.C.), these beautifully flaked flint tools provide the proof that man has entered the stage of humanity on his upward march to civilization.

Courtesy Field Museum of Natural History, Chicago.

Yet some things are familiar. The Field Museum in Chicago displays a cast iron stove of the Han Dynasty of China. With five holes for cooking pots and a chimney, this stove appears to be modern. Stoves similar to this, fired by wood or coal, were to last into the twentieth century even in advanced industrial countries like our own.

Man's environment and the materials he finds there—or can create—have always governed the things he has been able to conceive and produce. While it is true that technical accomplishments through the ages generate a cumulative benefit, it is a most significant fact that in just the last one hundred years we have developed more technological skill than in all the previous centuries together.

It was a half a million years ago, anthropologists tell us, when man first learned the use of fire and began to make recognizable tools. Not until 5000 B.C. did he learn to weave baskets and make crude pottery. By 3500 B.C. he had started to work copper, bronze, and gold. A thousand years later he found out how to make glass and in 2500 B.C. metal working in iron began.

The story of those accomplishments have been recorded in great

Vegetable strainers with a decorative pattern which raises them far above the merely utilitarian. Bronze, of course. From Pompeii, Italy.

Courtesy Field Museum of Natural History, Chicago.

The common folk used earthenware tripod vessels which could be conveniently set over a low fire. This more elaborate (and costly) bronze model was made for palace or temple use. From China, Chou Dynasty (the era of Confucius), 1100-200 B.C.

Courtesy Field Museum of Natural History, Chicago.

They were evidently popping corn way back, and this one is both beautiful and practical. 200 B.C. to 600 A.D. Peru, Mochica Culture.

Courtesy Field Museum of Natural History, Chicago.

Classic in design and function—a cooking vessel. Chinese, Han Dynasty, 200 B.C. to 200 A.D.

Courtesy Field Museum of Natural History, Chicago.

Some may remember the giant apple ice buckets of the 1930s. This melon-shaped motif preceded them by about a thousand years. From Peru.

Courtesy Field Museum of Natural History, Chicago.

An almost timeless item. Bronze iron, with a smooth bottom surface, the receptacle was filled with live charcoal. Handle usually of ivory. Decorative and, today, the perfect ash tray. Chinese.

Courtesy Robert J. Alexander.

Found in a bog at Castlederg, County Tyrone, Northern Ireland, this cauldron is made of beaten bronze sheeting. From about 700 B.C.

Courtesy National Museum of Ireland.

An elegantly decorated bronze kettle, ceremonial, or perhaps for the evening rice of a well-to-do family. Chinese, Han Dynasty, 200 B.C. to 200 A.D.

Courtesy Field Museum of Natural History, Chicago.

Sturdy stone mortars and pestles for the grinding of household grains and spices. From Mesopotamia, Old Babylonian, 2500 B.C.

Courtesy Field Museum of Natural History, Chicago.

Where else but from France—Gaul as it was known to the Romans—could have come this adjunct to the pastrycook's art. A charming item in the prevailing bronze-work. 200 A.D.

Courtesy Musée des Antiquités Nationales, St. Germain, France.

This looks like a whistling jar although it is not possible to test it today. 200 B.C. to 600 A.D. Mochica Culture, Peru.

Courtesy Field Museum of Natural History, Chicago.

All ready to receive a batch of popovers. An Etruscan bronze utensil for the oven. From Pompeii, Italy.

Courtesy Field Museum of Natural History, Chicago.

From the Mediterranean to China, jars of this shape were once universal for storage of oil, grains, wine, and even scrolls! They ranged in size from gigantic (six-foot high by six-foot across) on down. This one happens to be Chinese, Tang Dynasty, from 600-900 A.D.

Courtesy Field Museum of Natural History, Chicago.

detail over the centuries in endless shelves of books. A history of the relatively modern housewares industry would be woefully lacking without a brief, backward glance at its rich, ancient heritage. For that reason a few random examples of the past have been included here.

No one can look upon these treasures without marveling at the superb craftsmanship and exquisite sense of design and color they reveal. True, unlike the mass-produced conveniences of today which millions of people enjoy, many of these magnificent old artifacts are things made at great cost for the exclusive use of the rich and mighty. In other instances, they were created for some special religious or regal ceremony.

These ancient "housewares" tell at least part of the story of man's great source of ingenuity in creating devices with which to prepare, store, and cook his food, devices, which, in modified form, have managed to travel on down the centuries.

Here, then, is the briefest kind of glimpse at the housewares industry's immense and fascinating past.

An INDUSTRY Finds Itself

When was the first housewares show held? A good question.

But ask the next ten housewares people you meet and see how many can give you the correct answer. Actually, the first housewares show was held in New York in 1906.

The shows and conventions of the last sixty years or so are relatively recent developments. They are modern versions of the timeless fairs where artisans and traders would meet periodically to buy, sell, or barter one another's wares.

The very name *fair*, derived from the Latin *feriae*, meaning "feasts," provides an excellent clue to their origin. In the Middle Ages people from the countryside would gather at least once each year for some religious festival and celebrate by holding a feast.

Local "manufacturers" and "merchants" were quick to recognize the importance of these festivals. Like their present-day counterparts, they realized that "people are markets," and they would cater to the needs of those markets every time the people gathered to celebrate a religious festival.

Each succeeding fair seemed bigger and better—for very good reason. Religion was the dominating influence in the Middle Ages, and no one would willingly absent himself from an important church festival. It was a holy day, but the holiday aspect became very evident. There was always a good turnout of potential customers for the merchants.

Soon the church or the local ruling authorities (often one and the same), never slow to avail themselves of new sources of revenue, began to impose tolls and taxes on this thriving new commerce. The now inescapable exhibit fee had begun!

At least three of these early fairs became world-famous and still continue to flourish. They are worthy of special note here because housewares have been an important part of their exhibits for many, many years.

The well-known Frankfurt International Fair dates back to 1050; the Cologne International Fair started in 1360; and the Leipzig Trade Fair (now in East Germany) traces its beginnings to 1229.

Attendance at these events, usually held in spring and fall, was a must for every large department store and hardware-housewares

Opposite page: *The Copper Shop* by Dean Cornwell. The beginnings of an industry in a simpler age. This page: a tin peddler.

The Bettmann Archive.

25

26

The main hall and exterior of the Crystal Palace in London, 1851.
The Bettmann Archive.

wholesale buyer until the world wars all but destroyed their pre-eminence. "It is nothing new for American merchandisers to take advantage of the opportunities at the Leipzig Fair," reported *House Furnishing Review* (now *Housewares* magazine) in 1929, adding, "In fact, as far back as 1834 eight of them did so, crossing the Atlantic in sailing vessels and traveling to the fair by stage coach."

The commerce that took place at the early trade fairs over the centuries eventually resulted in the adoption of standards and practices so that strangers as well as acquaintances might readily do business. Standards of weight, measure, and quality were established; so were standards of value for mediums of exchange. Much of this later became the basis of commercial law.

One of the most important practices to emerge was credit. Originally all buying and selling at the fairs was consummated immediately, and the purchased goods were delivered on the spot. The limit to the amount of business one could do depended upon how much stock one could manage to bring along. But methods of transportation improved over the years, and the dangers of travel were reduced. With the use of credit, traders discovered not only that they could do business from a sample, but also that it was far more practical, enabling them to make many more sales than was previously possible under the cash and carry system. The relatively modern concept of the "sample fairs" emerged.

Modern Trade Shows

The worldwide scientific and industrial revolution that had been slowly developing during the first half of the nineteenth century undoubtedly helped to spawn the concept of great world fairs, where nations could compete with each other in exhibiting their technological achievements. The first of these was the unprecedented Exposition of the Industry of All Nations held at the breathtaking Crystal Palace in London in 1851. It was the first of some fifty similar world fairs that would be held during the next 120 years, each seeking to outshine its predecessor.

But these new world expositions, although wonderfully impressive for the general public and highly gratifying to national vanity, were too big and too broad to be of much immediate value to business and industry. So, as business and industry became more and more sophisticated, they began to develop their own specialized trade shows, just as the professions began holding their own annual meetings and conventions.

Trade shows became increasingly popular among American manufacturers, wholesalers, and retailers during the nineteenth century. Among the organizations of that era devoted to furthering the young nation's technological achievements, one of the most prestigious was (and still is) the Franklin Institute of the State of Pennsylvania for the Promotion of the Mechanic Arts, founded at Philadelphia in 1824.

In 1830 the Institute held the first of what, for many years, was to be its Annual Exhibition of American Manufacturers, perhaps the first, and certainly one of the earliest, formal exhibits in which "housekeeping articles" were included. The event came to be something of an official showcase, so to speak, of America's fast-emerging industries.

"Our present exhibition presents highly gratifying evidence of the growth of American manufacturers, and gives a prescience of the perfection they are destined to attain," declared Owen Evans, chairman of the committee on exhibitions, in opening the seventeenth show in 1847. Evans proceeded to make a rather profound observation,

> Every year there is a curtailment of our dependence upon the workshops of other countries.... By dint of skill, perseverance and industry, we successfully compete with densely populated districts of other countries.... There is, in the American people, an innate energy seeming to have a latent existence that is equivalent to whatever task is imposed—material for any and every emergency. We have but to proclaim a want and it is met, let the obstacles be what they may.

EVERYBODY

WILL BE THERE

MEET US AT THE

BIG SHOW

Madison Square Garden

NEW YORK

AUGUST 6 to 11

House Furnishing Goods Exhibition Company

EXECUTIVE OFFICE: 59-61 PARK PLACE. NEW YORK

The very first house furnishing exhibition in the United States—and possibly the world—was held in 1906.

Courtesy House Furnishing Review.

Isbon Scott was the founder and editor of *House Furnishing Review* as well as the driving force behind the initial house furnishings exhibition.

Courtesy House Furnishing Review.

In a manner that is almost rhapsodic, Evans recognized the significance of housekeeping articles on display.

> Undoubtedly the circumstances of woman are greatly improved by the advancements in the arts of life....The home that is made more delightful by the multiplication of domestic comforts is more attractive to him in whose presence woman should delight. The freedom that a refined mind enjoys from former prescribed toil may be beautifully employed in augmenting and strengthening domestic and social affections....Those who are to profit by these changes should smile upon the means by which these changes are produced....Woman [he never refers to "women"] should come hither to cheer the efforts by which her domestic, her social and her religious condition is improved.

Housekeeping articles have never had such a buildup before or since. Among the "domestic comforts" he mentioned were a combination shower bath, washstand, and dressing table, a butter churn made so the dashers could be removed for cleaning, and an icebox lined with zinc and filled in with pulverized charcoal, with movable shelves. No prices were quoted since this was an exhibit, not a fair.

The Early Housewares Shows

During all those nineteenth-century years "kitchen furnishing goods" or, as they were later referred to, "house furnishings," had almost no identity of their own. They were regarded merely as a less important part of hardware. Of course hardware itself was considered most important. As the country became more industrialized it naturally developed facilities and skill with which to produce more "kitchen furnishing goods" along with industrial and commercial hardware.

As early as 1890, the hardware associations began to organize and hold annual conventions; but apparently none of these gatherings included any exhibits of merchandise. It was not until the twentieth century that house furnishings finally emerged from under the concealing shadows of hardware and achieved sufficient public recognition to warrant a show of their own. The man who made that possible has earned the everlasting esteem of the housewares industry.

Isbon B. Scott was a man of great vision and determination who lived to be ninety-one. He began his career as a cabin boy during the Civil War on "Old Ironsides," the U.S.S. Constitution. After leaving the navy in 1877 he became a newspaperman with the old *New York Evening Post.* He then took his journalistic experience to Philadelphia, where he participated in establishing a new trade journal, the *Upholsterer.*

But Scott was eager for a publication of his own. One day, while browsing through a New York department store where "housekeeping articles" were scattered throughout many departments, he got the idea to combine them all into one logical department.

He soon discovered that some stores had at least a semblance of a selection for "kitchen furnishings," but not much more. Yet he

Itinerant salesman selling housewares on a New York City street.
The Bettmann Archive

was encouraged by the potential he visualized for such merchandise and the support he felt could be obtained. In Philadelphia in June 1892 he launched a trade paper of his own: *House Furnishing Review*. It began to prosper right from the beginning, though modestly.

Within a few years after the first issue of the *Review* appeared, Scott became increasingly aware of the need for a house furnishings show. There was a greater assortment of products than ever before, gaining more recognition and attention all the time. A formal show like the automobile or sportsman shows, he reasoned, not only could be advantageous from a trade standpoint, it could be opened to the public as well. In that way, house furnishings would get great public exposure and everyone would benefit.

It was in 1905 that Isbon Scott finally decided to do something about it. He began making definite plans to promote a house fur-

From top: George T. Brown, who represented the A. L. Baron Manufacturing Company, did business with housewares buyers around the end of the century. In those days, housewares buyers for department stores were almost czars in authority—and often looked the part. Frank Leffler, who later became an important manufacturers sales rep, was housewares buyer for Lord & Taylor, then on Grand Street in New York. Squire Hess was buyer for Bloomingdale's in New York.

nishing show to be held the following year from August 6–11 in no less a place than New York's already famous Madison Square Garden.

Although it had already been the scene of various shows, including the first automobile show, the idea of holding a show for "kitchen furnishing goods" was totally new. Many persons, both in the trade as well as out of it, did not hesitate to say what they thought of such an idea. Not much.

But Scott was not one to be dismissed lightly. His successful trade magazine gave him the right vehicle for promoting his idea. And Scott was not content to merely be *in* an industry; he also had to be a large part *of* it.

One of the first things he did was to organize the House Furnishing Exhibition Company to handle the show. He was president; T. C. LeFevre was general manager.

Although this was to be primarily a trade gathering for the express purpose of making sales, it would also be open during the evening hours "to educate the public to the immensity of labor-saving devices and economical mechanisms" that the then infant industry was already making available to America's homemakers.

Isbon Scott proved to be as persuasive a salesman for his show idea as he was for his magazine, and by the time summer arrived the House Furnishing Goods Exhibition was a sure thing. It proved to be a historic first, and it established a precedent for a practice which would be repeated almost every year thereafter in some form or other.

The sponsors of Scott's ambitious undertaking were determined to make it a success. They enlisted the support of the lively and important Merchants Association of New York, which then arranged a railroad certificate plan for a special one and one-third round trip rate for buyers anywhere in the country who wanted to attend the New York show. It even mailed out 125,000 circulars to stores in the United States and in Mexico (whose railroads, incidentally, also extended the reduced fare).

The very first exhibition in this country, and probably the world, devoted exclusively to house furnishing was a "hot" show in more ways than one. When it opened its doors that Monday morning, New York City was in the grip of a scorching heat wave. The temperature was 103° in the shade and 120° in the sun, according to *The New York Times,* and caused fourteen deaths and countless prostrations.

Although the show was ignored as unimportant by the daily papers, editor Isbon Scott gave it a glowing account in the next (September) issue of *House Furnishing Review:*

Greatest of all events in the history of the house furnishing trade was the House Furnishing Goods Exhibition held in Madison Square Garden, New York City, the week of August 6-11. Planned to achieve the much desired result of facilitating the operations of both manufacturer and retailer, and to further commercial relationships and cement business friendships, as well as to give the trade a general uplift toward a higher round of prosperity, this Big Show established a record along these lines that shall never be broken save by itself. Upon no previous occasion were there so many buyers and sellers assembled under one roof.

A more personal account of the first show was recalled by John E. Postley who, before his death in 1968 had represented the S. J. Bailey & Sons line of unpainted furniture for many years. As a boy he had often assisted his father, a manufacturers sales representative who had attended the 1906 event.

> The success of that show, I often heard my father relate, was largely due to an immense bar conveniently situated along the entire length of the building. Much of the business, naturally, was done in the booths, where displays were set up in an old-fashioned way. But a great deal of it, he told me, was transacted at that bar. Various buyers, especially the more important ones from the big stores, held court at the bar, and as soon as a salesman finished his business with one buyer, he would go on to another.

The first Madison Square Garden Show was so successful that it was repeated the following August. It also initiated a whole series of shows that, for the next twenty-five or thirty years, were to be identified with the house furnishing industry. Some were primarily consumer oriented; others were confined to the trade; and often they were combinations of the two.

Such shows with prospects for a quick dollar have always held a particular appeal to promoters with little or no interest in the industry. Buyers were quick to recognize the shows that served their needs and began to refer to the others as "joke shows."

It was not until 1928 that the industry finally took itself and the show seriously by setting up its own association, primarily to conduct its own shows.

The Second Industry Show

The second (1907) show in Madison Square Garden was also operated by Isbon Scott's House Furnishing Goods Exhibition Company. And again the September issue of his *Review* reported the event— but with a marked lack of enthusiasm compared with the review of the first show. The story makes no reference to the unfavorable business conditions in the country at the time (culminating in the financial panic of 1907), which apparently had some effect on the show. What seemed more significant to the *Review* reporter, however, was the very existence of a second industry show. He relates:

> That the promoters of the first show were correct in their theory that the house furnishing goods field was large enough to warrant an exhibition of the products it embraced was exemplified in the initial show that was an unqualified success. That such a success could be repeated was demonstrated in the 1907 exhibition, which was larger in point of number of exhibitors, many of whom were patrons of the initial undertaking.

From top: More housewares buyers from the early part of this century... J. B. Sheridan followed Frank Leffler at Lord & Taylor, and John Postley, uncle of the John Postley who later became sales representative for S. J. Bailey & Sons Inc., was buyer for Posner Brothers, Baltimore.

View of the Second Annual National Housefurnishings show held in Madison Square Garden in New York, August 19 to 26, 1907. *Courtesy House Furnishing Review.*

In 1900 women buyers of house furnishings were almost unknown—except for such rare instances as Miss B. Beuhler at Shoneman Brothers, Philadelphia. She managed what was called the entire "below the sidewalk" store, including "housefurnishings, bric-a-brac, lamps, crockery, glassware, trunks, toys and dolls."

Again the show opened to the public in the evening. No figures are given, but "each succeeding day saw an increased attendance and in the evenings the vast expanse of the floor was actually crowded....As a commercial proposition the exhibition amply repaid every exhibitor for the trouble and expense gone to in making a display of his productions," adds the *Review.*

Whether because of the 1907 financial crisis or some other reason, that fall Isbon Scott sold his *Review* and dissolved the House Furnishing Goods Exhibition Company. Yet he announced that he had arranged with New York's Grand Central Palace to stage another show there in 1908, during the week of March 2.

"It will," he promised, "be conducted strictly as a trade show," which meant one thing: no consumers allowed. "All the objectional features of the House Furnishing Goods Exhibitions heretofore [he had never even mentioned them previously!] will be eliminated. Twenty thousand square feet have been allocated for it and arrangements will far surpass any former attempt in this line."

The third show was not an overwhelming success. "While not so large as previous shows, as regards the number of exhibitors," reported the *Review,* "it was no less successful in other respects. So far as the attendance at the show, there was much complaint by the exhibitors in the early part of the week. Before the week was over, it began to dawn on them that this was as it should be. The general public was excluded." The end of the 1908 show also marked the end of Isbon Scott's role in these events.

Two years would elapse before someone tried another show. Then, in 1910, a Philadelphia promoter named Charles D. Axman staged a house furnishing show in Philadelphia's Exposition Hall that attracted over seventy thousand persons in one week. Looking for even greater success, Axman announced a National Household Show for Madison Square Garden in late August.

Although the *Review* had earlier endorsed the idea of a show just for the trade, it came out wholeheartedly for this event, which was open to the public as well. It received only mild support from housewares manufacturers, but the show was a great success. "Every night the aisles were packed solid with a seething mass of humanity," said the *Review.*

"The only Sight-seeing Company stopping at Grant's Tomb"—a side trip from the 1906 Exhibition.
Courtesy House Furnishing Review.

New York's Madison Square Garden was the site for the first industry shows. This is the Garden circa 1903.

From top: John T. Leadstone in 1902 when he was buyer for the William Bingham Company, Cleveland. William J. Reid, housewares buyer for the William Barr Dry Goods Company, St. Louis.

This was how the first "Household Show" in Chicago looked. It was held in the Coliseum in May 1912 and "drew great crowds" since it was open to the public as well as the trade.
Courtesy House Furnishing Review.

From top: Jacob "Jake" Kohnfelder was a popular housewares buyer for the former A. I. Namm store in Brooklyn. Buyers changed jobs often; Kohnfelder later went to Pittsburgh's Gimbel's and then to Chicago's Siegel Cooper & Company. Max Funkenstein was housewares buyer in 1903 for Chicago's Siegel Cooper, which also had a store in New York.

Axman repeated his show in 1911. But by that time the feeling for a really good, representative trade show was so pronounced that *House Furnishing Review* finally declared:

> It is certain that out of town buyers have been fooled so often that they will no longer make an effort, or go very far out of their way to attend any more trade shows promoted and conducted by private individuals. In a word, it is up to the manufacturers...to promote and conduct these shows cooperatively if they expect the leading buyers in the trade to attend....Judging from opinions expressed by the management of this year's show [obviously Axman], private individuals are not likely to promote another household exhibition for some years to come.

But such a show was still a long way off. In May 1912 another group of promoters headed by David P. Convey put on an Exhibition of House Furnishing and Furniture at the Chicago Coliseum. According to *House Furnishing Review* the following month, "The exhibitors were well satisfied, so much so that they engaged space for the show next year, for it is practically settled that it will be an annual affair." Of course it did not become an annual event at that time, despite the observation of the reporter who covered the event that "the citizens of Chicago are alert and vigorous, full of the atmosphere of the West, and it is all the same to them whether it is a World's Fair or a strike, a cement show or a household show—they don't start anything they can't finish."

In the following year, 1913, a trade show came one step closer to reality, for reasons that sound very familiar today. "In the house furnishing trade we never had a truly representative show," said an editorial in *House Furnishing Review* in June 1913.

> The reason for this has been because the promoters in former years have asked prohibitive prices for space, which was further added to by the extra expense necessary when the exhibitor arrived at the ex-

34

hibition, for the decoration of the booth, extra charge for lights, night watchman fee, etc....Until a show is put on in New York that would allow a manufacturer to make a display of his goods, at a reasonable price, we would simply have a repetition of the "joke shows" held in this city for the past three or four years.

The editorial went on to endorse a strictly trade show set for Grand Central Palace, August 11–16, under the auspices of the Merchants and Manufacturers Exchange and managed by Charles D. Axman, who had staged the shows at Madison Square Garden in 1910 and 1911. The cost was to be twenty-five dollars for fifty square feet of space—"about one quarter of the price charged by professional show managers."

Even though the magazine predicted that "this will be the most successful House Furnishing Exhibition held in New York," it was obliged to report afterward that despite the presentation of more lines than ever before, "the attendance was disappointing—and no wonder when housewares shows heretofore have had such a black eye."

The promoters were persistent, however. By the time World War I was in full swing, another National Home Exposition and Household Show was announced for Madison Square Garden in February 1916. It was the third—and last—to be held there, thanks to its own mediocre success.

Of course, during the intervening years there were numerous other general merchandise trade shows of one kind or another in which housewares were usually represented to some extent. For example, there was the Manufacturers and Importers Association of America, which originally held shows specializing in merchandise to retail at five, ten, and twenty-five cents—a reflection of the keen hold the "five and ten" concept had on the marketplace. Later it changed its price range to "from 5¢ to $5" as merchants broadened their market. This group's tenth annual show was held at Chicago's Palmer House August 6–11, 1917.

The Pottery Shows

No report of the development of the housewares shows would be complete without including the activities of the Associated Pottery and Glass Manufacturers, which, beginning in 1881, held a trade show annually, usually in a Pittsburgh hotel because of that city's proximity to the Ohio potteries. One must remember that for a great many years little if any distinction was made by retail merchants between house furnishing and china, glass, and pottery. Usually it was the same buyer who bought all such merchandise.

"In Pittsburgh, the William Penn Hotel was always confined exclusively to exhibits by American potteries," recalled Joseph Block, veteran New York importer and manufacturer, whose marketing activities with his brother Irving under the name of J. and I. Block for well over half a century have included housewares and china.

From top: I. Halpern and Adolph Rosner were housewares buyers respectively for Stix, Baer & Fuller, St. Louis, and Ludwig Baumann & Company, New York. Around the turn of the century, there were no merchandise managers and buyers usually ran their departments as they saw fit, answering only to the owners of the business.

In 1908, long before "Women's Lib," at least three ladies had what it took to call on buyers as "salesmen" for companies in this business. Miss E. M. Evans was with A. L. Tribble and Company, Boston; Miss Jean Hawthorn was with Silverdip Company, New York; and Miss Helen Delp, Dover Manufacturing Company, Canal Dover, Ohio.

The Fort Pitt Hotel was designated for exhibits of importers. House furnishings were not supposed to be shown but we always bootlegged some enamelware which we would keep under the bed and did quite a business with it.

"The first show I ever attended was in 1914 when a few of us in the housewares business, such as Max Lowenstein (a very prominent manufacturers sales agent), Steinfeld Brothers, and I decided to show our lines in the Fort Pitt Hotel during the china and glass show," recalled the late Walter Beh, founder of the long established, well-known New York sales agency, Beh & Company. "But in about two or three years we were requested to go elsewhere, so eventually we went to Chicago, where the first trade show was held at the Morrison Hotel."

The idea of providing the house furnishings trade with a permanent year-round show facility rather than a temporary one-week show, had often been discussed. In 1919 two such ventures were launched almost simultaneously. One was in the then recently completed Bush Terminal Sales Building on East Forty-Second Street, New York, where beginning September 1, a house furnishing division was established. "Quality offerings of sixty-six representative manufacturers will be on the floor for your inspection and comparison.... Buy first at 'Merchandise Headquarters,' " said their advertisement.

Two weeks later the operators of New York's Grand Central Palace devoted the eight upper floors to permanent industrial expositions, one of which was called the International Hardware and House Furnishing Exchange. "The new enterprise enjoys phenomenal backing," reported *House Furnishing Review.* "The Nemours Trading Corporation, of which Alfred I. duPont is president, owns and controls the Merchants and Manufacturers Exchange" (the official name of Grand Central Palace).

The following February (1920) witnessed the first of the semiannual merchandise fairs that Grand Central Palace was to promote for its new tenants in all lines. It proved to be quite successful, and there were many who predicted a permanent future for the fair, according to *House Furnishing Review.* It also reported there was unanimity of opinion "on the most important point of the enterprise: the exhibitors one and all stood back of their products and endorsed the spirit of the fair, which encouraged the buyer to make his purchases upon actual comparison."

The fair was slated to be repeated in July, but soon after its first presentation, an announcement was made of a competitive "Imperial Houseware Exhibit" to be held in New York's Imperial Hotel, July 10–31, 1920. Exhibits were limited to hardware, house furnishings, glassware, and china. Like many other one-shot opportunistic ventures this one was not repeated.

One promoter who planned for a "big merchandise fair" at New York's Seventy-First Regiment Armory early in August 1921 repeated it immediately afterwards in the Chicago Coliseum. Both featured department store merchandise and had a special section for electric appliances.

Finally, in October 1921, the trade began to take the show business into its own hands with the formation of the Chicago Glass, Pottery, Lamps, and House Furnishing Association. It promptly announced it would hold a nonprofit show in February 1922 at the Morrison Hotel. John F. Bowman of the Chicago Association of Commerce and Industry was elected president of the new group; Henry Von Hagel of Sears Roebuck was elected vice-president; John Ling of Mandel Brothers was chosen to head the executive committee.

The Morrison Hotel show proved to be everything its sponsors hoped for. According to the reports, sixteen hundred buyers attended the two-week event and placed $4 million worth of business. In an interview in *House Furnishing Review* Mr. Ling said:

> The ambition of the organizers of this association is to make this city the Leipzig of America, not because our show was held in Chicago, but because its splendid position…makes it the most natural city in the world as a central market….To quote some of our exhibitors, our show was "the most wonderful ever conducted in our line."

Ling continued by citing plans for a 1923 show and predicted that the new association would be a "permanent organization that will not die out…and we will continue to impress on the minds of the manufacturers of America that this is the logical city of America for international trade in every line of merchandise." But despite its glowing beginning the show was repeated only once more, in 1923, and then only as a kind of "market week." Before long both the show and the association faded into oblivion.

There were no more house furnishing shows until 1925 when the American Furniture Mart in Chicago decided to use some of its excess floor space, designated as the American Exposition Palace, for such an exhibition. But the trade preferred a hotel location for its show, and in January 1926 the Sherman Hotel was the scene of the National Housewares and Home Furnishing Exposition under the management of D. E. Crum, who had also conducted the show at the American Furniture Mart.

The Sherman Hotel show was repeated in January 1927, but for some reason Crum did not manage it, though he did a repeat show at the American Furniture Mart, the last to be held there.

That show, too, marked the end of an era of such shows in the housewares business. For the previous twenty-five years its merchants and manufacturers had been groping and fumbling with all kinds of expositions. Yet none of them, despite all the reports in the trade papers, were ever entirely satisfactory or provided the lusty young industry with what it needed to fulfill its marketing and merchandising requirements.

Perhaps up to that time the industry really didn't know what its requirements were. But at least long experience had given it a pretty good idea of the kind of shows it did *not* want.

Walter Beh, founder of the Beh Housewares Corporation, was among those who helped organize the New York Housewares Manufacturers Association.

Leaders of the housewares industry, meanwhile, had been giving the matter a lot of thought. Finally they agreed the time had come for a major change in their approach to a housewares show, and in the following year (1928) that change took place. It marked the start of a whole new era for this business.

From Idea to Reality

During the first quarter of this century, American housewares manufacturers and merchants had been prisoners of their own hopes. Since the turn of the century they had been thinking and talking about a trade show run exclusively by and for the people in their business. It seemed like a good idea, and, as events later proved, it was a very good idea. But for people to have hopes about determining the future of their industry is one thing. Actually making those hopes a reality is something else.

On several occasions during those years, more by accident than by design, the industry came close to achieving its goal. Each experience strengthened the resolve but fell short of initiating the action required to do something. The housewares business, it must be remembered, was still very small, especially compared with what it is today. It was a vaguely defined industry, composed of many disparate segments, that found itself resorting again and again to momentary expedients for solutions. And of course they contributed nothing in terms of constructive, lasting values. Nothing, that is, except to fan the fires of determination.

The Chicago Group

No one was more determined or was fanning those fires more diligently than the house furnishing buyer for The Fair Store in Chicago, Charles S. Maginnis. A fine merchant and excellent executive (who later became president of that big State Street organization), he recognized the need and opportunity for a nonprofit, industry-managed trade show. Probably more than any other single individual, he deserves credit for not only envisioning the potentials of such a show but, more important, turning the idea into a reality.

Charlie Maginnis, like most of his contemporaries, was keenly aware of the power and influence that important buyers for big department stores wielded over manufacturers; they were their giant customers. He believed, along with some other buyers, that a house furnishing buyers club could go far toward getting the manufacturers to set up their own show organization. On the evening of June 30, 1925, their thinking began to take shape.

That was the night when about fifty buyers took time out from the Chicago Home Furnishings Exposition being held at the American Furniture Mart to attend a dinner in the Furniture Club, at which they organized the National Pot and Kettle Club. Its purpose, as *House Furnishing Review* reported at the time, was "the building of good will,...cooperation, and the promotion of good fellowship."

Charles S. Maginnis, house furnishing buyer for Chicago's The Fair Store and later its president, saw the potential of an industry-wide housewares exhibition.

38

Apparently they were all so carried away by what they were doing that they completely forgot that little more than a year before, in January 1924, a Pot and Kettle Club had been organized for a similar purpose in Los Angeles. (Since then chapters of it have been formed in other West Coast cities, and it is now the Associated Pot and Kettle Clubs of America.) But there were no West Coast buyers on hand that night at the Furniture Club in Chicago, when W. H. Fergus, housewares buyer of the Boston Store of Chicago, was elected president and Maginnis was elected vice-president of the new organization.

Right from the start, Charlie Maginnis began "selling" the industry-run show concept. But by the time he had become president of the Pot and Kettle Club in 1927, he had really shifted his powers of persuasion into high gear. Fortunately, almost everyone he talked with welcomed the idea; it was just a question of time.

"Why not a National Housewares Association?" asked the *House Furnishing Review* editorially in March 1927, reflecting the intense feeling that

> house furnishing manufacturers are considering the formation of a national association for the purpose of conducting a national exhibition. Of the many retail lines in the United States doing more than a billion dollar business every year, there are few which do not have a national association devoted to the growth of the industry it represents.
>
> Conspicuous among this inactive minority is the house furnishing business, which offers nothing to be compared with the national organizations serving the other prominent retail fields....Such organizations, while they serve consistently throughout the year, do their most signal work in the proper presentation of products to the trade, generally at a national exhibition. An association organized for this purpose soon takes its natural place in the business and social life of the retailer.

Then, citing the fact that house furnishings do about $1 billion of business annually, the *Review* went on to report that meetings had been held earlier at local promoter-staged shows in Pittsburgh and Chicago, where "sentiment was decidedly in favor of a national organization....The idea of such an organization, promoted by manufacturers, for the purpose of holding an exhibition on a new high scale of magnitude and importance, is one that cannot be treated in cavalier fashion."

It wasn't! In November 1927, the industry, through its leading manufacturers, made one of its most important decisions. It was officially announced in a dignified full-page advertisement in the *Review* that:

> The National House Furnishing Manufacturers Association announces the formation of an organization for the purpose of promoting the best interests of the industry and to hold an Annual Exhibition of House Furnishing Merchandise.
>
> The first exhibition will be held at Chicago during the week of January 3-7, 1928, at the Stevens Hotel....For full particulars write the secretary...666 Lake Shore Drive, Chicago, Illinois.

That was all. But it was more than enough—it was tremendous.

Stan L. Hanssen, then president of the Hanson Scale Company, was elected president of the NHFMA. "Charlie Maginnis was unquestionably the 'work horse' behind the scenes in getting our group started," Hanssen said in a 1970 interview.

As buyer of what was then the largest house furnishings department in Chicago, if not the country, he carried a great deal of weight with the manufacturers and commanded everyone's respect. To assist us he headed a buyers' advisory committee consisting of seven leading buyers, including such figures as John Henry of the J. L. Hudson Company, Detroit, and John Boston of the Famous and Barr Company, St. Louis.

Other officers of the new organization included Warren Edwards, editor of *House Furnishing Review,* as secretary; J. S. Weinberg of Peyton Wood Products, treasurer (he was almost immediately replaced by W. H. Doherty of Queen Manufacturing Company, who held the post continuously until he was named president in 1936). W. F. Mellon, Wagner Manufacturing Company, and W. J. Vollrath, Polar Ware Company, were named directors. An office was opened in the Chicago Furniture Mart, and reservations for exhibition space began coming in immediately

The industry's first house furnishing exhibit in "the world's largest hotel" (then the Stevens, now the Conrad Hilton) proved a great success. It boasted 115 exhibitors with "a record number of buyers in attendance," and, as the *Review* added in its report, "the show proved on the first day of its existence that it would become truly an annual feature"—a prediction which, for the first time, turned out to be correct. It added:

> The exhibition also proved the need of a national housewares show to be held annually in Chicago by the manufacturers themselves, along nonprofit lines....This show will be long remembered for still another reason—it was the first style and color show in the history of the industry. Color gave this event an interest and appeal which otherwise would have been lacking. Color in the kitchen was an outstanding feature of the exhibit.
>
> The total amount of business placed during the week went far beyond anticipation, despite the fact that many of the manufacturers neither expected nor solicited orders during the exhibit.

Everyone connected with the event was, of course, delighted, especially Charlie Maginnis, who almost got a callus shaking congratulatory hands. And it surprised no one when the Second Annual Exhibition was promptly announced for 1929. For the next ten years the Stevens was the site of the annual January show.

Each successive show served to confirm the soundness and importance of the show concept for house furnishings and the wisdom of having the industry run its own exhibition. Each show attracted more exhibitors—and more buyers. As the saying goes, "word gets around," and the show became an absolute must.

40

Warren Edwards was editor of *House Furnishing Review* as well as involved in the National House Furnishing Manufacturers Association from its inception.

Courtesy House Furnishing Review.

It is interesting to note that it was also in 1928 that the Chicago marketplace was surprised by an unusual real estate announcement. The city would soon have a gigantic Merchandise Mart, a permanent showroom-exhibition building with four million square feet of space—the biggest building in the world. (It would be double the size of the Furniture Mart.) And house furnishings, of course, would be well represented among the tenants.

The New York Group: AHA

The resounding success of the Stevens Hotel show and then the news about the great new Merchandise Mart did not go unnoticed in New York housewares circles. To put it bluntly, New York was jealous of Chicago, and it showed. There was nothing new about the idea of having a house furnishing show in New York run by the industry itself on a nonprofit basis. It had been talked about for years. Now Chicago had not only proved it could be done but had beat New York in doing it. What was even worse was the fear among eastern manufacturers and sales representatives about where this might leave them. Chicago was unquestionably growing in importance as a housewares market. But the fact remained that New York had long been the industry's traditional commercial center. Now its position was being challenged and trade sentiment to take some effective counter-action assumed an ever increasing urgency.

"In those days there weren't nearly as many manufacturers' reps as there are today—or as many stores either," Abe Garner, retired president of Worldsbest Industries, recalled in a later interview. At the time to which he referred, the early 1930s, he had just formed the Housewares Sales Corporation and represented several lines over a large section of the country. His reactions were typical.

We had to have a big territory in order to make a living in those days of the Great Depression. But it meant traveling at least forty or fifty weeks of the year and it was plenty rough—nothing like traveling is today.... But everyone accepted it; there was no choice.

I had rented desk room for my few samples in the office of Francis Leffler, a former housewares buyer for Lord and Taylor when they were still way downtown. He had become one of the deans among the sales reps and one of the most important figures in the business. Each time I'd get back from a long trip I'd unburden my troubles on him. Like most of the other eastern salesmen I had talked with on the road, we began to worry about that Chicago show situation. I hoped Frank would use his position and influence to improve the situation.

"Frank, if something isn't done soon to develop the New York market, we'll end up being a small second fiddle to Chicago. Do you know what buyers are saying now? They say that with that Stevens Hotel show and that new Merchandise Mart, Chicago will become to the house furnishing industry what Wall Street is to banking. They ask why they should bother coming to New York."

Not long after one of these talks, he called me to say, "I had a visit from Flo English. She knows somebody in Philadelphia who runs a gift show over there who would like to run a housewares show here in New York."

By now, however, there was another and far more pressing reason than mere local pride to prompt New Yorkers to think seriously about holding a local show—the Great Depression. There was an urgent need to try to generate business in the marketplace and a desperate hope that something could be done.

Just a short time before the Depression began, newspapers were filled with optimistic promises from the Hoover administration: "A chicken in every pot and a car in every garage!" But suddenly the beautiful bubble burst. And in those few but never-to-be-forgotten weeks in the fall of 1929, the country was rudely awakened from its golden dream of endless riches when more than $32 billion worth of equities slipped out of the stock market into a painful nothingness. But that was only the prelude. The suffering and the despair, the breadlines and the suicides were to follow.

It was at this time that Mrs. George English entered the scene. Flo English represented several manufacturers, more in giftwares than housewares. A very capable and ambitious businesswoman whose husband was associated with a Wall Street brokerage firm, she was in business by choice rather than necessity. But the giftware business failed to generate much enthusiasm in Flo. More and more she recognized the larger potential of housewares. Her interest in it had been considerably heightened a couple of years earlier when, while returning from a European vacation on the S. S. Leviathan with her sister, she happened to meet J. I. Flynn, housewares buyer for Kaufmann's in Pittsburgh. They became good friends.

One of the biggest and most important buyers at that time, Flynn was among those easterners strongly in favor of a New York show, if for no other reason than to offset the apparent Chicago housewares monopoly. His views made a deep impression on her. When she expressed an interest in furthering the idea of a New York show, Flynn not only encouraged it but also volunteered to help if it ever materialized.

"I've had it," she recalled telling her husband George at dinner one evening in 1929, right after the close of the first New York Gift Show at the Pennsylvania Hotel (now the New York Statler Hilton). "No more gift shows for me. If a little gift show like this can bring such a good turnout of buyers, why wouldn't this be a good place for a housewares show like the one in Chicago?"

She continued with her gift business, however, and subsequently met Warner Hays, a Philadelphia show promoter, who expressed an interest in staging a housewares show in New York.

"Naturally I became very enthusiastic about the possibility," she recalled, "and I told him I'd be glad to speak to some of the key people about it. The first person I went to see was Lee Koch, sales manager of Frank and Son, the woodenware and furniture company." She continued:

Lee listened very attentively as I outlined the show idea. While I talked he reached into the bottom drawer of his rolltop desk and fished up a bundle of old, yellowed papers. "I'm afraid you're just wasting your time," he said when I finished. "The idea was tried and it didn't work. I know—here are the records."

The old papers he showed her referred to the second New York show in 1907.

A good salesman, it has often been said, really begins to go to work when the prospect says no—and Flo English proved to be an excellent saleswoman. Finally she paid a visit to Frank Leffler, who, for reasons already mentioned, was not ready to dismiss the matter without giving it some consideration.

A meeting was soon arranged in Lee Koch's office. Those present included Lee Koch, Frank Leffler, Flo English, Abe Garner, Sam Lippe, representing the F. A. Whitney Company, of Leominster, Massachusetts, and Frank Lederle, sales representative of *House Furnishing Review*.

Those attending the meeting were strongly in favor of a New York show. But it was felt that its sponsorship should be more broadly based and include more eastern manufacturers. So another meeting was arranged at the Pennsylvania Hotel. In addition to the original group, those attending this meeting included Walter Beh, of Beh and Company; Stanley Williams, New York manager of the Vollrath Company; Joseph A. Kaplan, president of the Joseph A. Kaplan Company; Robert D. Price, New York manager of the Robeson Rochester Company; William B. Flanagan, A. Kreamer, Incorporated; Albert A. Bernardine, New York manager, National Enameling and Stamping Company; Ben S. Loeb, manufacturers representative; Ralph Gretsch, White Tar Company; Warren Bettes, New York manager, Landers, Frary and Clark; James Hardenbergh, New York manager, Corning Glass Works; and H. S. Trump, New York manager, Aluminum Cooking Utensil Company (Wear-Ever).

Enthusiasm ran high at the gathering. Sentiment in favor of a New York show already existed, and attendance at this meeting gave those present something constructive, something tangible to do about it. Moreover, it was an attempt to offset the dreadful impact of the depression. A show could be a great thing—who knew how much business an event of this kind might put into their little-used order books?

The first order of business was to organize and establish an association. But what to call it? Chicago was already using the term "national," and although some wanted to emphasize the "eastern" or "New York" character of the group, such sectionalism was frowned upon by others. Finally Abe Garner came up with a suggestion everyone accepted—"American Housewares Exhibit." And so the American Housewares Association was formed.

Despite his earlier skepticism about the plan, Lee Koch accepted the presidency of the new group. The Pennsylvania Hotel was selected as the location for their show, which was to be held June 24–30, 1932. Many details remained to be worked out, but on one basic point there was unanimity: it would be an industry-operated, nonprofit affair.

There was one slight problem, however; no one who attended the meeting had had any experience in running such a show. So an arrangement was made with Warner Hays, the Philadelphia promoter with whom Flo English had originally talked about a New York show, to provide the necessary management guidance and counsel.

Hays suggested hiring salesmen to sell space at a 15 percent commission—an idea promptly vetoed. Meanwhile, the weeks passed and manufacturers were slow to sign for the show. "Finally," Abe Garner recalled, "we got a bright idea. We announced that on such and such a date rooms would be allocated to show exhibitors. Suddenly everyone decided they had better reserve a room before it was too late."

Meanwhile, Mrs. English had taken the initiative in selling space at the show. "By the time the show opened, ninety-six rooms had been sold and I had the personal satisfaction of having sold every one of them," she recalled.

Flo added that she not only received no compensation for her selling efforts, but even paid for her own exhibition room. "But that never bothered me one little bit. After all, I did it voluntarily and I was doing something I had thought about and had wanted to try for a long time. Now I had my experience and my answer; I knew this was something I could handle."

With the tremendous buyer attendance that housewares shows now command, it is difficult to realize that a show with ninety-six exhibitors—an impressive number for that time—would attract only 502 buyers. Yet they were all that attended the first American Housewares Exhibit. It provides eloquent commentary on just how bad the economy was in the summer of 1932. Nevertheless, the show did help to generate some business, and *House Furnishing Review* even referred to it as "an outstanding success."

In 1933 housewares manufacturers demonstrated a faith in the infallible wisdom and professional skill of housewares buyers they never had shown before—or since. To help make the second New York Housewares Show at the Pennsylvania Hotel a success, they named an "Advisory Buyers Board" headed by Charles Cross of Abraham and Strauss, to help prevent the introduction of poor selling items!

A luncheon meeting was arranged for May 16, at which the board would

offer to any exhibitor the opportunity to appear individually before us to present any new items...upon which he wishes to ask our opinion ...so that, if possible, we can avoid the introduction of non-saleable items...or too many with only limited sales appeal.

We believe considerable loss can be eliminated...through a study of new items before they go into production; also much of the trouble and waste resulting from distressed merchandise.

44

Opposite page: An ad for the American Housewares Exhibit, 1932.

July 24 to 30

AMERICAN HOUSEWARES EXHIBIT

HOTEL PENNSYLVANIA

First Time in New York

NEVER has such a sales promotion enterprise been so essential and timely to the business of both Manufacturers and Retailers ... to improve business-getting methods through conferences and interchange of ideas with other Retailers, and to revive confidence and to stimulate profits.

As this is being printed, more than fifty Manufacturers have signed. Thus is established a complete and comprehensive exhibit of the newest merchandise in Housewares, Electric and Gas Appliances, Home and Garden Equipment and Supplies, and Labor Saving Devices.

Retailers must economize in time and buying expense and can now compare and purchase at one time and in one place, the latest devices and wares in the vast Housewares Merchandise Field. And Manufacturers and their Agents, whether or not they maintain permanent New York Exhibits, will make many profitable contacts with new accounts, important Retailers who will come to the Exhibit from all parts of the country. At the Exhibit Manufacturers will secure orders early to have their merchandise in Retailers' stores ready for the consumer buying of Housewares in the early Fall.

NEW YORK

Out of New York Buyers Will Save Money thru the Many Low Summer Travel Rates. See Your Local Ticket Agents.

The list of exhibitors grows daily. For Information and Rates, write Committee of Exhibitors, American Housewares Exhibit, Executive Offices, 45 E. 17th St., New York.

AMERICAN HOUSEWARES EXHIBIT

EXECUTIVE OFFICES, 45 EAST 17th STREET, NEW YORK

Say you saw it in THE HOUSE FURNISHING REVIEW with which is consolidated HOUSEWARES MERCHANDISING.

Whether their offer had any takers wasn't reported.

The confidence in the ability of buyers was also shown by those manufacturers when they named twelve leading buyers to serve as a "Police Committee" to "see that only people in the trade are admitted to the show and that exhibitors stay in their rooms and refrain from soliciting in the halls."

The show, somewhat surprisingly, gave the American Housewares Association renewed confidence in itself and (not surprisingly) in Flo English. Warner Hays's services were discontinued, and Mrs. English was prevailed upon to liquidate her giftwares business and take a position as the fulltime, permanent secretary of the association. Another show was planned in the same hotel for July 1933.

East Meets West

The New York and Chicago show groups were competitive and jealous of each other. But their personal feelings were fortunately often tempered by the realization that both were striving for a common goal. Thus there developed an unwritten and unofficial but clearly understood agreement that the January show would be held in Chicago and the July show in New York. The success of the Chicago show, especially its nonprofit policy, greatly influenced New York to pattern its operation along the same lines.

In January 1934, after New York had held only two shows, the thought of combining the two groups was developed during a private meeting at the Stevens Hotel while the Chicago show was in progress. Directors of both groups, after long discussion, finally reached an agreement to function jointly. Or they thought they had. But on February 13, 1934, H. H. Kimball, of Landers, Frary and Clark's Chicago office and then president of the NHFMA, found it necessary to write a five-page letter to Walter Beh, spokesman for the New York group, in which he declared:

> From your letter of February 5, it is very evident that you regret the agreement you entered into with us on January 10 and that it is not your intention to abide by its terms. We are at a loss to know why your New York Committee invited us in to conduct the New York show.... If you find it is impossible to give us immediate assurance that the original terms of the agreement...will be followed, we will have to take immediate steps also to withdraw from that agreement and an embarrassing situation.

Then followed weeks of activity during which industry people in both cities made all sorts of efforts to salvage what had been believed was a merger of the two groups. Finally on February 19 a meeting was held at the Aldine Club in New York to try to reach a new agreement. Kimball and Edwards represented Chicago. New York's group consisted of Beh, Koch, Loeb, Flanagan, Gretsch, Carlstein, Williams, Trump, Engstrom (E. E. Engstrom of National Can Company), Bettes, and Bernardine. It started pleasantly enough at noon with lunch, but by the time it finally ended after six o'clock, those who endured the stormy session were worn out and frustrated.

"Several members of the [New York] Committee," declared Warren Edwards in his detailed report of the meeting, "personally congratulated Mr. Kimball on the manner in which he had handled Beh's uncomplimentary remarks and impossible demands during the meeting. I later understood even Beh himself did so. It developed that apparently a majority of the committee was in favor of carrying out the agreement, but no vote was taken."

Typical of the issues was the matter of an association secretary. New York—or at least Walter Beh—was now insisting that there should be two permanent secretaries—Warren Edwards in Chicago and Flo English in New York—who, Beh declared, "should be able to work in harmony, corresponding constantly on association and show matters." But Chicago replied, "There is no need for two secretaries, two offices, two business organizations. If the two shows cannot be conducted with the one organization, then there is no reason we can see for being invited in and our reason for coming in—that of economy—no longer exists."

The discussion was continued the following day in Beh's office by Edwards, joined from time to time by Flo English, Williams, and Engstrom. It covered many subjects, including how much each group was paying for advertising its shows. However, the merger concept was not to be revived at this time. Instead, the NHFMA finally announced that a show committee of the New York association "has been given representation on the board of this association." It consisted of Walter Beh, Stanley Williams, A. A. Bernardine, Warren Bettes, Ralph Gretsch, E. E. Engstrom, Leo S. Koch, Joseph A. Kaplan, W. B. Flanagan, and R. D. Price. Flo English continued as secretary.

Having taken such a step, the New Yorkers decided it was time to change their name. In place of "American Housewares Association," they adopted "New York Housewares Manufacturers Association" as the organization's title and then proceeded to incorporate it on June 29, 1934.

NHFMA vs HFMAA

Meanwhile, in Chicago, the annual January show that the National House Furnishing Manufacturers Association originally had started in 1928 continued to flourish. Each year it attracted more exhibitors and buyers; each year it managed to produce more business. All things, including the Great Depression, considered, the Chicago show came through year after year remarkably well.

Until 1938. The frailities of human nature are just as weak and vulnerable in trade association relationships as in any other realm of human activity, and in that year personality clashes split the NHFMA in half. This resulted not only in two competitive associations, but what was worse, in two conflicting trade shows. Ironically, the situation was precipitated primarily by the man who had done more than anyone else to help start an association and an industry-run show—

Charles S. Maginnis. In a very real sense both were "his babies," or at least he felt that way.

By spring of 1938 Charlie had been named president of The Fair Store, a unique honor for one whose retail career began amid pots and pans rather than, according to tradition, coats and suits. Quiet spoken and mild mannered, the new president lacked the proverbial Irish temper—except when, finally, things in the association failed to go the way he thought they should.

"My suggestions for the benefit of the National House Furnishing Manufacturers Association have always been acted upon by the Board of Directors in a favorable manner," he declared in a formal statement issued in March 1938 that clearly reveals his feelings.

> Changes have been made lately that I do not and could not approve of and I could not have them rectified. So therefore I resigned from the advisory committee. I will continue to give whatever assistance I can to the promotion of house furnishings in all its branches, as I am now more vitally interested than ever and I am the last one who wants to see any hindrance to this industry.

Yet hindrance is precisely what his action caused. Unable or unwilling to recognize that the business had now begun to grow up and, more important, that it was no longer a one-man organization, he was determined to get his own way or resign.

One of the people who moved Maginnis to act as he did was Warren Edwards, secretary of the association. A former editor of *House Furnishing Review,* Edwards failed to realize that the approach needed for one job is not necessarily the right approach for another. More often than not, he unintentionally rubbed people the wrong way—a mannerism that apparently became increasingly evident as the shows became more successful.

There were other reasons too. Maginnis did not approve of the pay raise the directors had voted Edwards for the good job he did in handling the 1937 show, the biggest and best show to date. Nor did he see eye to eye with E. E. Engstrom of the National Can Company, who had just been elected president of the NHFMA to succeed A. W. Buddenberg of the Lisk Manufacturing Company (and a onetime housewares buyer for The Fair Store). Maginnis wanted Buddenberg reelected, although the bylaws had previously been amended to prevent any president from holding office for two successive terms. And so a group of the directors loyal to Maginnis pulled out and started their own association. With his unreserved blessing, of course.

Stan Hanssen was named head of the new group and immediately issued a statement on its behalf:

> Having differed as to administrative policy within that association and having made due and proper effort to reconcile these differences without result...we have decided to incorporate The House Furnishing Manufacturers Association of America. This will be a nonprofit organization.

48

Past presidents of the National Housewares Manufacturers Association: S. L. Hanssen, Hanson Scale Company, 1939 and 1953-54; A. W. Buddenberg, Lisk-Savory Corporation, 1940; W. N. Gallagher, the Automatic Washer Company, 1941; H. H. Kimball, Landers, Frary & Clark, 1945.

He added that it would hold a show in the Palmer House, January 8–14, 1939.

The announcement merely confirmed rumors which by now were rampant in the industry. Many manufacturers felt that Maginnis was using his considerable influence unfairly. But since The Fair Store was a big customer there was little they could do about it.

By now the industry was sharply divided over the issue, and feelings were bitter. Everyone realized the futility of having two simultaneous competitive shows, and their inability to do anything to stop it only added to their frustration and resentment. Meanwhile, some efforts toward a solution were taking place behind the scenes, although they were designed to "solve" the problem the way the Maginnis faction wanted.

"Confidentially, we are no more anxious for two shows than you or Grable [E. M. Grable, president of the Aluminum Cooking Utensil Company], but Grable agrees with me that the only possible way to bring the old organization to a showdown is to go ahead with plans for a second show," wrote A. W. Buddenberg on March 21, 1938, to Walter A. Ricker, then housewares merchandise manager of The Boston Store, Milwaukee. "Then, if the National group will meet the views of the manufacturers [in the Maginnis group, of course!], we will consolidate the old and the new and have only one show under the national banner."

Ricker, a friend of Maginnis, was in New York when he got the letter, and he had a long session with Engstrom, whose office was located there, about a possible reconciliation. But it was useless. The impression prevailed, according to Buddenberg, "that the NHFMA just wants to get by with making a lot of promises...not doing anything...along the lines we had discussed." Setting up a separate association, he urged, "is absolutely necessary to make the other fellows understand we mean business."

They did—but so did the others. Understandably, it was a prime topic of conversation during the New York Housewares Show in July. Finally the rumors got so out of hand that, in August, Engstrom found it necessary to issue a lengthy statement clarifying the position of the NHFMA.

Warren Edwards did *not* vote himself any salary increase recently as has been reported in some quarters of the trade. It is true he received a nominal increase accorded him by unanimous vote of the directors ...but it came as a surprise....The directors took this action in appreciation of the fact that he had successfully directed the largest and best show in our history.

The statement did not hesitate to point a finger of guilt at Maginnis.

He has been the cause of much concern on the part of many manufacturers....When the annual election approached some months ago, Mr. Maginnis made it known to the directors of the association that he

Past presidents of the NHMA: F. S. Turek, Hamilton Beach, 1942-43; H. M. Hammond, National Washboard Company, 1944.

desired the reelection of the retiring president—a procedure the bylaws prohibited. Mr. Maginnis's suggestion that the bylaws be changed to conform to his wishes were not followed.

Later, after Engstrom's unanimous election as president,

Stan L. Hanssen and H. B. Klusmeyer presented an ultimatum to its directors demanding that unless the newly elected directors and officers resign and call a special election to elect a new board of directors and president, with proxies to be held by Mr. A. W. Buddenberg, the president during the previous year, they would organize a new association for the purpose of holding a competing exhibit....Mr. Engstrom...sought a conference with Mr. Maginnis to adjust differences, if any existed, but Mr. Maginnis definitely refused to attend such a conference. This...is a matter of record.

The statement concludes by emphasizing that "two shows in Chicago are superfluous, unnecessary, inconvenient and *an imposition on the buyer*."

By 1939 the housewares industry had managed to throw off most of the shackles of the Great Depression. It had even begun to sense a few advance signs of the prosperity that national defense programs would generate. It hardly needed two trade associations and two trade shows. But that is exactly what happened, thanks to the shortsightedness of willful men determined to follow their individual, personal aims regardless of the consequences to others.

Understandably, the problem of trying to cope with two hotel shows aroused a storm of objections from the buyers, and numerous protests, both official and unofficial, were registered with both groups. But they proved futile.

One of the major stumbling blocks to a consolidation of the National House Furnishing Manufacturers Association (the so-called Edwards faction) and the House Furnishing Manufacturers Association of America (the so-called Maginnis group) was the demand of the former group that Warren Edwards immediately be named manager of both shows, something that was promptly rejected by the Maginnis group.

The Housewares Manufacturers Association

Nevertheless, by June 1939 some hopes for a solution emerged when a committee composed of three directors from each of the two associations met and issued a statement.

It was agreed by the committee that, because both associations have already made hotel commitments for the January 1940 show, it will be necessary to carry out these obligations. However, a standing committee composed of members of both associations has been appointed to work out a consolidation of the hotel shows for 1941. The Board of Directors of both associations are in complete agreement to accomplish this purpose in time to plan for the 1941 show.

It was all much easier said than done. There were numerous meetings, official and otherwise. And despite the knowledge of both sides that there was overwhelming trade sentiment for a single show, the negotiations almost reached a point of no return.

It is important to remember that the House Furnishing Manufacturers Association of America was in a position to lead from impressive strength. As was already noted, Charles S. Maginnis of The Fair Store, who was completely behind the HFMAA, had tremendous influence and prestige in the housewares industry. It was no surprise that most of the big and important manufacturers were on his side. But by November 1940, as the HFMAA minutes indicate, "all the details of the consolidation agreement of the two associations have been carried out in a way satisfactory to both associations." The important stipulations of the agreement were: a change of name to "Housewares Manufacturers Association"; adoption of the HFMAA bylaws; and agreement on priority lists for the shows, and so on. Once again there would be only one housewares show in January 1941—at the Palmer House—and only one "national" trade association. At least in Chicago. And at least for the time being!

Another stipulation dealt with the elimination of major appliances from the show. When the house furnishings shows were introduced, there were several major appliance manufacturers among the exhibitors. One reason for this is that when major appliances were first introduced the obvious place for them was in the housewares department. Traditionally it was the department that sold washing machines, stoves, and refrigerators. Not until much later, and only after considerable effort in prying them loose from housewares, did department stores begin a separate department for major appliances. The elimination of major appliances from the big shows didn't actually occur until 1948, and until that year the show was known as the National Housewares and Major Appliances Show.

Atlantic City

In the East the New York Housewares Manufacturers Association was having its own share of troubles. Ever since it held its first show at the Pennsylvania Hotel in 1932, the location had proved to be highly advantageous for the association and for the hotel as well. But in 1939 the hotel management decided that booking visitors to New York's World's Fair would be even more advantageous. And so the association was asked to take its show elsewhere.

The New York show moved to the old Hotel Astor. Flo English recalled:

> By that time the depression was practically over, war prosperity had just begun to make itself felt, and we were so desperate for exhibit room that every available foot of space from the roof garden on down to all the ballrooms and meeting rooms was used.

When the New York World's Fair announced it would reopen in 1940, the housewares show had to look elsewhere again. After the 1939 show was over, Mr. and Mrs. English went to Atlantic City—and discovered the recently completed Atlantic City Auditorium.

The Atlantic City Auditorium proved to be a popular success with the housewares industry when the first New York Housewares Manufacturers Association exhibition was held there in 1940.

Atlantic City's Mayor Altman presents a "key to the city" to Flo English, secretary of the NYHMA in 1940.

"I became so excited the first time I saw it as George and I were walking along the Boardwalk that I turned to him and said, 'What a wonderful place for the housewares show!'" she related. A little while later she talked with Art Skean, general manager of the Atlantic City Convention Bureau.

We spent all afternoon discussing the pros and cons of such a show. I told him that although I thought it was wonderful, the final decision would be up to the association's directors. "Maybe most of them feel as my husband does, that stores would never allow their buyers to attend a show here since this is the playground of the world—and who will do any work here?"

Of course the immense auditorium (at least it seemed immense to the housewares industry in those days) and the appeal of Atlantic City with its hundreds of hotels was a natural setting for the show. Soon after her first visit Flo English announced that the association would hold its July 1940 show there.

It proved to be a tremendous show, the biggest the New York group had ever held, with about 303 exhibitors. Atlantic City was an extremely popular choice. It provided a new, refreshing atmosphere for the show, which previously had been confined to cramped and congested hotel rooms.

But what contributed most to its success from a business standpoint was the lengthening shadow of the war clouds in Europe. Although "The Phony War," as it was called, seemed far away and the likelihood of American involvement appeared remote, far-sighted merchants thought it prudent to begin building their inventories.

With the success of the first Atlantic City show still fresh in everyone's mind, the New York Housewares Manufacturers Association announced that its July 1941 show would also be held there. But by July 1940 the world situation looked a lot different and much more serious. Poland had been taken and France was collapsing. The London blitz was on. There seemed to be no way to stop the Germans. Like the rest of the business world, the housewares industry soon became familiar with military priorities for metals and other materials normally used in making household products.

It was becoming increasingly difficult for most manufacturers to operate under tightening government war controls, but they managed remarkably well—that is, until the 1941 Atlantic City show. Leon Henderson, chief of the new United States Office of Price Administration, had been invited by the association to make the usual

Atlantic City proved a durable host—and the NHMA used its facilities for many shows including this July 1959 National Housewares Exhibit.

"appropriate remarks" at the formal opening of the show. Earlier there had been an official breakfast at which all was smiles. Now the OPA chief stood at the rail of the balcony of the huge auditorium, overlooking the entire show. The thousands of merchants and manufacturers watching him from the exhibit floor below listened intently as he spoke. It was a short speech that brought the whole industry to a sudden realization that business-as-usual was from now on a thing of the past. "The honeymoon is over," Henderson proclaimed, and one could hear a pin drop. From then on the industry knew it was just a question of time before the production of metal civilian goods would end. Henderson's remarks naturally gave order writing a tremendous boost. Buyers didn't have to be told twice that they had better get all the merchandise they could while the getting was still good.

And then, Pearl Harbor! It all happened so suddenly and unexpectedly that there was no opportunity and no time to do anything about calling off the Chicago housewares show, scheduled to open less than a month later on January 4. In the absence of any official request to cancel it, the show was held amid all the uncertainties with which a nation finds itself when it is suddenly plunged into a war not of its own making.

54

Officers and directors of the New York Housewares Manufacturers Association at the July 1941 show in Atlantic City: *front*—W. B. Flanagan, A. Kreamer Inc.; Flo English, secretary; Joseph A. Kaplan, president of the association and head of Joseph A. Kaplan Inc.; *back*—R. D. Price, Robeson Rochester Company; Warren Bettes, Landers, Frary & Clark; A. A. Bernardine, National Enameling & Stamping Company; James Hardenbergh, Corning Glass Works; S. T. Williams, Vollrath Company; Bert Owen, Landers, Frary & Clark.

One thing, at least, was unmistakably clear: it was a sellers' market, a boom market in terms of order placing. How much of that business could be delivered in wartime remained to be seen. At any rate, no one had to do any selling; buyers simply bought...and hoped they would get what they ordered.

Possibly the New York Housewares Manufacturers Association —like some others at the time—didn't fully realize how dreadfully serious the war would be or how long it would last. And looking back today from a vantage point of thirty years, it seems more than a little strange; but they went right ahead and announced their upcoming show would be held "as usual" in Atlantic City the week of July 12, 1942.

Wartime: "Is This Trip Necessary?"

As summer approached, the NYHMA felt it necessary to issue a statement about its July show. "Due to priorities, curtailed raw materials, and other war restrictions...perfectly reasonable questions have arisen as to the practicality of a Housewares Show in July," wrote Maurice E. Horn, president of the NYHMA and also manager of the Aluminum Cooking Utensil Company's New York branch.

> At the moment it appears that official emphasis is being placed upon increased production from existing plants rather than upon additional new plant construction....This means that factories not yet affected or affected but little by the war effort must depend upon the remaining civilian business if they are to continue to operate. The least this association can do is to provide a place where these manufacturers can display their merchandise and meet in a short time in one place the maximum number of interested buyers whose stores must continue to function.

But when it finally came to facing up to the test, *"Is this trip necessary?"* with which the government challenged all sorts of avoidable gatherings, the housewares show failed. With the shows suspended for the duration of the war, the association closed its offices and "released" Mrs. English—to use her own words—to do whatever she wished.

The English Rebellion

In 1945, shortly before V-J Day, Flo English met with the directors of the NYHMA and informed them she thought it was time to announce a date for its first postwar show. But they disagreed; when the time was right, they told her, she would be notified.

At that point Mrs. English rose and issued her ultimatum. "Thank you, gentlemen, for your time," she later recalled saying, "but since you are not going to run a show, I am."

With her considerable experience it was not long before her show plans were well under way. But the directors felt she was taking undue advantage of the association and very bitter feelings developed. Actually, as it turned out, she did what the association

55

World War II drastically slowed down the housewares industry and ended the shows for the duration. Its manufacturers earned well-deserved "E" awards and retailers' "Black Out Shops" provided civilians with timely essentials.
Courtesy House Furnishing Review.

itself should have done. The nation's economy was beginning to edge toward a peacetime basis, and stores were starved for merchandise. Chicago's January show proved—if proof was needed—how urgently the trade needed to resume its shows.

In January 1946, the Atlantic City Convention Bureau, which manages its Convention Hall, decided to award the lease for its use for a housewares show on a competitive basis. The contract would have to be for five shows in the next five years. The successful bidder was to be the one who guaranteed the largest sale of space above the specified minimum requirement. Sealed bids and a certified check for $20,000 attached to the outside of the sealed envelop containing the bid were to be received by the Convention Bureau management and opened in the presence of the bidders on Friday, July 26, 1946.

Atlantic City Mayor Tom Taggert was among the city officials present when George and Flo English, along with Stanley Williams of the Vollrath Company and Rudolph Neilsen of Landers, Frary and Clark, representing the New York Housewares Manufacturers Association, met in the Convention Bureau offices. On the table were two sealed envelopes—but only one had the required certified check attached to the outside.

"I see we have only one valid bid," said Mayor Taggert, examining the envelopes. That remark brought a loud protest from Williams. He insisted that as a financially responsible former customer of the Convention Bureau, the association's check was perfectly valid without certification. But the officials declined to see it that way. "There was a lengthy, unpleasant argument," Flo English recalled, "but when it was all over I had the hall along with an option on its use for the next five years."

Her victory, however, was rather short-lived.

The conflict between Flo English and the NYHMA underscored the importance of forming one truly national manufacturers association to run all trade shows on a nonprofit basis.

Meanwhile, the many advantages of a single national organization were beginning to command increasing attention from the members of both the New York Housewares Manufacturers Association and the Housewares Manufacturers Association in Chicago. Both groups began to appreciate that it was just a question of time before they would have to get together.

Flo English's successful 1946 show left a distinct impression on the directors of both the New York and the Chicago associations. If they were going to do something to consolidate their position, they had better act quickly—because Mrs. English had already announced her second show for Atlantic City to be held the week of May 27, 1947.

The National Housewares Manufacturers Association

Flo English's *pronunciamentó* encouraged further discussion between the Chicago and New York groups about possible consolida-

Tom Stackpole, housewares buyer, opened the Lord & Taylor housewares department featuring one of the best hardware sections in Manhattan.

tion. At its meeting in Chicago on April 30, 1946, the Housewares Manufacturers Association made two moves that gave a forecast of things to come. First, it voted to add the word "national" to its name. Second, as the minutes state, "a majority of the [NHMA] directors agreed that the Chicago hotel situation made it practically impossible to hold a satisfactory exhibition there." In January 1947, therefore, a committee was appointed to find a suitable alternative site.

At the same time, there began an almost endless series of meetings between Chicago and New York association representatives. The more they met and talked, the more the obstacles to consolidation began to disappear. In the minutes of the August 6, 1946, meeting of the National Housewares Manufacturers Association, one finds this entry:

> The board of directors agree to proceed with the merger of the New York Housewares Manufacturers Association and this association, on the basis of suggestions made by the committee representing this association and the committee representing the New York association at a meeting held in Chicago on May 7, 1946...[and] the [NHMA] committee is authorized to complete the merger of the two associations.

The long-cherished hope of a single, truly nationwide industry organization was about to become a reality!

These are the men who made up the two committees:

Representing New York: James B. Hardenbergh, Corning Glass Works; Joseph A. Kaplan, Joseph A. Kaplan and Sons; and D. E. Stratton, Aluminum Goods Manufacturing Company.

Representing Chicago: George Fritz, F. H. Lawson Company; S. L. Hanssen, Hanson Scale Company; H. H. Kimball, Landers, Frary and Clark; and A. W. Buddenberg, NHMA.

Upon completion of the merger, three Chicago area directors of the NHMA resigned so that three from the New York group could be elected in their place.

With the merger situation well in hand, the remaining problem was to find a location for the coming January 1947 show. Efforts to get the Atlantic City auditorium failed—Flo English, of course, had already obtained the contract. Finally, Philadelphia's Convention Hall was obtained. From the standpoint of facilities it left much to be desired, but there was no other choice at the time.

However, there was a wide choice of dates for this show. Since it represented a big break from the previously established Chicago hotel location, it was argued that there was no special reason it had to be held in January. So the week of April 27 was selected.

That, of course, was just one month before the time and sixty miles west of the place (Atlantic City) where Flo English planned to hold her own show. Although no one was sufficiently brash or undiplomatic to admit it publicly, the move was obviously designed to undercut her event.

But Flo English "wasn't born yesterday." No sooner had the Philadelphia show dates been released than she announced a change

57

Past presidents of the NHMA: George Fritz, Jr., F. H. Lawson Company, 1946-47; J. R. Caldwell, Rubbermaid, Inc., 1948; J. W. Alsdorf, Cory Corporation, 1949-50; J. A. Kaplan, J. A. Kaplan & Sons, Inc., 1951-52.

in dates for the Atlantic City show to the week of January 5, 1947—four months ahead of Philadelphia! Once again the industry was to be saddled with an excess of shows.

Such wasteful duplication of effort was hardly the way to promote business, because although some firms came away from the shows well pleased, there was general grumbling and displeasure over the show situation.

Then something quite unforeseen occurred. It changed things completely.

Soon after her 1947 show, Flo English's husband became seriously ill.

> I didn't feel that I wanted to shoulder the responsibility for running such a show without George's help. After all, we had been in this thing together. Besides, in his condition he would require all of my time. So I called Mr. A. W. Buddenberg, then secretary of the National Housewares Manufacturers Association in Chicago, and asked if his group would be interested in taking over the Atlantic City auditorium and assuming my option on it.

The NHMA was very definitely interested. A meeting was soon arranged in Atlantic City between A. W. Buddenberg and Stan L. Hanssen of that association, Mrs. English, Al Skean, chairman of the Atlantic City Convention Bureau, and other city representatives. An agreement was concluded whereby the NHMA took over the option to Convention Hall. The action marked the end of her direct association with the housewares show.

At long last, the housewares industry had achieved what it had been striving for—a single, national association in complete control of managing its own official and nonprofit housewares shows. Starting in January 1948, and for the next thirteen years, the housewares show would be held in Chicago in January and in Atlantic City in July.

The country had begun to make the difficult adjustment from fighting World War II to a peacetime economy, only to find itself in 1951 deeply involved in the Korean War. But although it served to sharply curtail the production of civilian goods made of metal for some time, the "police action" never created the hardships and severe restrictions that World War II had imposed on the industry.

Prelude to McCormick Place

Despite all the operational handicaps that Philadelphia's outdated Convention Hall presented, the 1947 show had given the Chicago group a firsthand taste of an open-booth type of show. And they liked it. The Atlantic City Auditorium had already begun to condition the industry to the advantages of a show not confined to the cramped facilities of a hotel. When the NHMA had to choose a site for its January 1948 show, it selected the old International Amphitheater adjacent to the Chicago stockyards. Never designed for a trade show of such size, it proved to be as deficient as Convention Hall in Philadelphia, if not worse.

The summer show was held in Atlantic City, May 30–June 4, 1948. But thereafter (and for the next twelve years) the January show would be held in another old Chicago structure, Navy Pier. Often inadequately heated, its long, narrow, and confining layout proved to be merely a change from, not an improvement on, the Amphitheater.

The housewares industry was something of a victim of its own success. The discomforts and inconveniences of the inadequate show facilities in which it found itself merely reflected its growing pains. Each year, because of the booming postwar economy and the impact of the Korean War, the industry and its shows kept getting bigger. Even in 1952, when the drill hall adjacent to Navy Pier was pressed into service for exhibit space, there were many who could not be accommodated. The association had explored the possibility of moving the January show to some other city, but invariably found itself obliged to stay in Navy Pier. No other city offers the appealing, centralized geographic location combined with an abundance of hotel accommodations that Chicago does. But its lack of a big, modern exhibition facility equal to the demands of the housewares industry was long the cause of its worst difficulties.

It is an indication of the dynamic growth of the housewares industry that in recent years there has never been enough space in the association's show to accommodate all the would-be exhibitors —even after the opening of McCormick Place. It is a problem no other trade show faces, and the situation is far from being solved.

Not long after the end of World War II the number of housewares manufacturers who were unable to get into the NHMA show had become large enough to prompt independent promoters to start sepa-

Past presidents of the NHMA: C. M. McCreery, Revere Copper & Brass Inc., 1955-56; C. O. Hamilton, Hamilton Cosco, Inc., 1957; W. H. Sahloff, General Electric Corporation, 1958-59; G. C. Kubitz, Mirro Aluminum, 1960-61.

59

The NHMA Directors in April 1951: *front*—S. L. Hanssen; J. A. Kaplan; A. W. Buddenberg; *back*—J. R. Caldwell; C. M. McCreery; Ralph Fawcett; J. W. Alsdorf; Errett Grable; George Fritz.

Overleaf: The excitement of a modern NHMA National Housewares Exposition.

An industry continues to define and refine itself twice a year at the National Housewares Expositions now held in McCormick Place II in Chicago. This building replaced the one so dramatically destroyed just before the January 1967 Housewares Exposition.

Arie Crown Theatre in the first McCormick Place was the site of the NHMA's 1964 VIP Merchandisers and Manufacturers Banquet, which was designed to give executives greater insight into the range, importance, and potential of housewares.

rate "independent shows." These quickly became catchalls for marginal housewares (and much nonhousewares) merchandise, and have continued to be held in one of the Chicago hotels or Navy Pier.

In 1939, when he was still a sales representative for the Lisk Manufacturing Company, A. W. Buddenberg first became identified with the NHMA. He subsequently severed his connection with Lisk and devoted all of his time to being secretary of the association. In September 1948 the duties of that post had become so heavy that the directors engaged young Dolph Zapfel, Chicago housewares reporter for *Retailing Daily* (later *Home Furnishings Daily*), to become his assistant. Eight years later, on February 1, 1956, "Bud" Buddenberg resigned. The NHMA directors unanimously named Zapfel as secretary.

The Big Showplace

For over fifty years civic leaders, business executives, and government officials in Chicago had been urging the city to build a large well-equipped and up-to-date exhibition hall and auditorium to help attract business to that mid-America metropolis. The need increased year by year; the idea was logical and obvious.

THE FORUM

A year after it held its first show in McCormick Place and became acclimated to its new setting, the NHMA staged an impressive VIP Merchandisers and Manufacturers Forum and Banquet there in connection with its July 1962 show.

"This forum, 'The Challenge of Tomorrow's Merchandising,'" declared Harry Schwartz, executive vice-president of Lincoln Metal Products Company (then president of the NHMA), in his welcoming speech, "has been designed to enable each of us to reaffirm faith in continuing progress....

This industry induces homemakers to spend more than $6 billion annually for the great variety of products we now offer. It all started with pots and pans and a few cleaning aids many, many years ago—back when a "million" was big and the word "billion" was only used in textbooks....

Today [1962] the NHMA has categorized housewares into no less than 72 different product classifications for the United States Commerce Department. But here in McCormick Place you had the opportunity to see more than 200,000 housewares products....

Big as this industry has grown in dollar volume, it remains basically a nationwide assemblage of small businesses and an industry made up of many industries....No industry has probed deeper into the needs of homemakers as its prime source of ideas for new products....Beauty has been added, too; 56 percent of our manufacturers now employ professional designers. Housewares has truly become the industry of profit, progress, and ideas.

Past presidents of the NHMA: Harry Schwartz, Lincoln Metal Products, 1962; H. J. McCormick, Revere Copper & Brass, Inc., 1962; R. Lee Waterman, Corning Glass Works, 1963; L. C. Nelson, Cal-Dak Company, 1964.

Finally, after innumerable setbacks and disappointments, a Metropolitan Fair and Exposition Authority was created after World War II, and funds were provided to erect "the best convention hall in America." By January 1961 McCormick Place had become a reality.

It was not only the best but the biggest structure of its kind. Its 36 million cubic feet of space had cost $34 million and provided 310,000 square feet of exhibition space—the equivalent of about six football fields. There was parking space for 7,500 cars, and the taxi terminals could handle 400 cabs. A full-service dining room accommodated 650 diners at one time, and three self-service restaurants could serve 1,800 persons an hour. There were also two handsome theaters, one designed to hold 500 persons and another, not unlike New York's Radio City Music Hall, with 5,000 seats.

There was nothing anywhere to compare with the impressive building, conveniently located on Chicago's lakefront. As Edward J. Lee, former general manager of the Exposition Authority (and, incidentally, a former manufacturer of housewares—he was vice-president of the old Waring Products Company), described it, "McCormick Place adds a whole new dimension to our concepts of trade shows."

The first trade group to take advantage of these new facilities was the housewares industry, and on the morning of January 16, 1961, the National Housewares Manufacturers Association opened its thirty-fourth exhibit. It was a memorable event, which dwarfed all previous housewares shows. But just six years later another housewares show in the same place proved even more memorable when it suddenly brought this great new building to a flaming end!

The January 1961 housewares show had a record number of 909 exhibitors, using 1,640 booths. Yet enormous as McCormick Place was, it still fell short of the needs of the burgeoning housewares industry, and many would-be exhibitors had to be turned

In 1965, the NHMA cooperated with the U.S. government in organizing the NHMA Housewares Operation Europe. Fifty-seven manufacturers and trade representatives went on a three-week mission to Europe.

away. Some idea of how the demand for space in the show had grown can be gained from the fact that the promoter of the "independent" housewares show held at Chicago's Morrison Hotel during the same period signed up 350 exhibitors.

That the enormous new McCormick Place could not fulfill the space requirements of the housewares show dramatized what had been obvious—that the industry was constantly growing in size and in scope. Of course the nation's economy was also growing. America had started on its longest and strongest business boom—headed toward the trillion-dollar gross national product which it was predicted would be reached early in the seventies.

But the growth seemed especially conspicuous in housewares. The industry attracted a great many new manufacturers, small and large, and growth was also evident in the tremendous proliferation of products, both new items and old ones in new forms and colors.

Meanwhile, the NHMA also continued to grow in importance. Its major function was, of course, to conduct the semiannual trade exhibits, which it was doing with increasing success each year. By now, these had attained worldwide recognition as the most important events of their kind anywhere, and the presence of buyers from distant countries had long ceased to be novel.

By now, too, the scope of the association's activities had begun to broaden. For example, it retained a professional market research organization to begin a continuing series of annual studies of the housewares industry. Because of its complex, heterogeneous character, such studies had never been undertaken by anyone. In 1972, the fifth of these was issued. Together, they provide a wealth of facts about the industry which were never before available.

In 1965, in accordance with the government's efforts to promote exports, the "NHMA Housewares Operation Europe" was organized in cooperation with the United States Department of Commerce. As

Past presidents of the NHMA: S. M. Ford, the Proctor-Silex Corporation, 1965; M. R. Bissell III, Bissell, Inc., 1966; D. E. Noble, Rubbermaid, Inc., 1967; J. B. Stevens, the International Silver Company, 1968.

65

The NHMA "Housewares U.S.A." program allowed the American housewares industry the opportunity to exhibit as a group at the Cologne Housewares Fair in Germany.

Press conference time in Europe...
the purposes of the housewares trade
mission were to interest foreign buyers
to attend the U.S. housewares shows
as well as allow Americans to study the
European market for American goods.

a result, on February 16 fifty-seven manufacturers and trade representatives left by charter plane on a three-week, "two-way" trade mission to West Germany, France, Italy, and England. It was the first time, according to the Department of Commerce, that an industry group of such size had undertaken the twin objectives of studying the market potential abroad and seeking to bring additional foreign buyers to the housewares shows at home. Then, as a supplement to the trade mission, for the next three years the NHMA offered its exhibitors a package deal whereby they exhibited as a group in the Cologne Housewares Fair in a "Housewares, USA" presentation.

The Design Award

The NHMA made another policy departure when, in January 1966, it announced the start of a housewares design award based on a contest. Long aware of the tremendous increase in the importance of good design in all areas of housewares, the directors searched for a way in which the industry could effectively encourage and promote this phase of the business and finally decided upon a contest approach.

Arrangements were made with the National Design Center in New York to select an impartial panel of six judges consisting of the foremost professional industrial designers. These judges spent several days assessing the exhibits at the January show and making preliminary selections. Subsequently all the selected items were assembled elsewhere so that the judges could make their final choices. The winners were announced at an industry dinner at the following July show.

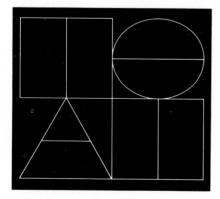

The NHMA sponsored three Design
Awards to encourage good design in
all areas of housewares.

The first "Design in Housewares Award" banquet took place during the week of the July 1966 housewares show and was held in McCormick Place. Nearly a thousand merchants and manufacturers attended. The guest speaker was the eminent director of Toronto University's Center for Culture and Technology, Marshall McLuhan, whose topic was "Communication through Design."

"This far-reaching program," explained the brochure distributed at the dinner, "seeks to foster the growing sophisticated image of the American housewares industry—and to do so where it counts: at the local retail level, where the consumer can see the best available designs in every major housewares category."

The banquet was conceived to be held on a biennial basis, and there have been three such events, the latest being the 1970/71 awards. The Art Institute of Chicago accorded the housewares industry a special honor by exhibiting some of the 1968-69 design award winners. This was a unique display of housewares, the first of its kind at the Art Institute. It is a significant sidelight on the ever-increasing sophistication of housewares that although sixty manufacturers received design awards at the first judging, only twenty-six firms were so honored at the latest event.

The Second Great Chicago Fire

The housewares shows, reflecting the nation's economy as well as the industry's emergence into a new era, broke all past records in the number of exhibitors and buyers who swarmed to McCormick Place in January 1967. By taking advantage of every square foot of exhibit space on both levels, the association was able to accommodate the unprecedented number of 1,236 exhibitors. Every indication seemed to assure that this would be the industry's biggest and best show. The weather, as usual in January, was very cold, but there was only a smattering of snow.

By Sunday evening, January 15, the three and one-half miles of red carpeting for the aisles which the association always provided at its shows was in place, ahead of schedule. The tardiest of the exhibitors had completed the finishing touches on their exhibits and were ready to leave for their downtown hotels which, by now, were packed with buyers eagerly waiting for the show to open.

Everything was set for that opening. Earlier in the evening Paul Demassey, the cleaning contractor for the exhibition halls, had been overheard telling a colleague, "Hell, things are in such fine shape this time the night crew will have practically nothing to do." In one way this turned out to be tragically true.

No one in the housewares business who witnessed that unforgettable night will ever need to be reminded of how disastrous it proved to be. By the time the fire was officially "struck out" at 9:46 the next morning, no less than five regular and four special alarms had brought five hundred firemen, ninety-four pieces of equipment, and three Civil Defense units into the fight. In the smoldering ruins

McCormick Place I always put out a welcome mat for the housewares shows —the biggest held in the center.

Unfortunately prophetic—just before the January 1967 Exposition, which was to be the thirteenth housewares show at McCormick Place.

The symbol of the shows in the old McCormick Place.

at daylight they found the body of a watchman who had failed to escape.

The unbelievable had become reality. It was the city's biggest and costliest conflagration since the great Chicago fire of 1871. The building alone was insured for $29,650,000 among seven companies, and three other insurers held $4 million in business interruption coverage. How many more millions would have to be added to those figures to cover the enormous direct and indirect losses of exhibitors and others would never be known.

"No single factor stands out as a major cause of the fire," concluded a special committee of experts named by Mayor Richard J. Daley to investigate. "However, the magnitude to which the fire grew is related to a progression of events and circumstances." Not unlike the sequence of events at Pearl Harbor, each successive mishap added fuel to the fire—in this case literally.

It originated, the investigators found, at the rear of booths 178-80-82, occupied by H & P House Furnishing Company. Two janitors discovered the fire. Efforts to beat it out with a broom and a piece of carpet were unsuccessful, and they could not control it. But no attempt was made to use a nearby standpipe and hose section. "The specific cause of the fire could not be fully determined," states the report, "due to the extent of the fire damage and because the committee was refused permission, after many efforts, to interview the contractor's electricians who wired the booth in question. Our investigation revealed that wiring methods used were temporary and contained many departures from recognized good practice. Reports of eyewitnesses who fought the fire initially indicate that it started in the vicinity of the booth's electrical wiring connections." The refusal of the electricians to testify at the hearing speaks eloquently for itself.

The haphazard fire-fighting efforts and the six-minute delay in sending in an alarm to the fire department had a significant effect on the extent of the loss, in the committee's opinion.

The first firemen arrived at 2:14 a.m., but by then twelve booths were already engulfed in flames. "Evidence indicates that the first arriving company laid out hose lines for an interior attack, had water for approximately four minutes and then lost the water."

Closed, partially closed, or inoperative private fire hydrants on the grounds of the building, at least in part because of the extensive construction work on the nearby Stevenson Expressway, created a major problem for the fire department. To make a bad situation even worse, the private pumping station supplying McCormick Place failed to function properly. "The fire department then had to resort to laying long lines of hose relays, using numerous pumpers to obtain water from the nearest available sources—hydrants 1 and 2, Lake Michigan, and South Parkway, located about one-quarter mile west of the building."

Fire fighting was seriously hampered not only by the lack of water, but also by the intense heat, the rapid spread of the fire, the collapse of the roof within three-quarters of an hour from the start of the fire, and the dangerously unstable large exterior wall panels, the report states. It goes on to criticize the fact that the building's "personnel, on the scene, were untrained and uninformed as to how to cope with an emergency of this type," and adds: "Had this fire occurred eight hours later when the exhibition hall could have been crowded with show patrons, egress facilities could have been taxed to their limit and the possibility of ensuing panic could have resulted in a great loss of life."

The report concludes with numerous recommendations for preventing a repetition of such a disaster, recommendations which, along with many others, were heeded in the design and construction of the new McCormick Place.

Somehow, the Show Goes On

The terrible fire incinerated all possibility of anyone's doing "business as usual" at the show. But it failed to destroy the determination of a great many sellers and buyers to make the most of the opportunity that remained. And so very early Monday morning, as word of the disaster spread by word of mouth and by radio and television news programs, a great many firms began improvising emergency sales facilities. Make-do displays were set up in hotel bedrooms. Samples were sometimes rushed over from local Chicago showrooms or even borrowed from State Street housewares departments. More often, catalog sheets and photographs had to suffice in place of the actual merchandise.

From long association and experience many buyers knew at which hotels their manufacturers were staying—and vice versa—so that it was possible for them to reach each other. In a great many instances it was imperative that buyers place their commitments for spring and summer merchandise before they left Chicago; otherwise they could find themselves in trouble later.

As the day wore on, an amazing number of such contacts had been established. It was a remarkable demonstration of buyers and sellers managing to carry on some semblance of business under the most difficult and inconvenient circumstances.

Yet helpful as these measures were, in the final analysis those relatively few instances were the exceptions. For most manufacturers and merchants the sudden destruction of the long-established show on which they depended so greatly demanded a far-reaching and costly revision of plans. An army of salesmen now set out across America to visit in their stores the buyers they had so confidently looked forward to seeing at McCormick Place. If some members of the trade had not fully appreciated the function of their show, they did so now that they had been deprived of it. As so often happens, the things we take for granted are not fully appreciated until they are gone.

69

Past presidents of the NHMA: R. B. Stone, the Dover Corporation, 1969; R. F. Draper, Sunbeam Corporation, 1970; V. K. Church, Aladdin Industries, 1971; L. L. Salton, Salton, Inc., 1972.

It is trite to say that in commerce, as in the theater, the show must go on; yet that is precisely true, and the NHMA's board of directors had meanwhile acted to see that it did. One of their first actions was to vote a 50 percent refund of all exhibit fees. Then—after having considered all other possibilities—they voted to move the upcoming summer show to Chicago's International Amphitheater. Compared with the spacious, modern, and pleasant location of McCormick Place, the old and outdated Amphitheater understandably was a rather depressing letdown for the industry. But the directors had no alternative. After McCormick Place it was still the largest exposition hall in the country at that time. And nowhere else could that amount of exhibit space be had together with the required hotel facilities.

All things considered, the industry adjusted to the conditions surprisingly well. And it is interesting that the number of exhibitors at the January 1968 show there—just a year after the fire—reached an all-time high of 1,283.

Nevertheless, the demand for space at the show continued unabated and once again a so-called independent show was held at Navy Pier, composed of companies who either were unable to get space in the Amphitheater or who were not qualified as actually being in the housewares business.

McCormick Place II

Meanwhile, a new and, it was hoped, bigger and better McCormick Place would rise in true Phoenix fashion from the wreckage on the lakefront. The move to rebuild it, however, immediately stirred up a bitter controversy. Some Chicagoans, aided especially by the *Chicago Sun-Times,* who had never wanted a McCormick Place in the first place, protested vigorously.

Nevertheless, planning went ahead. From various sources the Metropolitan Fair and Exposition Authority managed to round up over $80 million, and on May 17, 1968, ground was broken for a new building on the same site. Differences of opinion over the plans for the new structure developed and there were no less than three major changes in its design. Coming at a time when the country began to experience a period of serious inflation, these changes not only delayed the progress but also added substantially to the cost, so that the completed building ultimately exceeded the $100 million mark. Finally it was announced that it would be available for use in January 1971 and that again the NHMA housewares show would be the first major trade event to be held there.

"The trouble with the new McCormick Place, when you come to discuss it in any kind of casual way," a feature writer in the *Chicago Tribune* put it, "is that it is so frustratingly unique....There's nothing else anywhere that you can legitimately compare it with....So if you are going to talk about it at all, you are forced either to resort to a list of largely incomprehensible statistics...to prove how unique it really is, or what is worse, to play tricks with the building itself."

Where the buyer and seller get together —the big market place and the reason for the semi-annual National Housewares Exposition. The January 1972 show was a colorful amalgam of people and products.

It is so enormous that, as a spokesman for the architects remarked, "You could place both the John Hancock Center (a Chicago building 100 stories high) and the Empire State Building inside McCormick Place and still have room left over for two pretty good-sized high-rises." One critic declared, "It looks like an aircraft carrier that ran aground." Nevertheless, here are a few of its vital statistics:

It cost over $110 million.

It is one-quarter of a mile long and 590 feet wide. Its height is equivalent to an eleven-story building.

It contains almost 700,000 square feet of exposition space on three levels connected by escalators; the old building only had 480,000 square feet of such space.

The main reception lobby contains 73,000 square feet.

The electric generating capacity of the new building is enough to meet the normal demands of 1,200 single-family homes.

Food preparation and serving facilities in eight permanent restaurants can accommodate 20,000 persons a day.

Temperature, humidity, and air pollution are constantly moni-

SHOW RATES

For fifty-three exhibitions in thirty-one years, the National Housewares Manufacturers Association was able to maintain an unbroken record—probably unmatched in the trade-show field—of not raising its rates to exhibitors. But in January 1971 when the show was returned to the new McCormick Place, spiraling costs finally caught up with it.

Previously, the rate to housewares show exhibitors had been about two dollars per square foot. And that rate was always reduced later by the refund from the proceeds of the shows, since the NHMA has of course always been a nonprofit organization. To date it has refunded more than $3 million to exhibitors. Because of constantly increasing operating costs for the January 1971 show a new rate of $2.50 per square foot was set. But that is still substantially below the average rate for the national trade shows—six dollars per square foot.

We can gain some idea of the enormous increase in costs by comparing the January 1972 show expenses with those of January 1947, the first open-booth show held by the NHMA in Convention Hall, Philadelphia. The 1947 show had 412 exhibitors and cost $70,000. The 1942 show had 1,470 exhibitors and cost more than $750,000. Here are a few other comparisons:

	1947	1972
Advertising and promotion	$ 3,400	$ 70,000
Exhibit hall rent	$14,500	$186,500
Security service	$ 1,200	$ 31,000
Printing directory	$ 5,000	$ 45,000

For another example, there is the cost of free bus service for buyers, which wasn't available in 1947—another $25,000!

tored by 2,000 sensors located throughout the building to help insure maximum comfort.

There are fifty-four freight doors and fifty-four truck docks.

Taxi loading and unloading ramps, all underground, can accommodate 1,500 cabs.

There are thirty meeting rooms that seat from 35 to 1,800 persons; six theater-like meeting rooms seating between 550 and 1,800 persons. There are fifty-four rest rooms.

Telephone service for exhibitors is available from 6,000 outlet jacks.

The Arie Crown Theater seats 5,000, and there are six smaller theaters.

And, of course, fire detection and prevention facilities are greatly augmented. There are twenty fire-alarm pull boxes in the new building; there were nine in the old one. The new building has 20,000 sprinklers; there were 1,000 in the old one. In addition, there is an elaborate electronic fire detection system. Four hundred smoke detectors are located throughout the ventilating system, and there are one hundred heat-rise indicators in electrical and mechanical distribution systems, each of which will instantly report any changes to the central control station electronically.

Security in the new building is also under electronic control. Closed-circuit television cameras, under twenty-four-hour observation, will monitor all key areas from the central control station. Each door serving an event area is connected electronically to the central control station, from which it can be locked or unlocked; unauthorized opening of doors is instantly reported and guards are dispatched to the area.

No one watched the new McCormick Place emerge from the ashes with greater anticipation than the housewares industry. And when, early in 1970, Ed Lee, general manager of the building, assured Dolph Zapfel that it would be completed in time for the NHMA's coming January 1971 show, it was most welcome news. But the industry's enthusiastic anticipation was tempered with more than a little realistic apprehension. Would it—could it—really be ready on time? What if a prolonged strike or some other contingency arose? What if...

Their fears proved groundless. Although McCormick Place was far from being entirely completed, it was nevertheless sufficiently finished so that NHMA's fifty-fourth exhibition opened there right on schedule, Monday morning, January 11. Of course there were the usual minor annoyances and inconveniences always to be encountered in an unfinished building—occasional disturbing noises and little showers of plaster dust, limited eating facilities, and unopened rest rooms, to mention a few.

But no one paid the least attention to them. The overriding comfort and convenience of being "back home" in this great new exhibition facility was so satisfying that one heard nothing but praise for the building from buyers and sellers alike. What helped in no small measure was the excellent business climate; everyone seemed pleased with their sales.

Nevertheless, there was one disconcerting note—a very serious one. Dolph Zapfel expressed it when he said:

Our return to McCormick Place four years after the disastrous fire that wiped out our January 1967 exposition signals the start of an exciting and bright new era for the housewares industry. Unfortunately, however, the new McCormick Place, despite its great cost and the fact that it is the largest and most modern facility in the country, is still not completely adequate to meet the immediate, much less the future, actual needs of this rapidly expanding industry.

THIS IS HOW IT WAS...

A firsthand, personal account of what happened "the night a year went up in smoke" and McCormick Place burned down; an amplification of the report made the following day by the author in his column "If You Ask Me" in *Home Furnishings Daily.*

Not all the tired exhibitors were anxious to go downtown to their hotels that memorable Sunday evening, January 15, 1967, after they had finished setting up their booths in McCormick Place. Many decided to have dinner right in the President's Walk and then take in a performance of Herb Alpert's popular Tijuana Brass band, currently booked at the huge Arie Crown Theater there. It would be a relaxing prelude to the next morning, when they had to plunge into what was expected to be the greatest of all housewares shows.

Herb Alpert and his band were in exceptionally fine form that evening. There wasn't a vacant seat in the house. Their sharp, scintillating, satisfying music reverberated triumphantly throughout every corner of the immense theater, and the musicians appeared to be enjoying the evening every note as much as the highly appreciative audience, which is saying a lot. By the time the famous band finished its final encore one might easily have thought it had been some kind of historic farewell performance. In a way it was just that.

"That was great," remarked Dolph Zapfel as he, Dick Hochman—the association's public relations director—and I threaded our way through the departing throng toward a cab. "And it was really quite relaxing," he added a little wearily. He had good reason, of course, to feel more than a little weary; for weeks he and his staff had been working long hours putting the association's forty-sixth show together.

We finally got a cab. But once we were on our way downtown none of us felt much like talking. Presently Dolph spoke up about something that always bothered him, especially at show time.

"I think it's going to be a great show; it's cold but not snowing," he commented. "But if there were only more exhibit space to take care of the demand—that's what gets me. You know the Metropolitan Fair and Exposition Authority just allocated $15 million for adding 200,000 square feet to the exhibition hall. It can't come soon enough for me..." His voice trailed off. It was nearly midnight when we reached the Palmer House, and we parted to go to our rooms for some sleep. Tomorrow was the big day.

74

Opposite page: The fire, which wiped out the January 1967 NHMA show as well as Chicago's McCormick Place.

The aftermath, which pictures the utter destruction of the McCormick Place fire. Roof and walls collapsed, one man died, the entire housewares show destroyed. On the same site, a new McCormick Place arose, once again the scene for the National Housewares Expositions.

It was just two minutes to two, John McNellis, chief of the Kane Security guards at McCormick Place, recalled later, when he frantically dialed Ed Lee at his home. It seemed like hours before anyone answered his call; his eyes impatiently followed the crawling second hand on his watch. Actually, he had reached Ed Lee, general manager of McCormick Place, almost immediately.

"You'd better get over here right away, quick," McNellis shouted to his still half-awake listener. "The place is on fire...it looks pretty serious."

"No!" Ed managed to reply in disbelief. He mumbled a question or two, said he'd be right over, and hung up. As McNellis turned to leave his office a ribbon of black smoke curled in from the hall and snaked across the ceiling.

Ed Lee fumbled into some clothes and in no time was behind the wheel of his car, leaving his apartment building on North State Street; "pretty serious...pretty serious"—the words kept going through his mind.

By now the phone in room 2317W in the Palmer House was ringing. The irritating sound finally penetrated a dead-to-the-world Dolph Zapfel. More asleep than awake, he flicked the light switch, and as he groped for the intruding instrument he cursed those far-gone all-night carousers who never manage to dial the right room number.

"Hello," he growled. The voice that answered—or, more accurately, the words it spoke—instantly brought him wide awake. "Hello—is this Dolph Zapfel, the managing director of the housewares association? This is a reporter for the *Daily News.* McCormick Place is burning to the ground! What are you going to do about it?"

"What would you do about it?" he replied mechanically, not quite awake. Suddenly the meaning of the reporter's words registered; he began another question, but Dolph cut him short. "I... I can't stop to talk now...I'll see you over there right away." For a moment he sat on the edge of the bed as if stunned, trying to comprehend what had just happened. Through his mind raced those incredible words, "McCormick Place is on fire!" How? Where? What if...? But he couldn't even bring himself to finish framing such a question.

He called Dick Hochman's home and told Dick to meet him at McCormick Place as soon as possible. Zapfel then raced to a cab at the Wabash Avenue door of the hotel. "McCormick Place, and step on the gas—this is an emergency!" he told the driver as he numbly slid onto the seat.

Ed Lee's car, meanwhile, had reached the Outer Drive, and he swung south. Now no buildings obscured his view—and there it was! Unbelievable! Now he couldn't deny the awful meaning of that great bright glow that lit up the sky ahead.

"My God," he moaned. The horror of the sight froze his lips open. His heart, already pounding, hit an even more furious pace. His eyes were glued to the glow. Reflexively his right foot pressed down hard on the gas and the car leaped forward as if suddenly attracted by some giant magnet.

Before he realized it, Ed was at McCormick Place. He had seen that building under all conceivable conditions from the time it was only a blueprint, but now this! He stopped and took in the organized confusion of an army of fire fighters and their equipment, brought out into the bitter, 16-degree cold of the lakefront by a 5–11 alarm—which calls out the whole works. Piercing searchlights punctuated the leaping flames, and flying embers and the glow of flashlights in the hands of police and firemen darting in all directions illuminated the spectacle with an eerie impression of unreality.

The smoke eaters, their helmets and coats solidly encrusted with ice, seemed to be attacking the building from every side. Some pumpers were even drawing water from the lake through the ice; but the powerful silvery streams were having almost no effect. Suddenly there was an ominous, muffled roar and a sky-rocket of sparks; the roof had caved in. "It was a terrifying sight," Ed recalled later, "absolutely terrifying."

The cab in which Dolph had raced to the fire now stopped in a small open space away from the fire trucks and police cars, and he got out. Moments later Dick pulled up in another cab. They were numb, but not from the cold; they were far beyond that. Dolph stared in disbelief. What was all this, some kind of evil nightmare? Could it be real? Wasn't the housewares show to open here in just a few more hours, after months of preparation?

Yet there it was—the walls of the once-impressive McCormick Place collapsed...the acrid, swirling smoke and leaping flames... the clanging bells and shrill sirens...the shouted commands of the fire chiefs to their men silhouetted against the fiery glow—all only too real.

Dolph found himself standing beside someone's car. He glanced at the driver; it was Ed Lee, and he got in. Neither of them was surprised at such a chance meeting; nothing could surprise them anymore. Ed began to drive around the outside of the building in order to comprehend the full impact of the catastrophe, but neither of them spoke. At a time like this words could only be superfluous; silence communicated their thoughts far more eloquently.

It was the housewares show, they recalled, that was the first trade show at McCormick Place in 1961. Oh yes, come to think of it, this would have been the thirteenth housewares show here.... But now?

Now McCormick Place, the country's greatest exhibition and convention hall complex, which had cost $40 million, was being reduced to rubble before their eyes. Only a few hours earlier, the vast array of samples and displays, in which the industry had invested millions, was all set, neat and spittin' clean, ready to go.

But now? Now it began to sink in—finally, painfully, but undeniably. There would be no housewares show in McCormick Place today or for a great many more days. Moreover, there was nothing, absolutely nothing, that anyone could do to change things. And so about two hours later they drove slowly away.

In a magazine interview about the fire a year later, Dolph was quoted as saying, "January 17 would have been a good day for me to resign. There is just no way to determine how you will react when faced with a crisis; you don't know if you'll be a hero or a coward."

One needs little imagination to comprehend the personal impact such an unimaginable industry catastrophe must have upon the man who is at the core of it all. His actions at the time, however, speak eloquently; and throughout it all, as so many noted, his calm, self-possessed competence had the situation immediately under control—insofar, of course, as anyone could control it.

Back in his suite at the Palmer House, the managing director of the National Housewares Manufacturers Association, along with some of his staff, began to go into action. It was not yet five o'clock when he told the telephone operator, "I want to speak to Melville Bissell in Grand Rapids; and please hurry, it's urgent." Mel Bissell, former head of the Bissell Company and at that time president of the NHMA, had flown home to Grand Rapids the day before, right after the luncheon meeting of the association's board of directors. He had planned to return for the show early Monday in the company plane. Dolph told him what had happened and asked him to be at the NHMA offices in the Merchandise Mart at eight o'clock for an emergency meeting of the directors. "I'll be there as fast as I can round up our pilot," he replied.

Presently Dolph had Wayne Stetson, manager of the Atlantic City Convention Bureau, on the phone. Would the Auditorium there be available for a July housewares show? Someone else was trying to reach the manager of New York's Coliseum. Another had placed a call to Jack O'Connell, manager of Houston's Astrodome.

As these and other possible standby show sites were being checked out, calls were being made to round up the association's directors for the emergency board meeting at eight o'clock. And to add further strain to an already overwrought situation, there was a barrage of reporters and calls from the press seeking comment and information.

"The housewares industry," commented *Home Furnishings Daily* the next morning, "can be pleased and proud it has such a man in that very vital post as Dolph Zapfel."

79

CHANGING PATTERNS OF DISTRIBUTION

America's material greatness can be traced directly to its feat of pioneering the modern miracle of mass production and its indispensable corollary, mass distribution.

"Nowhere in the world has the art of selling at wholesale been developed to as high a point as it has in the United States," declares Walter Hoving, one of the country's eminent merchants and now chairman of Tiffany and Company, in his book *The Distribution Revolution.*

> No one in America believes the old adage that if you "build a better mousetrap the world will beat a path to your door." We found out long ago that this idea is as dead as the dodo. To achieve the mass distribution we must have, our sales executives must beat the path to the door of the *customer* instead of the other way around. That is why we have developed the art of salesmanship...to the point that it has reached. And that is why our distribution is far ahead of the rest of the world.[1]

Compared with today's mass production and mass distribution, trade in colonial America seems not three hundred years but light years away.

In Colonial Times

Until well into the eighteenth century, except for a relatively few things obtained from Europe, almost everything the early settlers required they had to make themselves, usually in their own homes. It was a "do-it-yourself-or-do-without" situation.

In such a setting surplus household products might be sold or bartered. A full-time craft occupation was rare, although a few trained craftsmen came to America on the very first boats—blacksmith James Reed to Jamestown in 1607, for example.

Rolla Milton Tryon, in *Household Manufacturers in the United States 1640-1860*, lists some of the common homemade articles: brooms, brushes, wooden trays, trenchers, bowls, platters, noggins, lamps, buckets, dye tubs, churns, firkins, doormats, baskets, wooden bread troughs, cheese-ladders, cheese-hoops, butter paddles, and washboards.[2]

In the towns and larger communities, especially along the coast, shops gradually began to appear. They were mostly a kind of general store. But Mary R. M. Goodwin, in a mimeographed manuscript "The Colonial Store" in the research library of Colonial Williamsburg, warns that "the colonial store should not be confused with the

80

NEW HOME
Sewing Machine Co.

Samuel Blastrick

Here is my card.
You will find my firm's name on the other side.

One of the most important forms of advertising in the nineteenth century was the simple business card. A big business in itself.

The Bettmann Archive.

Beloved to many generations and historically important in conquering the American frontier, "the old country store" was one of the original housewares market places.

Courtesy National Association of Manufacturers.

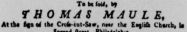

The Yankee peddler offering his wares to a group of housewives in a rural community. After a woodcut by C. G. Bush.

The Bettmann Archive.

From top: Housewares from other times: An 1876 Philadelphia centennial exhibition advertisement for Cedar Ware. The bottom photo notes that a colonial newspaper advertised the wares of iron merchant Thomas Maule. Limited in space but abounding in housewares-type merchandise.

Top, courtesy of the Society for the Preservation of New England Antiquities.

'country store' or 'general store' of the nineteenth century, as it contained a far wider range of merchandise, furnishing the colonists with almost all of their manufactured needs."

Specialization in the colonial economy developed slowly and only rarely in the early years was a shop devoted to one particular type of product.

"Shops may be roughly divided into four kinds," says Tunis in *Colonial Craftsmen,* "those of craftsmen who did bespoke work, that is, custom work to order; those of retailers who simply bought and sold; those of artisans who offered 'salework' on a take-it-or-leave-it basis, and those of specialists who performed some direct personal service for the public."[3]

Colonial trade as a whole was controlled by the British, very much to their own advantage. A long series of navigation acts, the Staple Act, and the Stamp Act imposed in the last half of the eighteenth century prohibited the export and import of many products except through British ports.

Production of pig iron—which Britain needed—was permitted to the colonists. But in 1750 they were forbidden to erect slitting mills to make nails and iron rods or to set up forges for making steel or finished iron items. The enterprising colonists were producing raw iron to such an extent that by 1775 the output was thirty thousand tons or one-seventh of the world's iron.

All agree on the difficulties of doing business in colonial America. Many of the basics now taken for granted were missing. The early colonists were forbidden to mint coins, and a hodgepodge of French, Spanish, English, and other money circulated, plus counterfeit!

However, in 1652 the general court established its own mint and limited legal current money to its own coins, according to Charles Andrews in his authoritative *The Colonial Period of American History.*[4]

Banking facilities were virtually nonexistent—there was no bank in pre-revolution New York, and the first to be established was the Bank of New York in 1784. In the late 1600s trade was conducted by barter, paper bills, and—always—extended credit advances.

The development of commercial banks, according to Harrington, was slow because to a considerable extent every important merchant was a private banker for himself and others, holding a deposit to the credit of each of his customers. "The net result of the system of credit, advances, inadequate currency, and lack of banks was to diminish the amount of cash at a merchant's call almost to the vanishing point,"[5] writes Harrington in the *New York Merchant.*

There was a lack of accurate and uniformly accepted standards of quality, fineness, and manufacture, so that conducting trade at a distance was constantly beset with problems and handicaps.

Rolla Milton Tryon sums up a portion of that transition thusly:

The history of household manufactures in the United States from 1640 to 1860 is mainly concerned with that slow transfer from goods made entirely in the home by the members of a family and from materials grown largely on the farm, to goods made wholly in shop or factory. This transfer was gradually going on during all the years between the foregoing dates. Its story would be a simple one if it had been marked with uniformity either in time or in place. Since this was not the case, such a story becomes a very complex one....

The fact that the country had a large frontier population during its entire history to 1860 made the transfer from household- to shop-and-factory-made goods something that was always taking place but never quite completed when the country as a whole is considered.[6]

The nineteenth-century tin peddler with his full wagon of pots and pans. Pen and ink drawing circa 1893.

The Bettmann Archive.

Then the gathering force of other patterns, summed up in the "industrial revolution" was to radically change every aspect of the "small shop and factory" economy which had dominated the American scene for two centuries.

Two inventions that have had their effect on business and distribution. The young lady above is working a Sholes typewriter, 1872. The woman below operates a telegraph machine of the same period.

The Bettmann Archive

HORSE SHOES OR FORKS—
FROM THE BLACKSMITH

The blacksmith in colonial times was called upon to provide some of the essential housewares, and in his *Colonial Craftsmen* Edwin Tunis describes it thus:

> If Mistress Hughes in Providence needed a long-handled cooking fork, her husband picked a smith who was especially good at such things and had him make it for her. This was a standard article and perhaps the smith had one made in advance that would serve. But there was no factory anywhere that turned out cooking forks in quantity, all alike, and no shop had a house furnishing department where Mrs. Hughes could look for the fork she wanted.
>
> The blacksmith who made the fork was prepared to make any cooking utensil, so long as it was wrought iron; a pot hook, a dripper, a strainer; a trivet on which to keep a pot warm near the fire; a broiler, either a plain square one or a fancy one with rotating circular top; a toaster with a rotating rack to simplify reversing the bread before the fire.
>
> The smith couldn't make skillets, waffle irons, stew pots and kettles—those were cast-iron foundry jobs or coppersmith's work—but he could forge handles for any of them.[7]

The Yankee Peddler

"It can hardly be said that anything deserving the name of interstate commerce existed in this country at the beginning of the present century [1800]," reports that monumental volume *One Hundred Years of American Commerce 1795-1895,* and it adds, "The Alleghenies constituted an almost impassable barrier between the East and the West, and such necessary products as the colonists could not obtain in their immediate neighborhoods were mostly brought from overseas."[8]

Along the seaport towns trade and commerce had begun to flourish and there one could find shops. In New York, for example, there were at least forty-four general stores by 1764. Yet only a relatively short distance from those coastal areas, shops were conspicuously absent. Factories, as such, were still unknown, and had anyone used the word "distribution" in the marketing sense no one would have had any idea what he was talking about.

As for "communication," the postal service was practically non-existent, and it would be years before the railroad arrived. Overland travel was possible only by horseback or stagecoach—unless one walked, as many did. Except for some of the more passable roads—usually toll roads—near the coast connecting communities like Boston, New York, and Philadelphia, roads leading elsewhere, particularly toward the frontier settlements in the interior, quickly deteriorated into Indian or animal trails. Back-country settlements were scarce and far apart and travel was often beset by all sorts of problems and dangers, not the least of which was the weather.

It was into such times and circumstances that one of the most important and colorful "distributors" of household goods emerged—the "Yankee peddler," a distributor of much-needed house furnishings, especially in the hinterlands, where the settlers had little or no other means of obtaining necessities for everyday living.

Often enough this "Yankee peddler" wasn't a Yankee at all. Immigrants—German, Jewish, Polish, Armenian, and others—often gravitated into such an occupation, sometimes ending up years later as merchant princes. The practice of peddling goes back to antiquity, but in the New England colonies, according to Dolan, it was at least stimulated in the seventeenth century by sailors' smuggling in small essential items from England for private speculation. "A sailor can pack a lot of needles, pins, buttons, combs, spools of thread, and spoons and knives for the table into a small bundle. (Forks were not yet generally used.) In Boston and in outlying settlements there was a ready market for such items, which were constantly wearing out or getting lost and had to be replaced."[9] Peddling was a natural career for an enterprising young man.

The beginners probably all started out with a pack on their backs —as Adam Gimbel from New Orleans did in 1830. He went on to found a department-store empire. Later they might graduate to a horse and eventually a regular peddler's wagon.

Pots and pans on sale at a later period. Street wares on Maxwell Street in Chicago about 1906.

Courtesy the Chicago Historical Society.

A boon to the housewares business and business in general, the telephone as of 1878....

Generally there was little love lost between the peddlers and the shopkeepers and merchants. The latter, often with little justification, charged the peddlers with taking away their business when, in fact, the peddlers for the most part traveled far out over the countryside serving customers who rarely could manage a trip into town.

As a trader the peddler had to be shrewder and sharper than his customers, a situation that took on added significance because money seldom played a part in the transaction. "From the town where he had acquainted himself with current prices, the peddler went into a thinly settled region and bartered his goods... the straw-chewing yokels could be persuaded to... pay in produce that, in the town, had a marketable value far in excess of what they had received in exchange," relates Richardson Wright in his authoritative *Hawkers and Walkers.* And, he points out, "there wasn't anything unusually dishonest about this sort of transaction; business standards up to fifty years ago [1875] were of that nature.... Commercial honesty had not yet cut its teeth."[10]

Roads in the new land were scarce, but rivers were plentiful. Raftloads of assorted merchandise were poled by the peddlers to the upriver settlements. It is probable that these raftloads of assorted merchandise gave birth to the general store as the up-river settlements became little towns.

Of most significance to the housewares industry were the tin peddlers. Although most peddlers stocked some tinware items, tin peddlers were something of a special breed. Generally they operated with a wagon or cart specially designed to meet the functional needs of the business, and the wagon was usually gaily painted in bright colors so it could be spotted at a distance. In Europe the tinsmiths were universally gypsies.

The peddling of tinware in America can be traced to 1740 when two Irishmen, William and Edgar Pattison, who had settled in Berlin, Connecticut, a couple of years before, decided to start making tin cooking utensils. Imported English tinware was costly; since there was little tin sheet to be had here they used imported sheets, beating out utensils on anvils with wooden mallets. There was such a demand for their wares that as they prospered others began producing tinware and Berlin soon became an important tinware center.

Wright relates that with the coming of the turnpikes, around 1790, the tin peddlers, based in Berlin, might cover twelve to fifteen hundred miles on a single trip.

Much of the tinware peddler's custom was in barter, which he conveyed to town to be converted into cash. All this seems very risky.

The first tinware peddlers weren't working for themselves; they were representatives of manufacturers in far away Connecticut. Here were hundreds of young men trusted with a stock, trusted with a team, trusted with bartering and depended upon to make honest reports and honest returns... [which] would seem almost expecting the impossible."

Yet the peddlers seem to have served their employers well.

Peddling grew and prospered. In his book *The Old Country Store*, Gerald Carson states that in 1850 there were 10,669 peddlers on the roads of this country; in 1860 there were 16,594. The nation's economy was growing and prospering too, and that marked the beginning of the end of peddling.

By the mid-nineteenth century the gathering impact of the developing industrial revolution had begun to make itself felt in endless ways. Mills and factories and foundries were being built throughout the country—railroads, highways, and canals were providing much-needed transportation, stores of all sorts were springing up everywhere, and newly formed wholesalers and jobbers—with their "drummers," as salesmen were then known—were ready to serve them.

The Yankee peddler was beginning to outlive his usefulness. For example, New York State, which had licensed 302 peddlers in 1841, licensed only 80 in 1871. But the spirit of the Yankee peddler didn't die—it was reincarnated later as the house-to-house salesman.

...perhaps being used by a housewares merchant and his secretary. "Hello, hello—how many?"

Woodcuts above and on preceding page, the Bettmann Archive

The Old Country Store

When the Yankee peddler tired of traveling and settled down, chances are that then and there a store was born. Maybe it was a frontier trading post or some likely upriver settlement. Gradually, in no fixed pattern, there emerged the country general store.

Shopkeepers of one kind or another had long since begun to appear in the larger towns along the East Coast, though often the "shops" were little more than a room in the craftsman's house. "But the general store was an American origination, something new under the sun, improvised to meet the raw conditions of a new continent," explains Gerald Carson in his richly nostalgic book *The Old Country Store.*

> In the days when men lived separate and solitary lives, it was the country store that tied the scattered farms into a community. The store was what made a neighborhood and gave it its central nervous system and a conscience. It also put some fun into life.
>
> The owner was invariably an important personality, a community leader ex-officio, a culture hero too. Around him gathered tales and incidents, one of the few instances of the businessman appearing as a character in folklore.
>
> For nearly a hundred and fifty years after the Revolution, the country store rendered a great variety of services not otherwise available in an unspecialized society. The successful storekeeper's ability to adjust nimbly to changing circumstances in times of war, financial panic, and depression, to make a profit in an orthodox manner at one time, and then at another to take a long chance, is a prime instance of American flexibility and durability, free enterprise in a very pure form.[12]

Carson quotes from an article on the "omnibus store" in the *Philadelphia Merchant* sometime in 1876, which notes that although the country general store is especially characteristic of newly settled areas of the west it is also found within forty miles of Philadelphia itself. It describes it thus:

> It is a grocery store...that seemed to have everything with tea, sugar, coffee, spices, molasses, dried fruits, etc. It is a hardware store with cutlery in variety, axes, rifles, divers mechanics' tools, kitchen utensils, agricultural implements, bar-iron, nails, etc. It is a shoe store, and men, women and children can alike be accommodated....It is a confectionery store, and there's a goodly row of glass jars of candies for the sweet tooth. It is a brush store, and bristles and broom-corn are in readiness for a customer. It is a crockery store, and you may buy queensware, earthenware, glassware and stoneware. It is a drug store....It is a trimming store....It is a jewelry store....It is a hat store....It is a book and stationery store....It is a tobacco store....It is also the post-office, and the merchant is the post-master. He will have almost any article you can call for, the *Philadelphia Merchant* said and will most agreeably make a note to get what he is "just out of."[13]

By and large the country general stores prospered. But America was prospering even more, and that, ironically, spelled the end of the general stores. The industrial revolution had taken off. More new manufacturers were producing more new products than ever before, and at every level of trade specialization became imperative. With constantly improving transportation and communication, distances were shrinking. Canals, roads, and railroads were providing ready access to new areas everywhere, and the telegraph and then that new marvel, the telephone, linked distances even more speedily.

But probably more than any of those things, the automobile proved fatal for the old general store. "One might...choose almost

The tinker's wagon, a very moving fixture throughout the nineteenth century.

Courtesy Old Museum Smith's Clove, Monroe, New York.

any year between 1891 and 1921 as the critical year for the general store,"[14] says Carson. It was in 1891 that Frank Duryea first made his homemade automobile run successfully in Springfield, Massachusetts. It was in 1909 that Henry Ford's first Model T rolled off the assembly line.

> The essential truth involved was that the car brought the paved road and the paved road took away the country store's customers. Of course it all happened gradually. The country merchant kept right on dusting his cases and sweeping out and wonder, sometimes, where all the drummers were. He did not know that he was a casualty of a transportation revolution.[15]

The Hardware Store

The first store for the sale of American-made and imported hardwares was set up by Amasa Goodyear in 1827 in Salem village, near Waterbury, Connecticut, an early hive of domestic industrial activity of all kinds. Among the tools, paint, shovels, axes and other ironmongery were housewares such as brass andirons, cast iron gridirons, Britannia tea and coffee pots, waffle irons, and several kinds of brushes. So relates J. Leander Bishop in his *History of American Manufactures.*

According to the 1970 U. S. Business Census, hardware comprises establishments primarily selling a number of basic hardware lines such as tools, builder's hardware, paint and glass, hardwares and household appliances, cutlery and roofing materials. No one of these categories accounts for 50 percent or more of a store's sales.

Of recent date there are over twenty-seven thousand hardware stores located in ten thousand communities. This contrasts with department stores which are massed in six hundred to seven hundred cities. Many of these hardware stores are located in fast-growing suburban and county seat areas.

Practically all of them (98 percent) have a housewares department which occupies an average 22.5 percent of the floor space and is generally located in a prime, up-front location.

Prodded by an active organization, the National Retail Hardware Association, the traditional hardware "jungle" is being radically upgraded into a "home center." Hardware stores are getting larger, the aisles wider, the display units free standing. In housewares, sectional displays for fireplace accessories, bath, closet, and kitchen have appeared. A conscious attempt is being made to attract women into these male strongholds: merchandise may be color-coded, or arranged in collections of copper or brass, or grouped by classification (pans, casseroles, etc.)

Housewares have in the past certainly been a very significant item in the hardware shop. At present it represents some 15 percent of the hardware business. Its share of the total housewares business amounting to over $400 million reflects the wide dispersal of hardware stores in communities large and small.

The house furnishings department in J. J. Gorman Company, Brooklyn. Located in the basement, of course. Standard housewares items of the time were milk pails (hanging from ceiling).

Courtesy House Furnishing Review.

89

Mail Order House

Several ingredients entered into Aaron Montgomery Ward's master plan, which he inaugurated in August 1872 in a shipping room at Clark and Kinzie Streets, Chicago.

He would buy goods at low cost for cash. He would sell mainly to country farmers, mechanics and country folk—that group then most victimized by manufacturers, salesmen, and retailers. All sales would be for cash. He would send out a circular describing his wares, and quality would be paramount. The articles would be sent by mail, freight or express delivery.

The most important ingredient was his base in Chicago, a hub of transportation. His capital at the time: $1600.

Among the housewares offered in his one-page circular were oil cloth table covers, one dozen white-handled knives and forks, and an ice pitcher. It was the original mail order catalog.

In a 1946 exhibit by the Grolier Club of New York, one hundred American books were chosen for their bearing on the life and culture of the American people. The mail order catalog was cited as perhaps the greatest single influence in increasing the standards of American middle-class living.

Continued the selection committee in exhibiting the pioneer Ward catalog: "...it brought the benefit of wholesale prices to city and hamlet, to the crossroads and prairie; it inculcated cash purchases against crippling credit; it urged millions of housewives to bring into their homes and place upon their backs and in their shelves and on their floors creature comforts which otherwise they

From an 1897 Sears Roebuck catalog, stove and kitchen tinware from the "cheapest supply house on earth."

never could have hoped for; and, above all, substituted sound quality for shoddy. As a final blow, the mail order catalog was, in many homes, the only illustrated book."

The 1874 Ward catalog had four pages and 394 items, including cutlery. For fall/winter 1875-76 there were 3,899 listings, including Rogers plated ware. The 1883 catalog was prepared to help you "walk, ride, dance, sleep, eat, go to church or stay at home." This catalog finally achieved the format that was to last till today—7½ by 11 inches. Thereafter its only alteration in dimension would be to get fatter as well as much more colorful and attractive.

In 1886 came the first sign of competition which was to create an even bigger giant in the mail order field, the association of Richard W. Sears, originally railroad telegrapher and agent of North Redwood, Minnesota, and Alvah C. Roebuck, watchmaker of Hammond, Indiana. On the strength of an "unwanted" shipment of watches, Sears founded the R. W. Sears Watch Company, first in Minneapolis, then moved to Chicago in 1887. Here Roebuck answered an advertisement for a watchmaker and in 1893 the partners incorporated the Sears, Roebuck Company. Their first catalog listed only watches, but this soon changed, and by 1895 a 507-page catalog was offering stoves, china, and glasses among hundreds of items.

Ward had actually tried to start an auxiliary retail outlet early on, with a store in Milwaukee, but the venture failed and neither Ward nor Sears Roebuck entered the retail store business to stay until the middle twenties, Sears in 1925 and Ward in 1926. By this time, population mobility by Ford and Chevy began to cut into the advantages of a purely mail order operation.

It was high time for retail outlets. In Sears' case, retail store sales surpassed the mail orders in the short space of six years, a trend that has continued even as gross sales have increased in both.

At the present time, all "Mail Orders" account for $261 million in retail sales for housewares.

The Department Store: What It Was Like

New ideas, the voice of experience has said, are first laughed at, then tolerated, and finally adopted. But adoption sometimes takes an astonishingly long time.

"We have many letters asking us about departmentalizing stores," begins an editorial headlined "Wide Awake Retailing" in a January 1901 issue of the *Dry Goods Economist* (now *Department Store Management),* a trade publication in retailing. "Departmentalizing is analyzing...and is the surest way to know what you are doing."

More than 70 years have passed since that editorial advocated a merchandising practice which, for decades, has been accepted as standard practice. What makes it notable is that it was still necessary at the turn of the century to preach the gospel of departmentalizing. For by then, the department store had already been on the scene for nearly fifty years!

PROPOSED MAIL ORDER MERGER

Sears-Roebuck and Montgomery Ward Reported as Contemplating Consolidation; Annual Business Exceeds $470,000,000

It is reported that a plan for the merger of Sears, Roebuck & Co. and Montgomery Ward & Co., big Chicago mail order concerns, is being worked out by the largest interests in both companies. It is said that informal negotiations have been conducted for several weeks and the preliminary basis for the merger discussed.

It is stated that plans have now reached a point where government sanction of the big consolidation will

What might have been...a 1926 news story that was never fulfilled.

Who deserves credit for "inventing" the department store and for opening the first one is controversial. Yet not until the department store began to flourish as a channel of distribution did the housewares business develop a real identity of its own and eventually emerge as an independent industry.

Comprised as it is of products from a great many different fields and/or industries, housewares does not—can not—really achieve recognition as such until those products converge at the retail level. Thus the advent of the department store played a significant though unwitting role in giving the housewares business its identity.

"Before the department store could become an actuality, several economic and scientific developments...were necessary,"[16] according to Frank M. Mayfield, in his highly regarded book *The Department Store Story* which he wrote after retiring as president of Scruggs, Vandervoort & Barney, the St. Louis department store.

These were, stated briefly, the growth of our cities, improvement in their transportation system, a rise in the standard of living, increased capital, the coming of the electrical age, and, by no means unimportant, the development of plate glass and of retail advertising. That all these took place in the same general period—immediately following the Civil War—accounts for the fact that the department store seemingly "mushroomed," although its background covers centuries.

To what extent Mayfield is correct in going back "centuries" is questionable. He recalls that Thomas Costain, in a novel called *The Moneyman,* mentions the existence of "department stores" in France in 1450 and tells that they were so plagued by shoplifters that detectives kept watch through slits in the walls; when a theft was observed, bells rang, the doors were closed and the thief caught! Be that as it may, up to the time of the Civil War no store existed on these shores which remotely resembled a modern department store.

Another housewares department located in the basement.
The William Doerflinger Company, LaCrosse, Wisconsin, about 1911.
Courtesy House Furnishing Review.

Ralph Hower in his *History of Macy's of New York* states: "The department store is one of the most complex of modern merchandising mechanisms. It is and always has been a dynamic institution: the department store of today bears little resemblance to its prototype of the nineteenth century...."[17]

Asserting that although the department store is a century old, it "resists definition," he goes on to say that

There seems to be general agreement, however, that the department store in its formative stage can best be identified by its *system* of merchandising, comprising the individual policies adopted by its proprietor or proprietors...[there are] specifically or by implication, eleven characteristics which identified the embryo department store in the period 1860 to 1880. These (not necessarily in order of relative importance) are:

    1—A central location.
    2—Many departments under one roof.
    3—Many "free" services such as the return of unsatisfactory merchandise for exchange or refund; merchandise delivery; reception, rest and writing rooms; wrapping and checking of parcels, etc.
    4—One price to all.
    5—Low mark-up.
    6—Selling for cash.
    7—Aggressive, specialized advertising and promotion.
    8—A large volume of business.
    9—Centralization of non-selling functions.
    10—Buying for cash.
    11—Organized disposal of old stock and special purchases through bargain sales.[18]

Unhappily there is little in the records to show precisely what—if anything—that great merchant pioneer carried in the housewares category of merchandise. Harry Resseguie touches upon it briefly:

Stewart's "Palace" [another nineteenth century operation] drygoods store did not include every characteristic...."Yankee notions" (which in modern merchandising terminology would be translated as housewares) were as near as he ever came to adding the so-called hard lines such as furniture, which further mark the development of the big departmentalized drygoods store into the department store.

If it is possible to assign any single date in answer to the question, "When did Macy's *start* to become a department store?", the answer is probably in the fall of 1860. At that time, by opening a fancy goods department, he launched his store on the course which eventually led to separate departments completely stocked with drugs and toilet goods, china and glassware, silver, housefurnishings (kitchenware, etc.)...and even books.[19]

The author finally focuses more closely on our particular interest:

In April, 1869, came a new department devoted to a wide selection of house furnishings: kitchen utensils, woodenware, baskets, bird cages, brushes, dusters, baby carriages, and a larger stock of plated ware. We cannot possibly comprehend today the horror with which Macy's rivals must have regarded this new step—the complacent ones be-

Also in 1911...Gimbel Brothers in New York has its house furnishings department on the eighth floor. A step up.

An Invitation

Every housekeeper in Chicago is especially
invited to visit our new Section of

Household Utilities

which will be opened to the public next Monday.
This Section will embrace Kitchen Furnishings
of all kinds, Laundry, Garden, and Household
Requisites.

It will occupy the entire Ninth Floor of the
new North Wabash Avenue building.

We are confident that this new Section will
soon be the talk of Chicago. Those who see it first
will be able to talk instead of listen. Many will
take pleasure in saying and remembering that they
saw this beautiful new Section the first day it was
opened. That day is next Monday, March 23rd.

MARSHALL FIELD
& COMPANY

A New Departure

Next week, Monday, March 23rd, we will open a new Section
of Kitchen Furnishings and kindred goods. Increased floor space
afforded by our two new buildings now enables us to handle additional lines which, together with similar merchandise heretofore
carried in various Sections, are now grouped in a new Section of

HOUSEHOLD UTILITIES
INCLUDING

Kitchen Utensils	Household Hard-	Bathroom Fixtures	Sewing Machines
Kitchen Furniture	ware	Electrical Sundries	Household Paints
Laundry Requisites	Garden Tools	Enamel Ware	Woodenware
Refrigerators	Lawn Mowers	Aluminum Ware	Vacuum Cleaners

And all the usual merchandise of this general character.

This new Section is the outgrowth of a general demand from our
customers for goods in these lines, and is another step forward in
the policy of this Store to render a complete service and make it
possible for our patrons to find here whatever they need in such
merchandise.

In keeping with the policy of Marshall Field & Company the
merchandise will be the best obtainable, the assortments most
complete, and the prices the lowest consistent with good quality.

Those contemplating purchases in these lines will find it to
their advantage to wait till next Monday, when the new Section
will be open for business. It will occupy the entire NINTH FLOOR
of the new North Wabash Avenue Building.

From top: Marshall Field in 1914 announced a ninth floor for household
utilities.

cause of the ridiculous folly of any attempt to combine such dissimilar
merchandise in one store, the smarter merchants because they sensed
the competitive threat involved in Macy's policy of diversification. If
a man could sell dry goods, silverware and house furnishings to the
customer who had formerly bought only dry goods at his store, his
expenses would be reduced. The variety displayed might itself attract
patronage, and lower expenses would lead to even lower prices and
even greater patronage; competitors would face ruin.[20]

Hower concludes that two New York City stores were tied in the
international race to become department stores—Lord & Taylor and
Macy's. But, he adds, "Of the two, Macy's was the first to establish
book, house furnishings, china and silverware departments."[21]

Upward From the Cellar

In true Cinderella fashion the department store chapter of the history
of housewares begins in the basement which is—or was in those days
—synonymous with the cellar. That is where housewares—if it was
stocked at all—was put and where most of the early departments
were started.

It isn't difficult to surmise the reasons for this. House furnishings
of this type, as distinguished from linens and domestic furniture and
carpets, symbolized the ruder and coarser aspects of home making—
the coal scuttles and wash boilers, the stoves and pots and pans, the
brooms and brushes and feather dusters. And while no one could or
would deny their essentialness, they were, in actual fact, either unattractive or downright ugly!

Basement lighting was then uniformly miserable. Electric lights
were a luxury and gas lights were generally considered adequate.
Sometimes an attempt was made to admit some rays of daylight by
means of small glass prisms set into an iron frame in the sidewalk
overhead. They soon became stained and dirty or cracked.

Worse if possible than the lighting was the ventilation, for the
reason that effective and efficient ventilating machinery simply had
not been invented. Stale and foul air vitiated customers and the sales
people alike.

Another reason why these goods were consigned to a basement
location was the very practical one of bulk and weight. Ice boxes,
stoves, baby go-carts and similar best-selling items had to be handled much less when they were in the basement near reserve stock
rooms and, more importantly, the delivery department from which
the horse-drawn delivery wagons departed.

In August 1904, in an article entitled "In The Basement," the
editor of *House Furnishing Review* had this to say on the subject:
"Ask any buyer of house furnishings if he doesn't think his department would fare better if it were removed upstairs to the third or
fourth floor and the answer will be an emphatic NO! 'The other
fellow,' he will say, 'can have any part of the upstairs section he
wants, but give me the basement.'"

Major Inventions and Developments of Basic Importance to Business

1830—Railroad: First significant steam line opened by the Baltimore and Ohio Railroad, a 14 mile run from Pratt Street, Baltimore, to Carrollton Viaduct. Fare 25 cents.

1844—Telegraph: First test line opened between Washington and Baltimore. Western Union formed in 1856 and cross-continent service inaugurated 1861.

1847—Postage Stamps: Use of adhesive stamps first authorized; then made compulsory in 1856.

1853—Plate Glass: First produced by James N. Richmond, in Cheshire, Massachusetts; made store show windows possible.

1863—Nation-Wide Mail Service: Distance restrictions that had been in effect on letter mail removed.

1864—Postal Money Orders: Service established.
Pullman Car Service: Begun when the "Pioneer" was put into service.

1866—Transatlantic Cable: Two cables laid by the S.S. Great Eastern opened service between United States and Europe.

1867—Typewriter: First practical machine invented by Christopher L. Sholes who also coined the word. First marketed by Remington.

1871—Corrugated Cartons: First patent for unlined corrugated paper granted to Albert L. Jones, New York; but corrugated packing boxes were not acceptable for freight shipments until 1906.

1876—Newspapers: First high-speed, steam-driven rotary newspaper presses put in use by the Philadelphia *Times*.

1877—Telephone: First test line opened between Boston and Salem, Massachusetts.

1879—Cash Register: Invented by James J. Ritty in Dayton, Ohio, and taken over by the National Cash Register Company in 1884.

1882—Electric Power: First generating plant opened on Pearl Street, New York City, by Thomas A. Edison.

1887—Adding Machine: Patented by Dorr E. Felt, Chicago, who called it the "comptometer."

1892-93—Automobile: Development of the first practical passenger motor vehicles.

1913—Parcel Post Service: Uniform service inaugurated January 1st.

1920—Radio: First radio station licensed to operate was KDKA, Pittsburgh. First radio advertising began in 1941 by the Longines Watch Company over station WXOR in New York City.

1928—Air Conditioned Building: First office building to be air conditioned was the Milam Building, San Antonio, Texas. First air conditioned train operated by the Baltimore and Ohio Railroad with Carrier equipment in 1931.

1931—Air Transportation: First commercial passenger service inaugurated by the Curtis Company with an 18 passenger Condor between New York and Miami.

1936—Television: First telecast made by the Radio Corporation of America from Radio City, New York, using the Empire State Building antenna.

1946—Electronic Computer: First one designed and built at the Moore School of Electrical Engineering, University of Pennsylvania, under the direction of Presper Eckert Jr. and John W. Mauchly. It contained 18,000 vacuum tubes and required a room 30 x 50 feet.

"The World's Greatest"—The Fair Store

One of the best known of those basements at the time was in The Fair in Chicago, then among the biggest and most important department stores in the country. Yet despite its lowly location, its housewares department often soared to merchandising fame with its promotions. It provides an excellent example of what the department store was like at the turn of the century and how its housewares buyer operated.

"Making the World's Greatest House Furnishing Department Still Greater," shouted the headline across the double-page ad of The Fair Store, Chicago, on Sunday, April 8, 1917, in *The Chicago Tribune.* "Our entire sixth floor has been beautifully and artistically refurnished, the stocks having been arranged with splendid and

An ad for Macy's in 1930.

A. F. Brockman, early housewares buyer for the Fair Store in Chicago.

Courtesy House Furnishing Review.

careful consideration for the practical requirements of every thrifty house-furnisher," added the sub-head.

Just two days before, the United States had declared war on Germany. But Chicago—like the rest of America—was much further away from Europe than it is today. The war didn't deter The Fair from formally opening what was then generally conceded to be the world's greatest housewares department.

Today The Fair exists only in memory, for in 1953 it was sold to Montgomery Ward & Company, its doors closed forever, to open again as that chain's State Street showcase. In 1875 when founder E. J. Lehmann opened it for the first time in that raw-boned Midwest crossroads, it was something of a merchandising marvel, one of those great new establishments, a department store. Not the only one because Field & Leiter was already well established, among some others. But it was "the last word" at the time, and it had a house furnishing department—in the basement, naturally.

In 1875, three years after the Chicago fire, when Field & Leiter (later Marshall Field & Company) and other merchants moved back to State Street, their establishments, they insisted, were primarily dry goods stores, despite the widening range of other wares.

"The only one who conceded he was the owner of an out-and-out 'department store' was a German-born newcomer named Edward J. Lehmann," so it states in *Give The Lady What She Wants—the story of Marshall Field & Co.* Lehmann had started business in a one-story frame building on State Street, featuring cheap jewelry, notions, crockery, kitchen utensils, and hardware.

> He called his store "The Fair" and blared that every item—"Everything for Everybody Under One Roof!"—was cheap. His low prices snared the interest of the hard-pressed citizens, who came to his store in such numbers that in four years he was able to buy out several bankrupt merchants and expand his store to four times its original size.
>
> Along with the kind of stock offered in less flashy stores, he piled high on tables on the sidewalk in front of The Fair, goods from auctions, bankruptcy sales, fire sales and similar disasters.[22]

"To the best of my recollection, The Fair was the first store in Chicago to have a house furnishing department as such. Soon after, The Boston Store, Siegel Cooper Company, and A. M. Rothchild Company on State Street began to carry some of this merchandise, but it was quite a bit later until Field's or Carson's had a house furnishings department," Louis Zinngrabe recalled during an interview in 1968.

A former buyer of that department, Louis Zinngrabe (who died in 1971 at the age of eighty-six) spent his entire business career—over fifty years—with The Fair. His vivid recollections about a long bygone era provided the rare opportunity of hearing personally from a merchant who actually participated in those formative years of the housewares industry.

The Bundle Boy

Born in Chicago in 1885, Louis Zinngrabe was only fifteen when he got a job at The Fair as a bundle boy in the house furnishing department.

Louis Zinngrabe, another pioneer housewares buyer for Chicago's Fair Store.

We had to be in the department at 7:25 each morning—there were six of us in house furnishings—and we had to sweep the floor. The store opened at eight o'clock and closed at six, including Saturday of course. We had half an hour for lunch. We got $3.50 a week, but salespeople got $8 a week, but no commission.

Two bundle boys were stationed at each of three big wrapping desks on the floor. There was a big bench there for the cash girls; registers of course were unknown then. After a sales clerk had finished making a sale he (or she) would rap loudly on the counter and yell "Cash! Cash! Cash!" Then a cash girl dressed in a conspicuous plaid apron would come dashing up to the counter shouting "42, 42, 42" or whatever her number happened to be, because the clerk would write her number on the sales slip. Then she'd bring the merchandise to the usher who presided over the wrapping desk. Then we'd bundle it so it could go on to the packing room for delivery.

When Zinngrabe joined The Fair, August Frederick Brockman was buyer of house furnishings, and it wasn't very long before Brockman had tagged the diligent newcomer as his own office boy. (Zinngrabe became a buyer in 1922, but didn't take over the whole department until 1935.) Louis spoke of Brockman as "the greatest merchant I have ever known, bar none."

In 1900 The Fair was already doing a tremendous house furnishing business for those days, even more than Macy's. (Incidentally, Brockman wasn't the first buyer; he was Jake Kesner and in 1886 when he was made general manager of the store Brockman took over. One of Brockman's assistants was A. W. Buddenberg, who later became secretary of the housewares association. But he and Brockman didn't get along, so Buddenberg took a selling job with Lisk enamelware.)

Today many people in this business think that the Housewares Carnivals or Bazaars that are often run by stores in connection with their annual promotions are a recent development. But in 1901 Brockman was already doing that. I have no way of knowing whether or not he was actually the first to use the idea, but he arranged a set-up of fifty-six booths, each with a demonstrator, all going at the same time. I can't recall the exact dates, but I know it was held for at least a month in the late fall and was so successful it was repeated the following spring.

The April 1902 issue of *House Furnishing Review,* however, duly recorded the dates—October 1 to November 15 and January 27 to March 15—as well as other significant details of what it headlined as "A Notable Exposition." "With the idea that the end justifies the means, no expense was spared....In order to make it purely a 'Fair' demonstration, Mr. Brockman resolved to bear all the expenses himself and not permit the various manufacturers to have any hand in the arrangements. As a rule manufacturers of kitchen utensils arrange and pay for their own demonstrations...."

Housewares Moves Up

Louis Zinngrabe recalled that in 1904 the management decided the store ought to follow a number of other big stores around the country and install a Bargain Basement. "That year we moved up to the sixth floor. I believe ours was the first house furnishing department to be moved out of the basement and after we did it others began to follow."

It took a lot of courage to take house furnishings out of the basement. For example, we had built up a big tool and hardware section, the biggest in Chicago. Being in the basement made it very convenient for men to drop in to shop on their limited lunch hour and that amounted to a lot of business. But I don't think it suffered seriously after we moved upstairs.

We did a tremendous business in enamelware. We carried twelve different lines. Much of it from Europe. Brockman, like buyers for most of the big stores made regular trips to Europe...John Henry of Hudson's, J. I. Flynn of Kaufmann's, Johnny Boston of Famous Barr, Tom Stackpole of the May Company...men like that were giants in this business then and had tremendous power and prestige far beyond anything that exists today. In those days you must remember, the buyer was king—and I mean KING! Everything revolved around a great, one-man operation. There was no such thing as a merchandise manager; the buyer reported right to the head of the store and except for that limitation practically did as he pleased.

Brockman, for example, was expected to show a gross profit of about 33 percent and for anything over that he'd get a bonus. His salary was $25,000 a year; I know because I used to take his checks to the bank for him. His bonus often went as high as $20,000.

But getting back to enamelware, that accounted for an enormous share of our business. I would guess 90 percent of our cooking utensil business; the rest was tinware. Many people believe that colored utensils are a relatively recent development, but there was a lot of colored enamelware already in those days, and I'm going back more than sixty years. I suppose we all sort of took it for granted, you might say; nobody ever thought about color much then in terms of decoration. Everything was judged simply from a practical standpoint.

We used to have sales on enamelware seconds in that basement that were a sensation! Later when we moved upstairs we became too aristocratic to handle seconds. But in the basement we would build special bins about four or six feet square all along the Adams Street side of the department. Then we dumped the seconds into those bins, sometimes piling them almost up to the ceiling, just as it was, naked and bare, just as it came from the factory. Remember, nothing was packed in cartons then.

The next morning when I'd get to the store soon after seven o'clock I could hardly get to the door because already there was a huge crowd of 500 or 1,000 people waiting to get in. They knew that our Friday Bargain Days offered legitimate values—no make-believe cut prices. Then at eight o'clock they'd all make a mad rush to the department and start climbing all over the bins picking out the pieces they wanted. We sold enamelware by the carload in that way. Sometimes I wondered where it all went.

He was asked if the stores held to the practice of delivering such sales items.

Deliver them? Why certainly we delivered them. We even delivered a package of tacks—and I'm not kidding. I remember that one of our biggest selling items was something called a bread raiser; most people baked their own bread in those days. It was made of tin and was a sort of dishpan-shaped, footed bowl with a ventilated cover. We'd buy them by the hundreds, pay nineteen cents each for them and sell them for twenty-three or twenty-nine cents or occasionally even at cost. Then we'd even deliver them—carefully packed in excelsior or straw! Sure, everything was delivered by horse and wagon too.

The first people to make aluminum cooking utensils which we considered acceptable was the Illinois Pure Aluminum Company in Lemont, Illinois. I believe their first item was a sauce pan which we sold for ten cents to help popularize this new lightweight cooking ware. I remember it as if it were only yesterday...they were wrapped individually in pink paper and I'd have to keep piling them up on the counters. We sold about 5,000 of them in one day.

Zinngrabe was asked if he thought buyers were more creative then they are today.

That's hard to say. Maybe it was easier to be creative then because merchandise was much less complicated than it is today; perhaps it was easier for a manufacturer to move on an idea then. For example, Fanny Stein—she started working at The Fair as a cash girl when I

A modern department store housewares section—this one at the Maison Blanche Store in New Orleans.

was a bundle boy—who was one of my assistants developed the idea of the metal vegetable bin. We were first with it and it became a tremendous item for a long time.

Private brands were not unknown in housewares in the 1920s, he recalled, and The Fair used "Fairview" as its own name on an electric iron, paint, and a few other things. The reasons for having them, he explained, was the same as that used later—the chance to make a better profit.

Asked what impresses him most when he visits a housewares department today, Zinngrabe promptly replied that the proliferation in color is most prominent:

> The tremendous array of colorful merchandise. Colored enamelware was around at least forty years ago, but the only firm that made anything else in color was August Kreamer & Co. in Brooklyn who made colored tinware—Japanned Ware we used to call it. Mostly bread boxes and cannister sets in white and blue and pink, but they never really sold. Only the black ones sold. But today color is practically universal in housewares; it's much more sophisticated than it used to be, it's much more fashion-conscious.
>
> It's interesting enough though, to see the stress today on porcelain-enameled cast iron. That stuff was made forty years ago—but not with the colors there are today. Then it was white inside with a pale blue outside and I can tell you who made it too; it was the Vollrath Company. They made cuspidors in the same colors.

How did the duties and responsibilities of being a buyer in "the old days" compare with more recent times, Zinngrabe was asked. There was no hesitation in his forthright description of what a buyer's life was like:

> Oh, there's no comparison—it used to be very much easier. You were your own merchandise manager and when you gave a salesman an order that was it. No one ever questioned Brockman's buying decisions. If he wanted to give you an order for, say, 5,000 wash baskets, that was it regardless of whether it was verbal or in writing. You could count on it—definitely.
>
> Brockman was probably always overbought because he would never pass up a good bet. That was one of the many things I learned from him. "When a salesman offers you a good buy on a closeout, whether it's 500 or 5,000 pieces, buy all he's got or don't buy any." The minute you leave him with some part of it he's liable to go right to your competitor and the minute two stores start offering the same special it's no longer a special.
>
> Generally speaking, that's sound merchandising philosophy, but sometimes you can misjudge an item and get badly hooked on something the way Brockman did once on the Half Moon Skimmer. That was a sort of half-moon-shaped ladle with a long handle designed for skimming the grease off the top of soup or anything else you were cooking that required removal of the fluid grease. The guy that made them went broke, which isn't surprising; after all how many people really need a skimmer? I think we bought all he had, about 150 gross. We bought 'em cheap all right—but we had them coming out of our ears for the next ten years! But that's all part of the game; you can't win 'em all.

100

RULES FOR EMPLOYEES

(Excerpts from the employees rule book of McCreery's, once an important New York Department store.)

No conversation between employees should be carried on in the presence of customers.

No reading of papers or books is allowed.

No eating except in lunch room.

Finger nails must not be attended to in the departments.

No alcoholic liquors, tobacco or chewing gum may be used in business hours.

Indifference to small buyers should be avoided; indeed this is a common breach of good manners and is in exceedingly bad taste.

To customers no infringement of good manners will be tolerated.

Sales clerks should never intimate that they have no goods so inexpensive as a customer may desire. Such an attitude invariably causes offense and is unpardonably rude.

Two views of the early "5 & 10¢" store: the cover of the S. S. Kresge "original post" catalog; and the opening of a Titus Company "five and dime" in Philadelphia, 1905.

*Top, the Bettmann Archive;
bottom, courtesy House Furnishing Review.*

"The Five and Dime" Variety Stores

The idea of selling articles at fixed basic prices geared to the currency is said to have occurred to Frank W. Woolworth when, as a sales clerk, he put up a sign "Anything on this table—5¢" and noticed how rapidly the merchandise disappeared. As related by Godfrey M. Lebhar in his *Chain Stores in America,* 1859-1962, this occurred in a Watertown, New York dry goods store, owned by William H. Moore. Woolworth opened his own store in Utica, New York based on this principle, and it did moderately well. But he shortly closed it and opened another on June 21, 1879 in Lancaster, Pennsylvania, and this one was very successful. To the basic five and ten idea, Woolworth almost from the start tied in the idea of multiple stores so that buying in quantity could ensure favorable prices.

By the turn of the century there were fifty-nine Woolworths, all doing well. In fact they were doing so well and the "5 & 10" concept was receiving so much favorable publicity that merchants, both large and small, everywhere began to follow a similar policy at least in part if not entirely. People like McCrory, Kress and Kresge had entered the field. And department stores gave serious consideration to installing a "5 & 10" section in their housewares departments.

In 1911 Woolworth consummated a giant merger of his own, 318 stores and those of five former associates holding 278 stores. Two of them were owned by his old boss, William H. Moore. Sales of the resulting F. W. Woolworth Company, New York went from some $60 million in 1912 to over a billion dollars by 1960.

Housewares—kitchen tools, brushes, flatware, china, glass, enamel and aluminum wares—appeared early on the flat or sloping,

Wool-like fabrics made from Soy Beans ...
Hats made from Milk ... Transparent knives
and forks made from Cellulose Acetate

97 AMERICAN MANUFACTURERS

show you how they are meeting consumer
needs in war-time by sending their ingenious new products for exhibition in the first

INGENUITY SHOW

Tuesday, May 12 through Saturday, May 23.
9 A. M. to 5:30 P. M. daily

• • •

SEE the fascinating
display panels arrang-
ed by Charles L. Simon
of the Industrial By-
Products & Research
Corp. of Philadelphia.

SEE the flexible plastic
cups that give you ice
cubes at the press of
your finger.

SEE draperies made of
paper, see bottles made
of flame proof glass,
leather made from,
pine trees.

SEE fluffy blankets
made from nylon,
pillows from milk
wool.

These, and scores of other marvels await you at America's
war-time Ingenuity Show May 12th—23rd.
Fourth Floor

Lewis & Conger is proud to being
New Yorkers this dramatic pre-
view of what Americans will be
using and wearing. Every woman
will want to see this amazing exhibit. You just won't believe your
eyes when you behold the scores
of products that are being developed for your comfort and convenience—and to replace such
vital war materials as wool, rubber, aluminum, steel. You'll be
grateful to the many manufacturers
who with typical American ingenuity, are evolving these practical, well-styled products for you
and for your home. Substitutes?
Yes ... but some may prove to
be even better than the products
they replace.

Come to the Ingenuity Show—
and then astonish your family and
friends with your knowledge of
"things to come."

LEWIS & CONGER
New York's Leading Housewares Store
6TH AVENUE AT 43TH STREET   NEW YORK
VAn. 6-1200

From top: The first Lewis & Conger Store at Herald Square, New York, 1882. Sixty years later, Lewis & Conger advertised a World War II-time ingenuity Show.

Both courtesy House Furnishing Review.

partitioned variety shop trays at the basic prices. With the lifting of the "nothing over ten cents" slogan in the thirties, housewares of every description became available at the varieties. These stores' annual share of the retail housewares business amounts to a hefty $490 million.

Today in addition to basic items, the variety stores offer toasters and coffee makers and chafing dishes at prices which, while competitive, would doubtless have astonished Frank W. Woolworth.

Discount Stores and Mass Merchandisers

The most misnamed channel of retail distribution is the "discount store." The term has come to be used loosely, its identity long eroded by widespread misuse, and is rapidly becoming as obsolete as the appelation "bargain basement." Today the term "discounter" is fast being replaced by "mass merchandiser"; and the trade association of the so-called discounters which, in 1962, carried the lofty misnomer, National Association of Consumer Organizations(!), is now the Mass Retailing Institute.

The name "discount house" was derived from the small entrepreneurs who, operating from hideaway walk-ups in office buildings in New York and later other cities, displayed catalogs of the latest national brand lines of appliances on their counters in place of the merchandise itself. The catalogs clearly indicated the "factory list price" on every item. Privileged people, equipped with a special identification or "membership" card issued by the discount house, could buy practically any item in the catalogs at a discount—usually from 10 percent to 30 percent below the established retail price. Customers had to return the following day for their merchandise—always bought for cash—which meanwhile had been picked up for them from a cooperating distributor or jobber. Major appliances would be shipped direct to the customer's house.

There is a widely held misconception that "discounting" did not exist before World War II. Although it is true that mass merchandising flourished during the postwar boom, the original discount houses came into being long before the war.

A feature article by this author in *Retailing Home Furnishings* (now *Home Furnishings Daily*), December 20, 1937, titled "They Can Get It for You Wholesale," recounts in detail the early history of this facet of retailing. This excerpt tells of its beginnings:

> The whole practice of giving discounts in electrical appliances had its origin no less than 27 years ago [1910!], according to George H. Jungen, vice president of the Baitinger Electric Co., 95 Chambers Street, New York, one of the oldest and largest electrical supply firms in the city....Mr. Jungen explains it thus: "Electricity was first used in factories and office buildings long before being introduced into the home.
>
> "Electrical appliances—such as they were at the time—couldn't readily be purchased by interested consumers from dealers simply

because there were few or no such dealers around. There were only five firms in the city then handling electrical goods: Stanley & Patterson; Latham; Manhattan Electric; Western Electric [now Graybar]; and J. H. Bunnell. Most of their business was done on electrical equipment. When a person wanted to get an electrical appliance, it was only natural, therefore, that they should think of getting it from the people who furnished them with other electrical supplies.

"In the larger firms—and they were often the first ones to adopt the then new-fangled idea of electricity—the purchasing agent of the company was the one to whom such orders were entrusted by other employes. Because the firm had been buying quite a lot of electrical equipment, these supply firms invariably extended a courtesy discount on purchases of appliances. It got to be the custom and still is, and I doubt if anybody can ever change it."

Before World War II the great success that "discount houses" were having, first with appliances and then with other well-established products that carried a list price, like cameras and luggage, prompted them to start stocking other products, particularly soft goods, in far greater amounts than the original hard lines. Most of this merchandise has traditionally never carried any list price; nevertheless, the term discount continued to be applied.

After World War II some of the pioneers like Eugene Ferkauf, founder of Korvette's, managed to increase their sales spectacularly. Discount stores mushroomed all over America. The discounters—or, more accurately now, the mass merchandisers—insist that they have brought a new and revolutionary form of retailing to fruition. Whether the mass merchandisers of 1972 are really a twentieth-century version of the original mass merchandisers like Sears, Roebuck and Company, which as early as the 1880s was building its growth and image on the slogan "Cheapest Supply House on Earth," constitutes an on-going debate.

Nevertheless, there is no denying the impressive record the mass merchandisers continue to set. The August 1971 issue of *Stores* magazine, published by the National Retail Merchants Association, quotes these figures from a comparative analysis made by Milton Goldberg, a consultant, of the three types of retailers during the past decade:

Conventional department stores' sales increased 78% in the '60s. National [meaning chain] retailers increased sales 157%. Discounters' sales jumped 529%.

In share of market, the conventionals went off 8%; the nationals gained 32% and the discounts gained 220%.

Lewis and Conger

The Civil War had been history for three years when, on an April morning 1868, workmen took down a weather-beaten sign on the building at 601 Broadway in downtown New York and replaced it with a freshly painted new one.

The old sign had said "J & C Berian"; the new one said "Lewis and Conger." The switch marked a change in ownership of an enter-

Whiskered gentleman is R. V. Lewis, who with Henry C. Conger took over the J. and C. Berian store after the Civil War.

103

"How Lewis & Conger advertise"... famously in a very distinctive style.

Courtesy House Furnishing Review.

A well-known housewares specialty store of the 1920s. Jantzen-Rallsback Company, in Los Angeles.

Courtesy House Furnishing Review.

prise that from its founding in 1835 to its 1957 demise was the country's most distinguished housewares specialty store in the east.

J. and C. Berian's "Crockery, China and Glass and Housefurnishings" store, right from its start in 1835, was aimed at "the carriage trade." House furnishings were then considered little more than a supplement to the much more important and profitable business in china, glass, and earthenware. Berian's stocked nothing but the best and attracted customers to match.

"My father, R. V. Lewis, was born in Welshpool, Wales, in December 1841 as Richard Vaughan and had been brought to the United States and adopted by his uncle, whereupon he became Richard Vaughan Lewis," R. V. Lewis, Jr., recalled during an interview in Saint Petersburg, Florida.

After a bit of schooling, R. V. Lewis started working for Berian's as a delivery boy alongside another youth named Henry C. Conger.

After Fort Sumter was fired on, Lewis volunteered for the Union army and served until the end of the Civil War. He returned to difficult times, and after three years was given the option of taking over. He was allowed to pick Henry C. Conger as his partner, and the Lewis and Conger sign went up in 1868 and was to remain, on one building or another, for ninety years.

Lewis and Conger moved uptown with the tide of New York's retail business, first to Herald Square, then to 132 West Forty-second Street, and finally, in 1922, into its own imposing nine-story building on Sixth Avenue and Forty-fifth Street.

The senior Lewis had died that year, and Conger, certain that moving uptown would be disastrous, disposed of his stock, although his son Harry remained in charge of special orders. R. V. Lewis, Jr., who had gone into the business in 1913, was now president, and his three brothers, Edmund, Arthur, and William, were managers.

The business flourished, and, although exact figures are no longer available, its peak was said to be close to $1½ million annually. Over the years it had developed a large following of the "chef and butler" trade, household staff from well-to-do families. Here they could always be certain of getting that particular duck press or wine cooler—or any one of scores of culinary items.

If the Lewis and Conger store interior was lacking in glamour and color, it more than compensated by its imaginative merchandising, its advertising, and its attention-compelling window displays.

As housewares took on more of a gift character, the firm began issuing a Christmas catalog. One of its earliest was a thirty-two-page booklet issued in 1923.

Probably its most famous and successful campaign was a series of advertisements headed "Shopping with Janet Gray at Lewis and Conger," prepared by the Manhattan advertising agency of Batten, Barton, Durstine and Osborn, Incorporated. A fictitious Miss Gray would tell, in a highly personal, chatty style, about the unusual things she saw at the store.

But the world of the fifties was different from the one of White Mountain iceboxes and Kent knife-cleaning machines. R. V. Lewis and his younger brother A. V. Lewis, who were the only ones then managing the business, were advised to sell and eventually did so to an outside group of investors, in July 1955.

Although business continued for a while with some of the old employees who were hired by the new management, the last years of Lewis and Conger were marked by confusion, recrimination, re-sale, resignations, and, finally closure in 1957. "The end came for a once famous store in a very ignoble manner," said R. V. Lewis, Jr.

But in 1970 the name suddenly reappeared. Hammacher Schlemmer, which had become a highly successful home-goods specialty store in the elite uptown Fifty-seventh Street shopping area, registered the Lewis and Conger name as its own for a new mail-order division. No reference whatever is made to that store's illustrious past—eloquent proof that the name speaks for itself.

"Two men but with a single vision," from a catalog of the period, William Schlemmer and his son, William F. Schlemmer.

Hammacher Schlemmer

One afternoon in the late 1960s Dominic Tampone, president of Hammacher Schlemmer on New York's fashionable West Fifty-seventh Street, happened to be standing just inside the store's main entrance chatting with Lewis Salton, president of Salton, Incorporated, as an unmistakable lady and a distinguished-looking gentleman entered. President Tampone nodded a friendly greeting as they passed.

"Of course I recognized Marlene Dietrich," asked Lew, "but who is that man?" "Oh, that's Baron Rothschild."

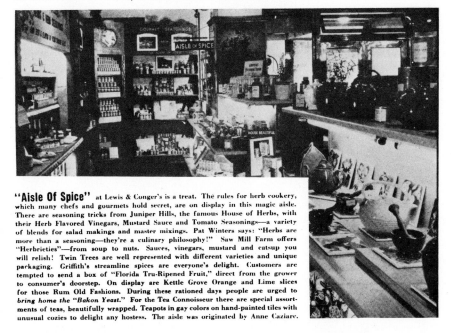

"Aisle Of Spice" at Lewis & Conger's is a treat. The rules for herb cookery, which many chefs and gourmets hold secret, are on display in this magic aisle. There are seasoning tricks from Juniper Hills, the famous House of Herbs, with their Herb Flavored Vinegars, Mustard Sauce and Tomato Seasonings—a variety of blends for salad makings and master mixings. Pat Winters says: "Herbs are more than a seasoning—they're a culinary philosophy!" Saw Mill Farm offers "Herbrieties"—from soup to nuts. Sauces, vinegars, mustard and catsup you will relish! Twin Trees are well represented with different varieties and unique packaging. Griffith's streamline spices are everyone's delight. Customers are tempted to send a box of "Florida Tru-Ripened Fruit," direct from the grower to consumer's doorstep. On display are Kettle Grove Orange and Lime slices for those Rum Old Fashions. During these rationed days people are urged to bring home the *"Bakon Yeast."* For the Tea Connoisseur there are special assortments of teas, beautifully wrapped. Teapots in gay colors on hand-painted tiles with unusual cozies to delight any hostess. The aisle was originated by Anne Caziare.

Lewis & Conger supplemented their gourmet-type cooking utensils with a colorful "aisle of spice."

Courtesy House Furnishing Review.

For a long time now both the famous and the not-so-famous from all parts of the world have been confidently flocking—and writing—to Hammacher Schlemmer, Manhattan's most glamorous and outstanding housewares and gifts specialty store where, they have come to learn, the unusual is the usual in its eight floors of merchandise and top quality permeates everything.

But in 1957 it looked as if this famous firm was finally approaching its end. Fifteen years later, however, and still doing business with a sophisticated, zestful flair that few younger firms can equal, Hammacher Schlemmer points with justifiable pride to its 114 years of continuous existence. Today it is more successful than ever.

The first known records of William Schlemmer's hardware store at 221 Broadway date from 1848, though it is believed to have started even earlier. In 1859 the business attracted A. Hammacher, and as Hammacher, Schlemmer and Company, it moved to larger quarters at 209 Bowery. Soon the thriving young company was making money in more ways than one—it coined its own. It was all legal. The start of the Civil War had created such a shortage of coins that the government authorized business firms to make their own, and Hammacher, Schlemmer was one of the first to issue these "copper heads" or "rebellion tokens," as they were called. Eventually the privilege was abused by so many people that the whole project was canceled by the government.

By 1904 the company had grown so big that it moved into a seven-story building on Fourth Avenue and Thirteenth Street, where it soon added three warehouses. William F. Schlemmer, son of the founder, was general manager. The business prided itself on carrying over a hundred thousand hardware items, including tools and supplies for railroads, factories, and institutions as well as individuals. There was also a large department devoted to piano materials and supplies and another for that newly emerging business, automotive supplies and equipment.

Things were going so well that William Schlemmer, now president, decided to add a branch store, and in 1926 he selected the site at 147 West Fifty-seventh Street to erect an eight-story building. At first it was just another very fine hardware store, as one would expect from that well-known company. But it was destined to become something quite different. That whole area of the city was slowly undergoing a change; in a few more years it came to be known as the "silk stocking" district, denoting the wealthy class of residents moving into it.

It came as something of a surprise to Mr. Schlemmer, but in response to customer demands the store began stocking such things as bar stools and the more luxurious type of bathroom and closet hardware, items for which there were no calls in the main store on Thirteenth Street and which no one had thought of stocking before. That was the beginning. By late 1927 the character of market potential for the Fifty-seventh Street store had become so evident that they decided to add housewares as a regular department. To get the right personnel for the new operation they lured the sales manager and some of the star salesmen from Lewis and Conger—then the finest housewares specialty store in New York, if not the country. Meanwhile business prospered—for a time.

By 1933 the Great Depression had taken a terrible toll, and Hammacher, Schlemmer and Company decided to close down its enormous, long-established hardware operation on Thirteenth Street and concentrate its attention on the uptown store. More and more it came to be less and less of a typical hardware store. By this time New Yorkers, referring to the city's best housewares specialty stores, would invariably mention Hammacher Schlemmer along with Lewis and Conger. And from the standpoint of location the former had a big advantage over Lewis and Conger, which was hidden away under the "L" tracks on noisy Sixth Avenue.

William F. Schlemmer died in 1945 and his wife, who had never been active in the business, took charge. In 1952 she decided to sell the business, and a syndicate composed of several men with retail backgrounds took over. Their approach to the business, however, was completely inconsistent with all the store had stood for. Sales began slipping badly and in 1955 they sold out—to another somewhat similar syndicate. Again the same story was repeated; the new owners completely misjudged the business and its potential.

"There didn't seem to be much hope left," said one of those who participated at the time. "So, almost as a last act of desperation, Dominic Tampone, who held the title of vice-president, was asked to take over. He could hardly make things any worse."

Dominic Tampone was a nice, rather ordinary-looking lad who had been hired in October 1929 as a temporary office boy in the

Dominic Tampone, president of Hammacher Schlemmer, launched a housewares import-wholesale operation for the company in 1961.

107

The Hammacher Schlemmer store on 57th Street, New York, built in 1926, put housewares right smack in the middle of the "silk stocking" district.

Hammacher Schlemmer

THE BOLD BLADE H5771 by INVENTO

Probably the world's sharpest knife. It's really a ten-inch razor blade housed in aluminum. Engineered for practicality, it is light and well made with a contoured... grip handle for all size hands. Encased in plastic scabbard with a side carborundum whet for sharpening. Cuts meats, fowl, tomatoes, cheese with astonishing ease. . . . 6.95

INSTANT PHONE ORDERS: (212) 937-8181 OR (914) 946-7725

Infra-Red Food Warmer

Now keep an entire meal hot, at its flavor peak for hours with infra-red energy. Food retains its moisture, color and flavor. Portable unit ideal for use in kitchen, dining room, patio. Warms plates, thaws frozen foods. 27x14½" high. By Invento H128 . . . 35.00

Keep Food and Plates Hot

Make Your Own Fresh Cream by Invento

Now make your own fresh cream with butter and milk—and for those on a low cholesterol diet, substitute margarine for butter and use skimmed milk. It's all so easy and so inexpensive. Simple, quick. Our Cream Maker also makes pouring cream for coffee and cereals, whipped cream, Devonshire cream, ice cream, cream jelly, salad dressings and mayonnaise. Complete with full instructions H125 . . . 10.00

For Low Cholesterol Dieters, Too

PLATE COVERS. Nylon net, plastic-covered hoods. Set of 7. 1 each: 8¼, 7, 8, 10, 11¼" sizes and 2 of the 9"... 8.95

PLATE SAVERS. Bound felt.
10" dia HPS10 . . . Doz. 8.95
9" dia HP9 . . . Doz. 8.95
8" dia HPS8 . . . Doz. 5.50
6" dia HPS6 . . . Doz. 4.95
4" dia HPS4 . . . Doz. 4.50

SYRUP DISPENSER. Drops sauces, honeys, syrups, without mess. Finger-release lever cuts flow. Honeycombed glass and chrome. Invento. . . 9.50

YOGURT MAKER. Whips up 1¼ qts. home-made yogurt at a 70% saving. Automatic temperature control; with instructions HYM . . . 9.95

BACON GRILL. Specially designed for cooking delicious, crisp bacon. Its shape allows grease to drain off. Cast aluminum. Teflon lined nox. 9.50

COFFEE STARTER. Plug into outlet, plug percolator into starter. This gadget wakes up before you do to start fresh-brewed coffee. . . 7.95

COFFEE STARTER HCST1-0

Hammacher Schlemmer

A typical and very distinctive Hammacher Schlemmer newspaper ad for the housewares specialties.

Fifty-seventh Street store. On the mezzanine of that store where its offices are situated, his "temporary" job became increasingly permanent. Presently he was promoted to the adjustment department, then to various others, finally ending up in 1932 in sales. With the exception of a stint with the United States Army in Europe from 1943 to 1946, he remained in the sales department until in 1956 he was named vice-president and sales manager. If his views about the various policy changes the different owners undertook were ever solicited, they were obviously seldom accepted. But now, with the game nearly over, they handed him the ball—there was no one else to give it to.

"It was all very flattering and offered me a tremendous opportunity," Dominic Tampone related in 1972,

> but the odds seemed overwhelming. At that point I had been with the company longer than anyone else. I had been able to observe the trends during its fat years and its lean years, and at that moment things were exceptionally lean. The mismanagement of the previous four years had put us in dire financial circumstances.
>
> My confidence in it—and in myself—amounted almost to zeal. And so as its new captain I was determined beyond any shadow of doubt to prove that the principles upon which the company had been founded and upon which it was nourished and grew were as good as they ever were. My job now was to get this venerable ship of trade back on its course; if I did that it could still make port and consummate a successful voyage. It was my contention then and still is now that the policy of the company toward our customers and purveyors alike is simply, "What can we do for you?" If we do well for a vendor, he does well for us; and if we do well for a customer, willy-nilly she spreads the news and does well for us too.

By the time he arrived at the January 1958 NHMA housewares show at Navy Pier in Chicago, Tampone knew precisely what he had to do and how he had to do it if Hammacher Schlemmer was to have a chance for survival. It was his first trip to a show.

The five-story building was the original Hammacher and Company store at 209 The Bowery, New York, in 1867. It is between Motts Oyster House and Clark Hardware Store.

Within a year the company was out of the woods and Dominic Tampone had been named president. Within a year too, he had begun a series of innovations and acquisitions that have made the company probably the largest and certainly one of the most outstanding in the industry.

In 1961 he launched a new housewares division called Invento Products, Incorporated, an import-wholesale operation for the company. "I realized that our role as a leading retailer in this business had always been to introduce unusual new items," he explained. "If the item was successful it was immediately picked up by the rest of the retail community and we'd be out of business on it. If the item was a failure we'd also end up being out of business. I'm happy to say Invento has made its mark. Through housewares advertising, Invento in 1972 is now known to hundreds of thousands of people, whether they have bought Invento items or not."

But what has probably contributed more than anything else (except its actual merchandise) to the remarkable public image Hammacher Schlemmer has created is its distinctive, consistent style of newspaper advertising. People often comment that it has "almost as much interest as the news columns."

"We are often told, especially by advertising people, that a change in our advertising style and layout is long overdue," Tampone commented. "They say it has outlived its usefulness and is showing its age. But it instantly identifies us to newspaper readers, and as long as they keep reading our ads and reacting to them the way they do we'll stay with it."

The Drug Store

There was a time when the American drug store dispensed only prescriptions and proprietary drugs and a few—very few—still claim to do so. But the vast majority have long since "diversified," and it has become a part of American folklore that the actual drug counter is hard to find.

Even back in 1850 there was a tendency for individual stores to expand into small chains, but multiplication ceased at three or four acquisitions. It is history that Charles R. Walgreen changed all that. He purchased his first store from his employer in 1901, and this date is usually given as that of the foundation of the Walgreen empire. By 1938 it had reached a peak of 540 stores. Today (1972) Walgreen with about five hundred (but considerably larger stores) remains first in the field, with sales of $745 million, followed by Rexall and Sterling.

Today, too, of course the so-called "drug" store has come to be more like the old country general store and in these "supermarkets" one can buy almost anything. The housewares industry has contributed importantly to its diversification and it is not uncommon to see a section clearly marked "Housewares."

The housewares "invasion" of this type of outlet began in the

From top: The facade of C. R. Walgreen's first drug store in Chicago. An important beginning. The interior shows his second store in 1911. As Walgreen's expanded, so did its housewares department.

109

1920s. One of the very first items was an electric curling iron, the "Hold Heet," made by the Russell Electric Company, Chicago, retailing for ninety-eight cents. Then there appeared a heating pad for about $2.98, far superior to the traditional rubber hot water bottle. Such prices were far below what similar items were selling for in department stores, and it didn't take long for them to become best sellers. Other items like electric vibrators, drink mixers and irons soon followed and an irreversible pattern was firmly established.

Today the drug stores' share of the housewares market is approaching the $200 million mark. And with no apparent limit to the housewares items they will sell, that figure is bound to increase.

Wholesaling

Wholesaling is an ancient and important function of the marketplace, but there was a time in America when it was difficult to determine when and where wholesaling became retailing.

In the course of time, all that changed. Not only did wholesaling and retailing become distinct and separate functions, but specialization followed. By the mid 1800s the wholesaler became a well-established cog in the growing nation's marketing mechanism, a highly important cog.

At one time the largest wholesale organization in the country was Butler Brothers, founded in Boston in 1877. Its volume reached a peak in 1920 when its eight huge branches did $90 million—only to drop the next year to $58 million, almost forcing it out of business. The reason, basically, was management's persistent refusal to replace or supplement its once famous catalog, "Our Drummer," with salesmen and its unswerving adherence to the prices published in its catalog regardless of the quantity purchased or of competitors' prices.

In "My 55 Years with Butler Brothers," an unpublished history of the firm written in 1941 by Frank S. Cunningham, its president from 1918 to 1927 and later chairman, he relates many fascinating aspects of that business.

> Printed on the cover of the catalogue was the slogan, "Our Drummer Is Our Only Salesman." Exclusive catalogue selling was so jealously guarded that it became treason even to think about selling goods through traveling men.... From the start the price printed in the catalogue was the only price. Maintenance of One Price became as jealously guarded as that of exclusive catalogue selling. Even though a customer was able and willing to give us chunky annual volume... large enough to reduce our handling cost, we refused to make any least reduction....
>
> Looking back it is clear that just about the turn of the century fundamental changes in the field of distribution began to multiply. But we of Butler Brothers hardly knew what was going on. We did not meet our customers face to face unless they came into our house. We lived in a world of our own.... About 1913 signs began to appear that the catalogue was losing its pulling power.... The saturation point was nearing for exclusive catalogue selling.

"Our drummer," Butler Brothers' only salesman—its complete catalog for spring 1897.

As the country grew and transportation improved, it was inevitable that the role of the wholesaler and the seemingly extra costs of dealing through him rather than with the manufacturer direct would be challenged by the larger retailers. Over the years the function and economic justification of "the middleman" was questioned and labeled as "unnecessary." Cunningham touches upon that development:

> During and after the first World War the growth of chains, mail order houses…(and other big retailers)…made it popular with bankers and economists to predict that the wholesaler and the independent merchant would be eliminated as mediums of distribution.
>
> Not until later did the world realize that the function of gathering goods from many concerns into warehouses convenient to the point of sale is an essential part of distribution, and that if the function is not to be performed by the wholesaler then it must be performed by …[the retailers]…at approximately the same expense.

Nevertheless, efforts of retailers to find ways to circumvent or at least reduce the cost of the wholesaling function of distribution have continued through the years. One of the most effective methods that has been developed is, of course, the creation of a dealer/cooperative-owned wholesale operation and many of them are to be found in various fields. In the housewares-hardware field the most outstanding example is the John Cotter Company, Chicago. Started by him in a modest way in 1947, this cooperative had over four thousand members in 1972, and its estimated volume for that year was approximately $330 million.

In the mid 1950s and early 60s over one hundred hardware-housewares wholesalers went into bankruptcy for over $7 million. Many others, including famous old-line firms that had been in business many years, decided to close down. In the Northwest, for example, M. Seller Company was liquidated.

The end of so many wholesalers within so short a time generated much speculation that maybe the end had truly arrived for this segment of distribution. "These jobbers have never been noted as shining examples of advanced merchandising," commented this writer in his column in *Home Furnishings Daily,* March 8, 1961.

What has happened to the hardware-housewares wholesalers in recent years is reflected in the following figures from *Hardware Age* magazine:

Year	Number of Firms
1940	500
1950	550
1960	525
1970	400

The magazine points out that from 1963 to 1968 these wholesalers enjoyed a 50 percent growth in sales, a compounded average of about 9 percent annually. To paraphrase a well-known TV commercial, the survivors must be doing something right and making a significant contribution to the nation's distribution system.

Direct Selling

Going from house-to-house, offering something for sale to the home owner, is one of the most ancient forms of selling. It dates back to biblical times.

Throughout Europe and elsewhere, peddlers of every trade and type have been commonplace. After the American Colonies took root, the Yankee peddler that emerged created a fame—and often a fortune—that placed him quite in a class by himself.

The legendary Yankee peddler has long since disappeared. But direct selling, as house-to-house merchandising is now known, was never more firmly established in the marketplace than it is today. Housewares have always accounted for a significant if not a major share of such distribution. Tinware was so important in the eighteenth century that a special class of tinware peddlers developed. And in the 1890s the Pittsburgh Reduction Company—later the Wear-Ever Aluminum Company—resorted to selling its new lightweight cookware direct to consumers because hardware stores declined to buy it at first. This policy led to the widespread use of door-to-door selling for cookware, a practice that continues to be followed today. The basic factors in the success of that merchandising method is creative selling and incentive compensation, this author explained in 1948 in his book, *More and More It's Door to Door*.

In the past years it was a simple matter for anyone to engage in this form of selling. With a pack on his back or his wagon loaded with goods, the peddler was ready to do business—here today and gone tomorrow. It isn't surprising, therefore, that over the years the business attracted its share of questionable characters and companies that did little credit to it. Yet while long-established, responsible firms in this business disowned such malpractices, they did little or nothing to correct the situation or to improve their public image.

In 1969 a completely reorganized Direct Selling Association (known before then as the National Association of Direct Selling Companies) moved out of its tradition-bound offices in Winona, Minnesota, to Washington, D.C., modernized in form and function and, even more importantly, in industry thinking. At long last it began to assume the public posture and new image it had earned for itself.

There are no accurate figures on the total volume of direct selling done in this country. In a story on this industry in its August 1, 1971 issue, *Forbes* magazine estimated 1970 volume to have been "over $4 billion." That, it explained, is only for companies "knocking on doors" and does not include direct mail or catalog sellers. "Overall," it adds, "the industry has just about doubled its sales and profits in the past five years."

Well-informed estimates place the number of companies engaged in direct selling at about twelve hundred. Membership in the Direct Selling Association has traditionally been comprised of the larger, nationally known companies in the field who manufacture what they sell. In 1972 it had ninety-four active members and sixty-four associate members, many well known in the housewares field.

In addition to the big companies there have always been small local or regional direct selling companies which, with very few exceptions, do no manufacturing but buy the items they sell. Widely scattered in different sections of the country, they had no identity as a group and even less of an image.

Selling on the installment plan is the very life blood of their business. And so, in the fall of 1950, when developments in the Korean War prompted the government to re-impose Regulation W to regulate consumer credit, these small operators were faced with a crisis with which they were not able to cope. As a result, for the first time, a group of them met to discuss the situation.

An association was formed—The National Association of House-to-House Installment Companies, since re-named the National Association of Installment Companies. It has proved to be a major factor in providing this field with effective and constructive leadership which includes holding an annual trade show, which had 135 exhibitors at the 1972 event. It publishes a monthly magazine for the trade and now has coordinated representation with which to approach legislative problems. As of 1972 it had 342 regular and 133 associate members enrolled. The association reports its members employ 13,000 outside salesmen who service five million families and collect payments on either a weekly, bi-weekly or monthly basis. About 75 percent of the members operate a store.

Stamp Plan Supplier Companies

The cash-discount trading stamp business was conceived and founded in 1896 by Thomas A. Sperry and Shelly B. Hutchinson and incorporated under its present name, the Sperry and Hutchinson Company in 1900. The company was acquired by the Beinicke family from the founders, went public in 1966, and remains the S & H (green stamp) Company. Its major business is the trading stamp, although it is beginning to diversify. Imitators have been fairly numerous, issuing stamps of every conceivable color.

The trading stamps in their commonest variety are given at the rate of one per ten cent cash purchase. The nominal value of a book of twelve hundred stamps is $1.20. However, merchandise can only be bought by stamp redemption, and this enables the company or companies to be competitive. The actual buying value of one S & H book (1970) was about $3.00.

Redemption centers, 725 of them, are scattered in cities across the country and there are an additional eighty-five mail order facilities. These are supplied by nine massive distribution centers scattered across the country.

The statistics of the S & H Company alone are remarkable. One hundred and fifty billion green stamps are issued annually, which is four times the number of U. S. postage stamps. Like the latter, they are always valid, no matter how old.

A 1934 Sperry and Hutchinson catalog showed many housewares items as premiums. An important industry outlet.

A contemporary S&H redemption center showroom demonstrating the importance of housewares items, contributing to the lure of green stamps.

In the S & H catalog of two thousand or more items, something over 20 percent represents merchandise in the housewares category, and this is probably standard in the business.

The stamp plan suppliers' housewares business now amounts to about $350 million annually.

Supermarkets

How did the little old corner grocery store happen to blossom forth into that uniquely American marketing "miracle" known as the supermarket?

According to Godfrey M. Lebhar in his book *Chain Stores in America, 1859-1962,* the supermarket was a development of the 1930s and was originally the brain child of the independents. But the idea was soon incorporated by chains as well, and gave rise to a rather surprising situation.

When the growth of a grocery chain like the Great Atlantic and Pacific Tea Company (A & P) is examined over a number of years, it is found that the total number of stores steadily increased from the time of its founding (1859, one store) to the middle thirties (1934, over fifteen thousand stores) and then began to decrease (1960, 4,350 stores). The loss of over ten thousand stores was much more than counterbalanced, however, by the increase in size of the individual stores, and sales increased from $1 billion annually in 1940 to $5 billion in the sixties.

Apart from size alone, the distinguishing features of the supermarket appear to be: all operations on a single level; self-service; large displays of groceries, meats, vegetables, and fruits; lowered prices derived from large volume and self service.

Right from the start supermarkets—like the old independent grocery store—had always carried some non-food items like soaps and cleaning preparations. But as competition on foods continued to increase (and the one-stop shopping concept became more popular), supermarkets discovered the non-food category to be one place where at least to some extent shrinking food profits might be bolstered with more profitable merchandise, especially housewares. And so, aided and abetted to no small degree by that specialized if opportunistic newcomer to the marketplace, the so-called rack jobber, housewares have been contributing an ever-larger share of sales—and usually profit—to supermarkets. In 1972 that share of sales was over $200 million. And as the marketing relationship between food and preparing it continues to become closer, many believe supermarkets will garner an ever-increasing share of the housewares business.

A housewares section in a present day supermarket, aided by the "rack jobber." Housewares sales in supermarkets was over $200 million in 1972.

TELEVISION MERCHANDISING

TV reaches countless thousands more people than the best demonstrator could ever hope to contact in person. Two interesting pitchmen, Ronald Popeil and Mel Korey developed the opportunity offered by TV into a multi-million dollar business selling small housewares items.

Popeil and Korey joined forces in 1964. "We decided we had enough experience to enter a major market and picked Kansas City. But there was no suitable TV time available for our standard two minute commercial," Mel recalled, "so we hurriedly made up a one minute pitch including nine seconds for the local tag line and that set the trend for such items in the industry."

In 1969 the firm became Ronco Teleproducts Incorporated. In 1971 their sales were well over the $20 million mark. "When we undertake to introduce a product," Korey explained, "we sell anywhere from 250,000 to 2 million pieces a year. By the time over 240 TV markets provide mass saturation, after one season, an item is established as a nationally known product."

Blenders and irons and bowls in the catalog-showroom of Antor Brothers in Cleveland.

Courtesy Barnett Store Fixture Corporation, Boston.

The Catalog-Showroom Firms

In 1972 the so-called catalog-showroom outlets were generally considered to be the newest and fastest growing version of retailing for housewares, giftwares, home entertainment and related hard goods items (usually no soft goods or major appliances). But the fact is that by then the concept was already at least fifty years old.

This is the merchandising approach whereby a retailer not only issues a catalog of the merchandise he carries and which can be ordered by mail in the usual manner, but in addition maintains a showroom where the merchandise can also be purchased in person. At the beginning of 1972, it was estimated, there were some six hundred firms in that business, a figure which it was believed would be close to the one thousand mark in 1973. By 1976, trade sources predicted, these outlets would account for at least $4 billion in annual sales, although many feel that at the rate they are expanding that goal will be reached much sooner.

In 1937 there were two well-established catalog showrooms doing business in New York and elsewhere, *Retailing Home Furnishings* reported on December 20. One, Bennett Brothers Incorporated, started doing business in 1900; the other, L. & C. Mayer Company, began about 1912. But there was one big difference; those firms concentrated on doing business with and through corporations with many employees, usually through the purchasing agent, and were not open to the general public.

Both those firms have (insofar as can be determined) long since been out of business and for some unknown reason the catalog showroom concept of merchandising remained dormant until the late 1960s. Unlike their early predecessors, today's firms in this business sell to the public generally.

Premiums

Few, if any, product category has provided more and more appealing items for use in the ever-burgeoning premium field than housewares. And there seems to be no limit. Perhaps the strangest use of housewares as a premium—or so it seemed when first started in California reportedly in the late fifties—was by savings banks to attract depositors. The practice soon spread to other cities and on one day alone—January 7, 1970—the *New York Times* carried seven nearly full-page ads of local banks offering housewares (and some other items) as a gift to new depositors. In 1970, housewares volume in the premium field was $63.5 million.

The Salesman

The hard lot of the "salesman" (no one then dignified that occupation with the word) in the eighties and nineties of the last century is recounted by Gerald Carson in his book *The Old Country Store.* Take Henry Dreshler, for example, from Newark, New Jersey, who was tossed into jail by the Baltimore police: the charge against him—selling goods without a license.

> Since it took him several weeks to get out of jail, and the penalty was a fine of from four hundred to six hundred dollars, it is unlikely that Dreshler ever troubled the merchants and police of Baltimore again. It may well be that he bitterly regretted ever becoming a "traveling agent" at all, for the same indignity might have been visited on him in Washington, D. C., Pittsburgh, Memphis, Cincinnati, St. Louis, Chicago or Philadelphia.[23]

America's mercantile provincialism was a die-hard hand-me-down from earlier years when a stiff license fee was demanded of peddlers not just for the ostensible purpose of keeping out suspicious characters but to protect local tradesmen from competition.

A premium advertisement from Vollrath, "in the stainless steel premium business with both feet."

117

The traveling salesman of the nineteenth century had to meet his train according to *its* schedule in any kind of weather. The traveling salesman literally put the housewares industry on the map.

The Bettmann Archive.

A traveling agent with bags, about to board his train; a latter day "bagman" or "drummer."

The Bettmann Archive.

Salesmen had long ago appeared in Europe, and Professor David L. Kurtz of Eastern Michigan University tells of the practice in the August 1970 issue of the University of Florida's *Business and Economic Dimensions:*

> The first true salesman appeared in the late eighteenth century at the time of the Industrial Revolution in England. These first salesmen—called "bagmen"—were instrumental in the economic growth of the period since they successfully marketed the goods produced by the developing factory system.
>
> The bagmen were the first real salesmen, since they were employees charged with performing the sales function by firms in which they typically did not have an ownership interest. This is the origin of professional selling as we know it today.[24]

Kurtz points out that the term "bagman" was derived from the "sample" bags these salesmen carried. This in itself indicated a marked change in attitude. Customers no longer insisted upon personal inspection of the goods.

Colonial America had no need for "bagmen;" the Yankee peddlers were doing a fine job of handling all the selling the times required. But by the start of the nineteenth century the whole picture began to change, and "drummers" and the "knights of the road," as salesmen were once called (only half in jest), would soon become a vital cog in the economy.

"Drummer" connotes one who "drums up" business. But Kurtz suggests that the name may derive from the very large trunks, often weighing several hundred pounds, that the salesmen used to carry their samples and their personal effects on the long trips. "The shape of these trunks caused them to be labeled 'drums,'" he says, and their owners "drummers." The era of the salesman had arrived. At first it was primarily the wholesalers or "jobbing houses" that used salesmen; only later would manufacturers become large enough to have their own.

"When I started on the road, the number of traveling salesmen, I think it safe to say, did not exceed one thousand in all the United States," recalled Edward P. Briggs, a hard-goods salesman from Kansas City, Missouri, who began his career in 1858. He represented the New York jobbing house of Hezekiah King at the time, and some insights into the conditions under which salesmen worked during the last half of the nineteenth century are revealed in his book *Fifty Years on the Road: The Autobiography of a Traveling Salesman,* published in 1911. He continued:

> Nearly all of them were from Eastern cities where were then located the wholesalers, importers and a few manufacturers. At present [1911] the estimate of the number of traveling men in the United States is six hundred thousand!...Whereas fifty years ago there were no jobbing houses outside of a few of the very largest Eastern cities, nowa-

days every town of ten thousand inhabitants has jobbing houses in one or more lines....

The life on the road is not altogether a happy one—in the opinion of many. The necessity of going when the train goes, at two, three or four o'clock in the morning, or nine or twelve o'clock at night, arriving at a destination at hours when all the inhabitants are asleep and all conveniences are not available. And the memory of the hotels of early days is far from pleasant, with their badly ventilated rooms, either too cold, or damp or too hot, with the necessity occasionally of sleeping in the same bed with a stranger. These memories are particularly of the hotels in my early days on the road, for there has undoubtedly been an immense change for the better in hotel accommodations and service....

In one case of which I knew, a salesman left a call for four o'clock in the morning. When that hour came it was raining very hard and he called out to the landlord that he "believed I won't go out in this storm." "Oh, yes you will," said the landlord with a loud, angry shout. "I have been sitting up all night to call you and you *will* go." And so the poor salesman was forced out in the storm against his will.[26]

Briggs recalled the ten-hour night trip from New York City to Washington, D. C., before the days of the Pullman sleeping car but with bunks made up on the order of ship travel, for which the charge was one dollar.

Growth and Changes

Even greater differences were beginning to affect America's marketplace by 1911. The industrial revolution brought an unprecedented variety of products and goods in quantities never before possible— or needed. Old sources of energy like water and steam were being replaced by electricity.

The nation's expanding population, increased still further by wave after wave of immigrants seeking their fortune in "the land of the free," kept creating new and larger markets. The telephone had begun to replace the telegram as a fast, convenient means of communication. The iron sinews of the ever expanding railroads, and networks of new and only occasionally paved roads, were reaching into every section of the land. And the new-fangled motor cars that alternately raised clouds of dust and sank up to their hubcaps in deep, muddy ruts, were starting to put harness and wagon makers out of business.

No one would be more affected by all these changes than the traditional commercial traveler or drummer, though few of them realized just what was happening. Marketing and merchandising as such were beginning to emerge. For one thing, as individual manufacturers grew and prospered they took increasing pride in their products from a competitive if not a personal standpoint, and made certain that their identity—their name or trademark—appeared on them. And then, impelled by competition, they began doing more and more advertising in the growing number of magazines that offered nationwide coverage.

"We sometimes wonder whether all merchants fully appreciate the fact that there is a third law of buying," editorialized *House Furnishing Review* in October 1911. "The established laws, recognized by all successful merchants, are as follows: First, Buy at the right prices; Second, Buy good goods. The third law is *Buy well advertised goods.*"

Meanwhile, a whole new era with its emphasis on brand names and national advertising was moving in—an era that stressed creative selling rather than mere order-taking—a time in which the emerging principles of sound business management would, henceforth, be applied as well to sales management—to marketing and merchandising and distribution—to territories and quotas—to budgets and expense control—yes, even aptitude tests and personality analysis for those who engage in selling. For selling had now not only become acceptable and "respectable" but important. And presently one of America's much-used, magical-sounding phrases, mass production, had a companion term: mass distribution. Meanwhile too, a world war came and went, a depression strangled almost all activity, and still another world war loomed. But regardless of it all the marketing concept, to use the economists' name, moved in and took over.

"A lot has happened," declared *Fortune* magazine in May 1952, in one of a series of articles on selling and salesmanship. "If one word could characterize the change, 'scientific' would be it; where once the salesman was fancied as an artist and an individualist who operated best left to his own devices, his activities have been brought more and more under home office control....He becomes, in a word, a *company* man."

The Manufacturers Rep

The role of the manufacturers sales representative—or sales rep as he is more popularly called—has an ancient heritage in the marketplace of the world.

A very substantial portion of the total housewares business is placed with sales reps and passes through their hands, but there are no actual figures available. The best-informed estimates place the reps' share of the business somewhere between 55 percent and 75 percent of the total, with the tendency to favor the higher figure. It is noteworthy that many large, and some smaller firms who are in a good position to have their own regular sales organization, prefer instead to use the services of manufacturers reps. Although there is no accurate count of the number of reps in the housewares field today, reliable estimates place the figure at about four thousand.

Veterans in the housewares business still recall with more than a trace of nostalgia some of the old-time reps who, in a very real sense, were regarded as "kingpins." One thinks of Max Lowenstein, the dean of the New York reps who handled the Amsterdam Broom Company's line for fifty years until his death. Or Frank Leffler... Walter Beh...Martin Carlstein...Charles Postley—whose son John was one of the more colorful representatives until his untimely death. The names of other well-known veterans in the field cross one's mind...Lou Gershon and Bert Clark in Kansas City...Walter Nye, Steinmetz and Kelly, Fred Edelston and Walter Jacobson in Chicago...Ernie Camos of St. Louis...Fred Wood of San Francisco ...Allan Carpenter in Denver...Frank Pfeiffer of Cleveland...the list is endless.

The manufacturers rep of 1972, however, is a very different breed; he has to be to survive. It is, perhaps, an over-simplification to say that friendship and loyalty played the major role in buyer-seller relationships in those relatively easy-going "good old days." Retail merchandising was primarily a process of by-guess and by-gosh, based as often as not on the whims and wishes of an all-powerful buyer usually responsible to no one but the owner of the store. It is also more than legend that buyers of that early era generally decided on their open-to-buy potential after walking through the stockrooms and noting in passing just how much stock remained on the shelves and in the bins.

There is a decided advantage especially for small manufacturers to use reps on a straight commission rather than hiring salesmen on a salary and expense basis. This became a widespread practice even among some of the larger companies during the Great Depression of the 1930s.

Today the most successful of the reps is a highly trained or experienced merchandising specialist, often a former buyer, and a professional in his approach. There's little place for a mere peddler —or the peddler's singleness of purpose in simply getting an order. Now the "professional" rep understands how and where his product or line can make the most effective contribution and he comes fully prepared—with factory backing—to help implement that contribution with creative merchandising.

This service is now being carried still further by what might be termed the "third generation" of reps. Today there is an increasing tendency toward specialization in a particular field such as premiums, stamp plan companies, mass merchandisers, etc. These men often handle quite a few lines but concentrate primarily in their chosen specialties which have become important enough to demand such concentrated attention.

A good insight into the current thinking of today's most successful reps is reflected in the statements of Edwin E. Bobrow, Lewell Associates Incorporated, well-known manufacturers rep in New York, in an interview in the *Agent and Representative Magazine* in 1971. "If I might make an analogy, our work is like a doctor's. Before he can prescribe, he must have a complete history and a diagnostic work-up of his patient. Before a sales effort can be made, our agency must have an accurate picture of the market position of the product. ...Only after we have assembled the facts and ascertained the implications are we in a position to tell a client what we can do for his

D. E. Sanford, founder of the
D. E. Sanford Company, a national
manufacturers rep organization.

122

product." He has elaborated that approach into what he calls the "concept of total marketing." Bobrow, who has become something of a spokesman for reps, has conducted a number of seminars on their function at college marketing classes and has published a book, *How To Make Big Money As An Independent Sales Agent.*

A Unique Rep Story

How many manufacturers sales representatives have dreamed—or still dream—of expanding their traditionally local business into a truly national operation no one can ever know. Nearly half a century ago two brothers, Dave and Fred Sanford, did build such an organization. The only one of its kind, at its peak in 1948 the D. E. Sanford Company did a volume of $35 million, with fourteen offices throughout the country and over one hundred employees.

The Sanford story begins in 1924 when, after selling housewares around New York, the brothers were caught up in the Florida land boom. Then they obtained a line of shirts to sell.

A restaurant came next. Again, less than a sensational success. They sold it just at the time two customers offered Fred a ride to Los Angeles, while Dave returned to New York.

In Los Angeles Fred became a salesman for the Parvin-Dohrman Company's hotel supply division. It also had a retail division and a wholesale division called Pacific Housewares for which Dave became a salesman when he arrived on the coast soon after. Both boys did so well that in 1927 Dave decided they could do even better by becoming manufacturers sales representatives and the D. E. Sanford Company was launched. Although they severed their financial ties in the business in 1937, they worked together closely for many years thereafter.

Their skill as salesmen, merchandisers and entrepreneurs was quickly evident. Branch offices were opened along the West Coast; then they spread eastward. They acquired an impressive list of lines —Kitchen Aid, Waring, Dazey, Ekco, Everhot, Taylor, Smith and Taylor—to mention a few.

The opening of an office in New York in 1945 at the end of World War II marked the first time any sales representatives had become a coast-to-coast operation. Also, the prestige the firm had developed was reflected in the announcement that A. C. Sanger, national sales manager of General Electric's housewares and major appliances, had resigned to become general manager of Sanford's Eastern division, and that James P. McIlhenny, a divisional sales manager for General Electric, had been named sales manager of the Sanford division.

The most profitable of all the Sanford Company's ventures was its creation of the "Desco" line of imported porcelain enamel cooking utensils in 1950—Desco for the initials of the company's full name. Sanford has since sold Desco to the General Housewares Corporation.

But even before Desco the Sanfords decided to curtail their nation-wide sales activities and cut back to a local office in Los Angeles. In the course of his interview Dave Sanford explained why:

There were three reasons, really. First, Fred and I were making twelve to fifteen cross-country trips a year, and although it was paying off we finally decided it was not worth the physical wear and tear. Remember, there were still no jet planes then. Second, we found we were obliged to neglect our wives and children far too much, and we missed them. And, finally, we were becoming convinced that having the exclusive, national sales representation of a line is an extremely difficult and often almost impossible assignment. Manufacturers in this category have no way of assessing regional or even overall performance. At the outset they are enamored with the elimination of territorial sales problems. But as time goes on they begin to question whether they are getting as much time and attention and volume as they think their products merit. At this point the honeymoon is over. That was our feeling in 1948 and, as far as I am concerned personally, it has not changed.

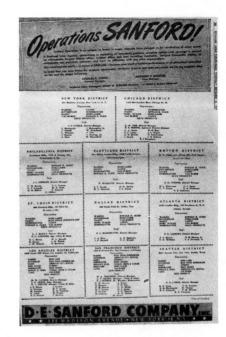

The first of a six-page trade newspaper ad used by D. E. Sanford announcing its nation-wide set up.

EVOLUTION of the Kitchen

The housewares industry reflects the development of America's high standard of living almost better than anything else. And nowhere can one see that reflection more clearly or find a more fascinating record of its remarkable progress over the years than in that all-important room of the house, the kitchen.

"The foundation of existence is home and about its walls are entwined all the sweet memories of earth....The basis upon which all homes should be founded is good living, and no matter how straitened the circumstances, how little there is to be spent, this can always be secured if housekeepers will begin at the beginning—that is in the kitchen," wrote Laura C. Holloway in 1883 in her celebrated book, *The Hearthstone, or Life at Home, a Household Manual.* She adds, "That they do not thus begin is the reason why there is so little real comfort in houses; so little restfulness and true pleasure found in what ought to be genuine homes."[1]

When one looks at the conditions under which the early settlers had to live, one wonders if they had—if they could have had—any comforts at all.

In the following pages the story will be told how, slowly but surely, the kitchen developed as a result of the contributions of the nation's housewares—and major appliance—manufacturers.

From 1800 to 1900

One of the earliest attempts to change people's ideas about housework in general and the kitchen in particular was made in 1838 when a popular author, William A. Alcott, wrote *The Young Housekeeper, or Thoughts on Food and Cookery.*

> A large proportion of the books which have been written professedly for house-keepers, are little more than large bundles of recipes for fashionable cookery. I know of no work in this department which contains, to any considerable extent, *important principles.*...A principal aim of this book has been to elevate the important profession for whom it is written instead of sinking it below its present unworthy level. I should be glad to convince the most skeptical that housekeeping is as much a science, and in view of its results in the formation of human health and character, as deserving of study—and of hard study too— as geography or mathematics. The duties and destinies of the housekeeper are too important to be misunderstood.[2]

125

This page: What the medieval kitchen may have lacked in modern convenience, it more than made up for in manpower. Circa 1643.

Courtesy New York Public Library, Astor, Lenox, and Tilden Foundations.

Opposite page: Two American kitchens a century apart show the results of progress and invention. A busy colonial kitchen is contrasted with the comparative luxury of a typical kitchen of the 1870s.

The Bettmann Archive.

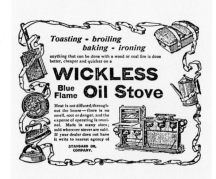

THE CRYSTAL WASHER

PAT'D APR 2.89

OUR Washer has a reversible rotary motion of both upper and lower wash-boards, giving the true hand-rubbing principle. Clothes never bunch while washing. From 15 to 20 shirts can be washed at a time.

For Circulars, Testimonials, Prices, Terms, Etc., Address

Crystal Washing Machine Co.
COLUMBUS, OHIO.

Toasting - broiling
baking - ironing

anything that can be done with a wood or coal fire is done better, cheaper and quicker on a

WICKLESS
Blue Flame Oil Stove

Heat is not diffused throughout the house—there is no smell, soot or danger, and the expense of operating is nominal. Made in many sizes; sold wherever stoves are sold. If your dealer does not have it write to nearest agency of

STANDARD OIL COMPANY.

126

From top: Two advertisements of the late nineteenth century selling "modern" amenities.

Courtesy House Furnishing Review.

The center illustration shows that the much treasured hearth of the frontier days was dirty, dusty, awkward, and often a dangerous place. But alas, there was no alternative.

Courtesy the Society for the Preservation of New England Antiquities.

Wood gathering was still an essential chore to power many stoves well into the twentieth century. A farm kitchen about 1900.

Courtesy General Electric Company.

Kitchen Principles

The first serious attempt to create some order and organization out of household disorder and inefficiency, then accepted as inevitable, was made in 1870. The impressive *Principles of Domestic Science as Applied to the Duties and Pleasures of Home,* written by Catherine E. Beecher and Harriet Beecher Stowe drew up a detailed plan showing just where and how all kitchen equipment and furnishings should be arranged, and provided a blue print to show how the kitchen could best be laid out in relation to the rest of the house.

"If all American housekeepers could be taught how to select and manage the most economical and convenient apparatus for cooking and for warming a house, many millions now wasted by ignorance and neglect would be saved,"[3] declared the authors. Their book was sub-titled, "A text book for the use of young ladies in schools, seminaries and colleges."

The Washboard

Since it was patented nearly 140 years ago the basic design of the washboard hasn't changed and despite the popularity of washing machines millions of washboards are still in use.

"We sell anywhere from 250,000 to 500,000 annually, depending on the state of the economy," reports E. K. Donahue, an executive of Wabash Incorporated, believed to be the world's largest manufacturer of that product. It began making washboards in 1885 in the town of Wabash, Indiana, and is now located in Memphis, Tennessee.

"Our biggest sales are to poor people in the Southeast and Southwest as well as the large cities," he added. "The pattern has been the same for many years—sales seem to improve as the general economy worsens."

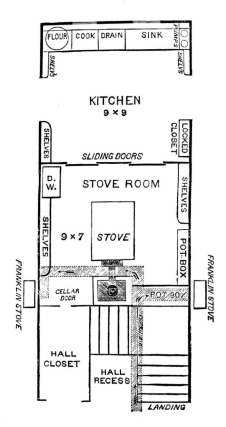

In 1870 an idealized kitchen layout demonstrated just where and how all kitchen equipment should be arranged. From *Principles of Domestic Science.*

127

THE "SERVANT PROBLEM" IS AN OLD, OLD STORY

"There is a cry for 'Help!' all over the land," wrote Laura C. Holloway nearly a century ago in her once very popular book, *The Hearthstone or Life at Home, A Household Manual,* published in 1883.

"It is not because our houses are on fire or we are besieged by burglars, or have fallen into the river and don't know how to swim. It is not because the highwayman holds a pistol to our nose and says 'Your money or your life!'

"It is not because the roof has fallen in and we are struggling in vain to get our limbs out of the ruins....

"It is none of these, although they are heard often enough. It is a cry for help, 'Up-stairs, down-stairs and in my lady's chamber.' It means, 'Can you tell me of a good servant?' "[4]

One hundred forty years old and still very much in use—the washboard.

From top: Keeping the cast iron stove in top shape required polish and elbow grease in 1860.

Courtesy Library of Congress.

The other advertisement demonstrates how furniture stores capitalized on the kitchen cabinet boom, promoting the "Hoosier Kitchen Cabinet Club," a facade for installment selling.

Courtesy House Furnishing Review.

SHOW ME THE KITCHEN

What food is to the body the kitchen should be to the home. Indeed, as Brillat-Savarin has said, "Tell me what you eat and I will tell you what you are"; so one may say, "Show me the kitchen and I can form a good idea of the home." As Laura Holloway says:

"As the comfort and happiness of home do not depend upon vast rooms and costly furniture—there is often far more peace and pleasure in a cottage than a palace. But as every human life depends for its support upon food, so every human home must have a kitchen in which that food is prepared. The person who neglects food soon gets sick, and the home in which the kitchen is neglected is not a healthy or a happy home."[5]

THE GARBAGE PAIL MARKET

"Philadelphia promises to become a great market for garbage pails. Last week the City Council there passed an ordinance compelling housekeepers to use a water-tight covered vessel as a receptacle for garbage and in order to enforce this rule, a penalty of $5 for each and every offense reported is imposed on the housekeeper," reported *House Furnishing Review* in July 1894.

Cabinets for the Kitchen

The woeful lack of cabinet storage space in their kitchen that had for so long plagued America's homemakers finally, around the turn of the century, penetrated the opportunity-consciousness of a few

America's first model electric kitchen was exhibited at the Columbian Exposition in Chicago, 1893. Note exposed water pipes, and porcelain screw-type outlets.

Courtesy Smithsonian Institution.

woodenware manufacturers, especially in northern Indiana. Then they did something about it, which created millions of happy customers and millions of dollars in business for themselves and their retailers.

Just why this enlightenment happened to strike then and there or exactly which company was hit first with the idea is not really known, but a somewhat revolutionary new type of storage unit began to be made. It was called a kitchen "Hoosier" or "Dutch" cabinet, depending on the maker.

Among these were the McDougall Company; Mutschler Brothers, (now a division of American Standard); Coppes Brothers & Zook; Kompass & Stoll Company; the Hoosier Manufacturing Company and others. Such cabinets were once enormously important to housewares departments because of their relatively high unit price ranging from around twenty-five dollars to well over one hundred dollars.

Moreover, the appearance of these cabinets marks the first step in the development of today's modern kitchen with its built-in cabinets and continuous counter work surfaces.

In 1899 J. S. McQuinn founded the Hoosier Manufacturing Company in Albany, Indiana. The factory was destroyed by fire and operations were then restarted in nearby New Castle, making kitchen cabinets.

In the early years of the company, according to the records of the New Castle Area Chamber of Commerce, the company employed only about a dozen men and produced from fifty to sixty cabinets a week. At that time the cabinets were only partially completed in what was called the machine room; then one of the skilled carpenters had

129

At the New York World's Fair in 1965, General Electric recreated this late nineteenth-century American kitchen, including "life-like" animated models.

Courtesy General Electric Company.

Kitchen cabinets, an important housewares product well into the 1930s, offered in wood or metal, complete kitchen functions. They were a significant furnishing before built-ins.

Bottom, courtesy House Furnishing Review.

to fit all the doors and drawers by hand. A good cabinet maker could complete only two cabinets a day.

Later on the parts were machined so completely and accurately that skilled cabinet makers were no longer necessary. It became an assembly-line, mass production operation and was started, it is claimed, even before the assembly-line was in operation at Ford.

At its peak the company employed seven hundred people in the factory, about sixty-five in the office and about fifty traveling salesmen. Average production was about seven hundred cabinets daily. It became the largest industry in New Castle and the biggest kitchen cabinet manufacturer in the United States. It created many innovations in its cabinets which, each year, became more elaborate as well as efficient with built-in flour bin complete with sifter; built-in sugar bin; spice rack; cutting board; cookbook rack; and later, what was especially popular, a porcelain enameled work surface.

The company promoted and advertised its cabinets extensively, with a budget averaging from $200,000 to $250,000 annually. Its last double-page color spread in the *Saturday Evening Post* cost $25,000. Young brides eagerly looked forward to the day they could own a Hoosier cabinet!

Another once well-known manufacturer of kitchen cabinets, the Wasmuth Endicott Company, Andrews, Indiana, attempted to cope with the new built-in trend by introducing a uniquely designed line of modular kitchen cabinet units. Called "Kitchen Maid Standard Unit Systems," these units ranged in size and purpose and could be arranged in any desired combination. Although the line was extensively advertised in national magazines and for a time met with considerable success, for unknown reasons the company eventually went out of business.

But something was happening beyond the control of all kitchen cabinet manufacturers—kitchens began to be designed with built-in cabinets so that free-standing cabinets were no longer necessary. Hoosier's management attempted to offset the downward trend by going into the built-in business and also promoting breakfast sets, but without success. The business was sold in 1942 and, largely due to war-time conditions, was liquidated by the purchasers.

The porcelain enameled work surface on those early kitchen cabinets—on some models tops could be pulled out about twelve inches or so to provide extra room—indirectly spawned another once extremely important product in the housewares business: the porcelain enameled-top kitchen table and breakfast set.

Right after World War I from 80 percent to 90 percent of this country's production of porcelain enameled ware was in pots and pans. But the development of new technologies had been expanding the production of porcelain enameled coatings on large flat surfaces such as table tops, signs, architectural panels, etc., to a degree not previously possible.

"The work-surface on the old kitchen cabinets originally was a

130

In the 1920s, Mutschler offered Porce-Namel cabinets as "aids to first class cooking." From a catalog of the period.

metal-finish surface called 'Nickeloid,'" W. N. Noble, group vice-president of the Ferro Corporation in Cleveland, recalled in 1970. Ferro is one of the largest producers of enamel frit.

"Sometime before 1910 the idea evolved to substitute a porcelain enameled work surface on those cabinets in place of the metallic finish then used. It was an instant success. Around 1920 this led to the creation of a porcelain enameled-top kitchen table, the most popular size of which was twenty-five by forty inches."

The many advantages of porcelain enamel made these tables and breakfast sets enormously popular, but not before there had been considerable missionary work done, according to Edward Mackasek, who was associated with the Porcelain Enamel Institute starting in 1921.

"Porcelain enameled table tops were just beginning to become big business, but our big problem was the fact that for the most part the public had no real understanding of the difference between it and paint. Sometimes it would be referred to as 'vitreous enamel,'" he related in 1970 from his retirement home in Florida.

"To prove its durability our Institute's literature placed great emphasis on the ancient history of the art of enameling and we used the Pyramids on our letterheads as a symbol of its permanence."

Broom and Linen Cabinets

Practical and efficient as they may have been—and they were both—the popular kitchen cabinets still didn't suffice to meet the need for storage space in the kitchens of America's homemakers. And so in the 1920s two new types of wooden cabinets appeared in the market-place—the "broom cabinet" and the "linen cabinet."

Generally they were about sixty inches high, about eighteen or twenty inches square, and whereas the broom cabinet had only one shelf about eight inches from the top, the linen cabinet had four or five. The name "linen" was really a misnomer; cereals, canned goods, and other things, but seldom linens were stored in them.

The origin of these cabinets is not known but they quickly became important best sellers in the housewares departments. Simple to make, local woodworking plants found them easy to copy and did so, thus minimizing, at least in part, the high handling cost of this bulky item. They were made in various colors, sold somewhere between ten dollars and fifteen dollars and were heavily promoted so that competition kept driving the prices down.

But presently the boom on these wood cabinets collapsed. Manufacturers of sheet metal goods found a way to duplicate them at close to the same price, and who would pay $9.95 for a wood cabinet if a far superior steel one could be had for the same amount?

Like their predecessors, the steel cabinets—in a proliferation of sizes and styles—became best sellers in stores throughout the country. Firms like Palley Manufacturing Company, Pittsburgh; Lyon Metal Products Incorporated, Aurora, Illinois; Interstate Metal Prod-

Free-standing kitchen cabinets, multi-purpose tables and other furniture were very important housewares before World War II. The completely accessorized Kitchen Maid cabinet above is the "missing link" between free standing and built-ins and offered most of the advantages of today's built-ins. Note the lower bin for flour under the porcelain table.

ucts Company Incorporated and M. Block & Sons Incorporated, Chicago; and E. J. McAleer & Company Incorporated, Philadelphia, were among the more important factories who supplied them.

World War II ended the production of these cabinets and after the war they never regained their early popularity. Something had developed during the previous decade which was having far-reaching effects on all aspects of the nation's kitchens. A ''new'' idea had taken hold. Kitchen design was being revolutionized and the once-wasted wall space was being equipped with built-in kitchen cabinets right at the time the house or apartment was built. From now on housewares departments would be providing a great many things for the new type of kitchens that was emerging, but cabinets would account for only a relatively small proportion of them.

The Modernization Bureau

The trend toward more up-to-date kitchens got a big boost in 1935 when the National Kitchen Modernization Bureau was established jointly by the Edison Electric Institute (now the Electric Energy Association) and the National Electrical Manufacturers Association to actively promote kitchen modernization throughout the country.

Tied in with the Federal Housing Bureau on general modernization of the home, the new Bureau launched an extensive program that included the creation of model modern kitchen displays; radio

132

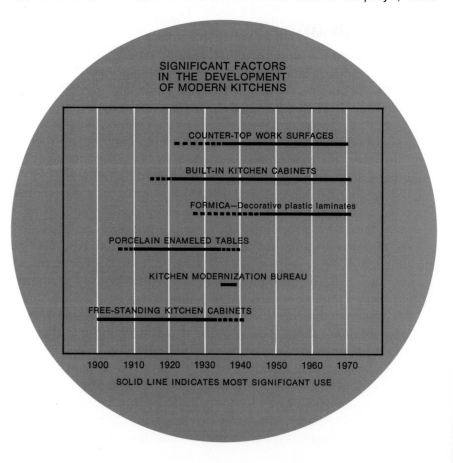

From top: A Porce-Namel decorated drop leaf table of the 1920s, a big selling item. Twenty years later, streamlined design, chrome, and laminated plastic merchandized this dinette set.

Courtesy House Furnishing Review.

From top: Department stores have long featured model kitchens in their housewares departments. Wanamaker's in New York presented this kitchen in 1905. Note the complete lack of storage cabinets and the inconvenience of the extreme height of the utensils on the upper hooks. The steel, porcelain enameled kitchen tables in the lower photo were sufficiently important to rate a window display in the early 1920s. This was a presentation of tables by the Porcelain Enamel and Manufacturing Company, Baltimore, in a May Company store.

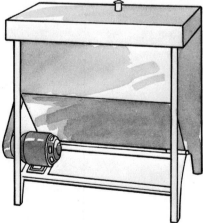

programs; distribution of modern electric kitchen plan books; a feature motion picture entitled "The Courage of Kay" in which the subject was dramatized with numerous tie-ins with retailers, appliance and kitchen equipment manufacturers, builders, and others.

World War II brought the whole program to a halt. It was revived in 1947 but with particular emphasis on the use of electrical appliances rather than modernization.

Fall and Rise of the Pantry

The checkered career of the pantry constitutes an important footnote to the story of the kitchen's evolution, and here in a 1972 interview, Margaret Davidson, well-known home management editor of the *Ladies Home Journal,* now retired, relates its entertaining details:

In the early days a pantry was considered a necessity for a well-

From top: Two methods of washing dishes with a little bit of help. The 1928 "practical dishwasher" featured a leak-proof attachment to fit any faucet and an "exclusive" brush for cleaning pots and pans. The Minit dishwasher was an early (circa 1914) device to electrically help with the chore of cleaning dirty dishes, pots, and pans.

Top, courtesy House Furnishing Review.

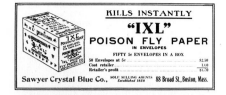

KILLS INSTANTLY

"IXL"
POISON FLY PAPER
IN ENVELOPES

FIFTY 5c ENVELOPES IN A BOX

50 Envelopes at 5c	$2.50
Cost retailer	1.40
Retailer's profit	$1.70

Sawyer Crystal Blue Co., SOLE SELLING AGENTS Established 1858 88 Broad St., Boston, Mass.

134

AMONG the knowing ones in the trade, the Consolidated Lamps always stand for originality of design and effectiveness of decoration. These qualities are what cause our lamps to *sell,* while other makes collect dust.

Our special December beauties are in so great demand that we expect to have more orders than we can deliver promptly; so see them and order them a good many days before you want them.

Railroads are unable to promptly move all the freight consigned to their care; so make allowance for possible delays en transit. And don't blame the manufacturer for that.

November First is not a day too soon for you to place your *final* holiday lamp orders.

Consolidated Lamp & Glass Co.
Coraopolis, Pa.

BRANCH SALESROOMS:

56 Murray Street, New York, E. H. Mays
1111 Market Street, Philadelphia, T. Downs, Jr.
1319 Michigan Avenue, Chicago, Wm. Kelley
Cor. 6th Ave. and Wood St., Pittsburg, McCombs Bros.

From top: As late as 1915 no well-stocked house furnishings department would think of being without fly paper. The 1902 version of today's aerosol bug-bomb. The "Kil-lol" sprayer produced a fine mist "which can be blown from ten to twelve feet" with a little lung power. Another important housewares item was the oil lamp for kitchen or dining room, sometimes a very decorative addition to the home.

All courtesy House Furnishing Review.

mannered kitchen. As far back as the days when the kitchen—or keeping room—was where the family really lived, the cooking needs were squirreled away in a pantry. As homes became more "advanced," menus more complex, and supplies more numerous, the kitchen developed as a working room, but the pantry was still the place where pots and pans were stowed, milk pans set out for the cream to rise, and cakes and pies lined up to cool.

About the turn of the century homes in which there was much entertaining had two pantries. One would be in the kitchen section for food and gear, and another connected the kitchen and dining room and was used for serving. In this second pantry, serving dishes and trays were kept, and wine was uncorked. Certain "clean" preparations were carried out there: salads, some desserts, and coffee. Also, dishes were washed there, so that they never went into the kitchen proper— the first dishwashers were often placed in such pantries.

In the twenties, pantries were considered old hat. For one thing, with an effort toward efficiency, kitchens were equipped with "Hoosier" cabinets and shelves, and it was thought that a good kitchen had storage "where needed." The pantry became passé.

Today, with informal living the rule, the kitchen sees many activities. Cooking is just one of them. As a result, they tend to be larger, and their appearance is becoming important. Also, people buy differently. There are more packaged and convenience foods to be stored. Foods come from supermarkets and are bought in large quantities (a carton of cokes, a dozen cans of baby food, etc.). Families expect more varied, often more exotic foods—and the stocks-on-hand must reflect this.

Where to store them? Lo and behold, back comes the pantry! Updated, of course, with spaces planned to hold special things—bulk foods and cans, large occasionally used utensils (canners, lobster cookers, special foreign cookers), supplies such as paper towels and napkins. Back comes the tall cupboard with shelves extending from the floor to the top. There are places for the plug-in appliances hitherto little used because they were inaccessible on a top shelf—the waffle irons, the sandwich grills, and the deep fryers. Women want pantries, and bigger homes are getting them; sooner, rather than later, they must reach the modest home, which is increasingly short of convenient storage.

Early Kitchen Cleaning Methods

Home cleaning equipment and materials constitute one of the most important categories of the housewares business today and go far toward making life easier, safer, and far more pleasant for homemakers. But things weren't always that way. Glance, for example, through a revealing volume called *The Hearthstone,* written by Laura C. Holloway. The time is 1883.

Here is some authoritative counsel on the care of brooms and carpets.

If brooms are wet in boiling suds once a week they will become tough, will not cut out a carpet, but last much longer and always sweep like a new broom—clean.

A handful or two of damp salt sprinkled on the carpet will attract and absorb the dust and carry it along with it, and make the carpet look fresh as new. Wet corn meal is also excellent and serves the same purpose. So do damp cabbage-leaves cut up small, if no other means are at hand.

The broom wears out carpets quite as much as feet do. A very dusty carpet may be cleaned by setting a pail of cold water outside the door, wet the broom in it, knock it to get all the drops, sweep a yard or so, then wash the broom and sweep again, so on till the whole is done....[7]

If all that seems like too much effort, there are other methods. "How to clean a carpet: Shake and beat it well, tack it firmly upon the floor, and then with clean flannel wash it over with a quart of bullock's gall mixed with three quarts of soft cold water, and rub it off with a clean flannel or house cloth." [8] There's advice for cleaning other things as well.

To clean knives with expedition and ease—Make a strong solution of the common washing-soda and water; after wiping them, dip the blades of the knives into the solution; then polish on a knifeboard; the same would, of course, be effectual for forks. Never put ivory-handled knives into warm water; it discolors and then cracks them. If knives are wrapped up in chamois leather they will never rust unless put away damp.

Soap would not be required in washing dishes if a stone jar was kept at hand filled with lye and the greasy dishes were dipped into it. If this lye becomes greasy, it should be poured into the tub in which all bones and extra grease is put, and, when a sufficient quantity is accumulated, it could be boiled and good soap made....

A strong alum-water is sure death to bugs of any description. Take two pounds of pulverized alum and dissolve in three quarts of boiling water, allowing it to remain over the fire until thoroughly dissolved. Apply while hot with a brush, or, what is better, use a syringe to force the liquid into the cracks of the walls and bedstead. Scatter powdered alum freely in all the places where they have appeared and the house will soon be rid of insects of every kind.

135

Maintaining yesteryear's oil lamp was a tedious kitchen task. Filling them and trimming the wicks were part of a continual job.

Courtesy Minnesota Historical Society.

In today's age of plastic and vinyl the word "oilcloth" is rarely heard, but in 1929 it was an important housewares category. Its numerous uses were of such widespread interest that a special broadcast was made from the windows of a department store in New York.

Courtesy House Furnishing Review.

The breakfast set was a standard housewares item in the 1920s. Note the popular "cottage" design of the times.

Courtesy Hobart Manufacturing Company.

White Mountain Freezers

WE have issued a large, new and complete catalogue, finely illustrated and fully describing our entire line. It has 32 pages of knowledge, both important and instructive regarding Ice Cream Freezers. *For free copy or information regarding prices or goods apply to Catalogue Department.

Are always used as a basis of comparison by other manufacturers because wherever introduced they at once establish a reputation to produce better ice cream and more of it, more economically and in less time than any other Freezer in the whole wide world.

Sizes 1 to 25 qt. inclusive.

Positively the Best Freezer Known

From top: Two early ice cream freezers contrast with a nostalgically clad, but very contemporary, electric machine. The upper two were powered by much manual labor.

Top, courtesy House Furnishing Review. Middle, the Bettmann Archive.

136

Old newspapers are excellent to put the polish on tinware, cutlery, silver spoons and to renew the polish of stoves and ranges....Nothing, not even chamois skin is as good as newspaper for polishing mirrors after they have first been wiped off with a cloth wrung out of strong suds....

To clean steel or iron, make a paste of two ounces of soft soap, and two of coarse emery powder and two of fine, apply; allow to remain a while, then rub off with wash-leather. For polishing steel, crocus powder, moistened with sweet oil, is best. "An ounce of prevention is worth a pound of cure," and if steel fire-sets and any steel articles that are to be put away for the season are well rubbed in sweet oil and done up in soft brown paper, they will keep free from rust....Wooden bowls or trays, if well rubbed inside and out with lard or any clear grease, before ever using, will never crack....

If you have a brass tea kettle it is all the rage now to bring it in to the table while you make the afternoon tea, and it must be polished so that it shines like gold. Buy five cents worth of oxalic acid, put it in an ordinary wine bottle and fill with cold water; when dissolved rub the kettle with a cloth dipped in the solution. Elbow grease is the only other necessity and if plenty of it is used, the result will be wonderful.[9]

Oh, for the good old days!

Home Made Ice Cream

"Until a woman named Nancy Johnson invented the first ice-cream freezer in 1864, ice cream was made at home by mixing the recipe and then beating it in a cooking pot packed in snow and ice with rock salt," G. Webster DeHoff, president of the Richmond Cedar Works Manufacturing Corporation related in 1971, discussing the remarkable durability of a venerable housewares item. "But nothing else is known about Nancy Johnson."

Mr. DeHoff's company has been in business since 1868 producing wooden pails, tubs, clothespins, and washing machines, and it began making a hand-operated, wooden-tub freezer about 1900. As early as 1888 the White Mountain Freezer Company in Nashua, New Hampshire, was advertising its "Sands patent triple motion freezer" as "the most perfect ever made."

Commercial production of ice cream started in this country in Baltimore in 1851, but for many years most Americans who wanted ice cream had to make it at home. For unexplained reasons the sales of ice cream freezers reached their peak right after World War I. About that time Ethel R. Peyser wrote:

To be 100% American each of us must eat at least 2¼ quarts of ice cream annually. This is the national American dish despite Boston's claim for the baked bean and the South's for beaten biscuits. Rich and poor, the be-butlered and the maidless, make their own ice cream. It is no longer a luxury; it is now recognized as a food.[10]

Webster DeHoff added that the principle of making ice cream is the same as it always was. Although materials for making the product have changed, nostalgia makes the hand-turned wooden-tub home freezer a popular sales unit despite large sales of electrically operated models.

The Color Revolution in Housewares

"I tell you I never saw so damn many one-quart saucepans in my life! And such colors—it seemed unbelievable!" recalled Joseph P. Kasper, a member of that relatively small and select group of housewares buyers who eventually succeeded to the executive suite. Mr. Kasper later also became president of the Associated Merchandising Corporation. He was recalling the start of one of the most important and significant housewares merchandising developments—color in the kitchen. His recollection is of 1927, when he was the buyer for what would later be known as Macy's famous Housewares Department.

Joe Kasper had been working on the development of colored enamel cooking utensils—colors unlike any that had ever been seen before. His efforts had led him to the Vollrath Company's plant in Sheboygan, Wisconsin, accompanied by Miss Katherine Kinane, probably the first housewares stylist in a department store (or any store) in the country. They made the journey to see unusually large color samples that had been specially prepared for them.

It would be a mistake to assume that there had never been any colored enamel cooking utensils prior to that time. Originally, of course, most enamelware was known as "Agate Ware," usually colored very dark blue or gray speckled with white—purely utilitarian with a drab, institutional look. Cooking utensil manufacturers had not learned how to make much else (at least commercially), and the very dark finishes covered a multitude of defects.

But the state of the art was progressing. German manufacturers were probably the first to come out with a gleaming white enamel, obviously something with great appeal for cooking utensils and other sanitary ware. For quite a while it gave them a tremendous competitive advantage, especially in the United States. Later, an Austrian manufacturer made something of a stir with the "Elite" brand line in robin's egg blue.

For the most part, however, these items were regarded and treated as novelties. No one in the housewares business attached any particular significance to them in terms of being an important basic merchandising potential. In fact, prior to the late twenties, nobody thought much about color in home furnishings at all. That was the era when even Henry Ford showed his feelings toward the faint rainbow beginning to appear over the marketplace by agreeing to sell his customers a Model T "in any color they want—as long as it's black."

But the times were changing. In New York City, for example, high rise apartments were appearing everywhere. Real estate competition became increasingly tough; and to give their buildings special appeal, some builders began to feature pink or blue tiles instead of the usual white in their bathrooms. But again, the colored tiles were only a novelty at the start.

Joe Kasper and his stylist found themselves in Sheboygan be-

From top: A common 1939 kitchen. Although it seems primitive, it was regarded as fairly up-to-date: note the one-piece working surface, unheard of earlier.

Courtesy Cornell University.

Much more than a touch of color and decorative art covered this General Electric "monitor top" electric refrigerator of the 1920s.

Courtesy House Furnishing Review.

cause of Jesse I. Straus, then Macy's president. Mr. Straus made frequent trips to Paris. On one of these trips he obtained pictures of decorative enamel pieces with very unusual colorings and, upon his return, asked Joe Kasper up to his office to discuss them.

"I remember it very well because neither of us had ever seen anything like them," Joe later recalled.

There were several cannisters, something like a cereal set, finished in white and with red streaks outlined in gold going up the sides; they looked like flames. He told me where they came from, a little shop on the outskirts of Paris, and suggested I visit it on my forthcoming trip there because, he felt, they held a lot of merchandising possibilities for enamelware in my housewares department. Well, I got to Paris, went to the shop, but found it to be more like an art gallery or studio. Furthermore, none of the new enamelware was for sale, despite my desperate eagerness to buy some. But what could I do? By some strange coincidence, when I unpacked my bags after returning to New York, there was one of those small, colorful cannisters mixed in with my clothes. One doesn't bother to ask questions at such good fortune. But the next day I showed it to Stanley Williams, then Vollrath's New York manager, and within the week we were out at the factory with it.

The Vollrath executives were quick to recognize the potentials of some striking new colors for cooking utensils, especially since Macy's was now thinking in terms of having many other housewares items also finished in color. "Color in the kitchen"—a coordinated program with a choice of several colors—was to be the new merchandising theme. DeWitt Reese, Vollrath's vice-president of sales, asked for a month's time to work out some samples, and now the Macy people were back in Sheboygan to see them.

"What a sight!" remembers Joe Kasper. "They had made up a one-quart saucepan for every college color combination in the country and arranged them all on shelves in their big sample room. They had black and orange for Princeton, green and white for Notre Dame …you name it and they had it. There was gray inside, red outside— and then it was reversed. It was really terrific!"

By a long and critically discriminating process of elimination, he and Miss Kinane finally selected the winners of this early "College Bowl" contest: Mandarin red, apple green, and Delft blue. And that was only the beginning. "What a time we had trying to get manufacturers of other merchandise to make up matching items, everything from paring knives to kitchen tables," Joe Kasper added.

"One of the most successful things were polka dot color combinations in oilcloth table covers. Sales were tremendous. Later on we even had refrigerators in color. Apparently people were becoming fed up with 'poorhouse white' in their kitchens, it was too much like a laboratory. Of course, we still continued to stock and sell speckled enamelware, but we were off on an exciting new track."

The Kitchen Comes of Age

While Macy's has usually been credited with originating "color in

138

AMERICAN HOUSEHOLD SCALES

The last word in popular Household Scales. Meet every need for reliability, endurance, long life and accuracy, being fully tested and approved by the standard of the U S Bureau of Weights and Measures. Made in the new popular American gray, also blue, white and black enameled body, with dial slanting at an angle of 25 degrees, making weighing and reading of weight simple, easy and practical. Prices are far below anything of a similar grade on the market and are so low as to make their purchase an every-day shopping affair for the housewife. Note the special bargains on this page. For list of other American scales write for special Scale Bulletin showing entire line of household, nursery, candy and grocers' scales.

Scale No. 3000

No. 5000—5½ inch steel platform. Weighs up to 25 lbs. by ounces. Slanting dial. Ship wt 4½ lbs., packed singly in individual cartons, six in a corrugated container weighing 30 lbs. Ready for immediate shipment from factory to your counter. Black enamel or gray. Retails for $3.00.

No. 5075—Same as 5000 but with scoop. Black enamel or gray. Retails for $3.50.

No. 5070—With tin scoop, as illustrated, double posts supporting claw and scoop. 25 lbs. by ounces. Ship wt 5½ lbs. Black or gray enameled. Retails for $3.40.

No. 3000—Black or gray enameled body. Double posts. Glass covered dial with nickel-plated sash, slanting at angle of 25 degrees. Flat steel top. Weighs to 25 lbs. by ounces. Same ship wt as 5000. Retails for $3.50 (see illustration).

Scale No. 5070

Exceptionally liberal dealers' discounts from these prices. American scales are priced so low that you can sell them like hot cakes. Try a bargain sale of these scales and you will marvel at the speed of your turnover. Clip the coupon now, today.

American Cutlery Co.
732 Mather St. Chicago

NEW YORK OFFICE,
Suite 615-16,
111-5th Av.
SAN FRANCISCO OFFICE,
180 New Montgomery
SEATTLE OFFICE,
L. C. Smith Bldg.

AMERICAN
CUTLERY CO.

Please ship me following scales, billing me special dealers' discount price for same:
...Doz. No. 5000, Color..
...Doz. No. 5075, Color....
....Doz. No. 5070, Color....
.....Doz. No. 3000, Color......
Note—Blue enameled scales 50c. extra, each; white enameled, $1 extra.

Name ....
Address ....
My jobber is ....

clip this coupon NOW!

Scales were and are a vital housewares item in the kitchen as well as the bath shop. These household scales were standard for years.

Courtesy House Furnishing Review.

the kitchen," Abraham & Straus contended in a large ad in October 1927 that it did so—and no less than a year before!

"No longer can the pot call the kettle black," declared its headline. "An idea launched by A & S a year ago and a reality today, has settled the argument. A year ago A & S presented the idea of colorful charm in kitchen utensils and accessories. A window display at the time was a sensation." The ad went on to say:

> The idea, which originated abroad, immediately caught the fancy and appealed to the artistic appreciation of women everywhere. Sooner than could possibly be foretold "Color in the Kitchen" has become a delightful drudgery-killing reality.
>
> A & S is proud to have a part in the movement which brings so much sunshine and real delight to a spot where hundreds of thousands of women have found only the endless monotony of hard work...The transformation of kitchens is one of the clearest indications that we are entering into a period of larger living....

At any rate the idea of making some change in the drab appearance of most kitchens had been coloring the thinking of people for some time. The scope of that new trend was described by Walter Redell Storey in an article in *The New York Times* in August 1927:

> The kitchen is now being definitely included in the decorative scheme of the home. One reason is that the mistress of the house has much more to do with the kitchen in these servantless days than she had heretofore. Also, the vogue of breakfast nooks, with only an imaginary line dividing them from the kitchen, has contributed to its decorative importance.
>
> One may have, of course, the kitchen which suggests obviously that it is the food laboratory of the home...in glistening white...yet as our bathrooms are changing in spirit from the old, ultra-chaste whiteness to more gracious and gayer interiors, so our kitchens are adding to their efficient equipment the charm of color.

The "color craze" proved to be something of a merchandising sensation. "There is no mistaking the importance of the color trend that is sweeping over New York," reported *House Furnishing Review* in October 1927. "While every large metropolitan department has gone in for color to an impressive degree, Macy's and Wanamaker's are outstanding examples."

This new merchandising rainbow was now radiating into every once drab corner of the housewares departments—as well as into every homemaker's kitchen. Some even predicted that "color in the kitchen" would provide the panacea for her problems.

Emerging from what was called "the White Enamel era," even that Johnny-come-lately, the electric refrigerator, had succumbed to the charms of color. "The refrigerator, having a number of plain surfaces, tempts the artist to ply his brush....They are to be hand-decorated patterns in every sort from simple flower groups to the last word in modernistic designs in color or metal....For those who do not require furnishings decorated especially for them, refrigerators are available already decorated in vermillion, with parrots perched on green branches," said the *Review*.

A very contemporary look in household scales is provided by this model with its simple, functional design.

The Need for Color Standards

In New York City Wanamaker's jumped on the color cavalcade by redecorating its widely-publicized "Six Little Kitchens" and renaming them "Six Little Colorful Kitchens." Ads for the kitchens emphasized "the triumph of color" in the kitchen as well as in the entire home. Housewares, of course, were important accessories to Wanamaker's colorful kitchens. Commented the *House Furnishing Review* in October 1927: "In them may be found a wide range of colors....Yet despite the great variety, everything has been synchronized and harmonized. Not a single jarring note can be detected."

It was not long, however, before it *could* be heard, loud and clear. At first there was a slowly emerging doubt—is this color stuff for keeps...or just a fad? Already the front offices in most stores had begun to nudge their buyers and point to the big increase in inventory and investment that color assortments demanded. Perhaps even more serious was the increasingly wide-spread variation of the same color that began to show up in merchandise from different manufacturers. Reds and blues and yellows—none of them matched. And as more and more manufacturers started seeking the pot of gold at the end of this alluringly colorful rainbow, the situation got worse. Walter A. Ricker, then buyer for the L. S. Donaldson Company, Minneapolis, often had the store painter repaint items in order to have them match and balance out his stock, a practice that was not uncommon in other stores.

"Our problems of stock-keeping were super-colossal," recalled Elliot V. Walter in 1971. In January 1928, he succeeded Joe Kasper as housewares buyer at Macy's, New York, when Kasper was made a merchandise counselor. (Walter became president of

140

When refrigerators were ice boxes they constituted a major housewares category. "Enviable profits" could be earned in 1924.

Courtesy House Furnishing Review.

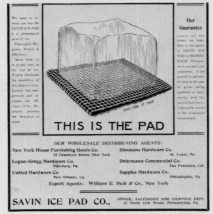

A variety of refrigerator and refrigerator accessory advertisements from the first quarter of this century stress conversions to electricity and porcelain interiors. The "Zone of Kelvination" could be installed in an existing refrigerator. The 1918 ad for Challenge refrigerators touted their one-piece lining for insulation and ease of cleaning. "Massive slabs" of stone made for frigid conditions according to White Mountain. But without a block of ice and its handy pad, the earliest refrigerators couldn't refrigerate very much. The gentlemen at right are examining an early refrigerator which also served as a major piece of furniture.

Above, courtesy
House Furnishing Review.

Macy's in 1956 and chairman of the board in 1958.) "The problem wasn't just at the retail level; it reached all the way back to the factories and it was even more aggravated in New York," Elliot Walter added.

We had kicked off our color program originally with Vollrath enamelware as our main line. But soon after the makers of Polar Ware enamelware jumped on the color cart with their own set of colors. Because of Macy's 6 percent policy at that time, most other New York stores stocked Polar Ware rather than Vollrath and within weeks from the time we started, both lines were being promoted heavily. Customers didn't care where the pots and pans came from originally; all they knew was that colors of one line didn't match the other and they were furious with the stores.

You must remember that in those days when the color concept was first registering with the public there was little sophisticated use of color. Almost everyone had the same idea—a red or blue or yellow kitchen, with the color of *all* the items matching. At least that was what the customers expected, but didn't get.

The situation became a "living color" nightmare for the manufacturers! They had started making our three Vollrath colors, then added the three Polar Ware colors and, as they began making special colors for other stores around the country suddenly found themselves making their line of fifty or one hundred items in a dozen or more different colors! Suddenly, too, they found themselves swimming in a sea of red ink when they audited their books. What this did to the delivery situation and the stores' stock assortments can easily be imagined. It was chaotic!

It is interesting to note that *House Furnishing Review* in January 1928, reported that a survey of buyers revealed that an overwhelming number voiced confidence in the color concept and felt it was here to stay. The future, of course, would prove them right, but in those days "color in the kitchen" was still a rather shaky proposition.

The whole color problem stemmed from the fact that there were no official or accepted color standards. When manufacturers of different products attempted to match each other's colors, they encountered problems. Porcelain enamel colors, being fired, always ended up being different from air-dried, sprayed lacquer utensil handles or bread boards, to cite examples. Even individual cannisters in ordinary painted cannister sets did not always match. Often the same paint, used under different conditions, would vary greatly if used on a wood or metal surface.

Scores of suggestions helped confuse matters even more. The ideas ranged from having the Pot & Kettle Club decide on color standards to taking a vote at the housewares exhibit. Then, Professor Arthur Hardy announced the invention of a "colorimeter" that, he claimed, would make possible the exact duplication of any shade or hue.

In mid-1930 another proposal was presented for ending "the chaos of color" in housewares. The Taylor System Incorporated in New York proposed "a basic line of 18 colors from which several thousand harmonious color schemes for kitchen decoration may be

Wanamaker's Now Announces

THE SIX LITTLE

COLORFUL!

KITCHENS

Completing the Triumph of COLOR Throughout the Home

A BEAUTIFUL rainbow has bent its arc through the Six Little Kitchens and splashed its brilliant hues on everything! Pots and pans, kitchen cabinets and gas ranges, tables and chairs, cutlery and clocks, percolators, toasters and waffle irons—throughout the six kitchens in their six different shapes and sizes—all are transformed by the magic touch.

See the Spanish Kitchen!

Modern American in equipment, reminiscent of far-off, romantic Spain in color effects and decoration...Classical in its combination of beauty and efficiency! Sunbronzed walls in a mottled, WASHABLE finish...Cabinet, range, refrigerator, table and chairs in a light olive tone, touched with red...Linoleum, curtains and utensils green.

Bring Color Into Your Kitchen!

Warm, cherry reds, cool blues, restful greens...any color you suggest...may be used to make YOUR kitchen as charming, cozy and inviting as any other room in your home!

The New Colored Enamelware Has Arrived

We can hardly keep it on display, so swiftly delighted home-makers whisk up everything that brings color to the kitchen.

Refurnishing Is Not Necessary

Sometimes just a line or spot of color is enough. All equipment may be purchased separately.

September Sale Economics

Now in effect in the housewares store. Thousands of work-lightening and time-saving kitchen accessories at the greatest economies of six months. Conveniently extended payments on major appliances. Furnishings painted to your order if desired, at small additional cost.

Visit the Six Little Colorful Kitchens for Ideas— Visit the September Sales for Savings

WANAMAKER'S—Seventh gallery, new building

Color comes to the kitchen. Wanamaker's in New York offer six bright ideas. Tired looking kitchens need the color cure according to this 1929 advertisement.

Bottom, courtesy Armstrong Cork Company.

142

evolved.... [This] is considered the solution to the color problems of the trade, the basis of the selection being the established consumer demand, the knowledge of consumer trends over a period of years, and the correct principles of interior decoration tied up with scientific knowledge of color harmony and familiarity with production processes of individual industries."

While the Taylor System generated considerable interest, very little ever came of it, and the "chaos of color" continued. It must be remembered that this situation did not by any means put an end to the sale of colored housewares; the basic concept was too valid to be halted merely because of poor color matching. "It is now a fact," declared Charles Hansen, then the buyer for the Powers Mercantile Company, Minneapolis, "that there is just as great a demand for style and color in housewares as in the other departments of any large store."

One day in the fall of 1936 Ted Blanke, then head of the merchandising division of the National Retail Dry Goods Association (now the National Retail Merchants Association), called on Elliot Walter at Macy's, who in the course of the visit casually mentioned the color problem.

"I was surprised that Blanke had taken our casual conversation so seriously," Mr. Walter later recalled. "But presently he had Mr. I. J. Fairchild from the U. S. Bureau of Standards call on me about this matter, and Blanke then offered to place the color problem on the program for the upcoming meeting of his association."

At that meeting in January 1937—a housewares session during the annual convention of the NRDGA at the Pennsylvania Hotel in New York—it was agreed that "the time for arguing was over and that color had to be standardized and controlled before it sank us all." At the time of that meeting there were probably hundreds of different colors and variations to be found in the housewares departments. Each had its own name, bestowed by some imaginative advertising manager—or perhaps the emerging newcomer in home goods merchandising, the store stylist.

Elliot Walter was named chairman of a Color Standardization Committee to which a number of other related organizations were later invited to name a representative. Working under the official aegis of the U. S. Commerce Department, the committee accomplished what many had thought would be impossible—the establishment of standards for bathroom as well as kitchen colors.

These now became part of the official "Commercial Standards" of the U. S. Commerce Department, formally published by the government printing office in 1937 in two booklets: "CS62-38 Colors For Kitchen Accessories" and "CS63-38 Colors For Bathroom Accessories." Both became effective January 1, 1938, and contain the following as the official "History of Project":

On February 8, 1937, the National Retail Dry Goods Association requested the establishment of a commercial standard for colors for

143

Delft blue, apple green, and mandarin red are the kitchen colors promoted by Macy's in this ad. After World War II colorful Formica plastic laminates soon replaced linoleum counter tops.

kitchen (and bathroom) accessories. A committee for the association had been studying the problem for several months prior to filing a request for such a standard and had selected certain colors on the basis of greatest general acceptance by purchasers.

Pursuant to the request, on April 9, invitations to a general conference or public hearing were mailed to a comprehensive list of trade associations, producer, distributor and user organizations, interested in kitchen (and bathroom) accessories.

On April 29, a meeting of the Color Committee of the National Retail Dry Goods Association was held and adjustments of the proposal were drafted on the basis of comment received. A revised draft was presented to the general conference at the Hotel Pennsylvania [now the Statler], New York City, on the following day, April 30, 1937, and adopted as the recommended commercial standard of the industry by vote of the conference.

The recommendations of the conference were circulated to the industry on May 21, for written acceptance and in the absence of active opposition, the establishment of the standard was announced on September 16, 1937.

Six standard colors were adopted for kitchen accessories: White, Kitchen Green, Ivory, Delphinium Blue, Royal Blue, and Red. Seven standard colors were adopted for bathroom accessories: White, Bath Green, Orchid, Ivory, Maize, Bath Blue, and Royal Blue.

"It took nine years from the time that the idea of 'Color in the Kitchens' first appeared until the colors were finally standardized," Elliot Walter recalled recently. "Incidentally, I think Ted Blanke and I. J. Fairchild are the unsung heroes of that accomplishment." Walter concluded:

> Despite all the early trials and tribulations it involved, I think that color in the kitchen was really the spark that ignited the imagination of homemakers—as well as manufacturers and merchants—and opened up a whole new era for the housewares business.
>
> Today (in 1970), of course, we have gone far beyond the original concept of merely matching the colors of everything. Homemakers have become far more sophisticated in their use of color and prefer to use it not only liberally but in contrasting, exciting ways no one ever dreamed of when the color revolution first started nearly fifty years ago.

Standards are Ignored

The war years, of course, put a temporary end to the color commotion just as they did to most other areas of this business. But with the post war boom the rainbow of color again arched over the marketplace. Most manufacturers and merchants were much too busy "filling the pipelines" and breaking sales records to remember the very official color standards that once had meant so much to them. But now they were sufficiently experienced to avoid extremes and move with care into color.

In 1946, long after the housewares industry's ambitious attempt to establish "official" kitchen and bathroom colors had been almost completely forgotten, *House & Garden* magazine announced the creation of a new color program for the home furnishings industry.

144

Contemporary apartment kitchens tend to be small and efficient. They aesthetically and practically benefit from the shapes and colors of present day kitchen housewares. A colorful appliance or cooking utensil does for the kitchen what paintings or objects d'art do for the rest of the house.

Top, copyright © 1972 Conde Nast Publications Incorporated. Bottom, courtesy Forecast Magazine.

From top: What of the future? In a limited space good form and shape are all-important. In the lower picture, housewares plays a significant role in accessorizing, even humanizing, an overly sleek cool look.

Bottom, courtesy House Beautiful.

On the basis of its own consumer research, it said, it would publish a color chart each year which would not only help guide the industry to focus upon the particular shades of color apparently most in demand with consumers, but thereby also provide a color standard which would enable different manufacturers of related products to achieve a color uniformity of those products to the advantage of all concerned. The program filled an obvious industry need. It soon developed a considerable following and has been continued ever since.

The original list contained twenty-two colors; in 1972 there were thirty-six basic colors. Each year, depending upon their sales performance, anywhere from three to twelve colors are replaced with others in greater demand. Color chips are available and each year the magazine publishes a detailed report entitled, "Economic Trends In Color."

"House & Garden Colors can hardly be the only answer to any or all problems," commented Paul Hornsleth, *H & G* publisher, in the 1972 issue of that report, "but our guided tour through the land of home products has been well plotted and...endured over twenty-four years....House & Garden Colors are not fixed standards, but living entities in a world of continuous change."

While these colors were by no means adopted universally, they

managed to gain considerable recognition and helped provide a degree of stability to the color picture in the marketplace.

By this time, homemakers were becoming quite imaginative in the use of color in their homes. Slowly, but unmistakably, housewares began to develop a very definite "fashion" character. Since the industry couldn't readily express itself with much degree of uniformity in its forms due to the tremendous variety of products, it nevertheless managed to do so in color. One of the most definite, early reflections of this was the manner in which "sand" (also sometimes called sandlewood) suddenly came to be the so-called "in" color in the early sixties. Before long it was being featured on everything from cannisters to can openers, with astonishingly little variation in shading—despite the absence of an official standard.

Unquestionably the most popular—sensational might be a better word—color to leave its beauty mark on housewares is "avocado." Curiously enough, this originated in the major appliance field when, in 1966, the General Electric Company introduced a whole new line of avocado-colored major appliances at a New York press party. It was a color that had never been used before, but by the following year there was so much of it in evidence at the housewares exhibition many were referring to it as the "avocado show."

Just why it has proved to be so extremely popular is hard to explain. Quite possibly, as Art BecVar, manager, industrial design operation, General Electric major appliance division, stated in 1971:

> It was the beginning of the period—which we are still in—when the richness and sophistication of the natural wood look was replacing the "cold" look of steel cabinets. Avocado is extremely compatible with the natural woods and goes very well with the softer tones women seem to prefer these days for their kitchens. It was picked by them from forty choices in a nationwide survey....One of the amazing things we have found about avocado is that every other color looks well with it. Perhaps the reason is that green—particularly the shade we have selected—is one of nature's colors.

Color continues to be the dominating factor in the so-called fashion aspect of housewares. But "housewares fashions" may be entering a more complex era, as is already widely evidenced in the cooking utensil field, where multi-color combinations with design are proliferating on all sides. And that applies as often to imports as to American products.

"Cookware manufacturers," observed *Home Furnishings Daily* in a story about a 1971 housewares show, "are trapping retailers in color, color and more color...that pose headaches in inventory and display." Perhaps, once again, the industry may find itself seriously considering the adoption of some new color standards.

147

From top: Any way you look at it, a rainbow of colors from the past. Enameled ware was among the first to offer color variety. Elliot V. Walter, a housewares buyer and later president of Macy's, was chairman of the industry committee on color standards for the kitchen and bathroom. Joseph P. Kasper helped launch Macy's "Color in the Kitchen" promotion. Later he served as president of the Associated Merchandising Corp.

Diuersi uasi

stufatoro

nauicella cõ piastrelle et quatro piedi

nauicella cõ piastrelle et 4 piedi

Conserua

nauicella senza piedi

nauicella senza piedi

stufator ouato

Conserua bassa

Conserua grande

padella p fare oui frittolate

stufatoro largo

tortera con il coperto

nauicella bassa

conca

nauicella alta

8

POTS&PANSPLUS

Of course, before the truth was known, no one in the old Massachusetts city of Lynn would ever have come right out and denied the story of the Saugus pot. The ancient legend that this cast iron pot was the very first cooking utensil made in America was something of which, at least in public, the people of Lynn might well be proud, even if privately they sometimes had doubts about its authenticity.

Certain facts, to be sure, were undeniable. Of the several New World efforts to establish an iron foundry early in the seventeenth century, the first successful venture was the Saugus project just outside of Lynn. The Saugus operation began in 1642 and was managed by Captain Robert Bridges and Thomas Dexter. It was a complete ironworks, with a huge furnace, a forge, a big hammer and an extensive water-power system. Also, there was a rolling and slitting mill, the first in America. (An exact replica of the Saugus Iron Works has been restored on the original site by the American Iron and Steel Institute.) One of the very first castings it produced was this small, three-legged, covered pot of about one-quart capacity. With walls almost 1½ inches thick it weighed 2¼ pounds. Crudely fashioned and unfinished by modern standards, it nevertheless presents a rugged dignity and simplicity of design which dramatically reflects the pioneer era. Scientific tests have long since proved that the origin of the Saugus pot is indeed a fact, not fiction.

Griswold Utensils

In the housewares industry—and among consumers—the name Griswold is not only synonymous with cooking utensils, but also enjoys the distinction of being the product brand name in the longest continuous use in this business—nearly one hundred years. Now it is part of the cookware group of the General Housewares Corporation which acquired it in 1969.

In 1865 when Matthew Griswold and Samuel Seldon founded the business as the Griswold Manufacturing Company in Erie, Pennsylvania, it made only household hardware, but cast iron cooking utensils were soon added. At that time, most cast iron cookware, popularly referred to as "common hollow," was made by prison labor, a fact that was obvious not only in its very low cost but proportionately low quality. Griswold, however, wanted no part of such merchandise and right from the start introduced a superior product known as "extra finish iron hollow ware." Women quickly came to recognize the difference and the small new company prospered. In later years when most states had outlawed the once widespread practice of selling products made by prison labor in competition with the free labor market, Griswold found itself and its already well-known brand name at a considerable advantage.

Griswold was one of the first to make and sell cast aluminum-

Opposite page: A collection of mid-seventeenth century cooking utensils as illustrated in the Scappi Cookbook. *This page:* Matthew Griswold who, with Samuel Seldon, founded the Griswold Manufacturing Company in 1865.

Opposite page, courtesy New York Public Library, Rare Book Division, Astor, Lenox and Tilden Foundations. This page, courtesy House Furnishing Review.

A display of aluminum utensils for waterless cooking in 1927. Note the famous trademark—"Griswold" in a cross within a circle.

Courtesy House Furnishing Review.

ware, and worked with the Aluminum Company of America in casting the first water kettles. Later a process for hardening the surface of cast aluminumware was developed. After being cast, the surface of the utensils were given a special electrical treatment which closed the pores of the metal and tempered and hardened it. In addition it resisted discoloration of the aluminum.

In 1955 the Griswold Manufacturing Company was acquired by McGraw Edison Incorporated and two years later they sold it to the Randall Company of Cincinnati, which four years earlier had acquired another cookware company, Wagner Manufacturing Company. Eventually, Griswold became part of the General Housewares Corporation.

Wagner Manufacturing Company

When the Wagner Manufacturing Company was founded in Sidney, Ohio, in 1881, the Griswold Manufacturing Company in Erie, Pennsylvania, had already been in business for sixteen years. Yet, like Griswold, Wagner was destined to survive and prosper to the present.

The manufacturing venture grew out of a retail store founded some years earlier by Mathias Wagner. Just what prompted the switch is not known, but the start was made in a tiny shop with a handful of employees using the relatively crude equipment then available for making cast iron cooking utensils.

One of the notable contributions to the quality of its ware was a pre-seasoning process. This began by thoroughly washing the cast iron utensils with soap and water, drying them quickly and then giving them a fine coating of pure bees wax that penetrated the pores of the metal and prevented rusting as well as sticking of foods.

Wagner got into the manufacture of cast aluminum ware early in the 1900s and gradually replaced most of its ironware with aluminum. It developed a special aluminum alloy with an extra bright permanent finish called "Magnalite" which it promoted with considerable success.

150

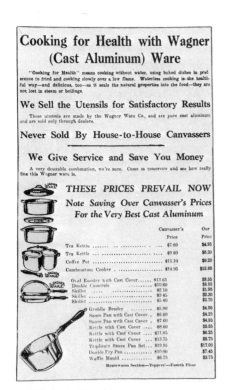

An ad for Wagner's aluminum utensils —cooking for health meant waterless cooking, sealing in the natural properties of the food.

Courtesy House Furnishing Review.

In November 1952, the company was purchased by the Randall Company, Cincinnati, a manufacturer of automobile stampings and leather working machinery, which, in 1957, also bought the Griswold Manufacturing Company from McGraw Edison. In 1959 Randall sold both cookware companies to Textron. Ten years later they were acquired by the General Housewares Corporation.

Enamelware

Along about 1750 an imaginative German with the improbable name of Johann Heinrich Gottlob von Justy, came up with the then unheard of idea that perhaps the smooth and durable porcelain enamel glaze so often found on jewelry and objects d'art, might make a nice, practical finish or coating on metal utensils used for food. After all, he probably reasoned, those porcelain enameled ornaments had retained their luster and hardness for centuries; in fact some Egyptian pieces have been traced back as far as 1400 B.C.

It was not until 1788, however, at the Königsbronn foundry in Wirtemberg, that a few cast iron pots were reportedly given a form of porcelain enameling coating. That development opened up a whole new commercial and culinary era by providing cooks with utensils they could keep clean more easily and conveniently than anything known before.

Later, chemists and metallurgists in Sweden and elsewhere also began work in this field. By 1838 an enameling plant had been set up by a German in Belgium, and about the same time a small plant in Birmingham, England, the Eagle Foundry, also began making a few pieces of the primitive porcelain enamelware.

After 1850 improved steel-making methods by Bessemer and others helped pave the way for the enameling industry. About this time the industrial enameling of sheet iron and steel ware began in Austria and Germany and the old records for the first time mention the names of such ancient and once well-known firms as Barthelmus, Hardt, Gnuechtel, Ulrich, Wupperman, and others, whose enameled utensils manufacturing plants were still in operation in pre-World War I central Europe. In England white enameled sanitary ware was introduced in 1887.

During the years from 1860 to 1870 the enamelware industry first emerged in the United States. But to more fully understand what happened in the American market, it is important to have some idea of the European developments.

Kitchenware dominated the enameling industry both in the United States and overseas for several decades. Around the turn of the century, however, we had only a few such plants while in Germany alone there were already about three hundred factories making enamelware.

To remain highly competitive, the European plants kept their methods and equipment up-dated, something they could readily do thanks to their highly developed machine and chemical industries.

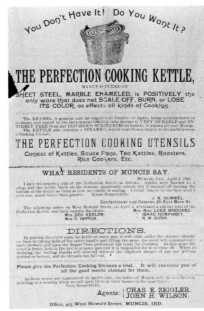

151

From top: An ingenious trade ad that combined a consumer ad with a pitch for hardware and other dealers to add Columbian Enameled Ware to their lines. Next, Charles Ziegler and John Wilson promoted Perfection Cooking Utensils in 1892. Ziegler and Wilson later joined Arthur Vining Davis and the Pittsburgh Reduction Company to operate its house-to-house sales force.

Both courtesy House Furnishing Review.

From top: Importing enamelware from Europe was a lucrative business, as illustrated in the top ad. But with the advent of World War I, American manufacturers really got going since European factories were needed for military production.

Both courtesy House Furnishing Review.

Their need to continually increase efficiency became more and more important as countries that had been customers now began producing their own enamelware. The old manufacturers had a difficult time meeting new competition that enjoyed protective duties and preferential tariffs.

In most other industrialized nations including Japan, the manufacture of such an important and useful product as porcelain enamelware was understandably pursued and developed diligently.

Meanwhile, the great technological strides being made throughout the world in chemistry and metallurgy continued to be reflected in constantly improved enamelware utensils, culminating in the present stain-resistant, almost chip-proof products.

Right from the start the United States has been one of if not the greatest markets for porcelain cooking utensils of both American as well as foreign manufacture. In the latter part of the nineteenth century when there were only a very few small producers operating here, European manufacturers, with the obvious advantage of a much earlier start, began to ship substantial quantities of utensils to this country.

Since price rather than quality (such as it was!) was the main consideration, the quantities of utensils even for such seemingly small dollar volume were enormous. Price was especially important on the East Coast and other areas where large segments of low-income, recent immigrants eagerly grabbed up the drab-looking gray agateware or dark, speckled blue pots and pans and pails.

It wasn't long until American producers began to develop greater production and move in for their fair share of the big U. S. market. Nevertheless it's interesting to note that by 1970—over a century since we first began to produce porcelain enamelware—this country continued to import it in astonishing quantities. In 1969, for example, such imports hit an all time high of over $9½ million.

The first real big break for the American manufacturers came with the arrival of World War I when European factories were commandeered for military needs. In 1913, the year before the war began, our enamelware exports were about $421,000, but by 1919 they had reached $4 million and U.S. production had hit a new all-time high of over $37½ million.

As it did with most other industries, the Great Depression of the 1930s made serious inroads into the enamelware industry. But that was only one cause of its slipping sales. Overseas manufacturers were again beginning to cut deeply into this market. But what was even more serious, probably, than both of those factors, was the competition the enamelware makers had been feeling in ever-increasing degree from that shiny and glamorous newcomer, aluminumware, as well as from glass cooking utensils. And as if that weren't enough still another serious contender for a share of the market was already peering over the horizon—stainless steel.

The situation finally deteriorated to such a point that some constructive action was imperative and, aided and abetted by the Porcelain Enamel Institute, the utensil manufacturers founded the Enameled Utensil Manufacturers Council. Under the direction of Prof. Fred A. Petersen, then of Ohio State University, the Council engaged in extensive tests in an effort to attempt to establish some kind of standards for enamelware. However, it met with little success and was eventually disbanded.

No doubt the markedly improving business climate brought about by the approach of World War II contributed to the end of those efforts. The industry was now too occupied with other things. Furthermore, with the price picture stiffening, there was no longer the necessity to quote low-cost figures.

Meanwhile, new technologies and better raw materials had improved quality enormously. But the once great popularity and volume of porcelain enameled steel utensils was rapidly decreasing. Perhaps the final blow to that popularity occurred in 1953 when porcelain enameled aluminumware was finally perfected.

Nevertheless, as the newer materials began taking over the market, one type of enamelware—cast iron—not only held its own but started a resurgence as a result of the ''gourmet'' cooking trend.

Vollrath Company

It was not until the last painful sounds of our bloody Civil War had died away that the first enameled cooking utensils were made in America. As sometimes happens in such situations, three different firms were struggling at the same time trying to learn the art of that German development. One of them, Jacob J. Vollrath, apparently accomplished it first.

"The first evidence of attempts being made in this country to apply this science commercially to hollow ware took place at some date between 1860 and 1870,'' wrote Jean C. Vollrath in 1935 in *The Enamelist* when he was president of the Vollrath Company which his grandfather Jacob had founded. "Three groups of men were primarily responsible for the extension and development of this science in this country at its inception. One group localized their activities at Sheboygan, Wisconsin, (Vollrath); one at St. Louis, Missouri, (St. Louis Stamping); and the third group at Woodhaven, L.I., N.Y., (Lalance & Grosjean). We believe that the primary experimental work was first performed by the small group in Sheboygan."

He goes on to cite the first cast-iron utensils: "pit and round-bottom kettles, tea kettles, maslin kettles, Scotch bowls as well as stove reservoirs...." It was all single-coat ware, the coating applied "through dipping or slushing."

Jean's father, C. A. W. Vollrath, who had preceded him as president (and who died in 1932), is even more specific. In a statement about the start of the company he wrote:

> Prior to 1874, my father was a foundryman and a manufacturer of steel. It was in 1874 that he first built his plant for the manufacture of

153

From top: The man credited with developing the art of enameling utensils in America is Jacob J. Vollrath. The importance of brand names on various kinds of enamelware is shown in the ad.

Bottom, courtesy House Furnishing Review.

cast iron enamelware, from which time my personal experience more distinctly relates.

In 1867, when I was a youth, I very vividly recall an experiment made by my father in attempting to coat a previously heated cast iron pan with a molten mass. He so manipulated the pan and mass as to evenly distribute the latter over the surface of the pan, allowing the surplus to run out and subjecting the pan to a reheating. The mass in the mix was red in color, leading me to believe that, no doubt, red lead in quantity had been used. The experiment must have been unsuccessful since nothing developed from it. My youth prevented me from knowing the full details of this experiment. It was in 1870, after extended experiments and progress in enameling, that we secured interesting and valuable formulae in Europe....

Jacob Vollrath was born in Germany in 1824 and as a boy was apprenticed to the iron-molding industry. At the age of eighteen he emigrated to America and in 1853 finally landed in Sheboygan, Wisconsin. Through correspondence with friends in Germany and as a result of several trips there, he learned about the newly developed "wet" enameling process, so that when he decided to go into business for himself in 1873 he was in a position to apply it to cast iron ware.

By 1886 he was doing so well that the Jacob J. Vollrath Manufacturing Company was incorporated and was expanded to include a complete line of cast iron utensils. It was not until 1892 that a line of stamped sheet steel utensils was added. "Before this date," explained C. A. W. Vollrath long afterwards, "sheet steel was of such composition that if [processed] as today poor ware would be produced....I cite this to show that the steel then produced in the United States was not fit for enameling...." He goes on to describe a foreign patent for "a mottled-gray enamel placed directly on steel. ...This was no doubt the beginning of the spreading of this industry in this country."

The steel utensils, he explained in *The Enamelist* article, "were in the nature of one or two coats in various shades of blue, brown, gray and black in the speckeled [sic] as well as mottled finishes. At that time shapes [of the utensils] were built up in parts and seamed together. It was not until the latter part of the nineteenth century that the modern so-called enameling steel was developed which could be readily drawn."

The customary one and occasionally two-coat ware produced by almost all of the early manufacturers was apparently due to economic considerations as well as technological limitations.

The Other Pioneers

What of the two other pioneers who, as mentioned earlier, also happened to be experimenting with the manufacture of porcelain enameled utensils elsewhere in this country?

About a thousand miles east of the Vollrath shop, in Woodhaven, Long Island, New York, the firm of Lalance and Grosjean, manu-

154

"The Greatest Sign in the World" advertises Vollrath Ware at Times Square in New York in 1911.

Courtesy House Furnishing Review.

facturers of stamped sheet metal ware, was closely—but independently—paralleling the Vollrath efforts. There are some who insist L & G had progressed every bit as far and fast in producing the first porcelain enamelware; perhaps it was a tie. The interesting Lalance & Grosjean story will be told later in this chapter.

In the meantime, the St. Louis Stamping Company was pursuing the development and manufacture of enamelware in another area of the country. An article about the company in *The Enamelist* magazine, October 1934, reports:

> In old St. Louis in the early 1860s on Cass Avenue, a sign on a factory building read, "St. Louis Stamping Co." It marked the location of a plant where two brothers, tinsmiths by trade, were well on their way to becoming prominent figures in the history of industrial development of St. Louis and the industry that produces pots and pans.
>
> These two boys, W. F. and F. A. Niedringhaus, saw the possibilities in mass production. They pooled what resources they had and started applying time and material saving methods to the manufacture of kitchen utensils.

Later, the report continues, after perfection of the Bessemer steel process, they also set up their own steel rolling mill. Exactly when the Niedringhaus brothers began their work on porcelain enameling isn't known. Then, in 1899, one of the first and certainly the largest merger of enamelware manufacturers took place with the formation of the National Enameling & Stamping Company. F. G. Niedringhaus became president and F. A. Niedringhaus vice-president. Included in the merger were: Kieckhefer Brothers, Milwaukee; Matthai & Ingram, Baltimore; Haberman Manufacturing Company, New York; Keen & Hagerty, Baltimore; and Haller Manufacturing Company, New Orleans. The company that later would come to be well known by its "Nesco" trade name was born. And long afterwards—in 1955—it would itself be merged into the Knapp-Monarch Company of St. Louis, which in 1969 was absorbed by the Hoover Company.

Geuder, Paeschke & Frey

Early on the morning of January 2, 1880, in Milwaukee, two serious-minded men, William Geuder and Charles A. Paeschke, were hard at work in a tin shop in the weather-beaten, two-story white frame building on North Third Street, the place where Mader's famous German restaurant now stands. Despite all the excitement in the city (a state reunion and parade of the Grand Army attended by General Grant and General Sherman), the two young men were much more conscious of the frequent reports of business failures that reached them. Their minds were on business and this was an important day in their lives.

Geuder's father had taught his son the tinsmith's trade and willed him the shop. Geuder had asked his brother-in-law Paeschke to join

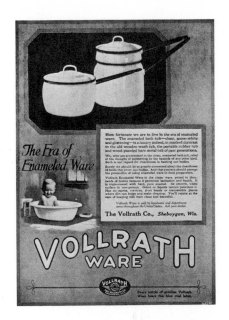

This ad in a 1922 issue of *Good Housekeeping* extols the clean, sanitary look of white enamelware. Food did have a tendency to look better in white pots rather than in the old blue and white speckled enamelware.

155

The Geuder & Paeschke Manufacturing Company's plant in Milwaukee in the 1880s, before Frey joined the firm.

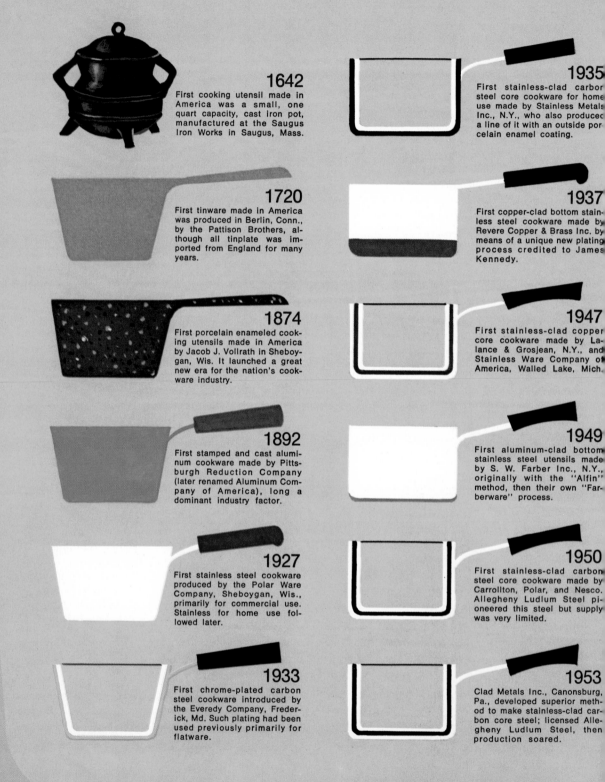

1642
First cooking utensil made in America was a small, one quart capacity, cast iron pot, manufactured at the Saugus Iron Works in Saugus, Mass.

1720
First tinware made in America was produced in Berlin, Conn., by the Pattison Brothers, although all tinplate was imported from England for many years.

1874
First porcelain enameled cooking utensils made in America by Jacob J. Vollrath in Sheboygan, Wis. It launched a great new era for the nation's cookware industry.

1892
First stamped and cast aluminum cookware made by Pittsburgh Reduction Company (later renamed Aluminum Company of America), long a dominant industry factor.

1927
First stainless steel cookware produced by the Polar Ware Company, Sheboygan, Wis., primarily for commercial use. Stainless for home use followed later.

1933
First chrome-plated carbon steel cookware introduced by the Everedy Company, Frederick, Md. Such plating had been used previously primarily for flatware.

1935
First stainless-clad carbon steel core cookware for home use made by Stainless Metals Inc., N.Y., who also produced a line of it with an outside porcelain enamel coating.

1937
First copper-clad bottom stainless steel cookware made by Revere Copper & Brass Inc. by means of a unique new plating process credited to James Kennedy.

1947
First stainless-clad copper core cookware made by Lalance & Grosjean, N.Y., and Stainless Ware Company of America, Walled Lake, Mich.

1949
First aluminum-clad bottom stainless steel utensils made by S. W. Farber Inc., N.Y., originally with the "Alfin" method, then their own "Farberware" process.

1950
First stainless-clad carbon steel core cookware made by Carrollton, Polar, and Nesco. Allegheny Ludlum Steel pioneered this steel but supply was very limited.

1953
Clad Metals Inc., Canonsburg, Pa., developed superior method to make stainless-clad carbon core steel; licensed Allegheny Ludlum Steel, then production soared.

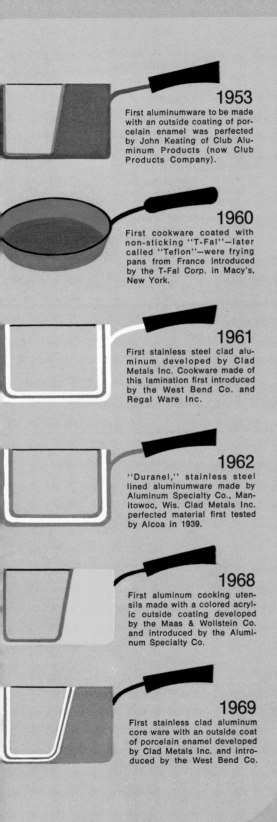

1953

First aluminumware to be made with an outside coating of porcelain enamel was perfected by John Keating of Club Aluminum Products (now Club Products Company).

1960

First cookware coated with non-sticking "T-Fal"—later called "Teflon"—were frying pans from France introduced by the T-Fal Corp. in Macy's, New York.

1961

First stainless steel clad aluminum developed by Clad Metals Inc. Cookware made of this lamination first introduced by the West Bend Co. and Regal Ware Inc.

1962

"Duranel," stainless steel lined aluminumware made by Aluminum Specialty Co., Manitowoc, Wis. Clad Metals Inc. perfected material first tested by Alcoa in 1939.

1968

First aluminum cooking utensils made with a colored acrylic outside coating developed by the Maas & Wollstein Co. and introduced by the Aluminum Specialty Co.

1969

First stainless clad aluminum core ware with an outside coat of porcelain enamel developed by Clad Metals Inc. and introduced by the West Bend Co.

Nothing illustrates the progress and development of the housewares industry more effectively than the history of cooking utensils.

From the time the first, modest little iron pot was cast in America in 1642, nearly a century would elapse before tinware manufacturing was begun, and over 150 years more would have to pass until, in 1874, we learned to make porcelain enameled ware.

By that time the industrial revolution had started and less than twenty-five years later aluminumware appeared. From then on, new materials and technologies in the cooking utensil industry—reflecting the nation's fabulous growth in other areas—came along with ever-increasing frequency as well as importance. As this somewhat simplified chart shows, more—and more far-reaching—developments have taken place in the last fifty years than in all the centuries before then.

Trying to single out the most significant achievements is almost an exercise in futility. One could cite the early work in the 1920s of companies such as Allegheny Ludlum Steel Corporation, Rustless Iron Corporation, and the Electro Metallurgical Company in developing the well-known basic 18/8 steel, (18 percent chromium, 8 percent nickel and 74 percent iron). Or the pioneering efforts of firms like Jessop Steel Company, Ingersoll Steel & Disc Incorporated, and Plykrome Corporation in developing stainless clad carbon steel.

Then there was the unique development of anodized aluminum cookware in 1946 by the Aluminum Cooking Utensil Company and the creation of stainless clad copper by American Clad Metals Company, Carnegie, Pennsylvania, the following year. Not to be overlooked, of course, is Club's John Keating's great contribution in 1953 in combining aluminum and porcelain enamel and the equally significant combining of stainless clad aluminum with porcelain enamel by Clad Metal's John Ulam in 1969.

Where will it all stop? It won't—anymore than the relentless dynamics of the housewares industry itself.

(The author acknowledges with thanks the special assistance of John B. Ulam of Clad Metals Incorporated and John Keating, special assistant to the president, Club Products Company, in the preparation of the facts for this chart.)

JUST THE THING FOR SUMMER SALES

THE NEW
Cream City
Kitchenette Cooking
and Refrigerator Set
With Detachable Wire Handle

GEUDER, PAESCHKE & FREY CO.
2-16 15th Street, Milwaukee, Wisconsin

Cream City Ware

158

From top: Geuder, Paeschke & Frey's Cream City Ware was named for the dairy industry around Milwaukee. Before development of the continuous, tunnel kilns for baking the frit-coated utensils that turned them into porcelain enamelware, individual kilns like these were in general use. Note the wheeled iron rack in the foreground, loaded with pans about to be placed in the oven. This picture was taken at the Geuder, Paeschke & Frey plant in 1911.

Top, courtesy House Furnishing Review. Bottom, courtesy Geuder, Paeschke & Frey.

him, and now the new enterprise of Geuder and Paeschke and Company was officially in business. Their move launched a firm—later to be known as Geuder, Paeschke and Frey—which, until it later discontinued its consumer goods operations, was one of the most important housewares manufacturers in the country.

In 1880, however, it was not much of a factory. It had a dozen employees, its equipment consisted of a few small presses, soldering irons, and other tinner's tools, and its early products were primarily basic cooking and baking tinware.

In 1882 the business was moved to Chicago, but it soon returned to Milwaukee, where in 1886 it was incorporated as the Geuder and Paeschke Manufacturing Company with Charles A. Paeschke as president. In 1908, when Frank J. Frey became secretary-treasurer, the firm became Geuder, Paeschke and Frey Company.

In 1892 it had begun to manufacture galvanized ware. This new rust-resistant material—thin sheet iron that had been dipped in molten tin to give it a protective covering—quickly replaced the customary wooden water pails and washtubs. Soon the new line included garbage and ash cans, coal scuttles, watering cans, etc.

In 1911 the retinned housewares items were gradually replaced with porcelain enamelware, which the company began manufacturing at that time. Later, it added aluminumware. It was this company that introduced, in 1939, an ironing table with a metal top; soon the "Met-L-Top" was made completely of metal, and its appearance marked the end of wooden ironing tables.

When new management assumed control of the company in 1955 they decided to concentrate on industrial and commercial products, and the consumer products division was disposed of in 1957.

Porcelain Enameled Ironware

Cast iron pots and pans may have been the very first kind to be porcelain enameled when that process was originally developed, but not until after World War II did such utensils achieve any real significance or sales volume in this country. Today, as part of the much-publicized "gourmet" trend, they have really come into their own.

A few people are primarily responsible for the widespread popularity of cast iron enamelware. Included are Dave and Fred Sanford who created "Descoware" and who, it is said, were the first to feature a full line rather than just separate items of such ironware; Schiller & Asmus Incorporated, who developed the Le Creuset line as a mainstay of their Gourmet Shop program; Sam Farber, whose sophisticated Copco line, and Ted Nierenberg, whose beautiful Dansk, speak for themselves. There are others...Graham Kerr, the "Galloping Gourmet;" Robert Carrier and his Cook Shop line, and so on.

In 1969 this country's imports of porcelain enamelware came close to $10 million, about twice the 1968 imports and far and away the largest quantity of such imports ever to cross our border. America apparently prefers imports to the locally produced variety.

In 1920 a young man in California had an exciting dream. "But it all seemed very real and imminent at the time," David E. Sanford recalled in 1971. Somebody, he dreamed—and the story is true—had perfected a way to make porcelain enamel cast iron cooking utensils in beautiful colors.

The Great Depression had already gripped America when, in 1932, Dave heard that the Crescent Iron Works in St. Louis had, in fact, developed porcelain enameled cast iron skillets. Within hours he was at that factory.

"The samples were beautiful; two sizes, one color. We tied it up," he related. "In a couple of weeks we had sold two carloads. That, remember, was in the depths of the depression and visions of sugar plums danced through our heads. Then, suddenly, it all evaporated like the original dream. Every piece, Crescent informed us, had crazed. The deal was off—but the dream went on."

In 1950 Dave was in Chicago just as Marshall Field & Company was promoting a United Nation's Exhibition including products of the member nations. "There it was!" recalled Dave. "A complete line of vibrant, flame-red porcelain enameled cast iron ware—the Le Creuset line from France."

Field's had been importing the line sporadically for about two years, the buyer told him with little enthusiasm. The reason: undependable deliveries, messy, cumbersome packing. But the quality, he emphasized, was excellent—chipping minor, crazing nil.

"Once again—spurred on by a dream that seemed awful real now!—I moved fast," continued Dave. "Getting to Europe required twenty-five hours. In Paris the sales manager met me and we drove to the LeCreuset plant in Fresnoy-le-Grand."

With an offer of an initial order for $100,000 worth of cookware —the biggest order the factory had ever seen—there was little problem in settling the details. Dave was to have it exclusively for the eleven western states; the line was to be reduced "to a manageable number of pieces," packed to specifications and—perhaps most important—would be sold under the "Descoware" trade name.

Spearhead of his all-out, shoot-the-works advertising and promotion program were one-hundred-thousand one-quart Creuset saucepans; usually $1.95, they were offered at one dollar.

Then, as they sometimes do, problems developed. In 1952, with two years experience Dave felt the line should be updated in color, shape, and packing.

"It was at this point," smiled Dave, "that we encountered the traditional French 'Resistance Movement':

Each of our requests was answered with the word "impossible," despite the track record we had made; our first year's total, I believe was over $500,000. It was at this point, too, we discovered the Belgium factory—Founderie Emaillerie of St. Trond, Belgium. We began carrying this line—also under the Descoware label—and, about a year later, dropped the French line.

The D. E. Sanford Company imported the line of porcelain enameled ironware from France and established it here under their Descoware brand.

159

Within a few years—in 1956—the Belgium management told us that since 80 percent of their total U. S. business was now coming from the eleven western states in which we had his line, he'd like us to take over the whole country, which we did. By 1960 our sales had outstripped their production and the management was reluctant to expand its facilities for one overseas customer taking 70 percent of the production. We attempted to buy the plant but it was not for sale. One interesting difference between American and European philosophy is that when business booms they're fearful it won't last and start preparing for the inevitable slump.

Dave Sanford was knighted by the King of Belgium in 1958 for his contributions to commerce between the two countries.

In September 1969, having gone long past the so-called retirement age—Dave was seventy—the brothers decided to sell out to General Housewares Corporation. Descoware, of course, continues to be a significant factor in the marketplace.

Copco and Dansk

When an enthusiastic amateur cook becomes increasingly unhappy with the pots and pans available in the marketplace to the point where he finally decides to do something about it, unusual things can happen. That's what resulted in the case of Sam Farber, the New Yorker who introduced the Copco Incorporated line of porcelain enameled ironware. Formerly in the silverware business, he had been thinking for sometime of starting an import operation.

"I had long held the conviction that almost all cooking utensils could easily be divided into one of two categories," he recalled in a conversation in 1971. "Either they were excellent from a functional

160

Country Forge is what West Bend calls its line of cast aluminum, porcelain enamel coated cooking utensils with no-stick interiors. Handles are of white ash, bottoms are flat for use on modern ranges.

PORCELAIN ENAMELED ALUMINUM

There was once a time when aluminumware was aluminumware and porcelain enameled ware was porcelain enameled ware; no one ever thought, much less said, "Never the twain shall meet." Everyone knew it was a technical impossibility.

Porcelain enamel (frit) had to be baked on to its steel base at 1,500 degrees F. (Even at that temperature it still did not fuse with the steel which usually has a melting point of about 2,700 degrees F. Thus when such a utensil happened to be exposed to sudden temperature changes when in use, it would often craze or chip right down to the steel, exposing it to rust and corrosion.)

Since aluminum melts at 1,250 degrees F., it was, obviously, completely impractical to attempt to apply a porcelain enamel coating to it. But around 1950 DuPont perfected and patented a so-called heavy metals frit which used either lead, cadmium, or antimony as a medium with the glass. This permitted baking at a temperature of only 1,000 to 1,050 degrees F., a heat so close to the melting point of aluminum that a very effective fusing of the frit and the metal takes place.

As a consequence porcelain enameled aluminumware can withstand a far greater thermal shock without damage; such a utensil, it is said, can be heated to 900 degrees F., and then quenched into cold water without crazing or other ill effects.

and utility standpoint but extremely deficient aesthetically—or they were very attractive but woefully lacking as good, practical cooking utensils. Why couldn't the best qualities of each be combined?"

In 1960, after surveying key retailers around the country, he decided to put his theory into practice and came up with Copco.

In 1955, the first year the Dansk Designs Limited Fjord line of stainless steel was introduced, Ted Nierenberg, president, decided to develop a line of enameled steel cookware attractive enough to be brought right to the table.

"I immediately wrote Jens Quistgaard who, as you know, is our designer in Denmark," he recalled in an interview. "I found that he had already developed some sketches of unusual-looking casseroles. Then, through the Federation of Danish Industries, I contacted Glud and Marstrand, an old-line firm which, among other things, fabricated metal household items. They had recently bought a huge new furnace from Ferro of Cleveland, Ohio." Nierenberg continued:

> Clearly G & M had excessive capacity. As we went over our ideas they were cooperative and competitive. I think Knud Hannover, the managing director, was somewhat dismayed that a young American—I was then thirty-one—was willing to gamble $40,000 for tools on such a product line. What was more amazing is the fact that I didn't have $40,000. But I did have $20,000 and offered to pay him half cash in advance, the balance on delivery of the first order.
>
> I was sufficiently confident and enthusiastic to feel sure I could sell a couple of hundred thousand dollars of this new collection and then finance those firm orders through my bank. Hannover bought the deal. But he insisted on a rather stiff contract—which prompted me to insist on a couple of rather stiff paragraphs too.
>
> The design of our new collection, which we named Kobenstyle, was—and still is—a manufacturing nightmare. The rest of 1955 was a grueling experience; we sold over 200,000 of the product line and the factory somehow delivered it. The handles were beautiful, but extremely vulnerable to chipping and it took several years until we overcame such problems.
>
> Meanwhile G & M's enormous new furnace never did run close to capacity and despite our growing business, they found it necessary to close the plant in 1965. That's when those stiff paragraphs in the contract became effective and in 1966 we relocated our tools with Japy and Aubecq in France where the line continues to be produced. The Kobenstyle collection has become one of our staples and now represents an annual volume of about $4 million throughout the world.

Tinware

There was a time when there were probably more things made of tin than anything else for use in the home. It was lighter and more easily fabricated than iron, less costly than copper and much more versatile than wood. Although originated in Bohemia about 1575, about one hundred years later England had learned to make a tin plate and the earliest arrivals in the New World often had a few pieces of tinware among their precious possessions.

Berlin, Connecticut developed into one of the best known and

From top: West Bend offers Stow-Aways, a four-piece porcelain enameled aluminum cookware set. All items nest into one compact unit for storage. A detachable, positive lock handle, which attaches to the saucepans and skillet, is one feature of this 1972 set. Copco's porcelain enameled ironware was designed by Michael Lax, an American, and Count Sigvard Bernadotte of Denmark for Sam Farber, a New Yorker. Farber launched gourmet cookware shops in specialty and gift stores as well as department stores to enlarge the appeal of these utensils.

Get Ready For More Business

DeLuxe

Extra Heavy Japanned Wear

Will Pull Customers to Your Store

Finished in white, oak, and imitation of Turquoise Blue Enamel.
It will create a ready demand, not only on account of its beautiful appearance, but also for its durability.

Get our Catalog and let us quote you on this profitable line

SCHLUETER MFG. COMPANY
ST. LOUIS, · MISSOURI

162

New Goods for 1904

Our 10 Cent Toaster.

We are constantly adding attractive, popular-priced articles to our line.

The buyer who is looking for goods that almost sell themselves should write us for samples and prices.

We manufacture everything in

TIN AND GALVANIZED IRON WARES

that is sold to the house-furnishing trade.

Sink Strainer.

The Standard.

The Vesuvius.

The Home Oil Stove.

NICHTHAUSER & LEVY
Office & Salesroom: 96 Beekman St., N. Y.

From top: A tin tea kettle of the mid-nineteenth century. Then, an ad for Japanned ware in the early 1900s. Note the extra large flour bin, reflecting the great amount of home baking done in that era. In 1904, Nichthauser & Levy advertised their tin and galvanized ironware.

Top, courtesy National Gallery of Art, Index of American Art. Middle and bottom, courtesy House Furnishing Review.

most important tinware centers in the colonies. Another place that developed a significant reputation for this merchandise was Stevens Plains, a small community just outside of Portland, Maine. Here in 1798 Zachariah Stevens began working tinplate in 1798. No one has explained why this remote spot became a tinware center. But by 1832 Stevens Plains had no less than eleven shops producing $27,300 worth of tinware annually.

The production, sale and use of tinware was of tremendous importance well into the nineteenth century. Some of the important manufacturers in the housewares business today trace their beginning to a small tin shop.

Production, of course, was all hand work—the tin was hammered over forms into the required shape and soldered in the individual shops of the tin smiths. Their raw material, the tin sheets, actually thin iron sheets dipped into melted tin, were all imported from England.

Decorated tinware, of course, was that which was painted and/or "Japanned," a term that continued to be used in the housewares business long after 1950. The term originated in England in the 1600s to describe the art of decorating furniture in the manner of the highly lacquered screens and cabinets imported from the Orient. After the Revolution it also became popular as a finish for tinware. A brown-black coating, made largely of asphaltum and varnish hardened by firing, was the usual background upon which the Japanner lavished his ornamental skill with bronzes, gold leaf, and colors.

Eventually the paint spray gun and modern, hard-surface lacquers—along with the high cost of labor—brought an end to the original, ornate Japanned type of decoration, but the name continues to linger on.

The popularity of the current so-called "gourmet" foods trend and the specialty housewares still made of tin have given this ancient metal something of a new lease on life. Actually, however, despite all the publicity such items have had, they still only represent a fraction of what the tinware business once was.

What did more than anything else to bring the important tinware era to an end was, of course, the introduction of new and more practical materials such as porcelain enamelware, aluminum, and stainless steel. But none of those ever made the inroads into tinware that plastics have made. From cannister sets to dustpans—you name it—the chances are that it is now not only made of plastic, but that it is also probably a far superior product in every way, from price to its impervious, colorful finish.

All that is not to say beautifully decorated tinware items—still sometimes referred to also by the old name "toleware"—are no longer available. Most certainly they are, though for the most part they are largely in the accessory category and take on more of the character of decoration than utility.

The booth of the Meriden Britannia Company at the Philadelphia Centennial Exhibition.

Courtesy National Antiques Magazine.

Meriden Britannia Company

Britannia ware is all but forgotten. Yet from 1830 to 1860 it was as important in the house furnishing business as stainless steel is today.

Promotion-minded English pewterers coined the name about 1750 to identify a newly perfected alloy. Usually Britannia metal consisted of about 150 parts tin, 3 parts copper, and 10 parts antimony. It was hard and resonant and had a bright sheen. Production of pewter ware had begun in Connecticut, especially in Meriden, about 1800. Two decades later, Britannia metal replaced it in popularity. It looked much more silvery than pewter and was easier to clean and polish. Also, it was considerably harder and more wear-resistant, which appealed to frugal homemakers.

In December 1852, despite the large number of firms already in the business, a group of aggressive and experienced manufacturers of tinware, pewter ware, and silverware consolidated to form the Meriden Britannia Company. I. C. Lewis was named president and H. C. Wilcox secretary and treasurer. The company soon became the largest in its field.

Sales for 1853 totaled $250,000. By 1855 the company was also offering hollow ware and flatware, to be supplied silver-plated if desired. In 1862, by agreement, the business of Rogers Brothers Manufacturing Company, manufacturers of silver-plated ware in Hartford, was moved to Meriden and added to the Britannia Company's line. After a disastrous fire on July 15, 1870, which destroyed much of the factory, the plant was soon rebuilt. Fortunately, the $250,000 loss was fully covered by insurance.

During the ensuing years the character of the market demand changed, and Britannia ware gradually lost out to silver-plated ware. Although the Meriden Britannia Company had achieved an excellent reputation as the world's largest manufacturer of Britannia ware, it was now being recognized as the world's largest manufacturer of silverware. By 1878 its sales had reached $2½ million annually, largely in silverware, but it clung to its long-established and widely known name. Finally, in 1893 Britannia was acquired by the International Silver Company.

Aluminumware

Back in 1890 everyone in Carlisle, Pennsylvania, who knew Charles Ziegler regarded him admiringly not only as a very personable but as a most determined young man. Desperately he wanted to go to medical school and be a doctor. But that required money he didn't have, so he started to earn it by going from house-to-house selling porcelain enamel cooking utensils. Sparked by such an incentive, he proved to be an excellent salesman and soon he had his friend, John H. Wilson, selling too.

Presently they learned of some unusual new utensils made of aluminum and imported from Europe. Within five years they had not only formed a little company, Ziegler, Wilson & Company to sell aluminumware, but Ziegler had invented the Ideal percolating coffee pot, while Wilson had invented the Gem cooking, steaming, and preserving kettle. Both were made of aluminum.

Aluminumware wasn't a complete stranger in the United States at that time. It had, of course, been known in Europe for over half a century; Napoleon served his guests dinner on aluminum plates since they cost more than gold. In 1852 this silvery new metal was priced at $545 per pound. By 1890 it only cost $2.25 a pound, but even at that figure only a little cookware and a few novelties could be produced.

On February 23, 1886, however, all that was destined to change when a twenty-two-year-old young inventor, Charles Martin Hall, working in his woodshed laboratory in Oberlin, Ohio, the year after he graduated college, unlocked the secret of producing aluminum inexpensively. It was a discovery which, by the time of his death in 1914, had rewarded him with about $30 million!

The remarkable story of how Hall finally interested Alfred E. Hunt of Hunt & Clapp, Pittsburgh metallurgists, in his discovery and how in July 1888 with $20,000 they organized the Pittsburgh Reduction Company—later renamed the Aluminum Company of America—to produce the new metal has often been told in fascinating detail.

Aluminum cooking utensils were one of the product categories the new company was most interested in. Such utensils were already being sold here; some were imported and a very few were being made in this country. Despite their unique appeal they met with great resistance. Compared to traditional cast iron and porcelain enamel-

From top: The German Aluminum Company picked the wrong time to start business in America. It wasn't long afterward that we were deep into World War I and even the name of the once-popular item, the Berlin Kettle, was discontinued—forever. Pioneer plant of the Pittsburgh Reduction Company was built on a rented lot on Smallman Street in Pittsburgh, 1888.

164

ware utensils, these newcomers were quite expensive. And unaccustomed to utensils of such unusually light weight, women were inclined to regard them with distrust and suspicion—an attitude which, more often than not, was justified by the poor quality and craftsmanship of those pots and pans. Manufacturers still had a great deal to learn about fabricating them.

The Pittsburgh Reduction Company had no intention of making utensils, but eagerly tried to encourage others to do so. To convince the long-established Griswold Company in Erie, Pennsylvania, for instance, it borrowed one of their iron molders and brought him to Pittsburgh to cast a tea kettle of aluminum. When Ely Griswold saw the advantages of using this attractive new material rather than iron he agreed enthusiastically—but instead of giving them an order for aluminum as they had expected, he gave them an order for two thousand kettles! So the new company had no choice but to go into the utensil fabricating business. (Griswold later began making cast aluminumware too.)

Meanwhile, Ziegler, Wilson & Company, though making excellent headway for a small, new company, was having trouble with the poor quality utensils they were getting from Sidney Shephard & Company in Chicago. So they got an enterprising new firm in Lemont, Illinois called the Illinois Pure Aluminum Company, formed in 1892, as well as a firm in Waltham, Massachusetts, Hill, Whitney & Wood, to provide them with better merchandise. (By now Ziegler,

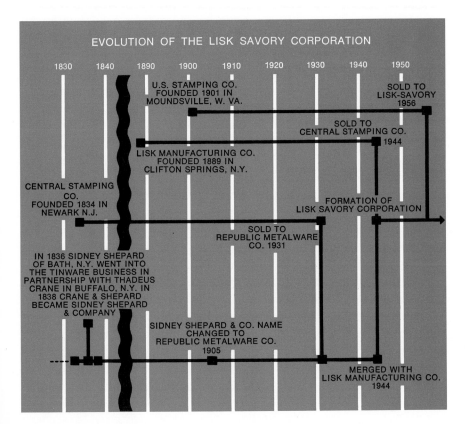

Lisk-Savory is one of the housewares manufacturers that has had a long and interesting history. Active and progressive today in enamelware, the company started out as a small tinware manufacturer. The Savory Roaster, the Tiffany of the cooking utensil field at the time, was one of its most famous products.

The BEST COOKS *use*
Aluminum

The chefs of many world-famous hotels preside over all-aluminum kitchens. They cook *everything* in aluminum—for they have found that aluminum cooks everything well.

Some of these experts praise the greater durability and economy of aluminum utensils. Others speak of the ease with which this ware is kept clean and sanitary. Still others call attention to its safety for all kinds of cooking.

Hospitals, too, and steamship lines, and railroads, and packers of food products are using aluminum more and more. And housewives, unwilling that the large user should monopolize such efficiency and economy, are deciding in increasing numbers that the all-aluminum kitchen is better than one equipped with a bit of everything. . . .

The best cooks use aluminum.

ALUMINUM WARES ASSOCIATION
Publicity Division, 844 Rush St., Chicago

This page: In 1927, ads like this marked the start of the Aluminum Wares Association's promotion program, which was expected to generate industry sales volume of $50 million in five years. Within two years, however, industry dissatisfaction with the campaign caused it to be discontinued.

Opposite page. A collection of cooking utensils that show the diversity in materials and colors now available for the homemaker.

Above, courtesy House Furnishing Review.

able to afford medical school, left the firm and it became Wilson Manufacturing Company.)

Not long afterward Hill, Whitney & Company, unable to continue the uphill fight to establish aluminumware, went bankrupt. The Pittsburgh Reduction Company, to whom it owed the most money, went through the Hill, Whitney accounts and were flabbergasted to find an unfilled order from a Wilson Manufacturing Company of Blue Island, Illinois, for an amazing twenty-eight hundred kettles!

Arthur Vining Davis, general manager of the Reduction Company at the time—who later achieved considerable fame as the long-time board chairman of Alcoa—immediately invited John Wilson to visit him so he could learn more of his operation. Also invited to attend that meeting was Wilson's former partner, now Dr. Charles Ziegler, an intern in Pittsburgh's Allegheny General Hospital. The upshot of the meeting was that Wilson and Ziegler agreed to join Davis' company and operate a house-to-house sales force.

In 1900 when the Reduction Company bought the defunct Hill, Whitney & Wood manufacturing equipment, less than 5 percent of all aluminum produced was used for cooking utensils. The equipment was moved into the old Excelsior Flint Glass Company plant in New Kensington and, using the old Hill, Whitney catalog as a base, a new line of utensils was soon developed.

A year later, the Reduction Company decided upon a name for its new manufacturing subsidiary and incorporated the United States Aluminum Company. At the same time it formed the Aluminum Cooking Utensil Company, which was to be the selling organization for the utensils. (The trade name "Wear-Ever" was not adopted until 1903.) When this operation was started it was expected that the house-to-house program would continue only long enough to educate housewives to the advantages of aluminum cookware and thereafter it would be sold entirely through retailers.

In 1902, to promote the sale of the new utensils through retail stores, the company hired E. N. Dillway and G. F. Cole. Dillway had been with Hill, Whitney & Wood calling on New England dealers. Cole had specialized in selling aluminum utensils at retail in Ohio.

Meanwhile, the as yet un-named "Wear-Ever" line was divided into two groups. In the first were the specialties which could be demonstrated in the home and were sold exclusively by the canvassers; the second consisted of the general line which—it was hoped—would be sold only through retail stores.

The first attempt at staging store demonstrations did not take place until 1903. Perhaps the most notable experiment took place in Wanamaker's, Philadelphia, where John Wilson conducted the demonstration personally. "Up to that time," the record relates, "J. F. Collins, Wanamaker's buyer, had refused to buy the line even at the maximum discount of 50%. Mr. Wilson had been instructed by his management to place the goods in that store even if he had to give them an additional 25% discount." Eventually, Wanamaker's agreed

BUCKEYE ALUMINUM CO.,
Wooster,   Ohio

Buckeye Aluminum Company, Wooster,
Ohio, advertised the solidity of their
material in 1916. Buckeye eventually
became part of Regal Ware Inc.

Courtesy House Furnishing Review.

168

to accept $250 worth of these shiny new utensils on a consignment basis.

"Mr. Wilson's first demonstration consisted of cooking apple butter without stirring. This seems simple enough now, but in those days it was a revelation to the housewives of Philadelphia. The result was the sale of $3,000 worth of preserving kettles and other utensils the first month."

As events proved, aluminum would have a future as bright and shiny as the metal itself. And, while it would take a half century to accomplish, by the 1950s new technologies would make it possible for the manufacturers to add to the basic, silver-like appeal of the utensils, the further appeal of aluminum utensils finished in gleaming porcelain enamel in all the colors of the rainbow.

But until then a great many things would happen in the aluminum cooking utensil industry. Overshadowing practically everything, at least until World War II, was Alcoa. Able to set the price of raw materials, Alcoa exerted influence on supply and demand of products—especially in aluminum cookware.

After Alcoa began producing utensils around the turn of the century, it wasn't long before others started to make aluminumware.

Probably the very first of the stamped aluminum cookware manufacturers to be established, as noted earlier, was the Illinois Pure Aluminum Company in Lemont, Illinois, in 1892, which is still very actively engaged in this business. At about the same time that Illinois was getting into the manufacture of stamped aluminum, two long established producers of cast ironware—both now part of General Housewares Corporation—began making cast aluminum. One, the Griswold Manufacturing Company first bought its tea kettles from Alcoa. Later, when it began its own production, it developed a process for hardening the ware and giving it a "tempered surface" which, it was claimed, "is positive proof against discoloration or absorption." As a result of this process its first big order for the new utensils came from London.

The other ironware producer who began making cast aluminum utensils was the Wagner Manufacturing Company, which started business in 1891 in Sidney, Ohio.

Mirro Aluminum Company

In 1895 the start of another new company, the Aluminum Manufacturing Company, became a matter of extraordinary significance. It marked the beginning of a large and important concentration of aluminumware production in a section of the country which, because of its relative remoteness from its raw material source and markets, would seem to be the place such a new industry would be least likely to succeed. James M. Rock, assistant professor of economics, University of Utah, who made an exhaustive study of the Wisconsin aluminum cookware industry, sums it up in these terms:

By the late 1800's the Northern Lake Michigan shore and 50 miles inland had been denuded of its giant white pines. The small lumbering towns were economically depressed; new industry was needed but aluminum manufacturing would not have seemed to be a good choice. Though unskilled labor was plentiful, skilled labor was not and transportation costs were high. The rudeness of the transportation and communication networks in Eastern Wisconsin at the close of the last century can be attested to by the locational compactness of the firms which make up this [aluminum] industry [today]. All the firms are located within a rectangular strip 80 miles long and 15 miles wide in Eastern Wisconsin.

What was the most important reason for the survival and growth of the aluminumware industry in such an illogical location and what was the most important influence on the location of the firms that were established there? "The answers to those questions," states Prof. Rock, "is the prideful men who founded the Wisconsin companies. This is not to deny the importance of other factors...but it does mean that entrepreneurship was the most important."

Joseph Koenig, who founded the Aluminum Manufacturing Company in Two Rivers in 1895, is generally acknowledged with having thereby also founded the aluminum industry in Wisconsin. He had displayed some German aluminum novelties at Chicago's World's Columbian Exposition in 1893 and became so impressed with their potential he decided to go into the business himself. His success soon prompted others to emulate him. In 1898 Henry Vits founded the Manitowoc Aluminum Novelty Company and in 1903 Albert Leyse began the Aluminum Sign Company in Two Rivers.

Competition began to intensify not only among these three companies but the New Jersey Aluminum Company in Newark, which had also begun to make novelties in 1898. None of these companies were as yet producing any cooking utensils. Finally in 1908, competition drove prices and profits to the point where Alcoa, fearful of losing customers if they went broke, stepped into the picture. The outcome was a consolidation of the Aluminum Manufacturing Company, the Aluminum Novelty Company, and the New Jersey Aluminum Company into a new firm called the Aluminum Goods Manufacturing Company (now Mirro Aluminum Company of Manitowoc, Wisconsin). In consideration of its efforts Alcoa was "permitted" to buy one-fourth of the stock of the new company and named as the exclusive source of its sheet and ingot supply.

Gustave A. Kruttschnitt and James C. Coleman, partners of the New Jersey Company, were named president-manager and secretary-treasurer respectively of the new company. Koenig and Vits were named vice-presidents and J. E. Hamilton, a Koenig associate, became chairman of the board.

The Mirro brand name appeared nationally in 1917 in aluminum cookware advertisements. At that time, Mirro was just one of several trade names of the Aluminum Goods Manufacturing Company, which had started mass producing aluminum cookware in 1913.

From top: Household specialties in aluminum from the Aluminum Goods Manufacturing Company, later called Mirro. Then, an early consumer ad in a 1902 *Ladies Home Journal* selling the qualities of lightness, durability, and purity of aluminum.

Top, courtesy House Furnishing Review.

Dissension soon developed. The New Jersey interests sold out to the others, George Vits was elected president and Alcoa took the opportunity to increase its holdings to 30 percent. Having a finger in the Aluminum Goods Company added just that much to its control for by then it was not only the largest producer of cooking utensils but accounted for 80 percent of all Wisconsin cookware production. Alcoa's "Wear-Ever" line was then the second largest in the country. The two companies accounted for 65 percent of all aluminumware made in America and provided Alcoa with the control it was determined to exercise over the industry. As of March 4, 1971 it still owned 19.7 percent of Mirro's outstanding stock.

"THERE IS NOTHING SO CONSTANT AS CHANGE"

The truth of that old adage is dramatically reflected in the changes that time and circumstances have caused in the aluminum cooking utensil business. And no one can speak with greater authority on that subject than Horatio B. Ebert, who was formerly national sales manager for Wear-Ever and who spent his entire business career with the Aluminum Cooking Utensil Company. In the course of a 1971 interview this keen and active octogenarian looked back on some of those changes.

One of our biggest problems was the effort needed to clean aluminum utensils; we didn't have the kind of alloys available today, and since stainless steel was so much easier to clean it began to make inroads right away.

To go back a bit, when I managed the St. Louis office, in the four states we had, Missouri, Kansas, Iowa, and Nebraska, our biggest volume came from preserving kettles, which we made in all sizes from two and one-half to twenty-four quarts. Women did all their own preserving, and I remember that it was nothing for my mother to have a couple of hundred jars of preserves on her shelves. That business was the first to disappear; the company hasn't made those kettles now for years. The next big item to go was the aluminum roaster. Incidentally, it was the aluminum roaster that all but put the once very popular porcelain enamel roaster out of business. People preferred aluminum roasters, and we made them oblong, oval, and round. They provided a big volume of business—until the electric roasters, people's eating habits, and other factors put an end to it.

Or take cake pans and pie plates, items we once sold by the millions. I'd give our production department a requisition for the quantities we'd need for the ensuing year on each item. We'd order No. 90 round cake pans 500,000 at a time—the same with pie plates. But the time eventually came when we couldn't order more than 10,000 pieces. In those small quantities it isn't even economically feasible to make them. What did it? Lots of things...Pyrex, frozen foods and cakes, prepared mixes....

Sink strainers were a tremendous item. But plastic strainers didn't discolor the sink the way ours did, so that disappeared from the scene. The dishpan business was enormous; we made round and oval, both in three sizes; now they're all plastic. All a woman needs in her kitchen today, it seems, is two or three saucepans and a frying pan. They just don't use those big items today on which we did such a volume.

When asked if Wear-Ever's management had ever seriously considered going into the plastics business, he replied, "No, they never did. That was a big mistake."

From top: Delivery trucks for the Aluminum Cooking Utensil Company in the early 1900s advertised a forty-five-cent saucepan for just fifteen cents with a coupon in daily newspapers that week. A bargain in any age. A much later Wear Ever display—the Hallite line. Note the free-form handles on the coffee and tea kettles.

Today Mirro is considered the world's largest manufacturer of aluminum cooking utensils. An impetus to this great growth was the introduction of the Mirro-Matic pressure cooker in 1945, an immediate success with millions sold over the years. In 1957 the corporate name was changed from the Aluminum Goods Manufacturing Company to Mirro Aluminum Company, an acknowledgment of brand name recognition in the marketplace.

Getting on the Bandwagon

The aluminum cooking utensil industry faced a very crucial period after World War I. Although the end of the war economy resulted in a recession in 1919, newcomers were entering the aluminum cookware industry at an almost unbelievable rate, according to Rock. Of the thirty-seven firms estimated to be in this business in 1923, about twenty-five started after World War I, not including at least five established firms that did not begin to stamp aluminum cookware until after the war.

As if the avalanche of newcomers didn't create enough of a competitive problem, a flood of low priced, poor quality aluminum cookware from Europe created an even bigger headache for the American manufacturers. Coming as it did into an already badly depressed market, these imports created havoc and provided the critics of aluminumware with plenty of ammunition for their persistent attacks on "those flimsy cooking utensils."

By 1924 there were at least forty manufacturers of stamped and cast aluminum cookware in this country and despite all the problems of the post war era, these new utensils were now making excellent progress. More and more retailers were stocking them and public acceptance of aluminumware was growing rapidly.

Alcoa, of course, was a major contributor to that development. In the course of its investigation of the aluminum industry the Federal Trade Commission was told by Alcoa that originally it had intended only to become involved in the manufacture of cooking utensils until the market was developed. But because of the great amount of "inferior quality" utensils coming from abroad and "the tendency of American manufacturers to produce ware of a similar quality," Alcoa "felt it incumbent upon itself to continue the manufacture of high grade utensils in order to protect the industry.... In other words, it was purely a matter of self-preservation that induced it to remain in the cooking utensil business."

Regal Ware Incorporated

There are many stories about how and where waterless cooking originated but which is the truth may never be known. It is known, however, that in 1922 James O. Reigle, an ambitious young house-to-house salesman—who had started out to be a minister—did such a remarkable job of selling West Bend's new Pioneer waterless cooker that he ended up establishing what is now the largest inde-

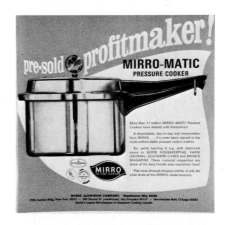

From top: Mirro joined the ranks of pressure cooker manufacturers in 1945. It and Presto are now the only ones in that business. The lower photo shows a determined approach to sell heavier gauge utensils—all the more interesting because it was launched during the Great Depression in 1932.

Bottom, courtesy House Furnishing Review.

171

From top: A contemporary development for Regal Ware—its Gourmet Cooker. Regal's three-quart Locklid strainer-saucepan was designed for low heat, waterless cooking. A twist of the cover let the cook drain water, cook the food, or take the lid off the pot. Then, James O. Reigle, founder and Chairman of the Board of Regal Ware, Inc.

pendent cookware manufacturer in the country, Regal Ware, Incorporated, in Kewaskum, Wisconsin. The company does not reveal its sales figures, but authoritative sources estimate that in 1972 its annual volume approached the $50 million mark. And its history represents an interesting example of the general merger trend so often evident in the housewares industry (see accompanying chart).

The house-to-house sales agency Reigle set up in Canton, Ohio, established something of a record by moving over half a million dollars worth of Pioneer cookers within five years. That performance landed him a job with the Enterprise Aluminum Company in Massilon, Ohio, with which he was associated for eighteen years, most of them as vice-president in charge of sales.

But Jim Reigle had long wanted a business of his own, and when, in 1945, he learned that the Kewaskum Aluminumware Company in Kewaskum, Wisconsin, was for sale, he and some associates bought it.

This company had been established in 1919, primarily by the influential local Rosenheimer family, apparently motivated by the increasing success of other aluminum cookware factories in that area. It marketed its line under the "Kewasko" brand.

Eight days after its new owners took over, World War II suddenly ended. They found themselves faced with terminating $3 million in government contracts, disposing of $500,000 worth of special, now unnecessary, equipment, and converting the whole operation to the production of civilian goods. At the time it was thought best to change the name only slightly, to the Kewaskum Utensil Company. But the name "Regal," which was used on many of its products and often identified the company itself, prompted a change in the corporate name in 1951 to Regal Ware, Incorporated.

Jim Reigle was doing very well; he was busy and happy but not so busy he didn't hear opportunity knock again in 1964. Regal Ware, Incorporated, answered by purchasing the Buckeye Division of the Mardigan Corporation in Wooster, Ohio.

The newly acquired company was originally established in 1902 in Doylestown, Ohio, as the Buckeye Aluminum Company. The men who started it had come from Quincy, Massachusetts, where in 1895 they were associated with one of the first companies in this business —the Bay State Aluminum Company. Civic-minded business leaders in Dolyestown had persuaded a group of the Bay State people, headed by Leon Ward, to start a plant in their city.

By 1911 it had prospered so much that F. H. Blake and his son G. W. Blake bought the company and moved it to Wooster where better transportation facilities were available. Two world wars and several corporate reorganizations later, in September 1954, Buckeye was bought by the Mardigan Corporation of Detroit, one of the largest tool and die firms in the country that specialized in the automotive field. As the Buckeye Division of the corporation it continued to produce cookware, and ten years later was acquired by Regal.

James O. Reigle retired from the presidency on September 16, 1965, but continued to serve as chairman of the company he had founded. His son James assumed the presidency; another son, Ronald, became vice-president for sales and management; and the third and youngest son, Richard, filled various posts until 1968, when he was named vice-president and general manager of Buckeye Ware, Incorporated, in Wooster, Ohio.

Another acquisition took place in 1967, when Regal purchased the housewares division of Norris Industries of Flora, Mississippi.

Two years later, in 1969, Regal Ware acquired controlling interest in the National Aluminum Manufacturing Company of Peoria, Illinois, an aluminum castings producer.

Today Regal Ware's operations include a wide variety of aluminum and stainless steel cookware. Among its innovations is the design of sets of cooking utensils with interchangeable parts so that various pieces can be used to make different cooking combinations. It developed the Locklid saucepan and a Push-Button whistling teakettle, and now includes numerous electric housewares items in its line. In 1950 it received an order from Lever Brothers Company for one million eight-inch fry pans and one million three-quart sauce pans, believed to be the largest single premium order ever booked in the aluminumware business.

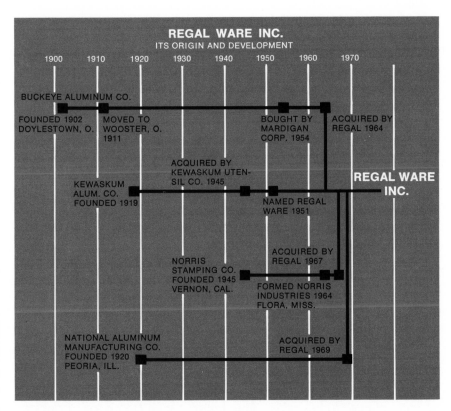

In 1945, James Reigle started to put together the company known today as Regal Ware Inc. The company's operations now include a wide variety of aluminum and stainless steel cookware.

MAKE YOUR SALE A SUCCESS
HANDLE
AMERICAN MAID ALUMINUM WARE
The Popular Price Line

A
Good
Sales
Feature

A
Quick
Profit
Maker

"American Maid"

FOR years we have had one main ideal in the manufacture of aluminum cooking utensils—"to produce and sell at a moderate cost a line to meet all demands, coupled with entire satisfaction." We have attained this in the production of the **American Maid** line.

MR. DEALER: You will find every housewife an enthusiastic buyer for **American Maid** ware—she cannot resist the popular prices; your sales will prove a success and your profits astonishing.

Ask Your Jobber for
American Maid Aluminum Ware

MANUFACTURERS

ILLINOIS PURE ALUMINUM CO.
LEMONT, ILLINOIS, U. S. A.

The Illinois Pure Aluminum Company was founded in 1892 and still very much in business in Lemont, Illinois. This 1921 ad offered their American Maid line.

174 *Courtesy House Furnishing Review.*

Illinois Pure Aluminum Company

In the Summer of 1892 a promoter from Cincinnati arrived in Lemont, Illinois, with a convincing tale of the great opportunity awaiting those who would go into the business of making specialties out of that remarkable new material called aluminum. At it turned out, he was absolutely right!

By August a group of local businessmen formally organized the Illinois Pure Aluminum Company. It would become a flourishing, family-owned business that is now one of the oldest manufacturers of aluminum cookware.

The company was capitalized at $50,000. But only $19,000 had been paid in and by the time a factory had been built there was no money left to start operations. A well-to-do retired building contractor named Edwin Walker finally agreed to provide funds to run the business and he was given notes on it as security. But more and still more money was needed. At the end of a year and a half he had invested so much in the venture that he persuaded his eighteen-year-old son, George S. Walker, to leave the Chicago bank where he was employed and join the aluminum company as his representative. Four years later, although only twenty-one years old, he was named president of the young company, a post he held until his death in 1947. In the intervening years he set the company on the successful course that has enabled it to survive.

A press was acquired and about 1897 the company added a foundry for making cast utensils. While others were already doing that, it claims to have been the first manufacturer to produce forged aluminum utensils. All that was discontinued in 1920 when the company specialized in drawn or stamped utensils from the lightest to the heaviest gauges.

Until that time the company's principal outlets had been hardware jobbers, general stores and the "bell ringer" trade, as the house-to-house operators were called. But in 1920 they abandoned direct selling ("sheriffs from small towns were forever bothering us in an effort to learn if Joe So-and-so was one of our salesmen!") It was around that time that the variety chains like Newberry, McLellan, Kresge and others were beginning to develop, and they soon became large customers.

George E. Walker, son of George S., became president in 1947 and held that post until 1970 when he was named chairman of the company. At that time his brother, Tracy Walker, assumed the presidency. Kenneth Walker, another brother, was sales manager from 1933 until his death in 1966.

Club Products Company

Who first developed "waterless cooking" is questionable. But there is no question that the Club Aluminum Utensil Company, organized in Chicago in 1923, brought that method of cooking to a sales boil.

Now located in Cleveland, having merged with the former Monarch Aluminum Manufacturing Company, it is known as the Club Products Company Division of Standard International Corporation, a conglomerate based in Andover, Massachusetts. It was acquired by Standard in 1968.

The marketing innovation on which Club built its success was a refinement of the house-to-house approach long practiced in the cookware field. It was a form of selling called the party plan.

Club's merchandise was made by Monarch, founded in 1913 by Raymond Deutsch to produce sand-cast aluminum parts for vacuum cleaners and some cookware. In 1920 this old method was replaced by a permanent mold process. Later the company developed a unique hammered finish for cast utensils, which were sold by Club under the "Hammercraft" name.

The 1929 stock market crash and the following depression brought progress in both companies to a halt. The following year H. J. Taylor, an officer of the Jewel Tea Company, Chicago, grocery and premium business also selling directly to the home, became president of Club. He tried to preserve the luncheon demonstration plan but, being unable to overcome the handicap of prevailing conditions, decided on a complete change in merchandising.

After first selling the Jewel Tea Company, Taylor began selling to department stores, kicking off with Gimbel's in New York. Retail prices were down to half what they had been and the new policy was so successful that within a couple of years both Monarch and Club were again doing very well.

During the late forties and early fifties Monarch, under Deutsch and his successor to the presidency, E. C. Bloomberg, and John Keating, vice-president of manufacturing, developed many innovations in production and products. Perhaps the most important of these was "Velvaglaze," invented in 1953, which for the first time made possible the production of porcelain-enameled aluminumware. This had a far-reaching impact on the cooking utensil business. Monarch scored another first in 1962 by pioneering in the use of Teflon coating on aluminumware, and in 1965 it introduced a ceramic-based Teflon finish.

In 1966 Club acquired the exclusive United States distribution rights for cookware of the Waterford Iron Founders of Waterford, Ireland. It is a porcelain-enameled cast iron line marketed under the Waterford name.

Today Club Products Company, although still primarily in the cookware and custom castings field, is a diversified producer of many lines and types of cookware, in both cast and heavy-gauge sheet metals.

West Bend Company

One of the most important developments in the aluminum cookware industry took place on September 27, 1911, in the then small town of West Bend, Wisconsin, when seven youthful men headed by twenty-

175

In October 1933, during the Depression, Monarch Aluminum Company, Cleveland, which made Club Aluminum's house-to-house line of waterless cast aluminum, offered Gimbel's of New York a big close-out of unbranded Club seconds. Gimbel's sold $90,000 in a month. Meanwhile, Club had filed a $5 million bankruptcy, decided to change its policy and sell through retail stores. Because of its earlier success, Gimbel's was given the opportunity in 1934 to be first with it and used this ad in five newspapers to do so. When the ad broke, buyers from other cities were on hand wanting Club for their stores.

seven-year-old Bernard C. Ziegler, organized the West Bend Aluminum Company, now the West Bend Company. Ziegler was obviously something of a boy wonder. By the time he had graduated from the local high school in 1901, he is said to have had his own full-fledged fire insurance company.

Keenly aware of the ever-increasing activity in his state in fabricating aluminum, when a pocket book plant in West Bend burned down and threw many people out of work, he and his associates finally decided upon an aluminum manufacturing plant. How wise that decision was and how skillfully that project has been managed since then is strikingly revealed by the fact that in 1968 (last year for which its figures are available) its sales were $70 million.

The company's first sales representative was S. S. Davis of Evanston, Illinois, whose orders from Sears provided half of West Bend's volume until 1919. In the 1920s it moved into the direct selling field as a result of an item called the "Waterless Cooker." Based on an enamelware item from Germany, it enabled the cook to prepare a whole meal over one range unit and proved to be the largest selling single item up to that time.

After World War II it acquired a number of other lines for direct-selling operations: Lifetime (1949); Advance Aluminum Castings (1958); and U. S. Industries (1964). Experiments on stainless steel began in 1940 and the first full line of stainless steel cooking utensils was produced in 1951. At about this time West Bend began expanding into the portable electric appliance field with the introduction of coffee makers—necessitating further plant expansion.

What is regarded as a turning point in the company's history took place in 1943. At that time president B. C. Ziegler (who died May 6, 1946) initiated an employee stock-purchase plan and today over 85 per cent of the stock is owned by present or retired employees or their families. On July 23, 1968 the company merged with the Rexall Drug and Chemical Company.

Northland Aluminum Products

The housewares industry is able to provide America's homemakers with whatever specialized equipment they may need.

Does someone require a Scandinavian Krumkake Iron? Or Ebelskiver and Platte pans? Or maybe a Rosette iron or a Bundt cake mold? For any of these—and others—the place to go is Northland Aluminum Products Incorporated, Minneapolis, Minnesota. Perhaps no company in this business has done more in the way of specializing in such items—or been more successful in the process. In just twenty-five years a $5,000 investment has been developed into a $12 million utensil and mail order operation.

In 1946 three determined young men, Mark and David Dalquist and their long-time friend Donald Nygren, launched a firm called Plastics for Industry. They made foundry patterns and models from liquid phenolic resins.

176

The original old iron Bundt cake mold which was brought to Northland Aluminum Products in 1949 to be copied. Brought over from Europe years ago, its ancient vintage is clearly evident in the two weld marks where it has had to be repaired on occasion.

Courtesy Northland Aluminum Products Inc.

Thereafter their course seemed to steer itself into the housewares field. After they had developed the patterns for some of the specialized Scandinavian baking utensils they advertised them in local Swedish, Norwegian, and Danish newspapers. Response was so gratifying it resulted in the formation of a mail order division called Maid of Scandinavia.

The 1950s ushered in an era of acquisitions and continued expansion for the small company. At this time it acquired a small company along with the name Northland Aluminum Products, and since it was so much better suited to the changed character of the company, it officially replaced Plastics for Industry as its name. Also in the acquisition was the trade name "Nordic Ware" and two more specialty products now in the company's line as "Anodized Steak Platter-Holder Sets" and a "Two Burner Griddle."

A third corporation, now called Northland Metal Finishers Incorporated, was formed in 1963. It includes a wide variety of specialized industrial products and services in its operation including Vikron electronic devices.

Today Northland manufactures more than two hundred different items of aluminum. But none of them have achieved anything like the consumer acceptance and popularity of its now famous Bundt® cake mold. In fact, president David Dalquist says, a Bundt pan can be found in one out of every nine homes in the country. And it has become a Northland trademark.

Northland's Bundt story begins in 1949 when it was approached by a fund raising committee of women from the Twin Cities Chapter of Hadassah, the Women's Zionist Organization of America. They had with them an obviously very old, badly worn and patched iron bundt pan that had been handed down through several generations. Since it was impossible to buy the required baking pan for it in any retail store, the committee asked Northland to reproduce the pans in aluminum so they could raise funds for Hadassah by selling them.

The unique idea was an obvious success. In fact it was so successful that presently women were asking housewares salespeople for a "bundt" pan; salespeople asked their buyers; buyers found out that Northland made it—and the Bundt Cake Mold took off for the national best seller list. Today of course, it is made in so many ways and colors that the old original iron pan would never believe they are all from the same mold.

Pressure Cookers

In London on the evening of April 12, 1682, the august members of the Royal Society sat down to a meal such as they had never eaten before. It was a history-making occasion. The meal was cooked by a Frenchman, Denis Papin, who had been especially invited for that purpose. For a long time thereafter, the astonishing event was an important topic of conversation. Even John Evelyn recorded it in his well-known diary.

From top: The Papin Digester of 1682. Then, one of the first pressure cookers, a Canner Retort, made by Presto (then known as Northwestern Steel and Iron Works) in 1905. The lower photo shows a 1920s model, which looked more like a piece of industrial equipment than a housewares item for the home.

Top, courtesy Cambridge and County Folk Museum, Cambridge, England.

PEAS-PERFECTLY
COOKED IN
Flex-Seal
IN 1 MINUTE

Never before such speed in cooking—with foods tasting so marvelously good. FLEX-SEAL has revolutionized cooking, just as "talkies" outmoded old-style movies. Remember that peas, cauliflower, beans, potatoes — all vegetables — and the toughest meats are cooked lightning fast, look and taste "like a million" when they're cooked the FLEX-SEAL way. Write for proposition:

VISCHER PRODUCTS COMPANY
MERCHANDISE MART, CHICAGO

From top: Alfred Vischer, Jr., and his Flex-Seal pressure saucepan first introduced in 1938. It revolutionized the pressure cooker business.

Bottom, courtesy House Furnishing Review.

The cause of all the excitement? Papin had cooked the meal in a new device called the "digester," which he had invented two years earlier. The society, having heard of it, was eager to observe a demonstration, and the first formal pressure-cooker dinner followed. Few people understood the principles of the "digester." Because the heat of the fire and pressures were so poorly regulated, many experiments with the unusual new cooker ended in serious accidents.

The "digester" was almost completely forgotten until 1811. That year Napoleon ("An army moves on its stomach"), desperate to find an answer for supplying proper food to his fast-moving troops, offered a handsome prize for the solution to his problem. Nicholas Appert, one of the forefathers of modern canning, revived interest in the pressure method initiated by Papin and developed the first successful and practical use of this means of food preservation.

The end of the nineteenth century saw the home preserving of fruits and vegetables, primarily in glass screw-top or clamp-top jars, greatly increase in popularity. Good homemakers prided themselves on their skill and industriousness in "putting up" such produce for the long winter months ahead. Not infrequently, however, these preserves caused illness—even death—when the food was improperly processed.

In 1917 the United States Department of Agriculture exploded something of a bombshell when it officially announced that the only really safe way to process low-acid foods was to use a pressure canner. Immediately there was a widespread demand for such canners, and a number of firms, especially those with an aluminum foundry, began manufacturing pressure cooker-canners.

For example, National Presto Industries, formed in 1905, had long been making "canner retorts" for commercial canners. Since it had an aluminum foundry, it promptly began making a household version of its "retorts." The company then changed its name to the National Pressure Cooker Company. Another long-established member of the field was Wagner Manufacturing Company, which introduced its pressure cooker early in 1922.

However, although all those cookers functioned (and presumably provided the safety assurance mentioned by the Department of Agriculture), they all shared the same deficiencies. They were heavy and hard for a woman to handle. It was a tiresome chore to screw down—and then unscrew—the six or eight wing nuts on the lid each time the cooker was used. When not in use, the cooker required considerable storage space. Whatever virtues its effective performance may have offered were more than offset by its inconveniences.

But all that was destined to be changed by a man named Alfred Vischer, Jr. Vischer practically revolutionized the pressure cooker itself and, along with it, the pressure cooker business, by developing a relatively small pressure saucepan replacing the traditional big pressure pot cooker.

Vischer's story began in 1917—the same year that the Department of Agriculture issued its statement on the importance of pressure cooking for preserving certain foods. At that time Vischer, mechanically inclined even as a boy, was a draftsman for the National Electric Signalling Company. A rather casual remark to Vischer by the chief engineer of the company triggered his thinking.

"Alfred, why don't you design a simple pressure cooker?" he recalled his boss's casually asking him one day. "The ones now on the market are too heavy, too complicated, too expensive, and too dangerous."

On the lookout for a hobby, Vischer was intrigued by the idea of a better pressure cooker. Finally he decided to make one using the principle employed by early inventors of the locomotive. He would make the body of the cooker of vitreous enameled steel, but the cover would be made of aluminum. The difference in the thermal coefficient of expansion of the two metals would, he was confident, automatically make a self-sealing cooker perfectly steamtight when the boiling water heated the cover. The concept worked so well that its inventor soon headed his Selfseal Pressure Cooker Company.

"In 1927 I had to face up to two serious problems," Vischer recalled. "First, either I had to devote my time to selling my Selfseal cookers and let someone else handle manufacturing—or get someone else to take over sales while I handled production. But I couldn't do both.

"The second problem involved my infant daughter, who had developed a severe case of asthma, necessitating our moving from damp Long Island to the mountains somewhere."

He solved both problems by moving to Wellsville, New York, in the foothills of the Allegheny Mountains, and making an arrangement with the Victor Aluminum Company, located there, to make and sell his cooker, thus freeing all his time for sales. "By 1928," he continued, "Victor failed dismally to produce a good product, causing sales to slump; and they made conflicting sales agreements that resulted in lawsuits."

While awaiting trial in New York City he took a job as draftsman with a firm making stock tickers for Dow Jones. After just two months he found himself in the hospital with a ruptured appendix.

I had seven weeks to think of all the shortcomings in the design of the Selfseal pressure cooker—shortcomings of which only I was aware. I had learned by then that an ideal pressure cooker would be one in which the force exerted by the steam pressure alone would make it steamtight, instead of the differential expansion idea covered by my patent.

So I decided I'd better solve the problem before someone beat me to a solution. I started solving it by sending my nurse to a nearby grocery for a carton of Quaker Oats—the kind that comes in a round box. After discarding the oats, I cut a hole in the top of the box, but left a one-half-inch edge to simulate the flange on the inside edge of a cooking pot. Then, from another flat piece of cardboard, I cut out a "lid"—but made it one-quarter inch larger in diameter than the hole

Kochfix

. . . it's the BLACK POT

HIT OF CHICAGO WORLD'S FAIR
and
1934 OUTSTANDING DEALER HIT ITEM

THE Qwick Cooker roasts a dinner in 10 minutes including meat and four vegetables.

Recommended by leading physicians because when foods are cooked in KOCHFIX they retain their mineral salts, vitamins, calories and individual flavors. Saves 75% in fuel and time.

Leading stores report KOCHFIX is one of the leading sellers.

Write now and make arrangements for demonstration and get in on KOCHFIX profits.

HOUSEHOLD SPECIALTIES, Inc.
327 S. La Salle Street . . . . Chicago

179

"ONLY SAFE CANNING METHOD"
SAYS U.S. GOVERNMENT

OVER 2,000,000 PRESSURE COOKERS IN USE FOR BOTH CANNING and COOKING

SAVE ¾ FUEL

COOK ENTIRE MEAL OVER ONE BURNER, TURNED LOW

The only safe method of canning meat, fish and non-acid vegetables.

WITH EVERY NATIONAL COMPLETE INSTRUCTIONS FOR COOKING AND CANNING

CHICKEN DINNER WITH VEGETABLES AND DESSERT 15 MIN

COOKS WITHOUT WATER

The Genuine and Only
NATIONAL PRESSURE COOKER

Learn the way to thrift and better living by using the safest, easiest canning method known—with the National Pressure Cooker. Don't be confused by other cookers made to resemble it. There is only ONE National Pressure Cooker.

SAVE FOOD FORMERLY WASTED

SPECIAL CANNER A new National Pressure Cooker designed especially for canning. Equipped with a wire basket and two cooking pans. Holds 20 No. 3 cans or 10 No. 4 cans. Ask to see it.

It's easy to can vegetables, fruits and meats the National Pressure way. Can your surplus food products and save money. Meals are also prepared so easily in this Pressure Cooker. No water used. Food cooks in steam of its own juices, retaining delicious natural flavors and healthful vitamins. Complete directions for cooking and canning come with every National.

A NATIONAL TO SUIT EVERY FAMILY

Before you buy any cooker, see the National Pressure Cooker in its various sizes to suit any family. Be sure it's a genuine National and is made by the makers of approximately 90% of all pressure cookers used in America.

National
PRESSURE COOKER COMPANY
EAU CLAIRE, WISCONSIN

ASK TO SEE THE IMPROVED CAN SEALER

New Seal-O Matic can sealer is scientifically automatic, seals tin cans as factory seals them. Also opens cans. Same cans may be used repeatedly.

LOOK FOR NAME The genuine has National Pressure Cooker, Eau Claire, Wisconsin, stamped on lid.

ASK YOUR DEALER

From top: Ads for pressure cookers emphasized their nutritional benefits as well as safety in canning. Northwestern Steel and Iron changed its name to National Pressure Cooker when it started making cookers for home use.

Top, courtesy House Furnishing Review.

From top: In 1946, Landers, Frary & Clark had their Universal name on a pressure cooker. Presto introduced the electric pressure cooker, a non-submersible model, in 1954. Two years later it was made with a removable control unit, as shown in the lower picture. The pan could be immersed for cleaning. Presto is the only maker of electric pressure cookers.

Top, courtesy House Furnishing Review.

I had cut in the round box top. Somehow, I was determined, the larger diameter "lid" would have to fit into the smaller hole in the "pot" —and then and there I conceived the Flex-Seal Speed Cooker.

It was accomplished, of course, by means of a flexible stainless steel lid which, when curved, slid sideways into the pot and then, flexed into place by its handle, fit snugly against the underside of the flanged edge of the pot. A special gasket helped to make the seal absolutely steam tight.

He tried to sell his new idea—and struck out three times. Automatic Canning Devices, Bellaire Enamel Works, and finally the Vollrath Company, all rejected his Flex-Seal Speed Cooker. Although Vischer had learned how to make the unusual covers on an experimental basis, producing them in quantity proved the stumbling block.

By March of 1938 the Vischer Products Company had been incorporated. By June the first samples were ready and were promptly put on display in the hopeful young firm's booth at the American Home Economics Association convention in Pittsburgh.

In the fall of 1938 the new Flex-Seal cooker was exhibited at the New York Premium Show in the Hotel Astor, where the most interested visitor was Mrs. Bessie Bissinger, housewares buyer for the Schuster Department Stores in Milwaukee. She was determined to have Schuster's present the Flex-Seal cooker first!

From then on sales mushroomed, and the cooker began to attract competition. National Pressure Cooker Company brought out a saucepan model it called "Presto," and Mirro Aluminum Company introduced its "Mirromatic" saucepan cooker. Meanwhile, in 1941, Vischer announced that Landers, Frary and Clark and the Aluminum Cooking Utensil Company had been licensed to produce Flex-Seal cookers after the war.

During the war the Vischer plant was working to capacity turning out stainless steel pressure cookers at the rate of ten thousand a month, exclusively for military use. But the day the war was over "competition really started in earnest. Almost overnight, eighty-five competitive pressure saucepans flooded the market—a market now clamoring for a pressure cooker to emulate the performance of Flex-Seal."

But quality varied as widely as prices. "Soon the bottom fell out of the prices, and it was not long before cheap, dangerous merchandise forced home pressure cookers off the general market." Vischer, of course, was also seriously affected by this contagious negative attitude on the part of homemakers.

To make up for the sales losses in the home market, a commercial cooker was developed. Although it failed to excite restaurateurs at the National Restaurant Show at Chicago's Navy Pier in 1952, medical men were intrigued by its possibilities as a sterilizer. As a result a contract was made with the Wilmot Castle Company of Rochester, New York, which, on an exclusive basis, purchased over one hundred thousand Vischer sterilizers in the next few years.

Eventually, on July 15, 1969, the Vischer Products Company was sold to the Hobart Manufacturing Company, Troy, Ohio, which now owns all its assets, including patents and trademarks.

Of all the hopefuls who entered cooker business after World War II, only Presto and Mirro, stayed with it. As a result, they now share the very sizable volume into which this important utensil has developed—or to be more accurate, into which their consistent advertising and promotional efforts have developed it.

Low Pressure Cookers

An interesting and important sidelight of the pressure cooker story is the tale of the short-lived but complicated low-pressure cooker. In 1884 a firm called the Peerless Cooker Company was formed in Buffalo, New York, by Charles E. Swartzbaugh, Sr. It was incorporated for $10,000 and organized to manufacture a then unique low-pressure steam cooker, a method of cooking whereby a homemaker could cook a complete meal over one burner on the then prevalent wood- and coal-burning stoves.

The original model consisted of a covered six-quart pot of heavy gauge tin equipped with an "extension" unit that fit snugly on top to increase its capacity when desired. The outside bottom of the pot was copper.

The cookers were sold by direct mail and also by house-to-house salesmen. The company probably had about five hundred sales agents, covering practically every state. To simplify their presentation each salesman was equipped with a portable miniature replica of the cooker. No exact volume figures are available, but Ted B. Swartzbaugh, one of the founder's sons now retired in Fort Lauderdale, Florida, estimates that at least two million were sold.

Fireless Cookers

The idea of conserving fuel by cooking a whole meal over one burner stimulated the elder Swartzbaugh's inventive ingenuity to other applications of that principle, and presently he announced a new invention—the "Fireless Cooker."

181

This Woman and 29 Others

comprising our traveling organization of 30 trained demonstrators.

Stage the Biggest Merchandising Events

in the house-furnishing goods field. They demonstrate

"IDEAL" and "DOMESTIC SCIENCE" Fireless Cookstoves

and their application to household economics, scientific home management, house-keeping efficiency, better cooking, etc., brings crowds to your store because these subjects are foremost today in the minds of those who have to solve the household problem. It not only sells "Ideal" and "Domestic Science" Fireless Cookstoves but is a drawing card for the entire store.

You can see what a rip-roaring, interest-arousing campaign such an attraction offers.

Let us open up the sale of fireless cookstoves in your store with one of these demonstrations.

THE CLUB PLAN of selling our fireless cookstoves is another TRADE WINNER.

Dealers tell us that our demonstrations and the club plan of selling (which can be worked separately or jointly) bring people to the store who never before were customers.

Write us for full details. We further co-operate with national advertising, dealers' helps, etc.

Write us for prices, catalogues, etc.

Do not delay, get in right with this line and be headquarters in your locality for these goods.

We also manufacture "IDEAL" aluminum cooking utensils, famous for their "Beauty–Service–Satisfaction"; and the IDEAL STEAM COOKER.

Address Sales Department

The Toledo Cooker Co.
Toledo, Ohio

Top: There was a market for fireless cookers in 1917. But by 1925, all fireless cookers were discontinued because of the development of the electric roaster. *At left:* A 1910 Sears catalog entry for a steam cooker with room for a whole meal in one unit.

Above, courtesy House Furnishing Review.

ECONOMICAL STEAM COOKER, $4⁸⁷

AT THIS REDUCED PRICE YOUR SAVING IS GREATER THAN EVER.

CAN YOU AFFORD TO DO WITHOUT AN ECONOMICAL COOKER WHEN IT SAVES THREE TIMES ITS COST IN FUEL ALONE DURING THE YEAR?

YOU CAN COOK ONIONS, CABBAGE, POTATOES AND PUDDING

in the Economical Cooker at the same time, and with less fuel than it would require to cook any one of them in the old way. Any combination of foods you desire can be cooked in this wonderful cooker with no danger of one smelling or tasting like another. The Economical Cooker is steam tight. The steam rises to the condensing dome at the top of the cooker, which is so constructed that the condensed steam runs back down the sides to the tank and does not drip on the food. It is impossible to burn or scorch food in the Economical Cooker, it requires but little attention, is equipped with whistle which begins to blow fifteen minutes before the tank boils dry, thus allowing ample time to refill the tank, and a self-regulating valve which holds the steam under pressure and makes it cook twice as quickly as the ordinary steam cooker. Food cooked in an Economical Steam Cooker loses nothing in evaporation, but retains all its savory juices.

THE ECONOMICAL STEAM COOKER is made of heavy XX (best grade) charcoal tin, has copper tank and will last a lifetime. It works equally well on wood, coal, oil, gas or gasoline stoves and has thick walls which retain the heat a long time after the fire is extinguished, thus keeping the food hot till it is ready to serve. The Economical has the greatest capacity of any cooker on the market. It is especially convenient for canning fruit. It will hold at one time a dozen 1-quart Mason jars, and cook the fruit perfectly. The Economical is easy to clean, and cuts the household work in half. The Economical Cooker has two swing doors, four compartments and we furnish with it two heavy seamless cooking pans. The Economical measures 12 inches square, 22 inches high and weighs, crated, about 20 pounds. Steam cookers that are in every way inferior to our Economical are sold by retailers and agents all over the country for from $8.50 to $10.00 each.

NO. 9K23843   Economical Steam Cooker, complete with instruction book containing 200 tested recipes.   Price...... **$4.87**

A hinged cover sealed the top of the container. Called the Ideal or Domestic Science Fireless Cookers, they functioned on the theory that when a previously heated aluminum pot of food was placed into the well (into which it was designed to fit snugly), the food would continue to cook from the heat tightly sealed inside.

"About 1918," Ted Swartzbaugh recalled, "we electrified the fireless cooker by means of a plug-in hot plate in the base. A bellows type of thermostat in the cover of the unit turned off the heat automatically to prevent burning."

But all fireless cookers, both electric and non electric, were discontinued about 1925 because something better was being developed.

Electric Roasters

The "something better" was the Everhot electric cooker Swartzbaugh developed in 1924. The company had contracted to produce 50,000 six-quart capacity thermic or insulated jugs for an eastern firm. In the course of production one of the engineers devised a way to electrify them.

After wrapping a thin asbestos pad around the outer wall of one of the jugs, he wound six hundred inches of electric wire, evenly spaced, over the asbestos. The whole outer wall was then covered with a special soapstone cement, and that in turn was covered with mineral wool insulation and an enameled steel casing that sealed everything in place. When the jug was plugged into an electric current, the wires heated up and produced uniform heat that was forced inward without developing any concentrated hot spots. The large amount of wire used prevented the wire from ever becoming hot enough to glow red; when the control switch was set at "high" it never exceeded 350 watts, and on "low" it was 100 watts. Since the imbedded wires could never touch each other it was impossible for them to arc or burn out, so it was virtually service free.

But it had one weakness—at least from the company's standpoint. Apparently there was no way the new item could be protected with patents. As a result, the introduction of these cookers sparked the development of a whole family of similar competitive products.

Ted Swartzbaugh pegs the start of this competitive race as 1932, when Al Smith, an enterprising promoter with some engineering background, took one of the cookers to the National Enameling and Stamping Company in Milwaukee. He sold them on copying it in a two-quart capacity unit and promptly announced it as the "Nesco Casserole." That started a competitive game of one-upmanship which later attracted other manufacturers. Swartzbaugh recalled:

> We met Nesco's move by bringing out a 3½-quart capacity casserole which boasted a thermostat control and a cooking pot that could readily be removed for easy cleaning. Nesco than came out with an oval model of six-quart capacity—so we went them one better with an eight-quart oval roaster. Then Nesco jumped to a ten-quart job.

Presenting ★ ★ ★

OUR NEW MODEL 900
Electric Roaster

— *Shipments Soon* —

● The advanced Everhot Electric Roaster, embodying unique, startling features of design, construction and performance combined with traditional Everhot quality and dependability is now ready for distribution . . . Completely engineered — thoroughly tested this new Everhot fully meets the expectation of dealer and consumer for extraordinary post-war advancement in such utilities.

Features That Make Sales

Advanced styling brings new beauty and symmetry to cabinet and roaster ensemble presenting sheer, easily cleaned surfaces, artistic trimmings, toe-in plate, and rigid reinforced door with concealed handle.

● Observation glass in lid.
● Combination in-built revolving temperature guide and cooking time-chart.
● New-type air and moisture control gives better flavor and appearance to all foods.
● Stain-proof cover.
● Turn-a-knob mechanical cover lifter.
● Deeper roasting pan assures more uniform cooking and better browning.
● Stainless steel covers for all utensils.
● In-built timer clock control optional.

The Swartzbaugh Mfg. Company . . . Toledo 6, Ohio
AUTHORIZED WHOLESALERS IN ALL MARKETS

EVERHOT
PRODUCTS
ROASTERS.. HEATERS.. APPLIANCES

This is a 1945 model of Swartzbaugh Manufacturing Company's Everhot roaster. The firm developed the first electric cooker in 1924.

Courtesy House Furnishing Review.

182

Finally we decided to bring out a rectangular roaster, first with a lift-off cover and then one with a hinged cover and a heat-control knob. By this time other manufacturers had come into the market and soon the "roaster" had been so improved and had become so versatile that in addition to merely roasting one could also use it to broil, barbecue, grill, fry, steam, bake—and even do cold-pack preserving.

Besides the basic improvements in the product, all sorts of accessories appeared, from automatic time clocks to special utensils and stands and cabinets that served as a base for the roaster.

The electric timing device was an exclusive Swartzbaugh development, Ted continued. Until 1930 all timing devices were ordinary clock mechanisms.

Swartzbaugh made many thousands of its roasters under contract for Westinghouse and General Electric. It also made various other appliances under the "Everhot" name, such as hot plates, waffle irons, broilers, and the original "Ray-vector" heaters. And it made much commercial and hospital equipment. "One reason the roasters became so popular," Ted explained, "is that they were often ahead of electric ranges in convenience and refinements. But as ranges improved, roaster sales began to drop. The smaller size of modern kitchens also tended to hurt sales. Roasters still sell, but primarily at Thanksgiving and Christmas."

By 1951 the Swartzbaugh Manufacturing Company had become the second oldest company in Toledo. But about that time a great deal of labor trouble developed at its plants, and it decided to sell the "Everhot" name, along with all the tools and dies, to the McGraw Electric Company.

Lalance and Grosjean

1855 was the year that the remarkable firm of Lalance and Grosjean was founded in Brooklyn by two young men from France. That immigrant enterprise was to become the largest and most prestigious of its kind in the country, surviving a variety of panics and depressions and no less than four wars—for each of which it was called upon to supply matériel. Then, in 1955, just one hundred years after it began, "L & G" found itself obliged to sell all its assets at auction and close its doors for good. Its story is fascinating for the American houseware industry in general and of particular interest to the cooking utensil business. Charles Lalance and Florian Grosjean first became associates in 1850 when they opened a small store in New York's Wall Street area and imported champagne, along with a smattering of household goods. "But why bother importing what we can make here?" they asked themselves after Grosjean had been granted patents on some corrugated-handle tinned spoons and forks. They then started a small, four-man factory on the lower East Side and the entrepreneurs were on their way to fortune.

The records of those early years are bare of any but the scantiest information about the company or its founders. Grosjean, seems to have been the dominating partner. He is said to have been born in

Florian Grosjean, one of the pioneer manufacturers of enamelware in America and one of the founders of Lalance & Grosjean.
Courtesy House Furnishing Review.

This TRADE MARK on

KITCHEN UTENSILS

IS A SIGN OF
Safety and Quality
We Make 1520 Kinds

NO POISON

Has Ever Been Found in the Enamel of
AGATE NICKEL-STEEL WARE

The BLUE LABEL

Protected by Decision of U. S. Court, pasted
on every piece, *Proves It.* If substitutes are offered, write us. *Sold by Firstclass
Department and Housefurnishing Stores.*
SEND FOR NEW BOOKLET

Lalance & Grosjean Mfg. Co.
NEW YORK   BOSTON   CHICAGO

LOSSES BY FIRE.

DESTRUCTION OF THE LALANCE AND GROS-
JEAN MANUFACTORY AT WOODHAVEN,
LONG ISLAND—LOSS $460,000.

A fire which destroyed over four hundred
thousand dollars' worth of property, and which will
cause nearly three hundred people to be thrown out
of employment, occurred at Woodhaven, near
Jamaica, Long Island, yesterday morning. The
property consumed was owned by the Lalance and
Grosjean Manufacturing Company of this City.

From top: The Lalance & Grosjean trademark for kitchen utensils. Then, part of *The New York Times* item about the disastrous fire at the L&G plant. The item appeared in the February 22, 1876, edition of the newspaper. The largest deep-drawing press for a stainless steel alloy was this one at the Lalance & Grosjean plant. It was so big that the building in which it stood had to be built around it after it was erected.

Switzerland in 1824. Very little is known about Charles Lalance.

Convinced by their Hester Street venture that they were on the right track, they formally began their major manufacturing effort in Brooklyn in 1855, but soon encountered growing pains from lack of space. In 1863, no longer able to keep up with the demand for their products—which consisted primarily of tin and stamped iron utensils—they decided to move "out to the country" in Woodhaven, Long Island—now one of the area's most densely populated sections. At its peak the plant employed about two thousand people.

In 1869 the original partnership was dissolved and a joint stock company formed under the same name. It was in this period that the company succeeded—simultaneously with Jacob Vollrath in Sheboygan and the St. Louis Stamping Company—in developing a process for the manufacture of porcelain enamel cooking utensils.

The company prospered beyond anything its founders had imagined. But on the night of February 21, 1876, fire destroyed the entire plant. Undaunted, the owners immediately set about rebuilding it, even bigger and better.

L & G's primary products in those years were of gray-mottled porcelain enamelware which it marketed under the brand name of "Agate Ware," a term that became so widely used that it served as a generic name for all similar enamelware. There was hardly a kitchen in the country that didn't have at least one piece of Agate Ware on its oilcloth-covered shelves. Protected by patents, the company was its exclusive manufacturer for about seventeen years.

The company provided equipment and supplies for the government during the Civil War and the Spanish American War, just as it would in the upcoming world wars. By this time it was recognized as one of the most skilled manufacturers in the country in know-how for metal stampings and especially deep drawings. Under the prideful guidance of Florian Grosjean, the company had always watched quality. There were times when it was obliged to auction off ten thousand cases of "enamelware seconds"—an action that clearly reflects its determination about what constituted first quality. Agate Ware had always been triple-dipped.

After World War I, European factories eager to help themselves, if not their countries, get back on their economic feet began flooding America with cheap enamelware. Import figures tripled and quadrupled while prices dropped lower and lower. L & G refused to get into a price war, and rather than start cutting quality and prices it simply lowered production.

The company had already been hit hard from another quarter. With the end of the war came the end of government orders for the services. And since the war-expanded steel industry could now turn out steel sheets more cheaply than ever, the L & G Harrisburg mill, which had been rolling about nine hundred tons a month, was no longer profitable and had to be sold.

At some point in this period, though just when is not clear, the

Woodhaven plant's production was curtailed more and more, and finally all manufacturing was moved to a much smaller plant in Long Island City, just across the river from New York City. During this period too—the 1920s—August J. Cordier, grandson of Florian Grosjean, became president of the company. "He was the 'go-getter' type," Elliot V. Walter of Macy's related not long before his death in 1971. "He had been a captain in World War I, had a fine personality, and was trying hard to turn the fortunes of the company around."

One of his greatest hopes for the survival of the venerable enterprise was the alluring gleam of stainless steel, then just beginning to beam its hopeful rays across the marketplace.

The management, emulating the shining, armor-clad crusader that was their trademark for the new stainless ware, ignored the gathering perils of the depression. But meanwhile, competition—like the new Revere Ware, to mention just one line—began cutting in. And on top of it all President "Gus" Cordier suddenly died of a heart attack.

World War II came and for the fourth time the skills and energies of L & G were directed toward supplying equipment and supplies to the armed forces, this time largely in the field it had come to know best, stainless steel. The war ended, and not too long after, for a combination of reasons, the end of the long, eventful road this remarkable company had traveled in the course of a century came into sight. In 1955 there was an auction sale, and when the final bid was hammered down it sounded the death knell of Lalance and Grosjean.

Stainless Steel—Revere Ware

Revere Ware provides a copper-bright example of modern cookware and of how one man's determination transformed what seemed like complete failure into glittering success.

Revere Copper and Brass, Incorporated, had long had a hand (if not an arm) in the cooking utensil field. As early as 1890 this Rome, New York, company, whose antecedents go back to Paul Revere, had been making copper pots, pans, pitchers, and other items which, to be usable, were lined with tin. Surprisingly, in the early 1920s this company also began producing a "full" line of aluminumware. In the late 1920s a "short" line of solid copper electric coffee makers was added; the depression of the thirties ended the venture. But that's getting away from the main story.

It starts with an enterprising inventor and promoter, Chester M. McCreery, who had done very well in the development of the first six-wheeled trucks for army use in World War I. He came back from a European vacation excited about developing copper cookware in this country like the items he had seen abroad. Since tin coating left much to be desired, he reasoned, why not chrome-plate the copper instead? Understandably he went directly to Revere—and was hired to develop the idea.

Revere's Contempora, a three-ply stainless steel cookware set introduced in 1971. As early as 1890 this company was making tin-lined copper pots, pans, and pitchers.

This was in the early 1930s, just about the time Donald Dallas, then president of Revere, sent his brilliant young assistant and protégé, James Kennedy, to the factory. "Go up to Rome [New York] and produce something worthwhile," he told the man who would soon become general manager of the Rome Manufacturing Division —and eventually president of Revere. What Kennedy did in Rome is well described by Isaac Marcosson in *Copper Heritage:*

> [When] it was discovered that chrome plating of any quality would be affected by the action of vegetable acids...Kennedy stopped the manufacture and sale of those items [and] created a Development Department to check and analyze all metals and combinations thereof in an effort to find a perfect cooking utensil. After almost endless tests, stainless steel proved to have the qualities needed....There was a hitch, however, because stainless steel lacked heat conductivity. The big problem was how to solve it.
>
> Kennedy had an inspiration. He knew that copper was the best commercial metal to distribute heat, so he reasoned: "Why not marry copper and stainless steel? Deposit copper on the outside bottom of the utensil and you will have the happy combination.[1]

But the problem turned out to be highly technical and difficult. It was necessary to use a copper deposit about one and half times as thick as the stainless steel material that composed the body of the utensil and to have the two indissolubly wedded. It was a marriage that precluded divorce. By February 1937, around-the-clock work in the Revere laboratories had finally produced an absolutely adherent plate. The final step was to deposit a smooth, heavy plate of copper thicker than the steel itself.

The cookware line was designed by A. Archibald Welden, Revere's director of design, and, in honor of the founder of America's copper industry, was named Revere Ware. Introduced at the Chicago Housewares Show in 1938, it created something of a sensation.

When it reached the retail counters it was an immediate success: Revere Ware suddenly became a "must" for brides. Just as suddenly, the beginning of America's involvement in World War II put an end to production.

After World War II, production of Revere Ware skyrocketed. Nothing quite like it had ever happened in the cooking utensil business. Revere "was cooking on all burners." It had demonstrated dramatically that American homemakers appreciated high-quality utensils and were able and willing to pay a good price for them.

The new Clinton plant had just about gotten under way when the Korean crisis broke out and, instead of cookware, Revere found itself making steel cartridge cases.

Chester McCreery, by then a vice-president in charge of the Rome Manufacturing, Riverside, and Clinton divisions, had directed Revere's entire marketing effort. His advocacy of Fair Trade and his development of a cooperative advertising program with dealers went far to help build the impressive image Revere Ware enjoyed.

But then that image began to fade—and so did sales. Just what

186

brought about the change is uncertain. This stainless steel-copper line was a glittering target for competition. In the early 1950s D. E. Sanford Company began a high-powered promotion on the West coast of the imported Le Creuset line of brightly colored porcelain enamelware. Californians loved it; it was new and colorful, and presently it was outselling Revere Ware.

In the East, S. W. Farber, Incorporated, was introducing its new line of Farberware aluminum-clad stainless steel with intensive store demonstrations. Like the Le Creuset ware, there was no copper bottom to polish. It too made steady, if sometimes slow, inroads into Revere's dominant position.

And then in 1958 what many think was the chief cause of Revere's fall from the top of the cookware shelf was the decision to drop its well-entrenched "Fair Trade" (or legal resale price maintenance) policy, perhaps prompted by a similar move by General Electric's housewares division. General Electric, it will be recalled, was the loser in a Fair Trade lawsuit brought by Masters discount stores.

With increasing competition, the arrival of more imported lines, and the advent of discount stores, things became steadily rougher for Revere Ware. There were management changes: John H. Eikenberg, Sr., who had come up through the copper rolling mill division of the company, succeeded to the presidency in 1961. In 1966 Clyde E. McDannald was named a vice-president and assigned the difficult task of restoring Revere Ware's position. Commenting on the situation in an interview with McDannald in the fall of 1969, *Home Furnishing Daily* stated:

> As in classical tragedy, Revere's fall was the result of hubris—the sin of overweening pride…the belief that one line could be all things to all retailers….The results [after taking its line off Fair Trade] were disastrous….Department stores discontinued it and the prestige that had accompanied the Revere name began to tarnish. In desperation the firm began to introduce one new line after another, dropping them as rapidly when they failed to please the gods of the marketplace.

Then McDannald began replacing Revere salesmen with manufacturers sales agents, policies firmed up, sales began to build, and market penetration grew. During the interim John Eikenberg became chairman of Revere, and in 1970, when McDannald resigned, John M. Eikenberg, Jr., was named group vice-president in charge of the cookware division. James Evans, formerly with General Electric, was named to replace McDannald and another former General Electric man, William Austin, became national sales manager.

Key stores that had practically dropped the line again featured it. The factory at Rome which had shut down for lack of business was reactivated in 1971 and scheduled to work full-time. The time was again ripe—copper-bottom stainless steel utensils, especially with the Revere name, meshed beautifully with the growing demand for "gourmet" cookware. After its temporary tarnish Revere regained its bright luster in the marketplace.

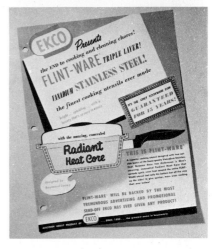

From top: One of the features of stainless steel cooking utensils was its ability to not discolor foods, even when left in a pan overnight. Ekco lauded the even-heating capabilities of its Flint-Ware triple layer line of stainless steel ware.

**By Popular Demand
For Sales!**

Here it is—a "Best Seller" according to the popular demand for the new McKee Range-tec Glass top-of-stove ware. It's made for the hot spot, either direct flame contact on top of the range, or for the buyer who is wondering how to maintain his stock of cooking utensils.

McKee Range-tec, by the makers of Glasbake, the largest line of glass ovenware in the world, is the answer. Write the factory for the new catalog, prices, counter displays, or ask our district representative to show you Range-tec.

GLASBAKE

McKEE GLASS COMPANY
Makers of "GLASBAKE"
Established 1853, Jeannette, Pa.

188

From top: Stoneware was once an essential in American kitchens. The Minnesota Stoneware Company in Red Wing made the largest and best-known line. The all-glass Range-tec skillet was advertised by the McKee Glass Company in trade papers in 1942. McKee had been licensed by Corning in 1921 to make ovenware under the Pyrex patents. McKee is now part of the Jeanette Corporation. The bottom photo shows one of Jeanette's current line of ovenware.

*Top, courtesy Minnesota Historical Society.
Middle, courtesy House Furnishing Review.*

Glass Cooking Utensils

"One of the most time-honored traditions of the household is the belief in the fragility and aloofness of glass," *House Furnishing Review* asserted in February 1920.

In the half century since that was written, glass utensils, of course, have not only become commonplace in the home, but the technology of glass/ceramic utensils has reached heights never even imagined in those days. Although heat-resistant glass had been developed in Germany by the end of the last century, it remained for an American company, the Corning Glass Works, to carry the concept further.

After Corning introduced its Pyrex ovenware in 1915, it licensed the Fry Glass Company in 1920 and the McKee Glass Company in 1921 to make it. Fry went out of business in 1933. For some years until it went out of business in the late 1940s, the Dunbar Glass Corporation, Dunbar, West Virginia, made glass cookware too.

Jeannette Corporation

The Jeannette Corporation, founded in the Pennsylvania city of that name in 1898, and now the largest manufacturer producing exclusively low-priced pressed table and kitchen ware in the U.S., got into the glass cooking utensil business via the acquisition route. In 1961 it purchased the McKee Glass Company and the well known "Glasbake" ovenware in order to round out its operations.

In 1921 McKee was licensed by Corning Glass Works to use its new formula for making ovenware and it introduced the "Glasbake" name on its own line of such utensils. Later, when Corning developed top-of-the-stove glass cookware, McKee was also licensed to make that and introduced a line of "Range-Tec" cookware.

Other acquisitions followed and in 1963 the company put in operation the world's largest electrically operated tank for the production of white heat resisting glass and in 1972 began building a second such tank. The corporation's sales in 1971 were $27,817,000.

ANCHOR HOCKING GLASS AND FIRE KING

The Anchor Hocking Glass Corporation of Lancaster, Ohio was established in 1905 and was primarily engaged in the production of glass containers, glass tableware and giftware. About 1940, it began the production of a line of "Fire-King" glass ovenware which it still markets under that brand. Originally light blue in color, over the years its color and shapes were often changed. For example, in the mid-forties it was changed to green and later to a straw yellow. In 1948 the first ivory colored Fire-King ovenware appeared and in 1951 the first crystal was introduced. At about that time ivory gave way to white and since then the line has been basically crystal and white. In recent years the white has been embellished with a series of decorations.

The Corning Glass Works

Soon after he arrived one morning in 1913 at the Corning Glass Works Research Laboratory in Corning, New York where he worked, a young scientist surprised his co-workers by offering them some cake. It was delicious, they acknowledged between bites—but cake in the morning? What was the special occasion?

"You fellows laughed at me when I suggested that you could cook in glass, so I've brought you first-hand evidence," explained Dr. J. T. Littleton, who later became vice-president and director of research at Corning. He had cut off the lower part of a glass battery jar and had his wife bake a cake in it. Actually it was a very special occasion, though none of them realized it, for it marked the start of Pyrex brand ovenware.

The results of Dr. Littleton's venture into gastronomical glassware promptly started the Corning laboratory staff off on a search for a glass formula more perfectly suited to that specific purpose. It succeeded far beyond all hopes.

Contrary to popular opinion, the Corning Glass Works, the leading producer of specialty glass, did not originate in Corning. It traces its beginning to Somerville, Massachusetts where, in 1851, Amory Houghton and some associates first established a glass business. (Incidentally, the 1972 chairman of the board and chief executive officer, Amory Houghton, Jr., is the great, great grandson of the founder.)

In 1864, Houghton and his two sons purchased the Brooklyn Flint Glass Works in Brooklyn, New York where they specialized in producing glass blanks for the manufacturers of cut glass tableware which was becoming popular. But the business didn't prosper and four years later, when a group of Corning businessmen invited the Houghtons to move upstate where coal was ample and rail as well as canal transportation excellent, they accepted. There it was renamed the Corning Flint Glass Works.

Following financial difficulties in 1875 it was incorporated as Corning Glass Works and began to concentrate on specialty glass products. One of these was hand-blown glass light bulbs for Edison's new incandescent lamp in 1880. Its commitment to specialty products—as opposed to making bottles or window glass—prompted it in 1908 to engage a young chemist, Dr. Eugene C. Sullivan, to organize a research laboratory for the company, the first in the glass industry and one of the first in American industry.

Continued research has been a major factor in the company's growth. In 1971 it reported sales of over $603 million, of which about $178.5 million or 30 percent was in consumer goods. How well its continued investment of what has been called "patient money" in research has paid off is revealed in its 1971 financial report which states "As a measure of the importance of this effort, 27% of today's total business comes from products introduced within the last five years."

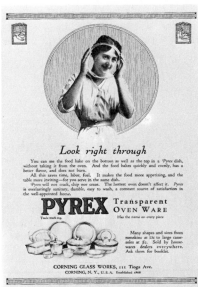

189

From top: The bottom of a glass battery jar, cut off like this, served as the baking dish in which Dr. Littleton's wife tried his idea of baking in glass in 1913. It led to the creation of Pyrex ovenware two years later. One of the first consumer ads on Pyrex ovenware; it ran in *National Geographic* in September 1916.

It considers glass an engineering material and in as much as it can be made using practically all the elements in the atomic table it considers the number of possible combinations as being almost infinite. For example it recently perfected a new type of glass that automatically darkens when exposed to bright light but resumes its normal clarity when the bright light is gone; it is a quality this type of glass retains permanently. The scope of the company's products is enormous, touching virtually every field of human activity and its operations are world-wide.

It was Dr. Sullivan and his associate, Dr. William C. Taylor, who in 1915 began to seriously explore the ideas Dr. Littleton had suggested. They were the ones whose previous work had developed Corning's heat-resistant glasses. Dr. Sullivan, who later became honorary vice-chairman of Corning's board of directors, was chief chemist at that time, and Dr. Taylor was then a chemist on Dr. Sullivan's staff. It was those two scientists whose work resulted in the new famous Sullivan-Taylor patents, applied for in 1915 and granted in 1919. One patent covers a series of borosilicate glasses which were heat resistant; the other covered a heat-resistant glass baking dish. (Sullivan and Taylor did not originate borosilicate glass; it had been invented by Schott in Europe in 1892. But this was the first specialized formulation for ovenware.)

The manufacture and marketing of this revolutionary new cookware had begun at the same time the patent applications were filed in 1915. It was decided to name it "Pyrex," not as many people believe, in keeping with the Greek "Pyra," meaning hearth, but because of the humble English word "pie" since the first product to be made was a nine-inch pie plate. Public acceptance for these new cooking utensils developed quickly.

Meanwhile Corning had started operations in a new plant in Tennessee. But then the so-called "inventory depression" hit the country, the bottom fell out of Pyrex ware sales and a few months after it started the new plant was shut down.

In 1919, a year in which over 4½ million pieces of Pyrex ware was sold "the glass was thick and heavy, and cords and blisters often marred its appearance, though they didn't affect the service of the ware," the company magazine, *The Gaffer* reported in 1946.

Another serious problem the company encountered was perfecting equipment whereby this new cookware could be made automatically—and thus quicker and cheaper. While an enormous press, "Big Bertha" had been built, not until 1927 was feeder equipment perfected that would handle the new types of borosilicate glasses that Pyrex ware demanded.

Pyrex has proved its excellence beyond any question in baking utensils. But cooking involves more than baking and if glass was to really become a contender for the cookware business it would have to be usable for top-of-the-stove cooking on an open flame. In 1931 during the depths of the Great Depression, when research funds

From top: A contemporary line of Pyrex ovenware. And Corning's Cook-Ahead set, featuring the idea of preparing and freezing a meal in dishes that can go directly from the freezer to the range and on to the table.

190

were one of the first casualties in most corporate budgets, Corning persisted in its research. It paid off, and in 1936 it announced Pyrex flameware. Now glass cooking utensils could be used for top-of-the-stove cooking as well as for baking.

Probably nothing has contributed more—or possibly as much, some say—to the success Corning has had with Pyrex and later with its other consumer products, than its marketing policy. Basically, the policy is based on the theory that unless all those that handle the line can make a reasonable profit for their efforts, and unless the policy is fair in every respect and treats all of a similar type of trade on a like basis, Corning would ultimately be hurt the most.

A New Glass Material: Corning Ware

In 1953 a Corning scientist, Dr. Donald Stookey, after completing some unusual experiments, produced a remarkable new ceramic-like glass material, the properties of which were amazing. By changing the batch formulation and the heating schedule he found that it could be varied widely; in fact he had found a whole new family of basic engineering materials possibly as versatile as glass itself. It was named Pyroceram.

One of the first and certainly the most dramatic application of this new material was its use as the nose cone of a space missile, the temperature of which must withstand the fierce heat of hundreds of degrees heat from air friction. Yet such heat had no effect on it whatever. A direct spin-off of Pyroceram is the unique line of cooking utensils Corning developed from it. They were introduced originally in 1958 under the name, "Corning Ware."

Cooking utensils made of this gleaming, snow white material can withstand use—and abuse—which no other glass or ceramic (and probably few metal utensils) can withstand without the slightest harm. Half a piece of Corning Ware can be frozen into a block of ice while the other half is subjected to the heat of a blow torch—and nothing happens to it. As a result of this remarkable characteristic, the company guarantees "to replace without charge the glass-ceramic part of any Corning Ware product that breaks from temperature extremes...." Incidentally, the introduction of Corning Ware also marked the company's entry into the portable appliance field. Today the line consists of over fifty items ranging from "Electromatic" percolators and skillets to roasters and serving platters. Moreover, it has provided a whole new dimension to cooking utensils which, with Corning Ware, can literally go from the freezer to the range—and then right on to the table as an attractive serving dish.

Corelle

Of all the many developments that the Corning Glass Works has contributed over the years, nothing can quite compare from either a technological or marketing standpoint with Corelle Livingware, a remarkable new product introduced in 1970.

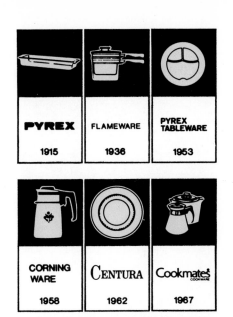

Some of the important milestones in Corning's long and impressive record of developing new products.

Corelle, break-resistant but with the look and feel of fine china, has been such a phenomenal success, Corning has been unable to keep up with demand.

Corning's latest addition is this
Creative Glass line introduced in 1972.

Unlike the earlier, break-resistant dishes Corning introduced in 1962 under the name of Centura Dinnerware, Corelle is never referred to as "dinnerware," but as "livingware" and with good reason. Before one of these unusual new dishes was ever placed on sale or even in production, an exhaustive research program was conducted in the U. S. and Europe to learn consumers' real practices and needs in tableware.

The findings of the study demolished many of the long-established, cherished traditions of dinnerware marketing. For example, in place of the usual composition—which invariably included a bread and butter plate—the new place-setting consists of a large plate, medium plate, bowl, cup and saucer. Four such settings were assembled in a new type of self-service package to retail for $19.95. Then in addition, a two-year guarantee—Corning calls it a "promise"—to replace free any piece that breaks within two years.

The research conclusions were sound as the rather sensational performance of Corelle in the marketplace bears out. Within eighteen months after it was first placed on sale in New England, *over forty million pieces of it had been sold*—an unprecedented record which no other type of tableware has even approached. As of December 1972, this line had been on the market for two years; sales totaled about 60 million pieces. Furthermore, as has been true ever since it was originally introduced, deliveries continue to be on a two to three months backlog; it has been impossible to keep up with the demand.

On the basis of those figures industry sources estimate that sales chalked up for the first year—1971—by Corelle came close to the $18 million mark—an impressive figure for a newcomer. And all this business goes to the housewares—not the china and glass—departments.

General Housewares Corporation

During the 1950s and 60s the housewares industry, like others, witnessed the growth of many long established firms largely as a result of mergers and acquisitions. The General Housewares Corporation, however, is a unique example of a company which was organized in May 1967, for the express purpose of developing, primarily through acquisitions as well as internal growth, a multi-product housewares manufacturing and marketing organization. By the end of 1972 its estimated sales had passed $55 million, and the corporation consisted of eleven companies comprising three major product groups: cookware, giftware, and leisure furniture products. Another acquisition had meanwhile been sold.

General Housewares Corporation's progress in developing what has now become one of the most important segments of the cooking utensil field is clearly shown by the accompanying chart of its Cookware Group. Its two other groups are:

Giftware Group: Holt-Howard Company, Stamford, Connecticut,

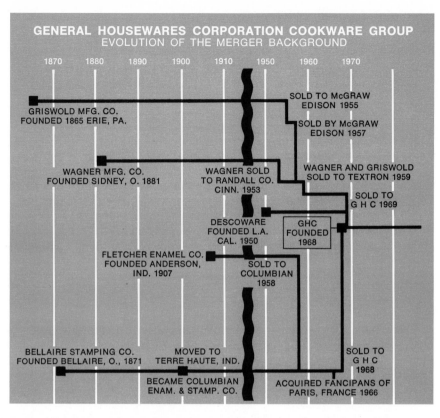

GENERAL HOUSEWARES CORPORATION COOKWARE GROUP
EVOLUTION OF THE MERGER BACKGROUND

1870 1880 1890 1900 1910 1950 1960 1970

GRISWOLD MFG. CO.
FOUNDED 1865 ERIE, PA.

SOLD TO McGRAW
EDISON 1955

SOLD BY McGRAW
EDISON 1957

WAGNER MFG. CO.
FOUNDED SIDNEY, O. 1881

WAGNER SOLD
TO RANDALL CO.
CINN. 1953

WAGNER AND GRISWOLD
SOLD TO TEXTRON 1959

SOLD TO
G H C 1969

DESCOWARE
FOUNDED L.A.
CAL. 1950

GHC
FOUNDED
1968

FLETCHER ENAMEL CO.
FOUNDED ANDERSON,
IND. 1907

SOLD TO
COLUMBIAN
1958

BELLAIRE STAMPING CO.
FOUNDED BELLAIRE, O., 1871

MOVED TO
TERRE HAUTE, IND.

BECAME COLUMBIAN
ENAM. & STAMP. CO.

SOLD TO
G H C
1968

ACQUIRED FANCIPANS OF
PARIS, FRANCE 1966

General Housewares Corporation now consists of three major product groups:
cookware, giftware, and leisure furniture products. The corporation is a result
of mergers and acquisitions.

acquired 1969; Colonial Candle Company, Hyannis, Massachusetts,
acquired 1970; and Carousel Candle Company, San Rafael, California, acquired 1971.

Leisure Furniture Group: Durham Manufacturing Company, Muncie, Indiana, acquired in 1969; Plantation Patterns Incorporated,
Birmingham, Alabama, acquired in 1970; and Vogue Rattan Manufacturing Company, acquired in 1970.

The Teflon Tale

During four years when Teflon-coated pans had been originated and
successfully sold and used in France, American housewares buyers
and manufacturers abroad cold-shouldered the idea. For two more
years all the efforts of one determined man failed to get a single
response in this country until Macy's George Edelstein decided to
give it a whirl in December 1960.

Thomas G. Hardie, formerly a foreign correspondent for United
Press and International News Service, and in 1970 president of a
textile machinery firm, Hardie International, Limited, went through
that frustrating experience. But if it hadn't been for him, "Teflon"
might not be what it is today.

The American Teflon Story begins in Baltimore in 1958 when

The first ad in America on Teflon-
coated cooking utensils was this
modest little offer of the T-Fal Satisfry
skillet by Macy's in *The New York Times*
on Sunday, July 31, 1961.

From top: T-Fal was advertised in magazines for the first time when this ad appeared in the *New Yorker,* July 8, 1961. The lower picture shows Teflon coating being sprayed onto cooking utensils.

Bottom, courtesy DuPont Company.

an old friend, Henry McNulty, gave Tom Hardie an aluminum skillet he had come upon in a Paris cookware shop. "Henry had been living in Paris for a number of years," Hardie related. "He knew of my admiration for French products and that I pretended to know something about French cooking.

The skillet had the odd trade name of "Tefal" and, I learned, had something to do with a DuPont plastic with the equally strange name of "Teflon." Henry explained that since the inside of the pan was coated with this plastic, it not only eliminated the need to use butter or oil for cooking but greatly simplified cleaning, since its slippery surface prevented food from sticking. Almost as an after-thought he added that "this might be a good item for the American market."

Thereupon I immediately flew to France to meet the managing director of the Tefal Company, Marc Gregoire, at the factory just outside Paris. He had started in a very small way, first doing the coating of the pans in his kitchen, and his wife had sold them on the sidewalks in Paris. They made an immediate hit and within a few years "Tefal" pans had become a *succès fou;* millions were sold by all major stores.

For most of the next two years, he called on nearly every important cooking utensil manufacturer in the United States, sometimes accompanied by DuPont executives, but with absolutely no success.

In the summer of 1960 when the Food and Drug Administration got around to issuing its official approval for the use of pure Teflon on cookware—which was what Hardie's process called for—he was sure this was the green light needed to move ahead. Once again he made the circuit of manufacturers, citing the continued great success it was having in Europe, but again he struck out.

By this time I had become emotionally involved; I simply had to prove my point. And though I knew nothing whatever about importing, in desperation I cabled the factory to ship me 3,000 pans by the next boat. When they arrived I shipped a free sample to each of the one hundred department stores in this country, along with full details. Not one buyer gave me an order.

With 2,900 pans building up charges in a warehouse I was getting increasingly nervous...and desperate. Finally, in a tiny basement office in Macy's in New York, George Edelstein, the housewares buyer —between lectures on his philosophy of marketing housewares!—gave me an order for 200 pans. I was so delighted I couldn't wait to send a victory cable to France.

The pans went on sale December 15, 1960, at $6.94 during one of the city's worst snowstorms. But within a few days they sold out, and Macy's began clamoring for more. Not until January 31, 1961, did the store run a very small advertisement on the skillets. "After that we were swamped with calls from all over the country," Hardie recalled.

"Of course our small inventory just melted away overnight. I was on the phone daily to France pleading for more pans." Hardie flew to France to urge an immediate increase in production:

Now I was even more desperate because I felt that the French factory was not equipped to meet the American demands. So I again went over and loaned the company $50,000 at low interest to assist them in building a new modern factory in the French Alps near their aluminum supplier. Although the company was most cooperative they were still never able to meet the tremendous American demand. Every housewife in this country, it seemed, now wanted nothing but Teflon utensils.

Finally, to supplement the French production I built a highly automated factory in Timonium, Maryland, which went "on stream" in October 1961. Unfortunately, at just about the same time every American cookware manufacturer decided to jump on the bandwagon.

The sensational success Tom Hardie achieved with his T-Fal skillet produced more than an ordinary reaction among American cookware manufacturers. And so by the latter part of 1961 what seemed like everyone in the cooking utensil manufacturing business began offering DuPont Teflon-coated utensils.

American manufacturers, however, lacked not only the patented process but adequate experience in such coating. The more responsible producers acted cautiously, but many others rushed ahead opportunistically. Soon the market was flooded with inferior utensils that failed miserably to provide homemakers the promised nonstick advantages. Teflon became "a dirty word"; stockrooms were loaded —but now customers wouldn't take Teflon-coated utensils as a gift.

Thomas Hardie's new factory never had a chance to get going before it was all but shut down. Later he turned over the entire distribution of T-Fal products to Royal Chambord, Incorporated, of Bellville, New Jersey.

No one, apparently, ever wanted to hear the word Teflon again. Even at the DuPont Company. One DuPont man who didn't think so was Paul Thomas, a young product technologist. Although he lacked marketing experience, he had unbounded faith in the potential of Teflon. And when DuPont decided it ought to reexamine the whole Teflon situation, Thomas asked for and got the assignment. DuPont researchers then canvassed everyone in the business as well as six thousand consumers about what was wrong with Teflon cookware. Basically, they learned, there was nothing wrong with it; and its convenience, they found, had far greater appeal than its "greaselessness." But faulty application of this slippery material by the utensil makers was destroying its usefulness.

As a result, in 1963 DuPont established an "official" certification seal of approval for Teflon cooking utensils and set manufacturing coating standards.

By 1968 DuPont had developed a new technique for applying Teflon whereby it not only prevented foods from sticking to utensils but, unlike the original applications, was also scratch resistant. Designated "Teflon II," it was promoted with a seal of certification like the original program. But by this time it had contributed so much toward increasing sales that it had earned respect at both the trade and the consumer level.

The Baths of Caracalla

the BATHshop

Nobody—but nobody—ever made as big a production of bathrooms and bathing as did the ancient Romans.

The idea did not originate with them, but they built the biggest, most impressive, most complete bathing establishments the world has ever known. Yet for all their sumptuous efficiency, made possible, of course, by slave labor, their baths cannot begin to compare with the personal luxury and convenience afforded by the modern appliance-appointed bathroom.

Had you been able to go to Rome's famous Baths of Caracalla, you would have undressed and been given a good coating of special skin oil, after which you would have stepped out into the courtyard for some vigorous exercise. Next you would have moved into the hot room, and then on to the steam room, where the body was scraped of oil and perspiration. By then you would have been ready for the warm room, followed by the cold bath. After that, food and drink, or the lecture hall or reading room.

It sounds very much like the arrangement in any men's club nowadays, only it was far bigger and catered to a great many more "members"—often as many as twenty-five hundred at one time. A similar facility was occasionally available for the ladies.

Yet long before the Romans became enamored of bathing, the Egyptians had already started it. Excavations by the Oriental Institute of Chicago reveal that it was the Egyptians who first conceived the idea of setting aside a separate room in the house for bathing. The Greeks carried the concept further. Aegean palaces provide well-preserved examples of bathrooms remarkable for their construction and for their advanced system of water supply and drainage. In fact the latter, according to the Plumbing-Heating-Cooling Information Bureau, was so elaborate that it was not equaled until comparatively recent times.

After Rome declined, bathing was all washed up for the next thousand years while the Dark Ages engulfed Europe. Bigotry and superstition about the evils and ill-effects of water were rampant, and in many places bathing was prohibited by law. Sanitation was nonexistent, and disease and epidemics wiped out whole populations.

With the Renaissance came a renewed interest in bathing, and public baths began to appear. But they became more like social clubs and generated widespread promiscuity: in Italy, for example, the word *bagnio* was used for either bath or brothel. Outraged morality all but ended bathing when priests and ministers denounced the practice. Subsequently, King Henry I and his Knights of the Order of the Bath helped start a bathing revival.

197

Opposite page: In Roman times bathing was public and ceremonial as seen in this cutaway drawing of the Baths of Caracalla.

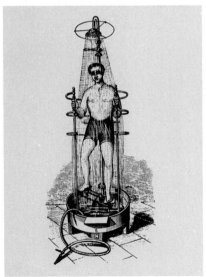

From top: Virginia stool shower, circa 1830-1840, an early Rube Goldberg type of invention. The "cold water cure," and a shower bath worked by foot-power.

Top, courtesy Crane Company. Middle and bottom, the Bettmann Archive.

America's First Bathtub

But the bathroom—and America itself—was still a long way in the future. It wasn't until 1790 that the first bathtub appeared in this country. Brought from France by Benjamin Franklin, it was shaped like a big shoe. A water-heating device was built into the heel, and a spigot for draining the water was in the toe. Franklin used this then somewhat sensational contraption, we are told, as much for a refuge as for bathing, and he is said to have spent hours in it not just for the luxury of soaking himself but to escape from his admirers and to catch up on his reading.

"To the average modern man a bath is a method of getting clean and cool," commented *Life* magazine on August 9, 1948, in a review of *Mechanization Takes Command,* a magnificent book by Siegfried Giedion, the historian of technology. "But to Giedion," continued the review, "it is a social ritual whose curious ramifications through the ages constitute a profound source of history and an index of changing social habit. The American bathtub would have been frowned upon by the highly developed civilizations of Rome, Alexandria and Islam. This is because modern society tends to regard bathing as a simple matter of ablution rather than as a social ritual whose purpose is 'regeneration,' the relaxation and stimulation of mind and body."[1]

The history of that other basic essential of every modern bathroom, the flush toilet, can be traced all the way back to the palace at Knossos in Crete, which as early as 1800 B.C. is said to have had a flushing toilet with a wooden seat in its bathing chamber.

But apparently only ancient royalty could manage such luxury, and it disappeared for centuries. In Europe the word later used for toilet according to Lawrence Wright, was *garderobe,* or a place to hang one's clothing; but by the sixteenth century the *garderobe* had been replaced by the "close stool." It was, he explains, "cosier for the user but harder on the servants,"[2] presumably because of the cleaning problems involved.

Although a patent was finally issued for a flush toilet in 1775, according to Wright, this important device, like the bathtub and the whole concept of the bathroom itself, made malodorously slow progress. As late as 1858, it is said, "public conveniences" were few, far, and foul even in a city the size of London.

Despite the propitious start that sanitary toilet facilities had at Knossos, it would be a long time before the advent of even the most elementary form of "modern" plumbing. What prevailed, of course, was the inescapable use of the pot or chamber.

It was not until after 1870 that the flush toilet slowly began to gain acceptance in America. And more than one hundred years elapsed after Benjamin Franklin used his fancy French tub before the bathtub became standard equipment, presaging the emergence of the modern bathroom. About 1920, according to Giedion, technology finally permitted the mass production of the double-shelled, porcelain-enameled one-piece tub. "It is a luxury article, which the combination of refined metallurgical and technical skills transformed into a democratic utensil."[3]

Meanwhile, man's ingenuity worked ceaselessly to evolve more convenient and comfortable solutions to the problems involved with the toilet and bath. A never ending array of inventions, contrivances, and contraptions were introduced, mostly in the homes of the well-to-do. No one fully understood what was happening, but the bathroom was on its way. And when it arrived, bath shops sprang up to serve it.

But plumbing still had a long way to go, especially in rural America. The outhouse was a familiar and unmistakable landmark behind every home. And whether it was a simple one-holer or a more elaborate two- or three-holer of the kind the comedian Chic Sales wrote about in *The Specialist,* all were equipped with last year's Sears, Roebuck or Montgomery Ward catalog to provide reading matter as well as serve more utilitarian purposes. "Look out for the pages with the barbed wire on them!" younger members of the family would be warned when they left the house for out back.

The chamber pot, or chamber pail, as it was sometimes called, continued to be used in this country until well after the turn of the century. Where there were no adequate bathroom facilities, this was the only practical solution to the problem. Originally these chamber pots were made of ceramic material much like those used in Europe in the past. They had a handle somewhat like that on a cup, and usually a cover. Ordinarily they were plain, but the more elaborate and expensive pots were decorated. Later, pots of gray porcelain

199

From top: A closet tub, about 1880. A spacious tub opened out, a bargain at $11.50. Milady's bath, Victorian style. At the time, women dressed modestly for bathing.

Top, courtesy Crane Company. Bottom, the Bettmann Archive.

Bathroom, circa 1890. The tub is glazed, enameled steel or other metal. Note the cast panel embellishment in an elaborate bathroom for the millionaire market.

By 1905 the potential of that great new convenience, a modern bathroom was already so promising that Macy's devoted one of its most important windows to featuring its accessories. Note the "Sitz Bath" or bidet at lower right and the hospital-type scale, left.

Courtesy House Furnishing Review.

200

Something of Interest

WE ARE offering this season a new Overhead Shower that will interest hundreds of your customers. The price has in the past barred many from the enjoyment and benefit of the shower bath. Our new STERNAU OVERHEAD SHOWER meets all the requirements, and is so very moderate in cost that all can afford it.

It is made of half-inch brass tubing, heavily nickel-plated and highly polished, fitted with Duck Curtain, Rings, six feet of ½-inch Rubber Tubing, with our Sternau "Holdfast" Combination Metal and Rubber Bath Connection, all complete.

It is so simple in construction that it can be put up by anyone.

Our latest novelty is the "STERNAU SPRABRUSH," a massage brush which solves the problem of cold water bathing for those who cannot endure the shock of the ordinary shower or a cold plunge. It is much like the ordinary spray with a Rubber Massage Brush fitted to the Spray-head and made with openings to allow a free flow of the water. There is an ebonized handle back of the Spray-head and the Rubber Tube attaches to the faucet by means of the Sternau "Holdfast" connection. The effect of the massage in conjunction with the flow of water is wonderfully exhilarating.

This, too, is moderate in price.

We should like to send you an ILLUSTRATED CATALOGUE of our complete line.

S. STERNAU & CO.

NEW YORK SHOW ROOMS:
Broadway and Park Place (Opposite Post Office)

OFFICE AND FACTORY:
195 Plymouth Street, Brooklyn, N. Y.

S. Sterno suggested "something of interest" at the turn of the century. A complete overhead shower, including all fittings and duck curtain.

Courtesy House Furnishing Review.

enamel on steel came into use, since there was no chance of breakage. They were known as "combinettes." For obvious reasons the item was not just a best but a very best seller, and many hundreds of thousands were sold. The unabating demand kept factories busy for years both here and overseas.

"We used to do a tremendous business on combinettes," recalled Joseph Block in an interview. Block's father started the J. L. Block and Son housewares importing firm in New York in 1892, and he began working with his father in 1910. "George Borgfeldt and Company [large importers, long out of business] were, of course, the biggest in that business, but I believe we were number two," said Block.

You must remember that in New York at that time, there was often no toilet inside a sprawling East Side tenement—it was down in the backyard. So even in the cities there was a constant demand for combinettes. We imported them from Germany.

For a long time the German manufacturers had a big advantage over the Americans in this field. In the first place, they made an allwhite combinette that had much more appearance appeal. Second, the imported combinettes were much more comfortable to use. American pails were made with a simple straight-edge rim around the top. But the Germans had developed a way to flare the top edge a couple of inches, so naturally everyone wanted the flared top.

In its 1897 catalog, Sears offered a covered gray enamel chamber pail about twelve inches high for $1.16. A small, seven-inch-high

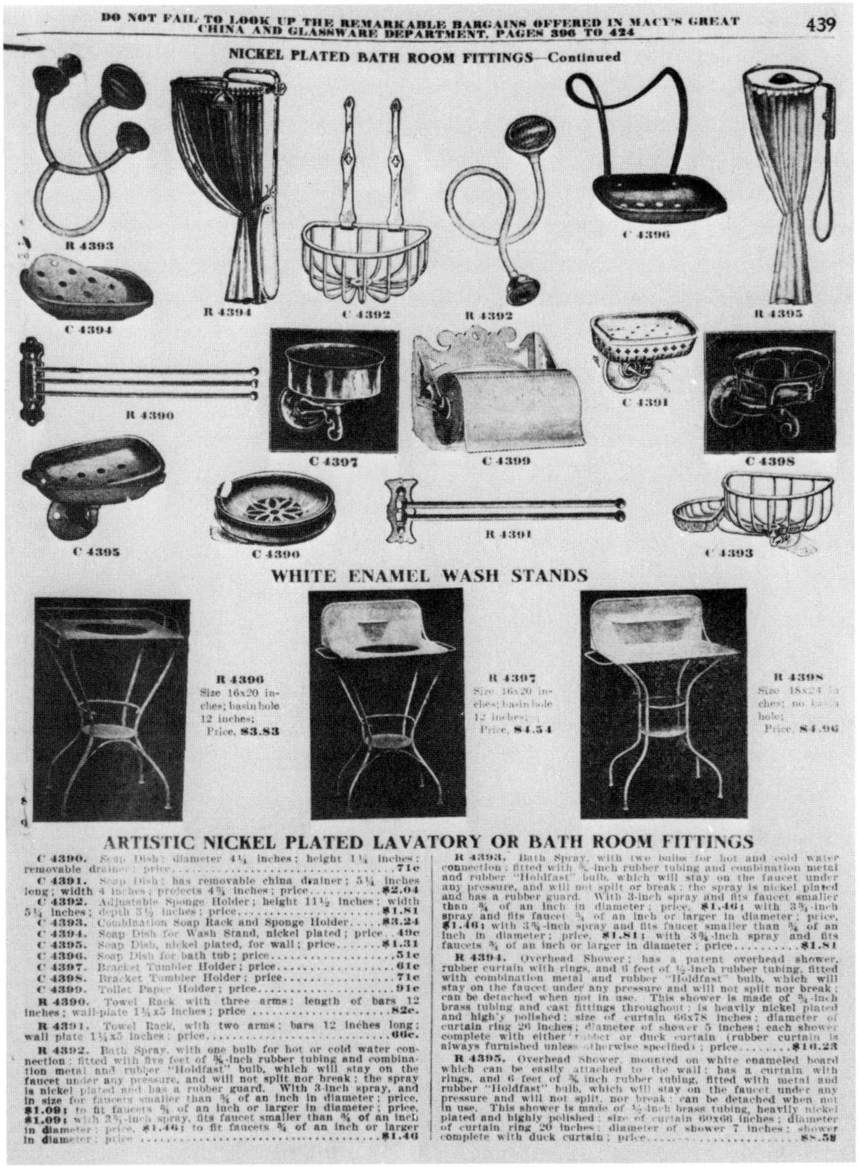
DO NOT FAIL TO LOOK UP THE REMARKABLE BARGAINS OFFERED IN MACY'S GREAT CHINA AND GLASSWARE DEPARTMENT, PAGES 396 TO 424 439

NICKEL PLATED BATH ROOM FITTINGS—Continued

R 4393
C 4394
R 4394
C 4392
R 4392
C 4396
R 4395
R 4390
C 4397
C 4399
C 4391
C 4398
C 4395
C 4390
R 4391
C 4393

WHITE ENAMEL WASH STANDS

R 4396 Size 16x20 inches; basin hole 12 inches; Price, $3.83

R 4397 Size 16x20 inches; basin hole 12 inches; Price, $4.54

R 4398 Size 18x24 inches; no basin hole; Price, $4.96

ARTISTIC NICKEL PLATED LAVATORY OR BATH ROOM FITTINGS

C 4390. Soap Dish; diameter 4¼ inches; height 1¼ inches; removable drainer; price........71c

C 4391. Soap Dish; has removable china drainer; 5¼ inches long; width 4 inches; projects 4¾ inches; price........$2.04

C 4392. Adjustable Sponge Holder; height 11½ inches; width 5¼ inches; depth 3½ inches; price........$1.81

C 4393. Combination Soap Rack and Sponge Holder........$3.24

C 4394. Soap Dish for Wash Stand, nickel plated; price........49c

C 4395. Soap Dish, nickel plated, for wall; price........$1.31

C 4396. Soap Dish for bath tub; price........51c

C 4397. Bracket Tumbler Holder; price........61c

C 4398. Bracket Tumbler Holder; price........71c

C 4399. Toilet Paper Holder; price........91c

R 4390. Towel Rack with three arms; length of bars 12 inches; wall-plate 1¼x5 inches; price........82c.

R 4391. Towel Rack, with two arms; bars 12 inches long; wall plate 1¼x5 inches; price........66c.

R 4392. Bath Spray, with one bulb for hot or cold water connection; fitted with five feet of ⅜-inch rubber tubing and combination metal and rubber "Holdfast" bulb, which will stay on the faucet under any pressure, and will not split nor break; the spray is nickel plated and has a rubber guard. With 3-inch spray, and in size for faucets smaller than ¾ of an inch in diameter; price, $1.09; to fit faucets ¾ of an inch or larger in diameter; price, $1.09; with 3¾-inch spray, fits faucet smaller than ¾ of an inch in diameter; price, $1.46; to fit faucets ¾ of an inch or larger in diameter; price........$1.46

R 4393. Bath Spray, with two bulbs for hot and cold water connection; fitted with ⅜-inch rubber tubing and combination metal and rubber "Holdfast" bulb, which will stay on the faucet under any pressure, and will not split or break; the spray is nickel plated and has a rubber guard. With 3-inch spray and fits faucet smaller than ¾ of an inch in diameter; price, $1.46; with 3¾-inch spray and fits faucet ¾ of an inch or larger in diameter; price, $1.46; with 3¾-inch spray and fits faucet smaller than ¾ of an inch in diameter; price, $1.81; with 3¾-inch spray and fits faucets ¾ of an inch or larger in diameter; price........$1.81

R 4394. Overhead Shower; has a patent overhead shower, rubber curtain with rings, and 6 feet of ½-inch rubber tubing, fitted with combination metal and rubber "Holdfast" bulb, which will stay on the faucet under any pressure and will not split nor break; can be detached when not in use. This shower is made of ¾-inch brass tubing and cast fittings throughout; is heavily nickel plated and highly polished; size of curtain 66x78 inches; diameter of curtain ring 26 inches; diameter of shower 5 inches; each shower complete with either rubber or duck curtain (rubber curtain is always furnished unless otherwise specified); price........$10.23

R 4395. Overhead Shower, mounted on white enameled board which can be easily attached to the wall; has a curtain with rings, and 6 feet of ⅜ inch rubber tubing, fitted with metal and rubber "Holdfast" bulb, which will stay on the faucet under any pressure and will not split, nor break; can be detached when not in use. This shower is made of ½-inch brass tubing, heavily nickel plated and highly polished; size of curtain 60x66 inches; diameter of curtain ring 20 inches; diameter of shower 7 inches; shower complete with duck curtain; price........$8.58

In 1907 Macy's offered a variety of bathroom fittings, from shower bath to soap dishes and wash stands.

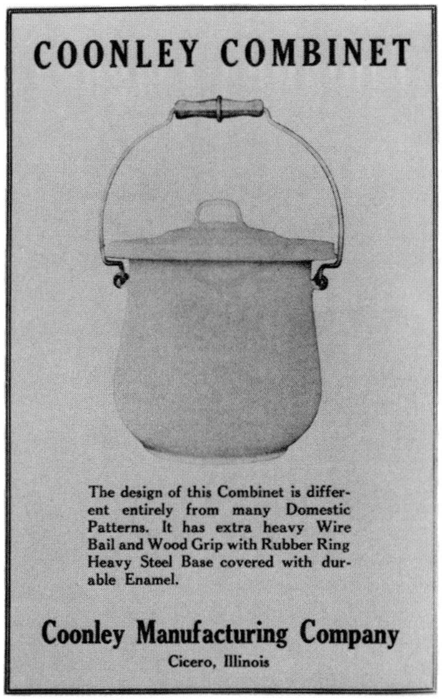
COONLEY COMBINET
The design of this Combinet is different entirely from many Domestic Patterns. It has extra heavy Wire Bail and Wood Grip with Rubber Ring Heavy Steel Base covered with durable Enamel.
Coonley Manufacturing Company
Cicero, Illinois

After World War I this portable necessity was still big business. Pictured here, the Coonley Combinet.

Courtesy House Furnishing Review.

uncovered enamel pot was ten cents, and the "Challenge Odorless Commode and Slop Bucket Combined" was no less than $3.25. At that price it also warranted some selling copy: "Beats everything of its kind.... Impossible for the foul air to escape even when the lid is removed as there is inside the lid a receptacle that holds a deodorizer.... Made of heavy galvanized iron and has no paint to hold stench or disease germs."

"I recall that when I was with Montgomery Ward we did a tremendous business on combinettes until the time farmhouses became modernized," Henry Forster, a housewares buyer until his retirement in 1946 when he then joined Ekco, reported in an interview. "We sold them by the carload. Most were white, but for promotions we'd use speckled gray that covered all the defects. Incidentally, the combinette was so shaped that nobody would ever mistake it for an enameled cooking utensil. Our nickname for it was 'the growler.'"

"In 1830 Sylvester Graham of graham cracker fame was crusading for a 'sound mind in a clean body' and advocating a warm-water bath three times a week," relates *Nation's Business* magazine for September 1947, adding, "Twenty years later the bathtub was a recognized social institution.... Glamor tubs got their real start in the '80's when one company offered a glazed porcelain job with a 'Grecian gold band' and 'turned porcelain feet.' You could have the tub fitted with a needle spray and shower. Ten vertical cage bars squirted water at the trapped bather, an arrangement in bathtub elegance costing about $800."[4]

A Saturday Night Ritual

Until the double-shelled, one-piece cast iron bathtub was accepted as the unofficial national standard, all manner of tubs and bath devices were tried, mostly, once again, in affluent homes. Usually made of wood lined with tin, copper, or galvanized iron, they were generally painted to prolong their life as well as to compensate for their lack of charm. Many times these tubs could be folded up into a special commode or closet made for the purpose and designed to match the bedroom furniture. There was even a canvas model that folded into a suitcase for travelers. Eventually the tubs were made of cast iron, painted or galvanized.

Although in the country the Saturday night bath-in-a-washtub ritual lingered well into the present century, the more affluent folks probably had a bathtub and most likely ordered it from the Sears catalog. As early as 1897 that alert merchandiser offered a "Plunge Bath [tub], made of heavy tin with wooden bottoms and handles at each end; japanned, blue inside, drab outside, trimmed in black, blue and gilt stripes, 4 feet long, $3.73; 6 feet, $5." An infant's bathtub could be had for only eighty cents; a "hip bath"—looking like a big tin armchair—twenty-seven inches in diameter was four dollars.

In New York, Macy's, doubtless taking a few leaves out of Mr. Sears' merchandising policy, published some catalogs of its own though not nearly as formidable. In 1904 its assortment of bathtubs included everything from "Oval Foot Tubs, size 0, 47¢" to "English Sponge Baths, 28 inch, $3.38."

Few newspaper advertisements of bath goods are to be found in those years, for advertising was limited and was reserved for more prestigious things like silks and gloves. One of the earliest advertising references to a bathroom or bathroom merchandise is a full-page 1908 advertisement of the long-departed Siegel Cooper and Company, "the big store," in Chicago. Launching a big "Household Show and Sale for Housekeepers," it features the introduction of "A model kitchen...a model laundry...and a model bathroom."

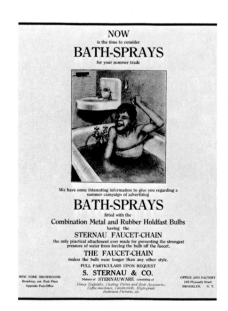

Before showers were commonplace, bath sprays were necessary merchandise. Even "the strongest pressure of water" can't force the bulb off this 1909 faucet!

Courtesy House Furnishing Review.

The contemporary bathroom displays a riot of color and design, utilizing modern fabrics and materials. From shower curtain and bath stool to wastepaper basket, tissue holder, and toilet seat, coordinated pattern is a big plus. Color and design ensembles are the important approach in selling today's bathroom accessories. Another approach is whimsey—an owl, stylized flowers and butterflies adorn these toilet seats.

Do You Realize the Profitable Field
there is for Chemical Toilets?

AMONG those who live in suburban homes on
farms, in camps and cottages. There is a surprisingly
large field which you can "cash in" on in a big way and
with comparatively little effort.

Iron Horse
Chemical Toilets

Simply display one
of these toilets in
your store. The
quality of the metal
used, the workman-
ship and finish —
these features, coupled
with the fact that it is
absolutely sanitary in
every way, will create a
volume of business that
will actually surprise
you.

Write today for descriptive matter and prices on this
equipment. We will gladly furnish you, without charge,
advertising matter for use in circularizing your trade.

Write us today, Now !!

ROCHESTER CAN COMPANY
ROCHESTER, N. Y.

204

New bath shop at Carson Pirie Scott's

A NEW Bath Shop was opened in June on the seventh floor at Carson Pirie Scott & Co., Chicago. Features of the new shop are two model powder rooms, in modern style. One introduces an unusual color note in brown and beige, with a flowered wall paper. The shop is well lighted, well laid out and offers a complete line of bathroom furnishings assembled in color harmonies. Below is a close-up of the wall panel on the left.

Such innovations were big news then. Bathing and bathrooms are taken for granted today, but fifty years ago they were just beginning to win acceptance, even among middle-class people. In 1852, for example, conditions were often so deplorable that the New York Association for Improving the Conditions for the Poor opened the first "public bath and wash house" in lower Manhattan.

A Bath in Every Room

Even the citizens who might have boasted about having a bathtub at home were frequently forced to do without during their travels, since few hotels were thus equipped. However, it is interesting that as early as 1829 the Tremont House in Boston was the first hotel to have toilets and baths: "8 privies and 8 bathing or washing rooms" in the basement. Commenting on it, Giedion notes that it marked "the first time in America if not the world that mechanical equipment became an important element in architectural design."[5]

During the next hundred years, very few hotels installed such facilities. It was not until 1908 that E. M. Statler built a hotel in Buffalo with a bath in every room. "A Room and a Bath for a Dollar and a Half" was an immediate success and set a pattern for others to emulate.

When homeowners in those days were fortunate enough to acquire both a bathtub and a flush toilet they then had a "bathroom"— or thought so until one realized how much was still missing. Where to hang the towels...the toilet tissue...or park the soap and the toothbrushes? Later came the need for a hamper and countless other accessories. It was the demand for these items that awakened retailers to the bathroom market. Since they rarely if ever got any of the tub or toilet business, for which they were not equipped, they began going after the fixtures. Department stores especially were quick to recognize the opportunity, and for many years this continued to be a most important category.

"This department has a very comprehensive assortment of everything for the bathroom," boasted the Fair Store in a double-page spread in the Chicago *Tribune* on April 8, 1917. Undaunted by the entry of the United States into World War I two days before, it went right ahead with its announcement of the opening of the remodeled "World's Greatest House Furnishing Department." It was still a long way from having the kind of bath shop that prevails today, but it had a section called "bathroom fittings" where "newly invented devices that add to the comfort of the bath are to be found."

The impending war had sent prices skyrocketing, but since the boom conditions kept purses well filled, no one seemed to mind. The "World's Greatest House Furnishing Department" was determined to live up to its self-designated title with opening day bargains to match. And so the bathroom fittings bargains included such things as an "18-inch brass, nickel-plated towel bar at 25¢; brass bathroom hook, nickel-plated 8¢; bath tub seat, oak finish, rubber-covered hangers 39¢; and a toilet paper holder, solid brass, heavily nickel-plated, 29¢."

By 1919, with the war over, the bathroom fixture business, free of production restrictions, began to boom. Now everyone, it seemed, suddenly wanted two things: a modern kitchen and a modern bathroom.

The Bath Accessory Boom

It was the gleam of that bath fixture business which was to attract an ex-doughboy, Joseph A. Kaplan—a twenty-four-year-old New Yorker born and raised on Manhattan's tough-as-nails West Side. Ready to take almost any kind of a promising job, he started off on a career in which he made significant and lasting contributions to the bathroom accessory business and became a leading figure in it.

In 1919 a friend put him in touch with a New York manufacturer of bathroom fixtures who was in need of a salesman—the Superior Brass Novelty Company.

"I knew as much about bathroom fixtures as an Eskimo knows about the hula-hula," he recalled in an interview in 1969. "But before the war I had sold paint and before that sold newspapers, and since this was supposed to be a great business I decided I could also sell towel bars and soap dishes."

His first port of call was Perth Amboy, New Jersey, and the McCormick Brothers hardware store.

To this day I don't quite know how it happened, but when I walked out I had an order for $450 in my pocket. When, the next day, I landed an $800 order from Miller Brothers in York, Pennsylvania, I decided I was really in the right business. By the end of the week my sales had totaled $1,500, which at 10 percent commission wasn't bad for those days. By now this new little company was doing all of $250,000 of business a year and I had finally been given the title of sales manager.

During the early 1920s the bathroom had become firmly established as an essential room in the home, and no one had to be sold on the idea. What now began to interest the manufacturers—just as they knew it would interest the consumers—was the possibility of further innovations. One of these was the one-piece, double-shell, flush-to-the-wall modern tub that began to replace the old tub with the claw-foot legs; another was the built-in shower bath.

Bathing under a stream of water was obviously not an original idea. The ancients had their slaves pour water over them. But during the early 1900s homes with built-in showers were the exception.

The average-income family had to be satisfied with a makeshift shower bath, usually improvised by using a spray nozzle connected to the faucet by a rubber tube. It was a risky method since very often the walls and the floor of the bathroom got as wet as the bather. Nevertheless, the continued demand for such sprays was an undeniable indication of how popular the idea of a shower was becoming.

Opposite page from top: An "exposed plumbing" bathroom circa 1915. The suburbs as well as farms offered a big market for chemical toilets in 1922. The mid-thirties saw new bath shop merchandising at Carson Pirie Scott in Chicago.
Courtesy House Furnishing Review.

This page: Integrated and contrasting color and fabric make bath accessories very sellable.

Joe Kaplan was soon to become especially aware of that:

In my calls on the hardware and plumbing-supply dealers I was struck by the frequent inquiries they made for a white-duck shower curtain. This was particularly true in Brooklyn and the Bronx, where large new apartment buildings were going up in record numbers. A modern bathroom, complete with built-in flush-to-the-wall bathtub and shower was one of the big attractions of these modern apartments, and soon the demand for shower curtains began to develop. White duck, of course, was the accepted standard: in fact there wasn't anything else.

I told my company I thought we ought to add such a curtain to our line, and presently we made arrangements with the Sanitary Bath Curtain Company on West 14th Street, New York. Their original business had been making canvas feedbags for horses and they had only recently begun to make shower curtains for some of the plumbing people, especially the Speakman Shower Company. They were eager to have Superior Brass as an outlet to retail channels, and so in 1921 we came to have a shower curtain in our line.

Wartime prosperity had made it possible for a great many formerly poor people to move into new high-rise apartments that were going up in New York and in other cities. Often they came from tenements where one dingy hall toilet was shared by four or five families; moving into a home with a modern white-tile bathroom must have seemed something like paradise for them.

But the development of these new bathrooms brought a far-reaching change in the merchandising scene. Till now the bathroom

206

The Bath Scene: Gimbel's very special bath shop in New York merchandises a total bathroom package with style and imagination.

fixture business had been tremendously important to house furnishing departments, Joe pointed out. But now the new tiled bathrooms included built-in tile fixtures and that marked the beginning of the end of the big metal fixture business in most of these stores.

One of my very good customers at that time—1922—was Sam Hughes of Bloomingdale's on 59th Street in New York. He was planning a sale and wanted something special—something really unusual. Now it so happens that some of the apartment builders, to get a competitive edge, had begun to introduce colored tile borders and then all colored tiles in their bathrooms instead of just plain white. That gave me an idea; why not have a colored shower curtain too?

Working with Sanitary, we selected a blue-striped cotton mattress ticking with a small floral design. I remember it vividly, even the pattern number, 5841. And because we wanted this to be unusual in quality as well as appearance, we sent the curtains to Philadelphia to the Alden Rubber Company to be rubber-coated. By present standards they were pretty primitive. But if the result can be called a decorative shower curtain, that unique concept was now a reality.

At any rate, I finally had something special and unusual for Sam Hughes. He was delighted and excited and immediately gave me an order for one hundred curtains to retail for $4.95. I think he paid me about $3.50. By noon on the day of the sale he was on the phone yelling for more curtains, and I immediately rushed more over in a taxi. By the time the day ended Bloomingdale's had sold over five hundred curtains. It set some kind of a record and everyone was delighted—most of all the customers.

What all this actually amounted to was that fashion timidly began to creep into the bathroom. That once strictly utilitarian and often odiferous ugly duckling was about to emerge from its past. The bath shop was on its way!

When, in 1924, the Superior Brass Company had a serious fire, Joe Kaplan decided to go into business for himself. He took on the Sanitary curtains and the American Ring Company's line of bath

Shower Curtains

OF

General Electric Company
OILED SILK

Transparent
Waterproof
Durable
Attractive

The General Electric Company Chemists have formulated a secret process especially for this SHOWER CURTAIN which makes it STRONG, DURABLE, WATERPROOF, TRANSPARENT, LIGHT IN WEIGHT. It can be DRY CLEANED or LAUNDERED, WILL NOT STICK, CRACK, HARDEN or GET LUMPY in any weather.

This fabric contains no rubber and will not deteriorate with age.

Although exceptionally light in weight it has phenomenal strength.

Made in nine attractive colors.

Samples and prices on request.

BLOSSOM MFG. CO.
79 Madison Ave.   New York

207

Oiled silk was once used as an insulator on electrical equipment; that's how GE's facilities came to be used for waterproofing shower curtains.

Courtesy House Furnishing Review

By 1955 the shower curtain business had become so style-conscious that Joseph A. Kaplan & Sons Inc. staged a fashion show of its new line for the press at the Waldorf Astoria Hotel, the first ever held. It concluded with one of the actresses taking a shower on stage.

fixtures. "A friend offered me space in his cellar, rent free, to keep my small stock. During the day I would call on buyers and make deliveries personally to the stores' receiving departments, and at night I used my friend's typewriter to make out invoices." In 1925 the Joseph A. Kaplan Company opened an office at 1107 Broadway, and Joe's brother Harry joined the firm.

The Department Store Bath Shop

By 1925 the concept of a bath shop in department stores was unmistakably on its way. But it would take a while for manufacturers to develop the type of glamorous, sophisticated fashion merchandise which today is taken for granted. It would take even longer for both the merchants and the manufacturers to fully recognize the tremendous potential of the bath shop.

A change in attitude was needed. There was a great deal of uncertainty among buyers and sellers whether the department store or the plumber should handle bathroom merchandising. But a department store excels at merchandising—a plumber usually doesn't. And that is why stores emerged the winners.

Presently a bathroom section—as opposed to the former bath fixture section—began to appear in more and more stores. Just who had the first real bath shop may never be officially established. But according to the best available information, Wanamakers of Philadelphia is the most qualified contender for that honor.

Besides shower curtains, retailers could now offer a bathroom scale, hampers, stools, and small rugs or bath mats as well as toilet seats, to mention some of the larger selling items. Understandably, this appealing new category attracted many manufacturers, few of whom managed to survive. As the bath shops began to blossom into more and more elaborate affairs—occasionally subsidized in some measure by the manufacturers—their growth and the ever increasing enthusiasm of homeowners to beautify their bathrooms spawned a multitude of accessories. Sponge-rubber tub pillows...bathtub vanity trays...bath tub mats...chenille toilet seat covers...bath sprays ...back brushes; the list is long and varied and changes constantly over the years.

Meanwhile, a new element entered the bath shop merchandising scene—internal store competition. The great success the housewares department had with this thriving and fast-growing category made some of the other departments, notably bath linens, curtains, and notions, want at least part of the action—especially shower curtains. Sometimes it was initiated by the buyer; often a manufacturer unable to get an order from the housewares buyer found he could get one elsewhere in the same store. And so the housewares department found its bath section faced not only with the growing competition from other housewares departments and numerous new bath shop specialty stores around town, but also from other departments under the same roof.

208

"BROKEN POTSHERDS TUMBLING DOWN"

One's life was at stake in the days before flush toilets, and not just because of the risk of contaminating diseases. One could easily be killed much more quickly.

"The enclosed chamber pot has generated a considerable literature, especially the practice that seems to have been universal at the time—what else was there to do?—of throwing its contents into the street at night through an upstairs window," Theodor Rosebury tells us in his delightfully informative *Life on Man*. And quoting Dryden's translation of Juvenal he adds, "Dryden...is evidently speaking of his own seventeenth-century London rather than second-century Rome when he writes:

> Return we to the dangers of the night;
> And, first behold our houses' dreadful height:
> From whence come broken potsherds tumbling down;
> And leaky ware, from garret windows thrown:
> Well may they break our heads, and mark the flinty stone.
> Tis want of sense to sup abroad too late;
> Unless thou first has settled thy estate.
> As many fates attend thy steps to meet,
> As there are waking windows in the street.
> Bless the good gods, and think thy chance is rare
> To have a piss pot only for thy share.[6]

Long before bathrooms existed the chamber pot was "it." This early engraving demonstrates their use in quelling noisy neighbors.

Courtesy the New York Public Library, Astor, Lenox and Tilden Foundations.

209

The Koroseal Story

Since before World War II, vinyl film has been universally accepted as the standard material best suited for shower curtains. How did it all start?

Back in the 1930s the Yokohama Rubber Company in Japan repayed certain obligations to the B. F. Goodrich Rubber Company in Akron, Ohio, with a lightweight, Mome silk rather than cash. During this period, Goodrich developed Koroseal, a unique synthetic material used only for industrial purposes. The catalyst in this story was Richard Dawson, housewares buyer at O'Neill's department store in Akron, who put in a long-distance call to his friend Joe Kaplan, the shower curtain manufacturer, in 1937.

"I have a gentleman in my office named Dr. Howard Fritz, the vice-president in charge of research for Goodrich," Dick Dawson told Joe that day. "He seems to think that a new material they have developed—I think he calls it a plastic—would make an excellent shower curtain. I'm very impressed and I think you ought to come right out here and look into it, Joe."

Joe Kaplan was not impressed. Yet there was a certain conviction in Dawson's voice that made him hesitate.

For years he had been searching without success for the ideal material for shower curtains. Every fabric and coating anyone had ever used was deficient in some manner as a shower curtain. He frequently characterized hot water, steam, soap, and sunlight—the things that caused the greatest and quickest deterioration of the

Designer shower curtains were successfully merchandised by New York's Lord & Taylor in this 1952 *New York Times* advertisement.

materials then available—as "the four horsemen" who brought death and destruction down upon shower curtains.

Manufacturers could make beautiful shower curtains, but they failed to stand up under the punishment of normal use. Rubber-coated curtains would soften and stick, dry and peel; oiled silk would crack and split; and practically all of them would mildew. It was bad for the customers, the stores, and especially for manufacturers. "We had tried all kinds of developments in an effort to lick the problem," Kaplan said, "and I assumed Dick Dawson simply had another false alarm."

Nevertheless, a few days later he met with Dr. Fritz in the Kaplan offices in Chicago's Merchandise Mart. For the first time, he was seeing a material that seemed too good to be true.

This new waterproof material had been perfected by Dr. Waldo Semen, a Goodrich scientist. It was basically polyvinyl chloride, and had many remarkable characteristics not found in other materials. Dr. Semen found a way to plasticize it, and Goodrich was using it in industrial applications.

"Unlike our ordinary shower-curtain materials," Kaplan continued, "this material would never mildew, crack, peel, or get gummy and sticky. Moreover, it could be fabricated or processed in film or sheets of various thicknesses.

"Then he showed me some lightweight Mome silk coated with Koroseal that he thought would make a good shower curtain. It was so interesting I agreed to stop off and visit him at the Goodrich plant on my way back to New York, which I did. I was even more impressed with what I found there."

Kaplan later learned that Goodrich had given Dr. Fritz one year to develop a significant sales volume for Koroseal or it would be discontinued. Their big inventory of Mome silk probably helped generate his idea for making shower curtains. Kaplan said of Dr. Fritz:

> He was a dedicated scientist and a fine gentleman. I didn't fully realize it at the time, but he was somewhat desperate; Koroseal was his baby, and he didn't want to see it tossed out. For my part, I was desperate too; for years I had been searching for the perfect shower-curtain material, and now maybe I had found it.
>
> I left for New York with a bundle of samples, and when I got back we—my brother Harry and I and Florence Isles, our designer for many years—did some more testing and checking. The more we tested the more excited we became. This, it seemed certain, was *it!* This was the "perfect" material for which we had been searching.
>
> The following week I was back in Akron. Dr. Fritz had arranged a meeting for me with his superiors, William Richardson, vice-president, and John Collyer, newly named Goodrich president. In a short time we had concluded an agreement whereby I would have Koroseal exclusively for shower curtains.
>
> Meanwhile, we were having problems. We had learned how to screen print shower-curtain designs on all kinds of material, but now we found ourselves stumped. No ink would adhere to vinyl. Finally, with the assistance of Goodrich technicians we licked the problem.

But there was another problem of even greater consequence. At that time silk prices were at an all time low of about 11¢ a yard, and competition had driven the prices of oiled-silk curtains down to ridiculous levels of $2.98 and even $1.98. Yet here we were thinking of marketing Koroseal curtains to sell for $4.98 and $6.98. Obviously a whole new approach was called for, and so we began to stress fashion and design more than ever before. We made our shower curtain box look like a book and used as our theme "a new volume in shower curtain sales." And as we had done years earlier with our first colored curtain, we introduced our first Koroseal curtain through Bloomingdale's.

Today, of course, vinyl has practically become the industry standard for shower curtains. Incidentally, Joe Kaplan was subsequently instrumental in promoting the use of Koroseal for many other consumer products, but it is its success as a shower curtain that he found most gratifying. Ironically, Goodrich's Koroseal has since disappeared from the shower curtain field.

THE EVOLUTION OF SHOWER CURTAIN MATERIALS

After shower bathing became popular early in this century, manufacturers began a long and often frustrating search for the ideal shower curtain material. The combination of hot water, steam, soaps and shampoos, sunlight, and mildew ruined just about everything—until vinyl film came along.

Before 1920—Most shower curtains were made of an eight-ounce white duck, generally sold through plumbing jobbers.

Early 1920s—First attempts were made to introduce color and design in curtains by rubberizing striped-cotton mattress ticking. Its quick acceptance led to the use of rayon and materials, all rubberized. But the rubber coating cracked, peeled, and finally disintegrated.

About 1924—Water-repellent treatments (such as those used on rain wear) were tried, but their effectiveness on shower curtains was short-lived.

About 1926—To achieve interesting new decorative treatments, undersea designs were air-brushed on fabrics before rubberizing. Pyroxylin coatings were introduced. Although they were an improvement over rubber, they soon deteriorated and failed.

About 1930—Specially designed screen- and roller-printed Celanese acetate curtains made their appearance. Treatment with the best water-repellents plus the natural water-repellency of acetate made these curtains desirable except for their tendency to fade readily when exposed to sunlight.

About 1932—Oiled silk curtains were introduced, using a special mixture of oil and varnish developed in connection with the waterproofing of wire and cable. Lightweight silk—low in price at the time—dipped in this mixture produced an attractive new curtain, but the coating aged badly in use and soon became sticky and evil-smelling.

About 1938—The B. F. Goodrich Company developed a new vinyl material, Koroseal. Waterproof and impervious to almost every element, it quickly proved ideal for shower curtains. Originally used as a coating for silk, lace, and other materials, vinyl in film form was soon used alone as the curtain. Rapid improvements in technnology such as special vinyl printing inks and heat-sealing provided a wide range of color and design potentials. In 1952 it became available in seventy-two-inch rather than thirty-six-inch widths, making a seamless curtain possible and enhancing its appeal even more.

Soon vinyl fabricators introduced such innovations as embossed vinyl, lenticular designs like the so-called "glass brick" curtain, and, later, heat-sealed treatments, making possible the "porthole" or "see-through" and other effects.

Vinyl unquestionably added a new dimension to the shower curtain business and attracted a number of producers. But the name Koroseal has vanished from the shower curtain field.

How the Hamper Was Born

Before anyone had ever heard of dirty linen hampers, there was dirty linen. In those "good old days," dirty linen was tossed into the family wash basket—a capacious and sturdy oval woven-willow affair fitted with a stout handle on each end to help in carrying a heavy load of wet wash out into the backyard where it could be hung up to dry.

Around the turn of the century, house furnishing merchants imported these simple but essential baskets from Poland, Austria, and Germany by the boatload. Once here, they were grabbed up by America's recent arrivals, who had always used them back in "the old country."

What they lacked in glamour they more than made up in utility. And little boys with a spirit of adventure found them to be unequaled as boats in which to sail off in perfect safety to the most distant never-never land of their imaginations.

As the willow wash baskets immigrated here from across the seas, imagination—as well as the thought of business potential—was stirring in the minds of American merchants and manufacturers. Few records remain to tell us about the early development and introduction of a separate covered basket or hamper for storing soiled clothes. Like so many similar developments, it probably emerged simply through circumstance. But no doubt it was spawned as an outgrowth of the basket business and by the emergence of the bathroom as an essential addition to the average American home.

In the latter half of the past century, when America's economy was primarily agricultural, the demand for containers in which to pack fruits and vegetables increased, leading to the establishment of numerous wooden crate and basket companies. Some became so big and successful that they even grew their own timber, like the Burlington Basket Company in Burlington, Iowa.

Established in 1888 by Emil A. Florang as the Burlington Woodenware Company, it was burned down and rebuilt three times, the last

From the mid-nineteenth century on, wicker was an important bath and laundry room ingredient. The above picture shows the author of this book illustrating some point about wash-basket hampers.

212

time in 1929. Burlington, which subsequently adopted "Hawkeye" as its trademark, made a wide variety of baskets for commercial, consumer, and farm use. In the early days, practically all baskets were hand woven. "For many years various types of reed, willow, and splint hampers were produced for the purpose of storing soiled laundry," A. O. Fausel, vice-president and general manager of Burlington recalled.

From these, the veneer-cut splint hamper was derived. Occasionally color was introduced in these hampers by using various dyes and weaving the different colored splints into a chain effect in the hamper.

As labor costs increased and the wood supply diminished, it was necessary to develop greater production efficiencies. This resulted in the development of loom-woven materials, which were wrapped around a wooden or metal frame and painted. Later, these were made with some form of plastic top. Progress in the hamper business has been made on a step-by-step basis, with the biggest step being the transition from hand-woven to loom-woven materials. Later, of course, the all-vinyl covered hamper we use today was introduced.

At the end of the last century the art of weaving reed, willow, and other materials—later twisted paper fiber especially—was by no means confined to making baskets. Much porch or "sun room" furniture and baby carriages were also woven or made, in part, by using loom-woven fiber "cloth," often in very ornate designs.

One such manufacturer was the F. A. Whitney Carriage Company in Leominster, Massachusetts. Even before World War I it began switching its production to hampers (probably before Burlington started making them), and, until the company went out of business during the Depression in the 1930s, it had become the leading producer of quality hampers in the small but important and fast-growing business.

Its first and best known hamper, called the "Whitney Pannier," (an old French term for bread basket), looked somewhat like a small, oblong bench fitted with spindle side handles and a hinged wooden lid. The name "Pannier" presently gave way to the more understandable "hamper," and soon not only Whitney but O. W. Siebert Company, Heywood Wakefield Company, the furniture manufacturers, and others were making hampers in a variety of styles. Another essential for the modern bathroom had "arrived."

Among the "other" firms referred to then was a small company called Gleitsman Incorporated. Today as the Pearl-Wick Corporation, it is one of the most important factors in the hamper (and related items) business. The company began most inconspicuously in 1898 when Louis Gleitsman took a small loft in a building on Mercer Street in downtown New York to launch a novelty basket business. A few years later when they were old enough, his two sons, Harold and Milton, joined him.

"Harold spent most of his time on the outside doing the selling,"

BEAUTY · UTILITY · QUALITY
A NEW LINE OF
WOVEN FIBRE HAMPERS

COLORFUL

WOVEN DESIGNS
SIX COLORS
EIGHT SHAPES

MODERNE

Phone or Write
S. J. LIPPE
220 Fifth Avenue
1150 Broadway
New York City

R. J. EHLERS CO.
206 Lexington Ave.
New York City

F. A. WHITNEY CGE. CO.
666 Lake Shore Drive
Chicago, Ill.

DISTINCTIVE

F. A. WHITNEY CARRIAGE CO.
The Home of Quality Merchandise.
LEOMINSTER   MASSACHUSETTS

213

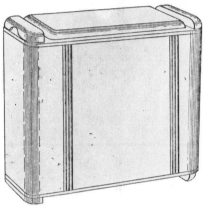

From top: The late twenties saw hampers as colorful, *moderne* and distinctive. The sketch of a 1938 hamper demonstrates a furniture console approach to design—rounded corners abound.

Top, courtesy House Furnishing Review.

Darwin Sussberg, his son-in-law and now president of the corporation recalled in 1971.

> One day in 1929, he often told me, while calling on Miss Mae Harvey, then the assistant buyer for flowers and for bathroom merchandise for Wanamakers in New York, she showed him a handsome, woven-fiber hamper with a hinged wooden lid that was covered with an imitation mother-of-pearl material. It should have been handsome; it was a French import and priced at $50.
>
> Knowing that Gleitsmans were making somewhat similar woven novelties, she suggested that he copy it—but at a popular price. She thought it would be a winner and Harold agreed. I recall him telling me how the first models were made with the wood from old egg and fruit crates for frames which were then covered with some type of burlap material. After being treated with a stiffener of glue sizing it was then sprayed with white paint.
>
> The wooden top was made the way toilet seats were once made, by glueing a pyroxylin plastic sheet to a wood base. Wanamakers promptly placed an order for these hampers, which proved to be an instant success when they were advertised for $5.95.

From that first, small hamper, crude by today's standards, the Gleitsman family built a big, new business. And, prompted by the make-up of its product, its name was changed to Pearl-Wick Incorporated.

Soon the "burlap material" used originally was being replaced with woven fiber purchased from the American Fiber Company. Well-made wood frames replaced the make-do egg crate lumber for the frames. And presently stores all over began asking for promotion-priced hampers. By 1928 the business had prospered so well that the company was able to invest in the purchase of the fiber weaving looms the Ypsilanti Fiber Company, Michigan, had decided to dispose of. Now the Gleitsmans would no longer need to buy this basic ingredient; they could weave their own fiber cloth.

In 1940 the business passed the magic million dollar mark and moved to greatly expanded plant facilities in Long Island City, New York. Right after World War II it had an opportunity to replace its old weaving looms with a new type of steel wire-reinforced fiber cloth looms acquired from the Lloyd Manufacturing Company in 1946. Since then the line has been broadened to include much related bathroom merchandise including a line of scales made for it by the Hanson Scale Company, and plastics of various types now dominate the hamper and stool items, among other things.

In 1967 the company acquired the Lincoln Metal Products Company, makers of cannister sets in Brooklyn, and in 1968 it purchased Hegeman Steel Products Company, producer of metal bathroom products. In 1972 Sussberg said that Pearl-Wick's present volume in bath shop merchandise alone "is now over $10 million," and that the company had become one of the top five family-owned firms in the housewares industry.

214

From top: Another hamper, this time with a southwest Indian design, to make it "different." Bloomingdale's found the Mariner sea-going padded toilet seat "see-worthy." This ad sold "cushion soft" qualities.

From top left
The modern bathroom is a
major selling point for real estate
developers. Always a production, it
sometimes becomes a confection of
plumbing fixtures and bath shop
accessories.

Courtesy House Beautiful.

Another bathroom emphasizes a la mode
accessories, this time in the pseudo-Empire
manner.

Copyright © Condé Nast Publications Inc.

One of the most successful merchandisers
of bath shop items—really an ensemble
approach—is Golden Dolphin Shops. Over
four hundred outlets glamorously package
bathroom fittings. Imaginative retailers have
vastly increased the status of the bathroom,
and bath shop volume.

Church PRESENTS NEW IDEAS IN PLANNED PROMOTIONS

SEE complete showing of Church Ensemble Bathroom Furnishings at Hotel Stevens—Chicago ROOMS 805 AND 806.

In 1934, a "new idea" in planned bathroom promotion.
Courtesy House Furnishing Review.

Church Bathroom Ensemble

"For over a dozen years now, department stores have been capitalizing on the ensemble idea in merchandising home furnishings," wrote a vice-president for Fuller and Smith and Ross, Incorporated, then (1933) the advertising agency for the C. F. Church Manufacturing Company of Holyoke, Massachusetts (now a division of American Standard). "First came the living room, then the bedroom and the dining room...finally the kitchen. What has been overlooked to date is the bathroom. In comparison with the merchandising attention, floor space, promotion, display and selling given by department stores to furnishings for other rooms, the bathroom has been 'the forgotten room.' "[7]

The company had surveyed fifteen hundred department stores in analyzing the problem and announced at the July housewares show that year that "the leading maker of toilet seats is now offering an entirely new line of bathroom furniture and furnishings built to meet today's needs of both the customer and the housewares buyer.... Called the 'Church Ensemble of Bathroom Furniture,' it was designed by Lurelle Guild. It is the first complete and authentically styled line of bathroom furniture."

Included besides hampers and toilet seats were stools, chairs, vanities, towel stands, mirrors, tables, cabinets, and so on. "In place of a bathroom department featuring towel bars, tumbler holders and other low-priced fixtures and gadgets, alert buyers have seen the greater volume and profit possibilities of selling ensembles of bathroom furnishings." But as sound as the "quality dollars versus dime gadgets" merchandising philosophy may have been, the desperate Depression (along with other factors) doomed the idea to failure. Within a couple of years it was just another memory.

Another Bath Shop Bonanza: The Scale

Through the centuries, the scale, one of man's earliest and most useful inventions, has helped make trade and commerce possible. But it was not until after the beginning of the present century that someone thought about a personal household scale on which to weigh oneself.

It was the Germans, with their penchant for the mechanical, who apparently first made such a scale. The first manufacturer may have been Jas Raveno and Son, who named their scale the "Jaraso." It had a small mirror suspended on chains in front at a forty-five-degree angle to enable the user to read the dial. It sold for a little under ten dollars.

Meanwhile, in Chicago in 1913 William Heinze, the buyer for Marshall Field and Company was planning for the opening of that great store's imposing new household utilities department. Naturally it would include a bathroom fixture section, and the Jaraso scale was among the special items he planned to feature.

The sheer variety and luxury of shower curtain fabrics gives them an haute couture association.

There were a number of good scale manufacturers in this country at that time, but since there was no demand for a bath or personal scale, none were being made. Kitchen scales, however, were a popular item. "Women are using kitchen scales more and more," declared the 1910 catalog of the Hanson Scale Company, then at 523 North Ada Street in Chicago. And, it continued, "Women not only check up on the weight from the grocer and butcher, but they are cooking by weight. Guessing at amounts…is too wasteful of valuable ingredients….One of the biggest services you can render a housewife is to urge her to cook by weight."

Making Scales Accurate

Seven years before the opening of Field's new household utilities department, a young man named Mathias C. Weber had left his native Hungary to seek his fortune in New York. A first-rate mechanic, he had had experience working on commercial scales. Soon after he arrived in America he got a job repairing scales at Charles Haller and Company on Leight Street. His pay was sixteen dollars a week.

In Horatio Alger fashion, he soon found himself in charge of service in the Manhattan office of the Olsgood Scale Company of Binghamton, New York, another manufacturer who made only commercial models.

"In those days accuracy was something you could find in the dictionary—but rarely in scales," he recalled during a 1971 interview in his home in Hollywood, Florida, where he retired.

It finally became such a serious problem that the New York City Bureau of Weights and Measures decided to register all scales used in business there. I remember that the bureau was headed at the time by a Mr. Steurla. He wanted some technical advice and someone had recommended me as an expert, although I was only twenty-one at the time. A big improvement in scale accuracy followed the registration program. For instance, Jacobs Brothers brought out a new model called the "J. B. Legal."

In 1912 he accepted an offer from Olsgood to become a special troubleshooter at the factory, and he moved to Binghamton. Less than two years later the business was sold. Weber continued:

I flirted rather seriously with the idea of going into the automobile business. Cars were just catching on then and everywhere you went people were mortgaging their homes so they could add a garage and buy a car.
But on February 16, 1914, a messenger from the First National Bank called at my home—we had no telephone in those days—to say they'd like to see me as soon as possible.

At the bank he was introduced to a representative of the A. C. McCord Manufacturing Company of Detroit, which owned the Mason,

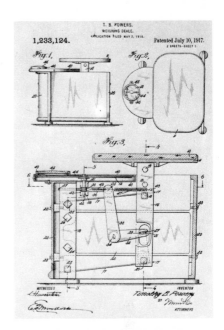

217

From top: A schematic of a 1917 bathroom scale. Next, the Madaco scale, one of Matt Weber's early scales. Mathias C. Weber, himself. With Alfred and Irving Hutchinson, he founded the Continental Scale Company in 1919.

Davis Stove Company and the Chicago Scale Company. He was told they were looking for "the best scale man in the country" and was promptly offered a contract. On March 11, 1914, he started his new job as superintendent of the Chicago Scale Company's plant at 7700 South Chicago Avenue. A. C. McCord's brother-in-law E. C. Rowe was president.

Within a few months the business climate everywhere began to change: World War I had started in Europe. New problems began to develop for everyone. One was that Marshall Field's, after having done so well with the Jaraso scale, now suddenly found its supply cut off. Could the Chicago Scale Company make such a scale for Field's? Heinze asked them. The company agreed to make the scale. "But I had ideas for improving it," said Weber.

Theirs was an ordinary, ball-bearing action mechanism. I had conceived a superimposed parallelogram platform scale using a spring suspension, something I later patented.

And we also made a big change in the arrangement of the dial. One day when all of us were leaving for lunch we decided to drive over to the Maryland Restaurant; during the short trip I happened to glance at the speedometer on the dashboard to make sure I wasn't speeding. I suddenly got an idea. "That's it!" I shouted at my astonished passengers. "That's it! We'll place the dial in such a position that it can be easily read when you're standing on the scale!" This eliminated the need for a small mirror attached to the scale.

Not long afterward our new scale was ready. We decided to call it the "Madaco," an abbreviation of Mason, Davis Stove Company, our parent company. It retailed for somewhere around $7.50, I think. And then one December morning in 1917, in the second mail, we got a letter from Germany—the Raveno people warned us of the serious consequences if we copied their scale! We had a good laugh and went back to work.

For some time now, Matt Weber had been aware that it might be a good time to start a new business—especially for a still almost unique product like a personal scale, about which, by now, he probably knew more than anyone else in the country. The war was over and things were prosperous; the postwar depression would come later. For some time he had been quietly working on the model of a new scale he thought was good. He called it the "Health-O-Meter." There was only one problem—he lacked sufficient capital.

Through his barber, he met Irving King Hutchinson.

I had been introduced to Irving—a real extrovert who drove a Stutz Bearcat, which was a great status symbol in those days!—and was meeting with him in his home, when in walked his brother Alfred, who had just returned from Mexico where, under Pershing, he had been chasing Pancho Villa.

By the time I had finished explaining the model of my new scale to the brothers they were just as excited about its potential as I was, and we agreed to get together. On January 17, 1919, we formally organized the Continental Scale Works.

Opposite page: Bath shop retailing has gone well beyond a small-department operation. The early 1970s saw "total bathroom" retail stores take an important share of this segment of the housewares industry. Attractive displays and backdrops create an atmosphere for buying. The Golden Dolphin Shops are among today's most successful bathroom packagers.

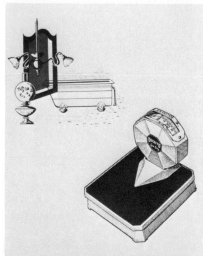

Scales, scales, scales. Some important examples from the past and present. Weight-watching provides a constant new impetus to the market.

Scales and the Diet Craze

What generated the rather sudden demand for a personal, or "bath" scale after World War I? For many years, people had weighed themselves in the penny slot machines that abounded in drugstores, railroad stations, and elsewhere. But there was no particular, certainly no urgent reason to weigh oneself. Presumably the diet craze provided the impetus. In the fifty years since the end of World War I, dieting has become a way of life for many people.

In the 1920s, reports James Young in *Medical Messiahs,*

style decreed that men must be lithe and athletic, women slim to the point of emaciation. "There seems, indeed, to have come upon the women of America," wrote the editor of the *Journal of the American Medical Association,* "a veritable craze for reduction which has passed the bounds of normality and driven women and young girls to a type of self-mutilation impossible to explain on any other basis than the faddism of the mob." "Fabulous sums are spent for...anti-fat frauds," says [FTC] Commissioner Humphrey, "since the female skeleton has become the fashion of this country."

The first general bulletin of the National Better Business Bureau dealt with this racket. Marmola [then one of the most widely advertised quack reducing remedies] told flaming youth and the would-be young about "the pleasant way to banish excess fat," and presented the testimony of actress Constance Talmadge: "The demand for figures is so universal that movie stars must have them. Not only beauty, but good health and vitality argue against excess fat."[8]

In any case, the slenderizing fad soon outgrew the fad stage and became a notable, as well as noticeable, characteristic of Americans. The phony reducing remedies, however, continued to grow fat and rich. There was, of course, nothing the least bit phony about the bath scales these weight-minded Americans demanded.

The first bathroom scale to be produced by the new Continental Scale Company was its Health-O-Meter model No. 100, brought out in 1919. Of cast iron frame construction with "hardened bearings, rack and pinion, made of best quality steel," it was finished in white, was eight inches high, and weighed twenty pounds. Its list price was sixteen dollars and its accuracy was guaranteed within one pound. It was an immediate success.

It fact it was so successful that it was soon being copied. During the next few years the Continental Scale Company found itself as occupied with patent suits as with producing scales for demanding retailers. "A patent in the scale business, it seems, is little more than a license to go to court and become involved in a lawsuit," philosophized Matt Weber, looking back on his forty-three years as a manufacturer.

Jacobs Brothers, he went on, was the first to jump on Health-O-Meter's newly discovered bath scale bandwagon and by 1921 had brought out a copy. "That was the start of a whole series of infringements with which we had to contend," he said.

THE DEBUT—AND THE DEPARTURE—OF "THE PRINCESS"

Probably the most sensational but short-lived development of the early days of the bath scale business was an order placed by Sears, Roebuck and Company at the January 1934 housewares show for 50,000 "Princess" scales at the incredibly low cost of $1.25 each—but they were never delivered.

"The Princess," recalled Mathias Weber, founder of the Continental Scale Company, was the first low-platform bath scale and was a design innovation which had influenced the industry ever since. It was the work of a young German immigrant, Carl Burkhardt, employed by the Narlor Heather Company of Goshen, Indiana, in 1933.

Sig Danziger, a manufacturers sales representative in Chicago, showed a handmade model at the January housewares show, where it not only bagged the immense Sears order, but also became "the talk of the show." Other scale makers couldn't even imagine such a low price.

When Mr. Weber examined the scale, he found to his amazement that its mechanism was an outright copy of the Health-O-Meter principle and promptly brought suit to stop it. "We had to chase the Princess from McCoomb to Cleveland and back again," said Mr. Weber, "but we finally succeeded in catching her with a consent decree in February 1934, and she never did get into production."

Thereafter the bath scale business proved to be very appealing, though often far from profitable, to nearly thirty firms. Competition became intense, especially during the Depression years, and quality, as well as price, became the victim, an old story in the housewares business.

But the leading manufacturers persisted, aided by the consumers' equally persistent determination to keep checking on their weight to protect their figures. By the time the Depression began to fade, bath scales had come to be an essential, basic stock item in that promising new section called the bath shop.

Scales and "Fashion"

Meanwhile, as color and design in housewares began to assert their importance—no one went so far as to use the word fashion yet—scales reflected the trend. After 1933, influenced by the radical "low profile" design of the ill-starred "Princess" scale, the awkward-looking, high boxlike scales began to disappear and endless variations of low platform models began to appear—in color.

It's often been said that when a girl reduces she is going out of her weigh to please some man. Be that as it may, it is nevertheless a fact that this once non-existent but now very important housewares product has reached the point where, in 1971 for example, over six million bath scales were sold to weight-conscious Americans who can buy them today in an array of shapes, colors and styles.

!!!THE TALK OF THE SHOW!!!

THE SALES OF PRINCESS BATHROOM SCALES DURING THE NATIONAL HOUSEFURNISHING SHOW HAVE SURPASSED ALL EXPECTATIONS

WE REACHED THE QUARTER MILLION MARK

OUR DELIVERIES WILL START PROMPTLY FEBRUARY 15th OR SOONER

PRINCESS Bathroom Scales
two-tone ivory and green
RETAIL at
$1.98

PRINCESS De Luxe Bathroom Scales
chromium and black
RETAIL at
$2.98

FULL SIZE 13½ x 9½
Fully Guaranteed

OUR ELECTRIC APPLIANCES, SANDWICH TOASTERS AND WAFFLE IRONS ARE STANDARD BEARERS IN THE POPULAR PRICE RANGE

S. H. DANZIGER, Inc.
1469 MERCHANDISE MART—CHICAGO

New York City 1150 Broadway — TORONTO — WINNIPEG — MONTREAL — Los Angeles, Calif. Transportation Bldg.

Wait Until You See "WATE-KING"

The First SPRINGLESS Bathroom Scale

Embodying the principles of the FINEST COMMERCIAL Scales.

NO SPRINGS—Accuracy to the Nth degree. KNIFE EDGE and BALL BEARING CONSTRUCTION. ONLY HEAVY STEEL USED—NO CAST IRON. AUTOMATIC PENDULUM LOCKING DEVICE—Insuring non-breakage of movable parts. STREAMLINED—CHROME PLATED. RUBBER FEET AND MAT.

A quality product at a price that will amaze you.

Don't Order a Bathroom Scale Until You See the Wate-King.

SPRINGLESS SCALE CORPORATION
910 West Jackson Blvd., CHICAGO

American Furniture Mart   Room 1433A—Merchandise Mart   CHICAGO

Space Saver Scale

A New Idea in Bath Scales

Get the scale off the floor yet ready to use. Here is a low cost scale (under $10.00) with the luxury of 24K gold plated handle, hang-up hook and ring, Model 950. The same in chrome plated, Model 951. Available in choice of four decorator colors. Capacity 300 lbs. by 1 lb. Instant-seal wall hook attaches to most wall surfaces without tools. Write Bob Rumpsa, Premium Dept., for personal attention.

HANSON SCALE COMPANY, Northbrook, Illinois 60062

Low price and new features ("springless," "off the floor") are touted.

MAJOR HIGHLIGHTS OF BATH SCALE DEVELOPMENT

1916 First U. S. Patent on a bath scale, No. 1,210,382, issued to M. J. Weber, Dec. 26, 1916, and assigned to Mason, Davis Company, Chicago. Used vertical drum dial for reading weight.

1917 First patent on a bathroom scale designed with leaf-type springs issued to T. B. Powers and assigned to Jacobs Brothers Company, (now Detecto).

1918 First bath scale to reflect some contemporary styling in its design and probably the first to be made of sheet steel instead of cast iron, patented by R. F. Chatillon. (The Chatillon Scale Company, New York, pursued the kitchen and commercial scale business, apparently in preference to the bath scale field.)

1918 Detecto Scales Incorporated obtain the rights to manufacture a bath scale being produced in Germany by Alexander Werk.

1921 First bath scale with a horizontal clock-face dial patented by M. J. Weber and assigned to Continental Scale Company.

1921 First "doctor's type" beam scale developed by M. J. Weber for Continental.

1921 First doctor's type beam scale developed by M. J. Weber for Continental.

1921 First scale to use springs to hold platform and base in fixed position developed by H. M. Cameron for Chatillon.

1931 First scale with horizontal weighing spring developed by H. M. Cameron for Chatillon.

1933 First scale weighing up to 300 pounds using a 100-pound dial with three rotations of weighing indicator, developed by M. J. Weber for Continental.

1935 First patent on a bath scale made with strip steel levers with free-floating rack, issued in England to H. W. K. Jennings, and assigned to Jacobs Brothers Company, (now Detecto).

1936 First scale using three indicators to read weight on a 100-pound face dial developed by P. J. Kircher for Detecto.

1936 First patent on a round scale design issued to A. J. Kurls and H. Hoyer and assigned to Jacobs Brothers Company, (now Detecto).

1936 First bath scale with a mechanism designed so that the support point is between the person being weighed and the weighing spring, invented by William Greenleaf and assigned to the George Borg Corporation. Later it became the Borg-Erickson Corporation and in 1953 for the first time marketed a scale embodying this mechanism. Designed by Raymond Loewy, it was called "Flight" and was less than two inches in height from the floor.

1937 First scale with an electrically (battery) illuminated dial developed by M. A. Provi for the Brearley Company.

1938 First bath scale designed with a stamped steel swinging pivot hanger, a significant basic improvement, developed by M. A. Provi for Brearley.

1939 First bath scale designed to be built into the wall and fold down when desired for use developed by William Greenleaf for the George Borg Corporation (later the Borg-Erickson Corporation), called the "Fold-a-Weigh" scale.

1939 First bath scale with a carrying handle designed by M. A. Provi for Brearley.

1939 First scale with a magnifying lens on the dial to provide greater legibility developed by Brearley and introduced by Sears, Roebuck & Company.

1940 First bath scale with a molded plastic housing designed by M. A. Provi for Brearley.

1944 First bath scale equipped with an external means for correcting or adjusting weight inaccuracy developed by M. A. Provi for Brearley.

1955 First scale made with a floating indicating mechanism permitting use of the scale on uneven floor or on carpet without affecting its accuracy, issued to the Krupp Works in Germany and assigned to Detecto.

1957 First bath scale equipped with device to lock dial with registered weight introduced by Borg Erickson.

1958 First bath scale designed to operate accurately on either a soft surface (carpet) or conventional hard surface—using the Mono-trol movement—developed by M. A. Provi for Brearley.

1960 First bath scale with a removable, transparent plastic platform cover so that any material with the color and design of the owner's preference can be readily inserted, designed by Vytant Aleks for Brearley.

222

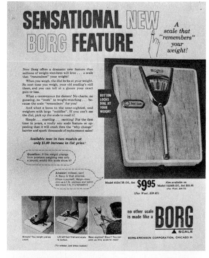

A scale that "remembers your weight" offered a special feature to the near-sighted and stout. Today's scale has a slim design and offers a "flip-top."

1960 First bath scale designed so that it could be hung on a hook on the wall when not in use introduced by the Hanson Scale Company.

1960 First stand-on-edge or store-away scale introduced by Brearley.

1961 First bath scale equipped with a magnetic stop for positive "zeroing" and correction of weight dial by the user developed by M. A. Provi for Brearley.

1963 First bath scale equipped with a mechanical stop for "zeroing" and correction of weight dial by user developed by Maxwell E. Jacobs and Charles Anselmo for Detecto.

1963 First scale with pile fur-fabric platform covering introduced by Borg Erickson Corporation.

1964 First mechanism to obviate the need for adjusting bath scales to zero called "Auto-Zero," introduced by Detecto.

1964 First bath scale to use a digital read-out projection numbers scale in place of the conventional drum or dial introduced by the Hanson Scale Company.

1964 First bath scale made with a platform of vinyl laminated aluminum introduced by Brearley.

1967 First bath scale using a novel leverage mechanism to achieve a very low profile developed by M. A. Provi for Brearley.

1969 First "Mod" or "Pop Art" designs in bath scales designed by O. B. Solie for Brearley.

For their special assistance in compiling this record, the author wishes to thank M. J. Weber, a retired founder of the Continental Scale Company, and M. A. Provi, vice-president, development and corporate planning, Brearley Company.

THE SCALE BUSINESS: SOME GAIN, SOME LOSE

Over the years many companies were attracted to the bath scale business, but only a few survived. For example:

1919 Continental Scale Company started the industry in Chicago with its "Health-O-Meter" to retail for $16.

1921 Jacobs Brothers of Brooklyn introduced the "Detecto."

1926 Hanson Scale Company of Chicago entered the bath scale field for the first time.

1928 Kleinsorg and Geometric Tool Company of Cleveland made a scale it then transferred to the Colson Company.

1928 Montgomery Ward and Company had its own factory in McComb, Illinois, make a scale under its name. Described as "very high and made of very heavy castings," it was not successful and was discontinued.

1928 Landers, Frary and Clark of New Britain, Connecticut, introduced its "Universal" bath scale, a high rotating dial attached to a platform.

1929 Pollock Manufacturing Company of Brooklyn made the "Hollywood" scale, low platform and high dial, to retail for $4.95. It was not successful and was dropped within two years.

1930 Club Aluminum Company of Chicago attempted to introduce a scale, but soon abandoned the project.

1932 Brearley Company of Rockford, Illinois, began with a low platform, high dial scale, and brought out a very low, rotating flat scale in 1934. In 1938 they brought out a low, rotating-dial model to retail for $2.95.

1933 Lion Electric Company failed within two years.

1933 Pace Manufacturing Company introduced the "Venus," a rotating dial scale. Not successful and soon quit.

1934 Forgings and Stampings Inc., Rockford, Illinois, an outgrowth of Brearley, brought out a scale called the "Corporal," but discontinued production within two years.

1934 Barler Heater, McComb, Illinois and Monarch Aluminum Company, Cleveland, announced the "Princess," to sell for $1.25 wholesale. Stopped by Continental Scale with lawsuit for patent infringement and was never produced.

1935 Floorman Company, New York, introduced a scale with no success; patents acquired by Jacobs Brothers.

1935 Geo. W. Borg Company, Chicago, introduced the "Borg" scale.

1938 Springless Scale Company, Chicago, introduced the "Wate-King," but discontinued it a year later.

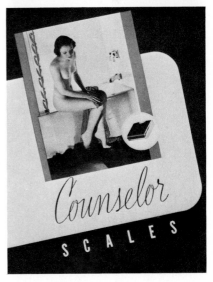

A French manufacturer entered the American market with this sleek bath scale designed by Marco Zanuso in 1971. Somewhat earlier, Counselor scales utilized another kind of sleek design in its advertisements.

THE ELECTRIC AGE

"Electricity is the coming power of the world. It is the sun-given power, generated by heat which is, at present, the master of man," Isbon Scott reported in the May 1895 issue of his recently established *House Furnishing Review.*

Three quarters of a century later, that power along with an overwhelming array of electrical housewares which perform countless functions, have now become the servants of man. In fact, there is also a rapidly growing number of electrical housewares that provide personal care to a degree no one ever imagined in the past.

All these appliances have now become such a commonplace, integral part of today's living and such an important part of the housewares industry, it seems surprising that there was a time when things were quite different. Those were the days, seventy years ago, when a great many people thought the "generating station" office (as the power company was often called) was the obvious place for appliances to be sold, rather than in department or hardware stores.

Yet even the power companies were often uninterested in selling appliances. "Strange as it may seem in retrospect, our efforts to convince the early power companies to sell these new current consuming devices as load builders, proved to be an approach that seemed to be entirely beyond their comprehension," Robert A. Kuhn, president of the American Electrical Heater Company, Detroit, related in 1971 in telling of his father's efforts to sell irons the company made beginning around 1900. "As far as they were concerned the only thing that mattered was the promotion of their electric lights in competition with gas lights. 'We have all the business we need by supplying power for our customers' light bulbs,' they said in effect."

One of the things that, at least indirectly, handicapped the development of appliances—certainly it didn't help—was the "Battle of the Currents" between d.c., direct current, and a.c., alternating current. Not until about 1900 did a.c. win out and even then it had much difficulty in overcoming tradition.

Edison, it so happened, had become dedicated to d.c., although it would have made no difference which current he had used for lighting purposes. When, in 1885, a new type of transformer, the "Z.B.C.," went into use in Europe, permitting long-distance power transmission at high voltage and then stepping it down at the point of use, it became "the technological darling of the moment," writes Robert Silverberg in *Light of the World.* Although "the forward-looking men of the industry were confident someone would invent a feasible A.C. electric motor" and that "alternating current was sure to win universal acceptance," nevertheless "Edison—nearly alone—fought the new trend."[1]

224

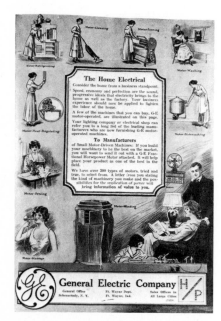

The home electrical, from 1918 (*above*) to 1972 (*opposite page*). What must have been astonishing in this General Electric Company advertisement—electrical sewing, dishwashing, refrigerating, and vacuum cleaning, circa World War I, is not less so today, with our wonderland of electrical housewares: juicers, extractors, appliance centers, mixers, broilers, blenders. A colorful collection of appliances from the past two decades.

Top, courtesy General Electric.

From top: An advertisement for electrical Christmas gifts in *Good Housekeeping Magazine,* December 1912. Note the electric samovar. "What Every Woman Wants"…an electric kitchen. One of a series of advertisements sponsored by the electric utilities in the 1920s.

George Westinghouse, relates Silverberg, "bold, ambitious, even reckless…sought to steal a march on Edison by getting control of that segment of the electrical field that Edison scorned; high voltage alternating equipment.…" In the ensuing "Battle of the Currents," he reports, "…Edison…persuaded the [New York State] legislature to legalize the electric chair for the execution of condemned criminals—and saw to it that the fatal chair used Westinghouse equipment. What better way to dramatize the lethal nature of alternating current?"[2]

And, adds Silverberg, "Out of bitterness and testiness Edison had elevated his original short-sightedness to the status of an inflexible policy; it was the worst mistake of his career.…In 1908 when he encountered George Stanley, son of the inventor of Westinghouse's transformer, he said to him, 'By the way, tell your father I was wrong.' "[3]

By 1906 many stores had begun to dabble a bit in selling—or trying to sell—some of these intriguing new household appliances. But the first department store to go into this business on a broad scale was Wanamaker's, New York, which in October of that year staged an "Electro-Domestic Science" exposition in its basement house furnishing department. Suggested and executed by Max Loewenthal, vice-president of the New York Electrical Society and president of the International Electric and Engineering Company, the presentation included a model electric kitchen and a bedroom to show how extensively electricity could be used.

But there were still many who were unsure of the appliance business. "How far shall I go in featuring and selling electrical household appliances?" headlined a story by Warren Edwards in the April 1920 issue of *House Furnishing Review,* which continued: "How far will you go in selling electrical housewares this year?"

The best answer to that question is the record of the electrical housewares industry itself. Since it was asked, the number of new time- and labor-saving conveniences on the market is exceeded only by the ingenuity, efficiency, and skill with which these appliances perform their tasks. And what is even more remarkable, perhaps, is the fact that there seems to be no end to the extent of such contributions to America's high standard of living.

Crude Beginnings

Ironing has long been one of mankind's—or more precisely womenkind's—minor but tiresome burdens. Through the ages, historians and anthropologists agree there has been an urge to make woven fabrics more attractive and more usable by removing wrinkles caused by use and washing. Likewise, fashion for men and women alike has demanded ruffles and pleats.

As early as the tenth century, the Vikings used a glass "linen smoother" that looked something like a flat inverted mushroom. The Greeks used a "goffering" iron to pleat their linen robes. In many places and periods people used a hand mangle—a flat mallet or paddle used to beat the fabric smooth and wrinkle-free.

Just when or where the idea of employing heat as well as pressure for ironing first developed is not clear. But by the sixteenth century in Russia and Europe, ironing was being done with a hollow, boxlike iron designed to hold hot charcoal.

Then irons appeared which were designed to hold a separate slug of cast iron; after being heated in the fire, these slugs were inserted into the hollow iron to be replaced with another hot slug when necessary. Women welcomed these improvements, which helped keep the soot of charcoal and fireplace off the clean linen.

Later as stoves came to replace the traditional fireplace, someone got the happy idea of casting irons in one solid piece and heating them on the stove, thus circumventing some of the dirt and inconvenience of the earlier methods. These were quickly named sadirons—not, as some have supposed, out of sympathy for the laundress, but because sad can mean compact or heavy.

After manufactured gas for illumination was introduced at the end of the nineteenth century, it wasn't long before this development began to be used for cooking and, shortly, for ironing. In the fall of 1894 the Bolgiano Manufacturing Company of Baltimore, Maryland, announced such an iron, perhaps the first of its kind.

This new iron may well have been "a neat, nickel-plated affair," but it requires little imagination to realize that the first of these devices were rather primitive, and often a potentially serious hazard to the user.

Yet with all their early handicaps and deficiencies, gas irons—in continually improved models—were far superior to the old sadirons. Millions of women showed their approval by buying one, more often than not from a door-to-door salesman, or sometimes from the local gas company; and invariably on the installment plan.

Three other types of irons were in use around the turn of the century: acetylene (gas) irons, similar to ordinary gas irons but with a different type of burner; alcohol irons, with an attached tank that held about half a pint of alcohol; and gasoline irons, which were of two types. One had an attached tank and operated like the alcohol iron, and the second was connected by a long tube to a large tank of fuel.

Early Electric Inventions

On June 6, 1882, a New Yorker named Henry W. Seely received United States patent number 259,054 on his invention of an electric iron—the first ever patented. He had filed his application the year before.

But the delay made little difference. The iron was of almost no practical use, since current was supplied to it only while it sat on its stand. Even if it had been designed better it would not have been practical, since there were no power companies until 1890.

227

Combination Lamp and Grill
Electrical Merchandising, January, 1925

Items from the past: a combination lamp and grill, "where space is at a premium;" a "beautiful piece of electric furniture"—a serving table and tea wagon. Before electricity, a "Uneedit" gas iron. Irons were among the first housewares items to "go electric."

Top, courtesy Merchandising Week.
Lower, courtesy House Furnishing Review.

Two pioneers of the electric iron: Earl H. Richardson, who developed the Hotpoint iron; and Joseph Myers, former vice president of Proctor Electric, who is credited with engineering the first successful adjustable automatic thermostat for irons.

From top: Fluting or ruffling irons were very important in the nineteenth century when costumes of the period demanded special pressing. The lower picture shows one of the first electric irons, necessarily of simple design.

Top, courtesy Margaret Davidson Collection.

Meanwhile that dazzling new wonder, electricity, was stimulating the inventive ingenuity of men all over the country. In 1889 in Minneapolis, Charles E. Carpenter, a cashier in a restaurant, discovered that he had talent he was to develop with great success.

Unfortunately, few facts are known about his early days. It is said that he constructed an electrically heated griddle which was placed in the window of the restaurant and became something of a sensation in attracting customers to watch—and eat—food cooked electrically.

Presumably Carpenter had, or acquired, an interest in the restaurant. At any rate his partner, a Mr. Nevins, who also owned a tailoring establishment, asked him if he could make a self-heating sadiron. He could and did.

What happened next is neatly summarized by an entry in the 1890/91 Minneapolis City Directory that lists "Charles E. Carpenter, Sec., Carpenter-Nevins Electric Heating Co."

Meanwhile he had gone to New York, where he formed the Carpenter Enclosed Resistance Company. In 1903 the firm was acquired by Cutler-Hammer, which then went into the appliance business. Their line included irons and hotplates, a heating unit for curling irons, and an electrically heated shaving mug. The company discontinued consumer goods after World War I.

The first known sale of an electric iron was made, it is said, in 1896, by the Ward Leonard Electric Company (located somewhere in Wisconsin). Details are scant, but the company made the first electrically heated flatiron with replaceable heating units, probably because iron—the only metal available at the time for heating elements—had a very short life.

But the development of the electric iron business—in fact the development of the entire electric appliance business—was seriously handicapped by a problem which was in no way the fault of the manufacturers: the scarcity of electric power. What was even worse, almost all the power companies—they would not be referred to as utilities until later—thought of electricity only in terms of lighting. "Load building" was unnecessary and had not even been considered. Only a very few of the largest power companies supplied electricity during daylight hours when women usually did their laundry.

But in 1903 at least one utility man had been thinking about this problem. He was Earl Richardson, plant superintendent of the power company in Ontario, California. Part of his duties included reading meters in the homes they served, and he frequently talked to homemakers about the idea of an electric iron. Few housewives wanted any part of the heavy, cumbersome irons they had seen.

Richardson's interest was twofold. For several years he himself had been experimenting with an iron. Also, if women began to use electric irons the demand for electricity would be increased, and then perhaps the power company could operate around the clock.

He went to work refining his earlier model, making it smaller and lighter. It had a glowing resistance wire wrapped around a large brass core which absorbed the heat and conducted it to the base of the iron.

Several dozen samples were made up and distributed to power company customers to try. He then convinced his management to generate electricity all day on Tuesdays so the customers could use the irons. They were a great success, and the demand grew so fast that the following year he left the power company and, with outside financial backing, formed the Pacific Electric Heating Company with four employees to manufacture electric laundry irons.

Then he ran into trouble; the expected demand for the new iron failed to materialize, but a lot of complaints came in from unhappy users. Yes, they conceded, Richardson's iron was better than the others they'd seen; but it had one major fault—it overheated in the center. When he asked his wife about it, she suggested he make an iron with more heat in the point, where it was needed to press around buttonholes, ruffles, pleats, and so on. He did just that, developing a new iron in which heating elements converged at the tip.

In 1905 he again placed samples with homemakers he knew. When he came back a week later none wanted to part with "the iron with the hot point." That was it! He had found the formula for success and a name. That year he made and sold under the new "Hotpoint" trademark more electric irons than any other company in America.

Meanwhile, a great deal of activity was taking place in the struggling appliance industry. One of the new companies destined to leave an impressive mark on the iron business was the American Electrical Heater Company of Detroit, which made the once well-known "American Beauty" iron.

Robert A. Kuhn, now president of the company, provides this interesting glimpse of its early days.

In the late 1890s, my father had started a small company in Detroit called the United Electric Heating Company. At about the same time, Ben Scranton started the American Electrical Heater Company. But until they chanced to meet one day while calling on the few available customers, neither knew the other existed. Since both were hardly able to stay alive and realized there wasn't room for both of them, shortly after 1900 they merged, American Electrical Heater being the survivor.

As electrical power became more widely understood and new power companies entered the field, other appliances were suggested. But since commercial buildings with electricity far outnumbered wired homes, the products took the form of space heaters, hotplates, hot water urns, tailor and laundry irons, and so on. The household market was virtually nonexistent.

The first flatirons for tailors were hand-machined and assembled one at a time. The biggest problem was getting resistance wire for the heating elements. The only source was Germany, yet even this material was not a true wire but rather a sintered material of resistance alloys in wire form. It had little tensile strength when cold and

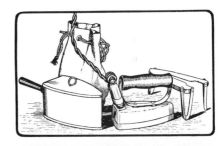

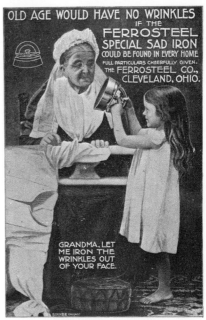

OLD AGE WOULD HAVE NO WRINKLES IF THE FERROSTEEL SPECIAL SAD IRON COULD BE FOUND IN EVERY HOME FULL PARTICULARS CHEERFULLY GIVEN. THE FERROSTEEL CO., CLEVELAND, OHIO.

GRANDMA, LET ME IRON THE WRINKLES OUT OF YOUR FACE.

THE FERROSTEEL CO.

CLEVELAND   NEW YORK   BOSTON   CHICAGO

From top: The historic sad iron is presented in this 1899 ad with a light touch. This early electric Hotpoint iron (bottom), a convenience in the boudoir, would also cook there if desired.

Courtesy House Furnishing Review.

Sales Volume of IRONS			
Year	Units	$ Volume (Retail)	Price
1922	3,300,000	20,000,000	$ 6
1930	2,362,500	10,867,000	5
1932	1,858,400	7,161,900	4
1940	5,171,000	18,853,500	4
1950	7,475,000	101,188,500	14
1960	6,410,000	91,678,000	14
1965	9,860,000	139,854,000	14
1970	9,275,000	159,210,000	17
1971	9,430,000	162,360,000	17

230

Few people recall it today, but the Sunbeam Corporation began in 1893 as a partnership to manufacture the Stewart mechanical horse clipper under the name of the Chicago Flexible Shaft Company. This old wood cut illustration is from one of the early catalogs. With the advent of electricity the firm began making electric clippers and in 1910 got started in the home appliance business with an electric iron, the Sunbeam. Appliances soon dominated the operation and in 1946 the corporate name was changed to the Sunbeam Corporation.

was extremely difficult to form on the windings of an element; and when it was heated it just fell apart at the strain points. Attempts to sandwich and clamp the wire with insulation led to early patents, but little true reliability.

The initial efforts to market household irons, he explained, consisted primarily in trying to convince the power companies to sell these current-consuming devices as load builders. Such an approach was quite beyond their comprehension.

"My father traveled all over the country and practically carried on a one-man crusade to convince the utility companies of the great business potential in selling electric irons. Not only would irons be used in the daytime when their customers were not using electricity for their lights, he reminded them, but in addition there was a nice profit to be made in selling these new 'appliances'," Robert Kuhn said.

It took time, but with far-sighted enthusiasts like the elder Kuhn and Earl Richardson, to mention only two, the power companies finally began to see beyond mere lighting.

Like the gas iron, the new electric iron was soon being promoted by house-to-house crews. And whereas the gas sales crews might often follow the lead of new pipelines and call on all the homes they reached, the electric iron salesmen simply looked for the streets and roadways where the new power line poles unmistakably announced that electricity had arrived.

"Free trial" merchandising plans and easy time-payment plans were widely used during this period. Often payment was made through a small extra charge on the monthly bill from the electric or gas company.

In 1912, Robert Kuhn recalled, the American Electrical Heater Company decided to produce an iron exclusively for household use. It was model 6½ B, retailing at six dollars, the first of the many "American Beauty" irons. "Finally we began to get carload orders from the utility companies," he added. "We had to start mass production to meet the demand, testing each iron as it moved into the shipping department. Except for the period during World War I, we made and shipped about four million of this one model until it was replaced about 1930 with an automatic thermostat model." After 1950, the firm stopped making consumer goods.

Technology Improves

Great strides were made during the next two decades in the development of electric irons and other products that used electricity. A whole new manufacturing technology emerged. Approval of products by the Underwriters' Laboratories became the accepted voluntary industry standard for safety. This has long been supplemented in many instances by the manufacturers' own efforts to impose even more stringent quality controls.

In 1927 the iron business took a tremendous leap forward with the perfection of the adjustable automatic thermostat. And right after that a revolutiontary new concept in household irons, the steam iron, appeared and eventually changed the whole character of the iron business. In fact, with this development the iron business was in a position to cope with the new demands of synthetic fabrics just coming on the market.

And then there was the new application of color and design to household irons. New plastics with remarkable performance characteristics, available in a rainbow of colors, have stimulated the nation's leading industrial designers to outdo each other year after year in transforming this once black and sooty Cinderella into a strikingly beautiful, highly efficient household convenience.

The Birth of the Automatic Iron

The invention of laundry irons with adjustable temperature and automatic heat control ushered the iron business into the modern era. And the acumen and curiosity of a keen fourteen-year-old boy, back in 1912 when electricity was still something of a miracle, had a great deal to do with the development of the automatic thermostat for irons.

Joseph W. Myers, who until his retirement in 1953 headed the research and development department for Proctor Electric Corporation (now Proctor-Silex Corporation), was that boy. He lived in Jackson, Michigan, at the time. He had been interested in electricity since he first learned of it, and he became excited one day when he saw a local furniture store advertisement offering an electric iron for $2.98. In an interview in 1971 he recalled:

> Somehow I managed to convince my mother she deserved to have this great new convenience. It was a Dover iron. And even though it had a plain, unplated iron soleplate and a nickel-plated shell, we thought it looked pretty swell.
>
> Compared to her old sadirons that had to be heated on the gas stove, the new iron did a wonderful job. But the attached cord, which ran directly inside the shell to the terminals, kept burning off because of the heat at that point.
>
> As a budding inventor, I thought this was urgently in need of improvement; so about four years later I undertook the job of providing the iron with an automatic heat control. It worked just well enough to encourage me—but not well enough to be worth anything.

When his job in a machine shop was ended by the 1921 depression, he decided he wanted to become a professional inventor and naturally turned to his automatic temperature control. By 1924 he had evolved a design he felt was good enough, and he made one hundred irons to try it out on. But then he was initiated into the problems of marketing them.

> I wrote Graybar Electric Company in New York, telling them all about my wonderful new iron. But they replied that since they had never had a call for an automatic flatiron they weren't interested. And they doubted any one would be.

The American Beauty iron. This model 6½ B was introduced in 1912 by the American Electrical Heater Company. For many years it was considered to be the standard of excellence.

From top: Before electricity, an example of sturdily built alcohol-powered iron. Another elaborately constructed iron, this time, electric. The 1922 Stahot boasted features to hold the heat longer and distribute it more evenly.

Bottom, courtesy The Jobber's Salesman.

TWO MODELS
GAS AND ELECTRIC

THE DUO POINT

A Six-Pound Double-Point Iron with Two Hot Points Instead of One

Thousands of women prefer a double point iron, because the same results can be obtained with the backward as with the forward movement of the iron.

IT IS MORE THAN THE ORDINARY IRON AND IS EQUIPPED WITH THE BEST MATERIAL AND WORKMANSHIP THROUGHOUT.

Hundreds of the largest department stores already sell the DUO POINT and are giving their customers an opportunity to choose between the double point and square back style.

Write To-day for Dealers' Prices

MANUFACTURED AND GUARANTEED BY

Central Flatiron Mfg. Co.

JOHNSON CITY, N. Y.

Suburb of Binghamton

Capitalize This Summer on the Easy Selling Qualities of Westinghouse Household Appliances

Westinghouse Electric & Manufacturing Company

Mansfield Works.   MANSFIELD, OHIO

Westinghouse

From top: The Duo Point offered two hot points, forward and back, and two models, gas and electric. Summer is the time to capitalize on the electric appliance market, Westinghouse noted in this trade ad.

Top, courtesy House Furnishing Review. Bottom, courtesy The Jobber's Salesman.

232

So I went out to the county fair and sold my irons for "five dollars and your old iron as a trade-in."

Then I approached the manufacturers. But they all turned me down. Hotpoint didn't think the industry was ready for an automatic iron; since they had most of the iron business anyway, why invite service trouble with something new and unknown?

American told me they had been trying for twenty-five years to make an automatic iron, and if such a thing were possible, they assured me, they certainly would have succeeded. Landers, Frary and Clark, turned my iron down because it operated only on a.c., not d.c., so it couldn't be used everywhere. Chicago Flexible Shaft interviewed everyone to whom I had sold my iron and said that they wanted to make such an iron under my license—but then they backed out. And so it went.

By this time the irons on my field test had been out about a year and were standing up perfectly—even in some commercial laundries. In desperation I went to a small firm that had been started in Cleveland during World War I, the Liberty Gauge and Instrument Company. They had become known as the world's largest exclusive manufacturers of electric hotplates and had a good line. But what was even better was their interest in my automatic iron. They investigated me and my field test and finally decided to go ahead with my development.

It was just at this time that Westinghouse came out with what they called their "million-dollar thermostat." But it was a simple on-and-off device, not adjustable as mine was. And so my iron, under the Liberty nameplate, became the first practical adjustable temperature control iron to be marketed. I use the word "practical" because some years earlier Dover had tried to market an adjustable temperature control iron called the "Dover-A-Besto." But the thermostat gave so much trouble that it was promptly taken off the market.

The Liberty Gauge and Instrument Company

What was the Liberty Gauge and Instrument Company? Nearly half a century ago it was purchased by Proctor and Schwartz, Incorporated, of Philadelphia for about $200,000 and renamed Proctor Electric Company (now Proctor-Silex). Lawrence Efferth, who was with both firms, served as the first vice-president for sales of Proctor Electric. In a 1971 interview at his house in Deerfield Beach, Florida, Efferth gave this account:

During World War I five Cleveland residents had financed the establishment of a machine shop to contract war work—in that wartime climate it was named "Liberty" Gauge and Instrument Company. After the war they were concerned because business had dropped off so sharply. One of them, J. A. Zimmer, a banker, happened to be a friend.

Jack Zimmer called to ask my opinion about the sales potential of an electric hotplate. Its inventor, John Ziola, had brought it to him claiming it could be made to retail for two dollars, far below competition. The trouble was that Liberty had had no experience whatever with consumer goods. To shorten a long story, I not only thought it was great, but promptly became Liberty's new sales manager.

In 1921, our first full year of production, I sold 200,000 of those hotplates. But all the profit we made on them was lost by the inactive machine shop; so I finally persuaded the company to sell it and concentrate on appliances.

The next year we added a "Hotspot" model for $3.85. I was a great believer in maintaining a fair price so dealers could make a profit, and so each hotplate had a tag with the retail price on one side and our one-year unconditional guarantee on the other.

Our jobbers kept urging us to make other items. But we didn't want to add anything unless it was as unusual as our two-dollar hotplate. Then one day we had a visit from Joe Myers from Jackson, Michigan, who showed us a new iron he had invented with an adjustable automatic temperature control. It looked very interesting.

To be certain that Joe Myers's new iron was really all it seemed to be, we took it to the Underwriters' Laboratories and *Good Housekeeping* magazine for their approval. We told UL to put the iron on a basket of laundry in their fireproof room for a few days and see what happened. Nothing did. We had a similar experience at *Good Housekeeping*.

Joe Myers's iron was *very* good. One day he confided to me how he had been able to perfect an adjustable thermostat for irons when others had failed. "It's because they didn't use virgin silver for their contact points," he told me. "That's the only way you can be sure of accurate, constant sensitivity to temperature."

Because Liberty was new in the iron business, the company decided to start first with Myer's earlier, nonadjustable thermostatic iron and not introduce the adjustable model until the following year.

Their ordinary automatic retailed for $7.95; the adjustable model for $8.95. Liberty took a booth that year—1926—at the Philadelphia Sesquicentennial Exposition, and Joe Tiers of Proctor and Schwartz, Incorporated, happened to see their iron display. His company had been trying to develop an automatic toaster without success, and so the thermostatic iron was of particular interest to him.

The eventual outcome of that chance meeting was the purchase of Liberty by Proctor, and Joe Tiers became president of the newly formed Proctor and Schwartz Electric Company.

CORDLESS ELECTRIC IRONS

The concept of a cordless iron—one that would provide the convenience of electricity without the annoyance of the seemingly inescapable connecting wire—has long intrigued inventors and promoters, but none of them ever met with more than limited success.

One of the earliest models was introduced in 1922 by the Nocord Electric Company of Los Angeles. The same basic approach—a cord in the iron stand—with variations was used by most of these would-be innovators. The Cotabl Electric Company of Chicago, for example, included two irons in their set so that one would always be available for use. "Because of their special constructions the irons hold their heat an unusually long time and it is possible to iron from five to twelve minutes without changing irons," it was claimed when the iron was announced in 1930. Even a radio manufacturer, F. A. D. Andrea, Incorporated, in New York, got into the act with an 1,100-watt iron in 1932. Some irons offered thermostatically controlled heat for different fabrics, and at least one manufacturer guaranteed his iron for ten years.

Real Economy in "Even Heat" Ironing

Whether for the family ironing, or for little pressings in your boudoir or sewing room, you can iron comfortably, coolly, economically with the "even heat" of the G-E Electric Iron.

You save money by ironing more quickly — thereby requiring less electricity. An average family ironing costs only 15 cents — and even this extra electricity can be saved if you light your home with Edison Mazda Lamps.

The G-E Iron's "even heat"— sustained and lasting—is secured by the special shape of the inside heating part of the iron. No cold

or half heated edges, where heat is needed most — no over-hot spots—just *even* heat everywhere—at the point, at the edges and in the centre, too.

The G-E Iron heats up quickly and stays hot so long that you can do a deal of ironing with the electricity turned off. This is because of a special arrangement of air spaces which store up the heat and drive it to the bottom and the point of the iron, where it is needed. And the G-E Iron is so handy and convenient.

The new heel-stand enables you to rest it anywhere—just by tipping it back. No separate stand is required. This is the quality iron—good for a life-time. The G-E trade mark assures that. It stands for the utmost in electrical skill and science.

Get the G-E Iron from your lighting company or nearest electrical dealer. Price, including cord and attaching plug, $4.25.

GENERAL ELECTRIC COMPANY
The Largest Electrical Manufacturer in the World

Sales Offices in all Large Cities   Agencies Everywhere

A NEW KIND OF ELECTRIC IRON!

THE **EUREKA**
CORDLESS

- No annoying cord to tangle and pull and get in your way!
- No cord or plug breakage!
- Fire hazard reduced to a minimum!
- Plenty of heat during the entire ironing period!

"PRECISION ENGINEERED FROM THE WOMAN'S POINT OF VIEW"

From top: An early (1913) advertisement for this "even heat" iron, which sold for $4.25. The ad appeared in *Good Housekeeping.* From 1948 to 1955 Eureka offered their cordless electric iron, especially for "meticulous ironers," who wanted to reach hard-to-reach places.

233

Electric Steaming Iron

Electrical Merchandising, May, 1926

Both ironing and pressing needs in the home are served by the "Eldec" steaming iron, brought out by the Eldec Company, Inc., 501 Fifth Avenue, New York City. It is a 6-lb. iron. Inside its insulated handle is a water reservoir with conduit leading to bottom plate. A small turn-screw valve regulates the flow of water which passes drop by drop to the heated plate. Through a series of tiny holes covering the plate, the water issues as steam, this steam forming on the garment or fabric being ironed as a mist-like film, evenly distributed between the iron and garment. The iron operates on the regulation 106-115 volt current. Its several parts are easily replaceable. The finish of iron and stand is nickel. This new steaming iron, it is pointed out, prevents scorching because there is even distribution of moisture. It likewise eliminates sprinkling action and the use of dampening cloths. Intended retail price, $10.

234

From top: The first electric steam iron, the Eldec, as reported in *Electrical Merchandising* magazine in 1926. It weighed six pounds and retailed at ten dollars. The lower picture is of the first —and last—steam iron ever marketed that had to be connected to a water faucet by means of a thirty-foot long tube—the Durabuilt Model 11, introduced in 1949 by Winsted Hardware Company. Its high price of $19.95 and water leakage forced it off the market.

THE STEAM IRON "HOLY WAR"

In terms of scoring a significant addition to the electric housewares business, the advent of the steam iron might well be called a hole-in-one. Actually, the first steam irons only had one hole—or possibly two or three holes—in the soleplate for steam to emerge. Later a few more were added. That generally seemed to satisfy everyone, especially the homemaker, for a long while.

But by the 1950s competition and creative ingenuity asserted themselves in the steam iron business to a much greater degree. And so, on the theory that if four holes are good eight holes must be twice as good, the iron manufacturers began what has aptly been called "the Holy War."

In 1952 Westinghouse came out with a fifteen-hole iron. That stayed the same until in 1958 Proctor-Silex introduced seventeen holes. The war escalated in 1964 when Sunbeam made an iron that had thirty-six holes and for the first time spread them out over the full length of the soleplate.

By 1971 Westinghouse had gone to sixty-five holes and Sears, never one to do things in a small way, to seventy holes. However, if one includes the holes in the spray vent, Presto's 1971 spray-steam iron is the winner with eighty holes!

The Steam Iron

In the 1960s, when every conceivable refinement in iron design and technology seemed to have been reached, the textile industry had just about perfected the "permanent press" or "no-iron" technology for fabrics, thus making the iron, at least in theory, obsolete. But right now that is academic, with the 1971 sales of irons of all types totaling over nine million units!

Steam irons for pressing garments were in use in commercial establishments before any attempt to introduce such an appliance for the home. In the spring of 1926 the Eldec Company in New York announced the first household model, an "electric steaming iron" to sell for ten dollars. Veterans in the iron business say it was an import from Switzerland, although trade sources there do not have a record of such an iron. Little more was heard of it after the original announcement, and it disappeared from the market.

The Great Depression stifled most new product development, but in 1936 the household steam iron again made its appearance with an announcement by the Steem-Electric of St. Louis of "an iron that dampens clothes as it irons." It weighed 6½ pounds, came equipped with a 1½-pint measure and funnel, and retailed for $9.85. If an existing illustration is accurate, it had no fewer than thirty holes in its soleplate.

In Ridgefield, Connecticut, Edward P. Schreyer, an inventor who earlier had introduced an iron with an aluminum soleplate, was trying to perfect a steam iron that would be safe and free of the operational "bugs" prone to lurk in this tricky appliance. He and his brother Milton formed the Edmilton Corporation.

By the time they were satisfied with its performance and safety, they had an all-aluminum iron weighing only 3½ pounds, with a soleplate of a special aluminum alloy. The iron could be set on its heel without spilling any water. They called it the "Steam-O-Matic" and priced it to sell for $9.95. It made its merchandising debut in 1938 in New York at Macy's and in Chicago at Marshall Field's, each starting off with an order of three hundred. It was a success.

Meanwhile others moved into the field. One notable early follower of the "Steam-O-Matic" was the Waring Products Corporation, owned by the band leader Fred Waring. The company had received widespread recognition for its unique Waring Blendor, and Ed Lee, Waring's merchandising director, wanted to add another appliance which would be equally distinctive.

Merrill M. Kistner, an inventor previously associated with the Maytag Company, had patented another version of the steam iron. But whereas the "Steam-O-Matic" iron was based on the "boiler" type of operation, the Kistner iron was developed on a "needle-valve or flash-boiler" principle. Soon Waring and Kistner had concluded a contract whereby Waring would produce and market the Waring steam iron.

Kistner had worked with a Chicago firm, Quality Hardware Company, to produce his iron, but after Waring took over, the General Electric Company also became interested. As a result, General Electric and Waring entered into an agreement in March 1941 whereby General Electric was to manufacture the iron under a license for sale under its own name and also on a contract basis for Waring.

If there had ever been any doubt whether the steam iron would really catch on, the last remnants of it vanished with the announcement that General Electric was in the business. This type of iron quickly became so popular with homemakers that traditional dry irons dropped to a minor part of the market.

Additional competitors appeared. During 1939, for example, the Steampoint Electric Company of New York introduced a steam-or-dry iron; Stillman Products Company of New York, the "Steam King"; and Chicago Motocoil Corporation, the "Challenger." The following year the Knapp-Monarch Company of St. Louis entered the field with a "Steam King"; Noma Electric Corporation of New York, with a "Steam Queen"; and the Silex Company of Hartford with a "Silex" steam iron.

In the same year the Proctor Electric Company of Philadelphia brought out an interesting variation of the steam iron by adding a water reservoir connected by a tube to its "Never Lift" iron. The reservoir clamped to the edge of the ironing table, and when steam was not wanted it could readily be disconnected. An even more unique version was the "Durabilt" steam iron introduced in 1949 by the Winsted Hardware Manufacturing Company, Winsted, Connecticut, designed to operate by means of a thirty-foot plastic tube connected to the nearest water faucet.

For the well-informed Buyer
THERE IS ONLY ONE STEAM-IRON
for trouble-free, profitable selling

9.95 *retail*

STEAM-O-MATIC

Only this Steam-Iron has ALL these features:

1. All-aluminum construction — weighs only 3½ lbs.
2. Aluminum sole plate, made of special alloy for long service, is absolutely rustproof.
3. Stands on its heel without spilling a drop of water.

Write for samples and further information

STEAM-O-MATIC CORP.
228 South First St.   Milwaukee, Wis.

235

The 1938 Steam-O-Matic could be set on its heel without spilling any water.

By the time America's entry into World War II put an end to the production of civilian goods the advantages of the steam iron had become firmly rooted among consumers.

New methods and materials, especially in the field of plastics, now permitted the realization of bold concepts of function and design. In the following years irons became larger but lighter and more colorful. However, although they were more efficient, they also became more complicated for the homemaker to use—or so it seemed at first.

A most welcome improvement in steam irons was that most of them now no longer required distilled water; ordinary tap water sufficed in most areas. Molded plastic handles began to assume a variety of shapes reminiscent of sculpture.

Innovations such as the General Electric steam travel iron appeared. Hoover introduced a stainless steel soleplate, and General Electric brought out a Teflon-coated soleplate and a steam iron designed especially for those who sew at home. Proctor-Silex contributed a technological and merchandising breakthrough with its "Lifelong" model, designed on a "replace-it-yourself" principle with snap-in replacement parts. Another significant breakthrough was achieved in 1972 when General Electric announced a self-cleaning steam, spray, and dry iron, the first such iron ever perfected.

One wonders if there's anything else left to develop. Indeed, further developments may be unnecessary. If fabric technology continues to perfect wrinkle-proof fabrics as it has been doing in recent years, the day may come when irons will be seen in museums rather than in housewares departments.

Ironing Tables

Ironing tables are still often called ironing boards. In the 1880s the family ironing was actually done on a plain board suspended between a table and a chair back. Frequently the board was padded and covered with sheeting. Eventually manufacturers began making "skirt boards" tapered at one end. They ranged from three to six feet long; the short ones were four to eight inches wide and the longer ones eleven to sixteen inches wide.

About 1898, for the first time, one of these boards came equipped with legs so that it could be set up anywhere. It was made by the J. R. Clark Company of Minneapolis, established in 1878, one of the largest manufacturers of woodenware and ladders. Today, it is known as the Rid-Jid Products Corporation in Spring Park, Minnesota.

K. B. Oberlander, who spent forty-five years with Clark before his retirement, recalls that first table and tells about it:

> They were called "four-legged devices" and were equipped with a leg in each corner. But folding and unfolding them required some acrobatic maneuvering. One simplified style employed pivoted sawbuck type legs that fit into a slotted bracket when set up for use.

236

In 1970 Norelco added a lightweight combination travel iron and pleat press. It operates on 110- or 220-voltage for world-wide use.

In 1928 the Rid-Jid ironing table was considered so outstanding it was even advertised as "the most appreciated" Christmas gift that five dollars would buy.

About 1914 a West Coast inventor named Springer patented an ironing-table leg structure that eliminated the annoying wiggle of the four-legged tables by using only three support points. His slogan was: "Will not wiggle, wobble, jiggle, slip, or slide."

Two years later George Kleinsorge, in Waukegan, Illinois, began manufacturing the Springer ironing table using the brand name "Rid-Jid." In 1921 Clark purchased the patents and the name and for a quarter of a century was the leading manufacturer of ironing tables.

Around 1921 Clark also introduced an automatically folding ironing table called the "Queen," with a top made of smooth basswood or cottonwood. In 1929, to help offset some of the basic problems of wood, the company patented the "Master Maid" model, which was lacquered so it would not absorb moisture, and was claimed to be washable, waterproof, and warp proof. Originally made entirely of wood with only a few metal components, the tables eventually were made with metal legs and finally metal tops. Clark discontinued wooden tables entirely in 1956.

"Although metal-top tables eliminated the warping and cracking that so often developed in wooden tops," Oberlander continued, "their tendency to rust despite careful painting created new difficulties. Often they would buckle under the heat of the iron, creating an annoying click, and condensation of vapor beneath the pad produced tiny pools of water."

These problems were eliminated when Edward T. John, Clark's production superintendent, hit on the idea of using metal mesh, which left 60 percent of the top open so that heat and steam could easily escape.

While Clark was the first to bring out a table using expanded metal for the top, the first all-metal ironing table had been introduced in 1939 when Geuder, Paschke & Frey Company, Milwaukee, announced the "Met-L-Top" table. It also claimed to have been first with an adjustable height table. Once one of the most important manufacturers of various types of metal housewares, it decided in the 1950s to discontinue manufacture of all consumer goods and has since concentrated exclusively on the commercial and industrial field.

Standing at the ironing table was tiring, and the possibility of sitting had long been discussed. From time to time various Rube Goldberg devices were suggested as a solution. In 1950 many home economics departments emphasized the health advantages of sitting while ironing. Finally K. B. Oberlander developed and patented for Clark a new ironing-table leg structure employing bent tubular steel so that a person could sit comfortably at the table. The "Rid-Jid Knee Room" table could be adjusted to any desired height, and when it was introduced at the January 1953 housewares show it understandably created considerable interest. It was soon copied by others, even in Europe, but infringers were promptly stopped by successful suits.

237

Two ironing tables, the Met-L-Top twins for "her" and "little her." In the 1920s this consumer is ecstatic over a J. R. Clark Company ironing table. From their catalog of the period.

Top, courtesy House Furnishing Review.

From top: Iron milestones. Sunbeam offered "All-Over" heating in 1925; also that year, the first non-adjustable automatic iron, by Westinghouse. In 1971 GE introduced this iron for home sewers.

Historical Milestones in the Development of Irons

Early—Until about 1900 most laundry irons were made with a hollow interior that could be filled with hot coal, charcoal, or a heated iron slug; or they were of the solid cast-iron type commonly known as "sadirons." Numerous attempts were made to market irons using alcohol, gasoline, and acetylene gas to generate heat, but they were dangerous to use and never achieved much success.

1874—First gas iron patents issued, according to the American Gas Association.

1882—First electric iron patent No. 259,054 issued to H. W. Seely of New York.

1903—Development of an electric iron with a hot point by Earl Richardson in California; became origin of the "Hotpoint" trademark now owned by General Electric.

First iron with detachable cord introduced by General Electric.

1906—First insulated, flat-mica heating elements made in the United States introduced by General Electric. Previously they had been imported from Germany.

1909—First iron with fusible over-temperature device on an iron used by Hotpoint.

First use of nickel-chromium alloy wire instead of iron wire for heating element used by General Electric. This was covered by the Marsh patents owned by General Electric and all appliance manufacturers who used such elements paid General Electric a royalty of twenty-five cents on each appliance.

First travel iron weighing only 3¼ pounds introduced by General Electric.

1910—First iron made with stamped, nickel-plated steel shell in place of cast iron introduced by General Electric. Previously some such shells, often coated with porcelain enamel and in color, were imported from Europe.

First iron with detachable cord set, GE.

1917—First beveled-edge soleplate iron "particularly applicable for fancy waists and lingerie" introduced by Westinghouse.

1919—First iron with the wooden "Thumb Rest" handle introduced by Hughes Electric Appliance Company, later acquired by General Electric.

1921—First iron made with imbedded "Calrod" heating element introduced by General Electric.

1922—First cordless electric iron introduced by the Nocord Electric Company.

1923—Landers, Frary and Clark (formerly in business in New Britain, Connecticut) introduced a rounded-heel iron that "irons backward without catching on pleats, etc."

First iron with a side rest introduced by Westinghouse.

1924—First automatic iron (non-adjustable) featuring the "Klixon" disc thermostat, introduced by Westinghouse.

1925—First chrome-plated irons, the "Hold Heet," produced by the Russell Electric Company, Chicago.

First use of molded plastic for an iron handle made by General Electric.

First irons with heel rests introduced by Westinghouse and General Electric.

1926—First "steaming iron" introduced by the Eldec Company (formerly in business in New York City. Said to have been a Swiss import.)

1927—First adjustable-temperature automatic iron, 660 watts, introduced by Liberty Gauge and Instrument Company of Cleveland (acquired by Proctor and Schwartz—now Proctor-Silex—in 1929.)*

1929—First iron with a "Button Nook" to facilitate ironing around buttons introduced by General Electric.

1930—First lightweight (non-travel) iron—under six pounds—introduced by Sunbeam.

1931—First iron with cast-aluminum soleplate introduced by General Electric.

First 1,000-watt iron introduced by Proctor and Schwartz Electric Company; had a permanent cord connected to cool outside terminals.

1932—First 1,000-watt, 4½-pound iron introduced by Westinghouse; designed with a sloping "fatigue-proof" handle covered with molded sponge rubber.

1933—First iron with a one-piece, all-plastic handle introduced by Birtman Electric Company, Chicago.

1934—First iron with a built-in snap-out stand, called the "Snap Stand" iron, introduced by Proctor and Schwartz Electric Company (now Proctor-Silex Corporation). Later in improved form it became the "Neverlift" iron.

First thumb-tip temperature control introduced by Sunbeam.

First iron with a double-pole automatic thermostat introduced by Sunbeam.

1937—First steam iron made in the United States, "Steem-Electric" introduced by Steem-Electric Company (formerly in business in St. Louis).

First folding travel iron, "Durabilt," 500 watts, 1½ pounds, introduced by Winsted Hardware Company of Winsted, Connecticut. Since acquired by Waring Products.

1939—First steam iron to get Underwriters' Laboratories approval, the "Steam-O-Matic" introduced by Steam-O-Matic Corporation, Milwaukee.

Knapp-Monarch (since acquired by Hoover) introduced a circular "pie plate" shaped iron designed especially for flatwork.

1940—Waverly Tool Company (formerly in business in Irvington, New Jersey) introduced "Petipoint," an air-cooled automatic iron with a dual soleplate, the smaller one extending at an upward angle from the rear into a point for ironing frills and so on.

Manning-Bowman (formerly of Meriden, Connecticut, but since acquired by McGraw-Edison) introduced "the iron that wags its tail," the cord of which was connected to the back of the iron with a swivel joint so it could swing readily in any direction and be out of the user's way.

1941—First steam iron using the "needle valve" or "flash boiler" principle introduced by Waring Products. After World War II General Electric produced such an iron under agreement with Waring and the inventor, Merrill Kistner.

1946—Yale & Towne (now part of the Eaton Corporation) introduced the "Tip-Toe" dry iron equipped with a hinged tip to facilitate ironing pleats. It was later acquired by McGraw-Edison Company.

1948—First front-fill steam iron introduced by General Electric.

1949—Winsted Hardware Company introduced steam iron operating by means of a thirty-foot long tube attached to water faucet.

1953—First steam travel iron introduced by General Electric.

1954—First steam/dry iron with "channeled" steam in a stainless-steel-clad, cast-aluminum soleplate introduced by Hoover.

1957—First spray/steam iron introduced by General Electric.

First color-coded fabric temperature guide on an iron to show proper setting for each type of fabric, including new synthetics, introduced by General Electric.

1960—First United States-made travel iron for worldwide use having combination 110/120 volt AD-DC utility, introduced by General Electric. Previously some such irons were imported from Europe.

1961—First steam and dry iron with a single control for temperature and steam introduced by Westinghouse.

First steam iron with built-in water gauge introduced by General Electric.

1962—First spray-mist steam iron introduced by Sunbeam.

1963—First iron designed with "snap-in" replaceable components for do-it-yourself repairs introduced by Proctor-Silex in the "Lifelong" iron.

First steam/dry travel iron for use anywhere on either 110 or 230 volt current introduced by General Electric.

1965—First iron with a Teflon-coated soleplate introduced by General Electric.

1967—First spray-steam iron with choice of two spray settings introduced by General Electric.

First iron combining a heel rest and cord storage compartment introduced by General Electric.

1968—First iron with wide heel rest to provide added stability introduced by Sunbeam.

1969—First iron with a trigger-controlled "Shot-of-Steam" ejector introduced by Sunbeam.

1971—First iron designed specifically for home sewers introduced by General Electric.

1972—First "self-cleaning" steam, spray, and dry iron introduced by General Electric.

*The Dover Manufacturing Company (formerly in business in Dover, Ohio) brought out an adjustable temperature-controlled automatic iron in 1916, according to Joseph W. Myers, retired engineer for Proctor Electric Company. It was called "Dover-A-Besto," but proved to be so unreliable only a very few were ever produced. Subsequently Hotpoint attempted to market one but had so much trouble with it that it was discontinued.

(For their special assistance in compiling this list the author wishes to thank Joseph W. Myers, retired vice-president for engineering, Proctor-Silex Corporation; Walter McMahon, retired vice-president of sales for the Still-Man Manufacturing Company; E. J.

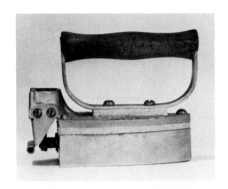

SELF CLEANING Spray, Steam, and Dry Iron
MODEL F110WH

From top: Interesting irons, past and present. In 1904 General Electric offered this iron made of cast iron and weighing eight pounds. Weight was then regarded as the most important factor in effective ironing. The 1940 Yale & Towne "tip-toe" model. A first: in 1972 a self-cleaning steam iron introduced by General Electric.

The full line of Universal "serviceable gifts for sensible people." Appliances with the Universal trademark included a percolator, toaster, and chafing dish.

Courtesy House Furnishing Review.

240

Wray, manager product safety and standards, housewares division, General Electric Company, and J. W. Harrison, formerly manager design engineering, portable appliances, for the Westinghouse Electric Corporation.)

The Saga of Landers, Frary & Clark

"This is the story of Landers, Frary & Clark and its service to the American home. For more than a century three able men, active in the industrial, political and cultural life in New Britain and in Connecticut, were the principal actors in our little story. But the real theme is the changing pattern of American living in the past 100 years and of the company's contribution to this changing pattern, because Landers has been making products for the American home for nearly twelve decades and its success has been due to ability to change products with the changing times."

Those were the words with which Richard L. White, then chairman of the board of directors of Landers, Frary & Clark, began a speech on his company's history at a meeting of The Newcomen Society in Noank, Connecticut, August 12, 1955. (Mr. White resigned as chairman in 1958. B. C. Neece continued as president of the company. The following year he was named chairman but retired in 1960. Harry T. Silverman, who had been president and was then elected chairman, was the last to hold that post.)

In 1965 though, this great company, once one of the best known and most prestigious in the housewares and hardware business, closed its doors permanently. The unbelievable had happened. While rumors of its impending doom had long been zig-zagging throughout the marketplace, the final reality came as a shock to the thousands of retailers who had known and dealt with the company for so long.

On May 17, 1965 its illustrious "Universal" trademark along with the remaining assets, inventory and equipment were acquired by the General Electric Company's Housewares Division, though not until after some rather frantic last minute meetings with government officials in Washington who wanted to satisfy themselves the acquisition involved no "monopolistic" aspects.

The number of products manufactured by Landers over the years was enormous and their scope amazing. They made stainless steel bull-nose rings and electric ranges, kitchen scales and vacuum bottles, window hardware and ice skates, mouse traps and percolators, can openers, cutlery and aluminum cookware, and thousands of other products. And somehow, almost until the very end, it seemed to work out profitably.

Landers, Frary & Clark traces its start to the time George Landers, age sixteen, arrived in New Britain, Connecticut in 1829 looking for a job. He soon went to work for Josiah Dewey who, seven years earlier, had started a small foundry making cupboard latches and other hardware. After Dewey's death, it became Landers & Smith

Manufacturing Company in 1853. As president, Landers' salary was seven hundred dollars a year.

In 1862 the small but prosperous company made another of the many acquisitions that were to mark its history and growth in future years. It acquired the firm of Frary, Clark & Company, of Meriden, Connecticut; the company name changed to Landers, Frary & Clark, which it retained for the next full century of its existence.

Probably the most important item introduced around this period was a household scale, "the first product designed particularly for the American housewife," White explained in his speech.

The company and the extent of its line continued to grow...now it had added meat choppers and sausage stuffers, screw eyes and strap hooks, door handles and floor scrapers, molasses gates and faucets, meat hooks and harness hooks, cast iron match boxes and curry combs, fancy brass hat hooks and eyes with porcelain knob ends—and even toys.

In 1870, George Landers, having turned fifty-seven, decided to retire from active management, but to stay on as vice-president and director. His son was now secretary of the company.

In the 1890s the trade name "Universal" was adopted for the company's products. And it was in the same period that it introduced a series of quite revolutionary household products that were to help establish it as a leader in the housewares field.

One of these, explained Richard White to the Newcomen Society, was the "Universal" bread maker.

In those days breadmaking was a common household chore...the days of baker's bread were still far away. In the "Universal" bread maker, dough was prepared in the evening, left in the machine to rise overnight, ready for baking in the morning. That business was one of the mainstays of the company.

The second product to become a household necessity was the "Universal" food chopper. Choppers were not new, but this one ground not merely meats but vegetables as well....Odds and ends could be turned into hashes and casseroles with ease....The *identical* model food chopper first produced in 1897 is an active item in our line now in 1955—58 years later.

The third, and to us, the most important invention of the period was the "Universal" coffee percolator (first produced in 1905). Here was a brand new method of brewing coffee below the boiling point, with resultant improvement in clarity and flavor....Today percolators outsell other types of coffee makers. This percolator of the nineties was a simple one, heated on the stove. The day of electricity was only dawning.

A stock clerk named Charles F. Smith had gone to work for Landers in 1882, and in 1900 on the death of Charles Landers, son of the founder, he was elected president. Until his death in 1938, Smith was responsible for the tremendous growth of the company.

Beginning with a patent it received in 1908 for the development of an electrical unit to be used on percolators, the company moved head-on into the appliance field.

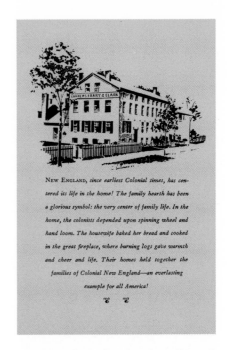

A sketch of the first Landers, Frary & Clark factory.

241

The Universal Bread Maker established LF&C as a leader in housewares.

A gallery of contemporary electric housewares embracing new ideas and new applications of old ideas. The ancient Chinese wok takes on new character electrified. Oven broilers toast and broil, as well as bake and roast. Coffee grinders do their thing miniaturized. This toaster, turned upside down, becomes a broiler. Eggs are cooked automatically electrically while the iron is designed with snap-into-place replacement parts to minimize service problems.

The first "Universal" appliance appeared in 1912 when a "thermo cell" electric iron was introduced. Percolators, toasters and ranges soon followed. By 1915 it was already making electric ranges. Then came World War I when all production was devoted to military needs.

After the war the company greatly intensified its entry into electrical household products, an era Richard White referred to as the second or "electrical phase" of its development. "Today [1955], while Landers is manufacturing many non-electrical products for the home, its principal products are in the electrical field," he said.

It is noteworthy that in the early 1920s Landers, in order to exercise more complete quality control over its appliances, adopted a policy of making all its own parts as far as possible. At the time it claimed that six out of every ten homes in the country had at least one "Universal" product. Its capitalization in 1923 had reached $10.5 million and it employed over three thousand people.

In 1919 the Barnes & Kovell Company and the next year the Columbia Heating Pad Company were added to produce its own "Universal" line. In 1940 it acquired the O-Pan-Top Manufacturing Company, producers of a top-opening carpet sweeper.

Throughout the many years of its growth Landers had developed a conservative, intensely quality-minded image; here, it seemed, was a company so solidly rooted "it'll go on forever." So in 1950, when it announced the discontinuance of its cutlery division after eighty-four years of operation, the trade was shocked. Landers, they would tell you, acquired businesses—it didn't drop them.

But the next few years saw acquisitions. In 1954 Landers bought the Dazey Corporation with a big line of can openers, juicers, and other items. The following year it bought the Electric Steam Radiator Corporation, Paris, Kentucky, adding the name "Electresteem." In 1956 the Standard Products Company, Whitman, Massachusetts, was purchased and its line of portable appliances marketed through a new subsidiary, Handy-Hannah Products Corporation under the "Handy Hannah" brand. The same year a Canadian firm, Ever-Bright Limited, was bought. It made copper-clad utensils and portable appliances. To house the operation making private brand merchandise, Landers bought a big new plant in Ft. Smith, Arkansas, the Eastern Metal Products Company. In the next couple of years Landers also brought out a line of "Cookamatic" copper-cored stainless steel appliances, operated by a single control.

A great effort was made to develop new products, especially in portable appliances, using new principles of design. Yet an ominous cloud of doubt still hovered over the company's future.

The complicated closing chapters of Landers, Frary & Clark can be well summarized by these excerpts from an account of those developments which appeared in the New Britain (Connecticut) *Herald*, April 21, 1965:

> Concern over the future of L F & C in New Britain, its birthplace, reached large proportions in 1957 with the purchase of the modern

Eastern Metal Products plant in Fort Smith, Arkansas....President Bret Neece advised stockholders on March 3, 1958 there would be greater utilization of subsidiary facilities....

Final days of true local control of L F & C were early in 1959. Frederick W. Richmond of New York, called a modern "empire builder" and "financial wizard," came onto the L F & C scene in 1958 by way of a "blind offer" to buy stock. The Franklin National Bank of Long Island made the offer.

Richmond, still in his thirties at the time, headed an investment firm which wound up with one hundred thousand shares of L F & C. Richmond soon became chairman of the board.

He was unseated in June 1960. A group, headed by another New Yorker, Harry T. Silverman, became the largest shareholders....

Silverman expressed confidence at the outset, predicting the number of employees would double within a year. Approximately 1800 were on the payroll then, about one-half the 3600 peak.

By the Spring of 1961 Silverman, the chairman of the board, the president and other holders of large blocks of stock, turned their ears to offers.

On March 30, Silverman announced a tender to acquire controlling stock of L F & C by J. B. Williams Company, a leading producer of pharmaceuticals. Within six weeks J. B. Williams had ownership of 80% of some 404,000 outstanding shares.

Matthew B. Rosenhaus, president of J. B. Williams, came to New Britain before the stock was actually acquired. He spoke optimistically of the future. Williams paid $22 per share or approximately $9 million for the stock. The total investment of the Rosenhaus group, Silverman estimated, would be $25 million. Williams officials have maintained L F & C has been a losing proposition.

The efforts to diversify, to strike out in new areas continued. In 1964, for example, with much fanfare, it introduced what was said to be the first, mass-produced, pure nickel electroformed coffeemaker under the brand name of "Permatel." Research and development for this project cost $500,000 and cost of installing production equipment was $1 million.

But a year later it was all over. Landers, Frary & Clark was now another famous name that had passed into history where, with the years, its former fame would soon fade away.

Coffee Makers—A Profusion of Devices

The virtues and delights attributed to coffee from ancient times to current TV commercials are exceeded only by the number of devices man has invented during that period for brewing it. And no people have devoted as much skill and ingenuity to the creation of coffee makers as Americans.

Despite the great variety of coffee makers now available and their increasing sales, the consumption of coffee in this country has declined during the past two decades from an average annual per capita consumption of 16.1 pounds to 14 pounds by 1970.

The experts say that the causes of poor coffee are improper

In the early 1870s Manning-Bowman and Company offered these percolators based on the French "biggin" concept.

Courtesy House Furnishing Review.

244

brewing, too little or too much coffee, unclean pots, and, insist others, an unwillingness to grind coffee fresh each time it is brewed.

Like the coffee importers, the manufacturers of coffee makers have never suffered from over-modesty. In looking over their advertisements through the years one is struck by the number who unblushingly claim that their coffee pot is without question the best that has ever been developed!

Until the invention of the French biggin in 1800 and, in fact, for a great many years thereafter, coffee was made simply by boiling ground coffee in water "until it smelled good," as some unknown "authority" once put it. The biggin was named after its inventor and was a form of drip pot, designed so that water percolated down through the ground coffee in a separate compartment above the coffee pot.

The early coffee pots were usually made of tin, sometimes of copper or pewter. After porcelain enamel utensils began to be made in this country in 1875, that new material was widely used for coffee pots. Then by the end of the century nickelplated pots appeared.

The first known American adaptation of the French biggin was patented in 1873 and was made by Manning-Bowman & Company. It was, explained *House Furnishing Review* in August 1911 in an article about the company's early pots, "a combination of the French biggin idea and a drip percolator, differing from the regular biggin in consequence of the press or interior strainer. The press was operated by a wooden block, which was forced down on the wet coffee grounds to extract the coffee by pressure."

But what might be termed the final transition of the percolator to its present form was a model Manning-Bowman introduced in 1890. Said the *Review*: "This...is practically the same thing as many of the present percolators now [1911] being made...even to the glass cover. The only difference between this old model and the latest of Manning-Bowman percolators really is that it has no small water pocket, and will not pump cold water in less than twenty minutes, and, for that matter, few of the so-called modern ones will...."

An Innovation

The very first to have just such a percolator was Landers, Frary & Clark. In 1908 it introduced its first electric appliance, a "Universal" percolator with a remarkable innovation called the "cold water pump." In ordinary electric percolators then just beginning to be manufactured, the element had to heat all the water in the pot to about 190 degrees before it began to "perk." The Universal model was designed with a small well or recess in the base around which the heating element was brazed. Thus the concentrated heat on a small quantity of water started perking action in only two or three minutes. The "cold water pump" percolator quickly gained fame as well as sales and promptly outmoded all ordinary models.

Variations and adaptations of the cold water pump concept soon

A turn-of-the-century coffee maker, which made toast and waffles as well, as advertised in *Good Housekeeping*.

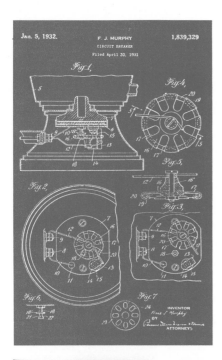

From top: A patent illustration of the unique fuse replacement unit used on the first Farberware percolator in 1930. That company's Coffee Robot as advertised by the Cincinnati Gas and Electric Company in 1937.

followed. One interesting version was developed by the Metal Ware Corporation in Two Rivers, Wisconsin in 1916, when, according to V. F. Trastek, vice-president, it obtained the first patent on an immersion type heating unit with a valveless pump for its percolators. It also produced three-minute percolation and, with some modification, is still used extensively today.

Meanwhile even during this period—and long before the advent of "consumer protection"—the matter of safety of home appliances in general and coffee makers in particular was already getting careful attention.

"The most important development in electrical cooking appliances," wrote Lewis Stephenson of Landers, Frary & Clark in an article entitled "Safety First" in *House Furnishing Review*, May 1915, "has been the installation of safety devices [in those designed to hold a liquid] for the prevention of fire, burned out heating units or other injury to the appliance through carelessness in leaving the device connected after the water has become exhausted or through use on excessive voltage." He goes on to describe a new lead fuse or Safety Plug just developed for use on Universal appliances, which acted as a circuit breaker. "With an ordinary screwdriver a new plug can be inserted in a moment's time and the appliance is ready for use again."

A unique gravity-operated safety device was introduced by the Robeson Rochester Company in 1924. It was described as a safety switch that not only prevented burn outs if and when the percolator ran dry, but eliminated the need to replace the blown out fuse. "Simply invert or shake the pot and it reconnects on the gravity principle and the appliance is again ready for use." Another early maker to stress safety was the Dover Manufacturing Company, Dover, Ohio, which in 1925 offered a percolator with its "Vea No Burn Out" heating element equipped with a safety fuse and guaranteed free replacement if it did.

In 1931 the Knapp-Monarch Company, now part of the Hoover Company, introduced a group of "Therm-A-Magic" percolators designed to shut off the current after pre-determined interval of time and after reaching a predetermined temperature. However, they did not maintain a warming temperature.

S. W. Farber Incorporated, New York, moved into the percolator field in 1930 with an ingenious safety device called the eight-in-one fuse, developed by one of its engineers, F. J. Murphy, and granted a patent January 5, 1932. Basically it consisted of a rotating disc on the base of the percolator equipped with eight separate fuses. If for any reason one fuse should blow, simply turning the disc until the next fuse snapped into place made the percolator immediately usable.

The Farberware "Coffee Robot" appeared in 1937. Featured as a coffee maker that "does about everything but buy the coffee," this vacuum-type brewer made the coffee, shut off the current when it was finished and with a thermostat control kept it hot indefinitely.

The simplicity, speed, and satisfactory performance of the percolator made it highly popular—so popular in fact that it prompted several big cooking utensil manufacturers to start making percolators and thus move into the appliance business. They had a considerable advantage since aluminum percolators could be produced to retail for much less than chrome-plated pots. An early entrant was the Aluminum Goods Manufacturing Company (now Mirror Aluminum Company). According to Al G. Vraney, advertising manager, "during the 1920s our company had the reputation for producing well over 50 percent of all the electric percolators in the country. This was a non-automatic percolator with a patented, very durable flat-type element." It made aluminum percolators to retail—with a guaranteed element—for as little as $1.75 for a five-cup size. Later, chrome-plated percolators were added but still priced much below percolators in the regular appliance lines.

During the late 1920s and early 1930s several manufacturers introduced coffee makers with separate bases containing the heating units, a design possibly suggested by the separate stove used for the then new Silex coffee maker. In 1927 the Permway Electric Manufacturing Company, St. Charles, Missouri, introduced an aluminum "Thoro-Perk" with a detachable base to sell for seven dollars; in 1928 the Economy Aluminum Company, Chicago, produced a model with a stove that projected up against a recess in the percolator, an eight-cup model retailing for four dollars. Sunbeam Corporation in 1935 (then the Chicago Flexible Shaft Company) was another entry in this category with its "Maxwelton Braes" seven-cup vacuum-type coffee maker retailing for $6.95.

If the percolator was—and still may be—the most popular type of coffee maker in America, a very close second was the vacuum drip or Silex type. It was the introduction of the Silex about the time of World War I that generated the greatest interest: the novelty of a glass coffee maker was enough to attract a lot of attention. In addition, its widespread use in many fine restaurants and hotels made it a real status symbol. Later, during World War II, when metal for most consumer goods was prohibited, a glass coffee pot had a great merchandising advantage.

As a result almost all manufacturers of coffee makers included glass vacuum-drip models in their line. Despite the obvious disadvantage of breakage and the many all-metal versions introduced, the glass models maintained their popularity for a long time and while they have passed their peak, are still very much in evidence.

The Perfect Coffee Machine

"What seems to be a perfect coffee machine on a small scale is the patent of an Englishman," reported *House Furnishing Review* in January 1894. "It consists of a glass globe or boiler which hangs by means of trunnions from an ornamental stand, the base of which is a spirit lamp....A funnel-shaped vessel, terminating in a long, glass

A specially designed drip-type coffee pot, the BrewOlator was developed by Joseph A. Bender during the 1960s. Despite some initial enthusiasm for the coffee pot, the BrewOlator failed to take off in the market place.

The first trade ad for the Silex coffee maker appeared in 1914. Note the interesting explanation of S-I-L-E-X.

Courtesy House Furnishing Review.

248

tube, the junction being surrounded with a cork...fitting the mouth of the boiler, forms the remaining portion of the appliance."

The report proceeds to explain how it works and concludes: "...as the steam in the boiler condenses, the coffee will strain into the boiler, from which...the coffee is drawn off as required."

It makes no mention of the word "Silex," but there is reason to believe its description of the "perfect coffee machine" unquestionably fits the Silex coffee maker that operates on the vacuum-drip principle and which, for more than half a century, has played a prominent role in the American housewares market. (However, Frank E. Wolcott, Jr., retired son of the founder of the company that sold it, when asked about it in 1972, said it was his impression Silex had originated in Germany, but he couldn't be certain.)

It is also not certain just how, in 1909, two sisters in Malden, Massachusetts, Mrs. Ann Bridges and Mrs. Sutton, acquired the rights to such a glass coffee maker. About that time Mrs. Bridges approached the Frank E. Wolcott Manufacturing Company in Hartford, Connecticut, which had begun to make a line of appliances under the "Torrid" brand, and asked Mr. Wolcott if he could make "a small electrical stove" for a new glass coffee maker called "Silex" she wanted to market. It was made of the just-developed "Pyrex" glass. Wolcott not only agreed, he was so impressed with its potential he undertook to aid in selling it.

William G. Church, who was eastern sales manager for the "Torrid" line and was later sales manager for the Silex Company, recalled some of the early developments during a conversation in West Hartford, Connecticut in 1972: "In 1927 Mr. Wolcott sold a half interest in his business to Charles E. Beardsley of the Novelty Manufacturing Company, in Waterbury, Connecticut. The firm became the Beardsley and Wolcott Manufacturing Company and production was transferred to Waterbury. Not long afterward, Frank sent the company treasurer, William Turner, to see Mrs. Bridges with the idea of buying the Silex Company and in 1929 consummated the deal."

On June 25, 1929 a holding company, Wolcott Incorporated, was organized in Hartford, along with a wholly owned subsidiary corporation called the Silex Company, the latter conducting all the manufacturing and selling operations of the coffee maker. In 1936 Wolcott Incorporated changed its name to the Silex Company and dissolved the subsidiary.

Gross sales for Silex in 1929, according to a statement of accounts that Mrs. Bridges gave Bill Church when he took over as sales manager, were just over $97,000.

"Silex was originally designed primarily for home use but we got a lot of business from restaurants," Vinc Lonergan, a retired manufacturers sales rep who handled the line in Chicago for many years, recalled during a conversation in 1971.

For example, in 1930 we had all the B&G sandwich shops using Silex on their counters which gave us a continuous public demonstration.

That was most helpful in getting public acceptance. And many of the best hotels in Chicago also used it.

One of the biggest boosts we got was from the old Majestic Radio Company with whom I arranged a nation-wide dealer-consumer promotion. They made a very attractive Silex coffee maker window display for their dealers who then gave one away free to the person in the neighborhood with the lowest serial number on a Majestic radio. We sold many thousands and got lots of free publicity that helped us get Silex into more stores.

In those days the reps used to refer to Silex as "the gasoline lamp" or "the chemical retort." It was a good product to demonstrate and we all drank lots of coffee, but at the start it wasn't easy to ring the cash register often enough for a good balanced diet.

A 1971 version of at least half a solution to the problem of breakage with glass coffee makers is this Cory Vacuum Brewer—the upper bowl of which is of taste-free, high density plastic and dishwasher safe, it is said.

Sales grew steadily and reached a peak of over $11 million in 1947, which was three years after Frank Wolcott's death. Unlike metal coffee makers, there were fewer restrictions on glassware during the war and in the immediate postwar period due to industry overproduction and accumulated inventories of these products, sales slumped sharply. In 1948 the Silex Company showed a loss of over $900,000 and over $300,000 in 1949. "Attempts were made to diversify the company's product line with only limited success," reports a study of the company by W. Keyser Manly, dated January 10, 1955, "and small profits were shown in 1950 and 1951 followed by further losses ($342,000) in 1952." The report continued:

In late 1952, a new group, realizing the value of the Silex name, bought a substantial stockholding in the company. They believed that a more diversified product line and experienced management was needed if the company was to prosper. The Chicago Electric Manufacturing Company which had been making rapid strides since 1946 under the management of S. M. Ford, a former General Electric appliance executive, was brought to their attention. Negotiations with the owners of Chicago Electric Manufacturing were begun and in June 1953 all shares of that company were acquired by Silex for $900,000 cash.

A preliminary prospectus of the Silex Company dated August 12, 1953, offering 201,563 shares of common stock (per share par value) at $3.50, stipulates: "The company and Stanley M. Ford entered into an agreement on December 22, 1952, whereby Mr. Ford was employed as General Manager of the company...such agreement to continue to December 31, 1954 and during each calendar year thereafter until terminated by written notice given by either party...."

Besides coffee makers, the Silex line at this time included the "Freeze-O-Tray" ice cream freezer for use in a household refrigerator, a steam iron and additional commercial items. The products of the Chicago Electric Manufacturing Company, now the Chicago Division of the company, included a portable electric washing machine, ice cream freezers, juicers, mixer, irons among other items, all marketed under the company's "Handyhot" name.

The merger was effective in reversing the downward sales curve and by 1958 had reached $5 million. In 1960 the company was ac-

Besides an interest in everything from gunpowder to the theory of heat, Count Benjamin Thompson Rumford also found time in the early 1800s to formulate thoughts on coffee and the best means of brewing it. In a long essay on the subject he presented his designs for pots as well as detailed instructions for brewing. This pot's dimensions were "...most proper for making four cups of coffee at once."

From The Complete Works of Count Rumford.

250

quired by the Proctor Electric Company, whereupon the name became Proctor-Silex Company. In 1966 it was acquired by the SCM Corporation of which it is now a subsidiary.

To date the little glass "perfect coffee machine" has had a long and varied journey.

A HISTORY OF THE SILEX COMPANY

1929—Frank E. Wolcott in Hartford, Connecticut, incorporates a holding company, Wolcott Incorporated, and a subsidiary called Silex Company.

1936—Wolcott Incorporated name changed to the Silex Company and subsidiary corporation dissolved.

1951—Silex Company becomes publicly owned corporation.

1953—Silex acquires the Chicago Electric Manufacturing Company, a fifty-year-old manufacturer of appliances.

1955—Silex glassware products operation sold to Corning Glass Works.

1956—Silex acquires the Enterprise Manufacturing Company, Philadelphia, manufacturer of coffee grinders, meat choppers, irons and other products, established in 1864.

1958—All Enterprise commercial products are sold to U. S. Slicing Machine Company. Consumer products sold to Chop Rite Incorporated.

1960—Silex is sold to the Proctor Electric Division of Proctor & Schwartz, Philadelphia, which becomes Proctor-Silex Corporation.

1966—Proctor-Silex Corporation acquired by the SCM Corporation, of which it becomes a subsidiary.

Simple and Successful—Chemex

On July 10, 1956 a rather unusual ad appeared in the *New York Times.*

"Hello New York!" it began. "The chemist who invented in this city and who manufactures in this city the Chemex coffee maker would like to say a word of thanks....Today is my sixtieth birthday. Having left Berlin University at the ripe student age of thirty and having the choice of many pleasant abodes, I picked...New York as the place to live and work as inventor and manufacturer. Where else do you feel the world's pulse as clearly as at its Hudson vein? Where else is such a magnetic field which induces an inventor 'to do something about it'? Nowhere....You have to start the ball rolling in New York...there is nothing like New York. Thank you New Yorkers! Dr. Peter Schlumbohm."

That brief excerpt reflects something of the uninhibited character of the inventor of one of the most simple and successful coffee makers—an adaptation of the chemist's basic laboratory filtering principle to making coffee. Moreover, its success was, literally, a one-man achievement, for until after his death in 1962, there was never another salesman for Chemex. (Burt Sloane, well-known New York manufacturers sales rep, relates how delighted he was when,

Dr. Peter Schlumbohm, inventor of the Chemex coffee maker.

some years ago, he asked for the Chemex line and its inventor readily agreed—until Sloane asked how much commission it paid. "Commission?" Schlumbohm thundered. "I never pay a commission! You have the honor of handling Chemex.")

Born in Kiel, Germany and educated to be a chemist, he was almost killed fighting in World War I and in 1939 decided to come to America. Never hesitant in speaking of himself, in 1960 he published a booklet describing how he came to produce the Chemex:

> The success of the Chemex coffee maker has been riding on the Bauhaus style...[namely] a table must be a table, a chair must be a chair, a bed must be a bed....When, in 1938, the personal desire for coffee came up (I had been a tea drinker), my aspect simply was: A coffee maker must make coffee and then I applied my knowledge of physics and chemistry....
>
> Strangely, I was "forced" into this venture. Except for having filed the patent and having had such a coffee maker made up by a glass blower for my personal use, I had no plans for its commercial exploitation....[In 1941 financial circumstances obliged me to] take an appraising look at...my new patent for the coffee maker....Within a week I sold half-an-interest in it for $5,000 and planned to license it. Practically every famous appliance maker in the country turned it down. It is amusing to read their letters today. At the time it was less funny....
>
> During my discussion with those potential licensees I had studied their products, their carload mentality and their limitations. For the first time I realized the merit of my invention....So, in 1941...I designed the quart size model which—except for minor details—has never changed in all these 19 years. I coined the mark Chemex... and formed Chemex Corporation. The patent partner went along for a while until I could buy him out at a very high price.

It took months, he continues, until he had a finished product. (It was made for him of Pyrex by Corning.) Then he showed it to the housewares buyer at Macy who said it wasn't a coffee maker "because it doesn't look like one." He finally prevailed upon the buyer to take it home and try it. Next morning he got a phone call. "Okay, Doc, we'll run an ad on May 24th." Macy's sold fifty-four the first week.

> But then we got a letter from Corning Glass Works: "Unless you can produce an A-5 Priority Rating [from the War Production Board] we can no longer supply you." That seemed the end...I wrote President Roosevelt about our plight, heading the letter with *"Minima rex non curat,"* (a king does not bother with details), *"President curat et minima,"* (a president cares even about details).
>
> The Latin pun probably did it. Three days later the phone rang. "This is the WPB. Are you Dr. — I can't pronounce the name?" "Yes." "Well you have a helluva nerve to bother the President with your goddamned coffee maker....But it seems to be a goddamned good coffee maker. What rating do you need?" "A-5." "Well, you have it. Good luck."

Who could ask for anything more—a wartime okay to produce an all-glass coffee maker at a time when almost all other coffee maker production had ended! To a great extent his "sales" problem

CHEMEX

U. S. Patent 2,241,368
Trademark Reg. U. S. Pat. Off.

"The Coffeemaker without parts..."

Retail: **$5.00**

One single piece of strong-walled "PYREX" Brand Glass, with beautiful Birchwood Handle in natural color with Satin Finish.
Each CHEMEX carefully packed in strong, attractive box, 6 boxes in master-box. F.o.b. Charleroi, Pa.

Dr. Schlumbohm's famous Chemex coffee maker, "based on a Bauhaus concept of simplicity."

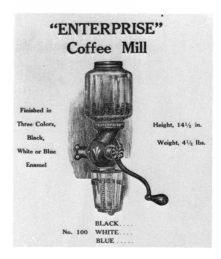

"ENTERPRISE"
Coffee Mill

Finished in
Three Colors,
Black,
White or Blue
Enamel

Height, 14½ in.

Weight, 4½ lbs.

BLACK....
No. 100 WHITE....
BLUE.....

Before World War I, the Enterprise
Manufacturing Co., Philadelphia,
offered this utilitarian, wall-mounted
coffee grinder, which probably got
daily use.

252

In 1908 in Germany, Mrs. Melitta Bentz
felt her family deserved better coffee.
So she took a tin can and punched the
bottom full of holes. Then she cut a
round disc from blotter paper to fit the
bottom of the can. She placed the can
over the coffee pot, put coffee in the
can and poured boiling water over it.
This crude but effective filtering device
produced a great brew. Thus was born
the Melitta coffee maker. In 1964,
Melitta Inc. of Cherry Hill, New Jersey,
was marketing a full line of these coffee
makers. Shown here is a white china
two- to six-cup capacity model.

thereafter became largely a matter of allocation. He sold only the
stores he felt could and would do justice to his Chemex—and only,
but only, if they agreed to maintain the established retail prices.
Apart from everything else, he could offer the added appeal of constant repeat business for the stores on the filter paper.

Although he held patents on some three hundred inventions,
none of them achieved anywhere near the success of Chemex; but
with that he proved himself to be as good a marketing man as an
inventor. Now owned by others, the business continues under the
Chemex name.

Instant Coffee Inroads?

Will there ever come a time when coffee brewing appliances will be
obsolete—when instant coffee will have become so popular as to
make them useless? "Absolutely not!" one can hear the real coffee
lovers shout. But despite the advantages of instant coffee, the record shows that the sale of coffee makers continues to go merrily
upward. In 1960, according to *Merchandising Week*'s annual industry statistical report, 4,695,000 coffee makers were sold. In 1971 that
figure had practically doubled and reached 8,550,000 units. (In
many homes, it is believed, percolators are often used just for heating water for instant coffee.)

Water soluble coffee is nothing new. Over a century ago it was
already being experimented with and in 1901 a Japanese living in
Chicago demonstrated his version of it. But it remained for a chemist
named G. Washington, who invented a new process in 1906 to be
the first to market instant coffee commercially in the United States
in 1909 under his own name. Since then, of course, there have been
great improvements in the technology involved, notably the freeze-
dried process, and many newcomers have entered the instant coffee
and instant tea field as well.

Coffee Grinders

Tea, coffee, and chocolate were brought to colonial America toward
the end of the seventeenth century and Mary Earl Gould in *The Early
American Home* reports:

> The early way of preparing it was strange indeed. The leaves were
> boiled, the liquid thrown out and the leaves buttered and salted and
> eaten—with none too much relish. Tea was also made from herbs—a
> custom carried on for many years. A license had to be obtained to
> sell tea....
> Coffee drinking was a general habit first acquired at the time of
> the Revolution, although coffee had been served as early as 1670.
> Chocolate, spelled chockolett, appeared in the colonies in 1697....
> Mills were invented to grind this bean or seed, as were mills for grind-
> ing coffee; such mills were boxes of wood, with an iron holder, blades
> and crank.[4]

The need to roast or at least grind one's own coffee lasted for
many years, and a coffee mill was an essential in every well-ordered

home. According to *Kane's Famous First Facts,* the first patent issued in this country for a coffee mill was to James Carrington, Wallingford, Connecticut, April 3, 1892. In his *History of Manufacturers in the United States,* Victor Clark writes: "As early as 1831 a New England manufacturer estimated that 300,000 coffee mills were being made annually in the U.S."[5]

The variety of grinders was endless. There were models to mount on the wall, the table or even hold on our lap while doing the grinding. There were wooden cases, iron cases, steel cases and some with a quart-size glass reservoir in which to keep the beans till needed. Some provided adjustments for fine or coarse grind and often considerably decorative embellishments in gold trim and floral designs were lavished on these early housewares items.

One of the most important producers of mills was the Enterprise Manufacturing Company, Philadelphia (later acquired by the Silex Company), which specialized in cast iron mills and meat grinders for home as well as commercial use. "Our grinders," it emphasized, "are warranted equal to steel." Its wall model grinders, states its catalog, are "adapted for steamboats, butchers, lumber camps or wherever it is desirable."

In 1900 or thereabouts, specialized coffee and tea stores as well as many grocery stores were equipped with grinders and, as part of their service, ground the coffee the customers bought. As a result the demand for a household grinder began to diminish rapidly. Later when canned and vacuum-packed coffee appeared, there was even less need for the average homeowner to have a coffee grinder.

An electric coffee grinder for household use first made its appearance in this country in 1937. Made by the KitchenAid Division of the Hobart Manufacturing Company, Troy, Ohio, it was known as Model A-10, was adjustable for different grinds, and retailed for $12.75. In 1970 it was replaced with an improved modern version, Model KCM, selling for $26.75.

Meanwhile other electric coffee mills appeared. Braun North America introduced a grinder in 1965, Model KMM 1, made in West Germany, featuring nine different grind adjustments and subsequently supplemented by another mill, KMM 2, with a built-in coffee bean container. In 1969 it added the colorful Braun Mini Coffee Grinders, 6½ inches high and weighing only two pounds. In that year too, Salton, Incorporated entered the field with a sleekly designed coffee mill of plastic to retail for around twenty dollars. Since then, others have been introduced.

It is noteworthy that despite the fact it becomes increasingly difficult for the average homemaker to buy coffee beans, the loyal devotees of good coffee still manage to buy it and grind it.

From top: Hobart's Model A-10 was the first electric coffee mill. Introduced in 1937. In 1965, the sleek, handsome Braun "aromatic" coffee grinder.

Whistling Tea Kettles

Just who should be credited with inventing the whistling tea kettle? One can find examples of whistles on utensils (which had to be

This electric coffee grinder by Salton has settings for grind size and a detachable container for refrigeration of coffee beans.

254

For non-coffee drinkers, there's always tea. Its method of preparation remains basically the same: a steaming kettle of water is primary. This 1968 advertisement shows a wide variety of tea kettles.

blown by mouth, however) on some of the earliest, primitive clay utensils. But if anyone preceded Joseph Block in developing a whistling tea kettle, history is unaware of him.

Joe Block, though long past the traditional retirement age, continues to be active as head of his New York firm of cookware importers, Steelmasters Incorporated. Previously he and his brother Irving operated the firm of J and I Block, continuing a jobbing firm established by their father in lower Manhattan in the 1880s.

"I remember," he recalled readily in 1971, "a model of a potato cooker my father devised many years ago. Like almost all other utensils at that time, it was made of tin, and he had added a whistle to it which, supposedly, blew when the potatoes were cooked." Joe continued:

He never tried to manufacture it. But years later, when I was in Germany right after World War I, I happened to think of it. I was in the Werdohl enamelware manufacturing area, visiting the plant of Gebruder Hansel in Westphalia. I saw them making a small aluminum teakettle. Recalling my father's idea, I had them put a whistle in the spout which blew when the water boiled.

They made up thirty-six pieces by hand and the following Saturday morning I arranged to put them on sale with a demonstrator in Wertheim's Department Store in Berlin. By noon they were all sold. The item soon became a best seller. I immediately ordered some for the United States, and they arrived just in time for the housewares show—I'm not sure, but I believe it was at the Morrison Hotel in Chicago in 1922. I had water boiling in one all week; the whistle almost drove us crazy. But for all our trouble we made only one sale—forty-eight pieces to Wanamaker's in New York.

That enterprising store, he continued, didn't fare much better than he had. "It proved to be a slow starter." But eventually it began to click.

Where once we couldn't get any interest in the item at all, sales zoomed until we were getting orders for 35,000 kettles a month from W. T. Grant alone. By then the kettles were made for us by the Aluminum Products Company of La Grange, Illinois. They had colored plastic handles and they retailed for one dollar. But by that time, as everybody else was getting into the business, we phased out.

The Toaster

"Something wonderful happens to bread when it's toasted," some unknown lover of that great American breakfast staple once wrote.

The ancient Egyptians are said to have scorched or parched bread to remove the moisture as a form of preservation. History notes that the Roman conquerors of Britain brought the custom north with them. By the seventeenth and eighteenth centuries toasting had become British and American common practice. (Latins prefer rolls.) Early English and colonial toasters were a toasting fork or crude wrought iron devices contrived by the local smithy. Between the toaster and the vagaries of the fireplace the quality of the product was quite variable.

Jim's Toaster

An indispensable article for gasoline or gas stoves. Toasts **4** slices in **2** minutes. A leader and seller in department stores.

FOR SALE BY THE MANUFACTURERS

HARKINS & WILLIS, - ANN ARBOR, MICH.

New York Agency: FRED FEAR & CO., 15 Jay St.

Write for prices.

Not gone, but often forgotten is this top-of-the-stove toaster. As the ad says, it was an "indispensable article" long before electricity and is still sold today.

The first regularly manufactured toasters in this country were probably the tin and wire affairs designed to set over a coal stove opening or a gas burner and hold four slices of bread tilted toward the center. Surprising as it may seem, these types are still made by the Bromwell Wire Goods Company in Michigan City, Indiana, a firm founded in 1819.

Not until 1910 did the arrival of electricity bring with it the "modern" toaster. In June of that year a Westinghouse ad in the *Saturday Evening Post* was headlined, "Breakfast without going into the kitchen" and introduced the toaster-stove—"ready for service any hour of the day or night."

The idea of an appliance designed for just one function was still a bit strange, and it was not uncommon for manufacturers to bring out dual-utility items. The Armstrong Electric and Manufacturing Company, Huntington, West Virginia, offered a three-in-one combination grill, hotplate, and toaster to retail for $8.85.

The next two decades witnessed considerable innovation and progress as manufacturers mastered the handling of electricity for household tasks. In 1922 the Estate Stove Company, Hamilton, Ohio, came out with an ingeniously designed four-slice toaster on which "one movement of the lever knob turns over all four racks." In the same year "The newest turnover toaster—a Hotpoint servant," was introduced by the Edison Electric Appliance Company.

The popular sandwich toasters now appeared on the market. One of the first was the "Hostess" made by the All Rite Company, Rushville, Indiana; another pioneer in this category was the uniquely designed sandwich toaster of the Fitzgerald Manufacturing Company, now Son-Chief Electric Incorporated, of Winsted, Connecticut.

Designers vied with unusual shapes and concepts for toasters. In 1922 a Detroit firm, the Best Stove and Stamping Company, came out with perhaps the first "oven type" toaster with an in-and-out sliding bread rack, an interesting idea which Landers, Frary & Clark of New Britain, Connecticut used the following year in a "Universal" toaster.

But the most significant development was the automatic toaster. That distinction belongs to D. A. Rogers of South Minneapolis, Minnesota, who in 1924—two years ahead of Toastmaster—designed a toaster equipped with a dial somewhat like that on a telephone. By

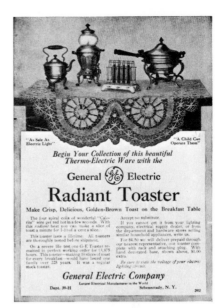

"As Safe As Electric Light"   "A Child Can Operate Them"

Begin Your Collection of this beautiful Thermo-Electric Ware with the

General **GE** Electric

Radiant Toaster

Make Crisp, Delicious, Golden-Brown Toast on the Breakfast Table

General Electric Company

Largest Electrical Manufacturer in the World

Dept. 39-H   Schenectady, N. Y.

Four Pieces at a Time!

READY for service—an electric toaster that makes four pieces of toast at a time. A real, exclusive specialty. You know what that means to a salesman.

The illustration below shows the mechanism of this innovation in toasters.

One movement of the lever knob to right or left turns over all four racks. Turns them positively —no jamming or sticking.

A strong, sturdy appliance—built for long and efficient service. Heating element made of genuine Nichrome wire.

Nickel finish, with all parts easily accessible for cleaning.

Equipped with cord, plug and off-and-on switch.

Ask "the house" to order a sample for you. You'll find that it sells on sight.

Estate
ELECTRIC TOASTER

MADE BY THE ESTATE STOVE CO., HAMILTON, OHIO

MAKERS OF ESTATE ELECTRIC RANGES

From top: In 1912, General Electric's Radiant Toaster, so simple "a child can operate." In 1922, Estate advertised the first electric toaster that could make four pieces of toast at a time.

Bottom, courtesy The Jobber's Salesman.

Now! Automatic toast for breakfast ... *Made like this*

Just drop a slice of bread into the oven slot as illustrated below.

Then press down the two levers. This automatically turns on the current and adjusts timer.

Pop! up comes the toast when it's done—and the current is automatically turned off.

This amazing new invention makes perfect toast *every time*—without watching, without turning, without burning

How many times *each week* do you have to throw out burned slices of toast? You leave the room for a minute—and return to find the bread burned to a crisp. Often it burns before your very eyes. Now a new invention ends this annoying and wasteful methods.

The Toastmaster *automatically* makes the kind of toast everyone likes. An even golden brown. Crisply tender. And always sizzling hot. Does it *every time*—without watching or turning. This is how.

Three fascinating operations

First, you drop a slice of bread into the oven slot. Second, you press down

THE commercial Toastmaster has proved to be a veritable gold mine for hotels, restaurants, cafeterias, coffee and sandwich shops ... made in four sizes—1-slice, 4-slice, 5-slice and a new 2-slice. A postcard will bring full details without obligation.

the two levers. This automatically turns on the current and sets the timing device. Third, Pop! up comes the toast automatically when it's done, and the current is automatically turned off. The toast is made in a jiffy because both sides are toasted *at the same time.*

There is no guesswork. No danger of the bread burning, whether you watch or not. And because both sides are toasted *at the same time* in an enclosed oven, all the flavor is *sealed in*—and the toast is so hot when served that the butter melts and disappears in an instant.

A beauty to own or give

Finished in gleaming nickel, the Toastmaster

is an attractive piece for the dining table or server. With it you can make toast at the table the minute you want it.

While the Toastmaster is brand new it has been thoroughly tested. For it is a small brother of the big Toastmaster which has been used for many years by famous Restaurants, Hotels and Sandwich Shops.

Now at your dealer's— or order direct

This is National Toaster Month. Your Electric Light Company, department store and electric dealer are now displaying the new Toastmaster. See it. Examine it. Operate it. You'll be won to it at once. In case your dealer cannot supply you, send us a money order for $12.50. We will ship you a Toastmaster on 30-days trial. Money back if you aren't delighted with it. Waters-Genter Co., 231 N. Second St., Minneapolis, Minn.

The TOASTMASTER

The *Saturday Evening Post* of March 5, 1927 celebrated National Toaster month with this Toastmaster ad. "Pop! Up comes the toast when it's done...."

From top: The Bersted Manufacturing Company, brought out this version of a two-slice automatic model in 1928. "It rings a bell when toast is ready and at the same time a switch automatically turns off the current." In the thirties, Merit-Made introduced this *moderne* coffee maker and toaster. "It toasts... it cooks...it brews."

256

setting the dial to the desired type of toast, the toaster then operated until automatically shut off, at which point the hinged sides would drop down so the toast could be removed. Although Rogers made and announced such a toaster, little more is known about it and for whatever reasons it was short-lived.

With the Toastmaster it was a different story. It had its beginnings in a plant in Stillwater, Minnesota where, during World War I, a master mechanic, Charles Strite, became fed up with the burned toast he got for breakfast in the company lunch room.

Working in his home shop, he developed a crude model of an automatic toaster incorporating a spring, motor, and switch—the forerunner of the automatic Toastmaster—which, after being refined and improved, was patented on May 29, 1919. He custom-built a few four-slice units for restaurant use and the following year Glen Waters supported him with some financing. Of the first one hundred commercial toasters shipped to the Childs restaurant chain, one hundred came back. But only minor adjustments were needed and the idea worked.

In 1921 Harold Genter invested in the idea and the Waters Genter Company was formed. But production was only one commercial toaster a day. The idea of a household toaster seemed a good one but was scrapped when it took months to produce ten single-slice toasters.

Then in 1925, the year the name "Toastmaster" was registered, Murray Ireland joined the company as factory superintendent. It was he who designed Model 1 A 1, the first household toaster. Marketed in 1926 it launched the company in the housewares field to make toaster history.

In 1926 Max McGraw bought the Waters Genter Company. The move provided additional working capital and experience in the appliance business. With the same staff, the McGraw Electric Company was incorporated and the business began the steady growth that has marked it since.

"When we first contacted distributors and retailers with our first Toastmaster and told them it would have to sell for $12.50 they told us we were crazy to even think of a toaster at that price," Glen Waters said in 1944 in a memorandum in the company's files. "But I guess we were just dumb enough to try. The wholesalers insisted our 40% discount was far too low, but despite that and the warnings that 'it couldn't be done,' our business developed."

Success of the automatic toaster idea set other manufacturers to emulate it. Thomas A. Edison Incorporated with "Edicraft," Bersted, General Electric, Landers, Frary & Clark with "Universal," and others began competing for the automatic toaster business from consumers who, by then, were reluctant to buy any other kind.

Yet despite their convenience, automatic toasters didn't always produce perfect toast. Factors such as the starting temperature of the toaster, the moisture content of the bread as well as the operating temperature and timing of the toaster remained to be reconciled. For example, directions for using the first Toastmaster suggested operating it once without bread so as to raise the temperature. In later models this was corrected by adding a piece of bi-metal to the speed regulator of the clock mechanism. The engineers called this a "compensated toaster," and while it made fairly uniform toast regardless of the starting temperature of the toaster, it did not compensate for variations in the moisture content of bread. That was finally accomplished by another refinement—the "color selector."

In the 1930s engineering ingenuity began to produce further refinements in automatic toasters and the tic-toc of the standard clock mechanism gave way to silent controls. In 1930 Proctor brought out a toaster that operated on the basis of surface temperature of the bread and the temperature of the toasting space rather than on any fixed time of operation, and regardless of moisture content of the bread or the temperature of the toaster itself, made toast of a fairly uniform color. In 1935 Knapp-Monarch announced its "Tel-A-Matic" (Model 514) toaster with a timing device employing

THE *NEW* TOASTER SENSATION
that will make your customers
STOP, LOOK AND LOOSEN!

THERE won't be any regrets when you advertise this ultra-modern HANDY HOT toaster. It's a successful seller on sight alone. Stream-lined in the newest manner, it will instantly attract the attention of the public and it will be the treasured possession of every housewife who acquires one.

Model 405
Cord Attached
Underwriters Approved

See this beautiful new Toaster and the most complete line of popular priced household electric appliances in

ROOM 536-A
NATIONAL
HOUSE FURNISHING EXHIBIT
Stevens Hotel, Chicago
January 6th to 12th, 1935

The surprisingly moderate price makes this Toaster the finest value you've ever offered . . . Write for our catalog and prices today!

A reliable Handyhot product.

CHICAGO ELECTRIC MANUFACTURING CO.
2801-35 SOUTH HALSTED ST. - CHICAGO, ILL.
NEW YORK OFFICE, Room 1129, Fifth Ave. Bldg.

257

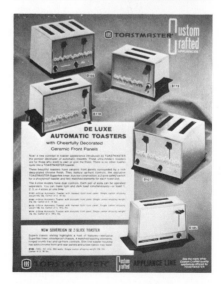

TORSTMASTER Custom Crafted APPLIANCE LINE

DE LUXE
AUTOMATIC TOASTERS
with Cheerfully Decorated
Ceramic Front Panels

NEW SOVEREIGN IV 2 SLICE TOASTER

From top: The Handyhot "new toaster sensation" featured streamlining that was the vogue in 1935. The lower picture has a variety of toasters offered in color with "cheerfully" decorated ceramic front panels.

Top, courtesy House Furnishing Review.

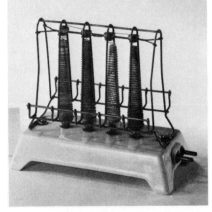

From top: Three early electric toasters: GE's very first, the 1905 model X2. In 1909, General Electric's model D12 boasted a porcelain base. The electric toaster-stove was Westinghouse's entry into the toaster business, 1910.

bi-metal construction. It had nothing to do with the moisture content of the bread. But it required a definite time for each cycle to heat and cool and "remembered" to allow more time for a cold toaster and less time for a very hot one.

Sunbeam entered its new silent automatic in 1949, a bi-metal operated unit which it called "radiant control" and which introduced a novel feature—bread placed in it lowered itself automatically and emerged as toast automatically.

Apart from continued improvement in design refinements in timing and control devices and similar niceties after the automatic toaster became the generally accepted standard for the industry, little or no significant innovation took place until 1956 when General Electric introduced its "Toast-R-Oven."

Combining an automatic, pop-up type toaster with an oven warming drawer, the new concept promptly created a new trend, the end of which is nowhere in sight. All these variations and innovations have combined to make an entirely new kind of appliance out of that which once was known simply as a toaster.

Major Highlights of Toaster Development

Early Era—Bread was originally toasted at the fireplace in wrought-iron holders. In the late 1800s tin and wire toasters designed to fit over a gas or oil stove were introduced. These are still being made and sold in 1972.

1909—First electric toasters introduced by General Electric and Westinghouse. They were of completely open construction and lacked any type of cover or shell.

1918—First combination toaster and percolator introduced by Armstrong Electric and Manufacturing Company of Huntington, West Virginia (now Armstrong Products Company).

1920s—First "flip-flop" toaster that turned over bread by lowering a side panel made its appearance. It was the basic standard for many years, but who made it first is not known.

1922—First four-slice electric toaster, designed somewhat along the lines of the square tin gas toasters, but capable of manually reversing all four slices of bread at once, introduced by the Estate Stove Company of Hamilton, Ohio.

First "oven type" toaster introduced by the Best Stove and Stamping Company of Detroit. The toaster was enclosed on all sides but one and was equipped with a tray to hold two slices of bread vertically; the tray was pushed into the toaster, then pulled out when the bread was toasted as desired.

1924—First automatic toaster announced by D. A. Rogers of South Minneapolis, Minnesota. It was equipped with a dial like a telephone to regulate timing, but was not commercially successful.

First combination flat toaster and table grill introduced by the Sunbeam Corporation (then called the Chicago Flexible Shaft Company).

First combination toaster and corn popper introduced by the Acme Electric and Manufacturing Company of Cleveland.

1926—First commercially successful automatic toaster, the "Toastmaster," introduced by Waters Genter Company of Minneapolis, Minnesota, and acquired the same year by McGraw Electric Company (now McGraw-Edison Company). It operated by means of a clock-type timing device adjustable to the desired type of toast; it shut off the current and ejected the toast when finished.

1930—First automatic toaster using a silent, bimetallic heat sensor in place of the then-standard clock-type control introduced by Proctor Electric Company (now Proctor-Silex Corporation). The sensor, adjusted for the desired type toast activated current shut-off switch and signal light or bell when toast was finished.

First "drop down" type of toaster introduced by the Beardsley and Wolcott Manufacturing Company of Waterbury, Connecticut. The bread, inserted in slots at the top, dropped into a tray in the base when toasted.

1933—First toaster designed to accommodate rolls as well as bread introduced by the Samson United Corporation of Rochester, New York.

1937—First toaster using a conveyer device introduced by the Toast-O-Lator Company of New York. The bread was inserted at one end, passed through heaters, and emerged as toast at the other end.

1940—First toaster with a "keep warm" feature introduced by General Electric. Its mechanism was designed so that after the heater was turned off the toast could be held down inside the toaster, where residual heat would keep it warm until it was wanted.

1947—First toaster equipped with separate control governing the crispness of toast introduced by Proctor. It made possible a choice of any type of toast from light to melba.

First "long slot" toaster designed with bread slots end-to-end rather than parallel, resulting in a long, narrow toaster, introduced by Samson United Corporation.

1949—First automatic toaster using a radiation-type of bimetallic sensor control introduced by the Sunbeam Corporation. The bread lowered itself automatically; the sensor, set to the desired type of toast, operated on heat reflected from the bread, shut off the current and ejected the toast when finished.

1955—First toaster using vertical toasting and equipped with a drawer type of oven for heating buns or other food introduced by General Electric. Heat from a single element was used for toasting bread or, deflected downward, food in drawer.

1956—First four-slice well-type toaster introduced by Proctor.

1959—First toaster designed with a double-pole main switch at end of toast cycle introduced by General Electric. This was considered a major safety improvement in reducing potential shock hazard.

1961—First oven type of toaster using horizontal toasting and equipped with oven compartment for preparing frozen foods as well as baking introduced by General Electric. In 1971 a "king-size" version was introduced.

1968—First toaster equipped with push-button controls introduced by Westinghouse.

Waffle Irons

Waffle irons and wafer irons date to the fourteenth century and were often used in connection with religious services, Mary Earle Gould relates in *The Early American House*.

> They had long handles (so the user could stand as far from the heat of the fireplace as possible), with two heads, shutting like pincers. The waffle iron had oblong heads of different sizes, while the wafer iron had round or elliptical heads. The waffle iron, just as today, had a waffle pattern on each head, which gave it its name; later ones made in factories have a number and date of manufacture.... It was customary to give the bride a wafer iron on which were her initials, the date of the wedding and a hex mark for luck.[6]

The Griswold Manufacturing Company of Erie, Pennsylvania, the earliest recorded firm in the business, was founded in 1865 to produce all types of iron cookware. (It is now part of the General Housewares Corporation Cookware Group). A waffle iron was one of its early products. Although it later added aluminum utensils, the popularity of iron for making waffles persisted for a long time.

Not until after World War I did the electric waffle iron appear. One of the first was "a waffle iron for lamp socket use" introduced in 1918 by Landers, Frary & Clark of New Britain, Connecticut. Two years later the Armstrong Electric and Manufacturing Company of Huntington, West Virginia, introduced one with a heat-indicator to show when it was ready to use. In 1930 the Waters Genter Company, which had brought out the automatic toaster, introduced a companion "Waffle Master," which was also automatic.

Innovations followed: the twin reversible; the double-decker;

The 1949 Westinghouse model TO-91 had a push-up feature to prevent burned fingers.

259

Sales Volume of TOASTERS			
Year	Units	$ Volume (Retail)	Price
1922	400,000	2,000,000	$ 5
1930	1,263,000	6,946,500	6
1932	960,000	3,100,000	3
1940	2,272,000	15,000,000	7
1950	4,525,000	80,142,700	18
1960	3,345,000	60,043,000	18
1965	4,750,000	73,625,000	16
1970	5,975,000	107,550,000	18
1971	6,400,000	115,200,000	18

From top: Sun Chief Electric's sandwich toaster in nickel or chrome. Circa 1925. In the early 1930s this waffle iron in the middle picture made by the Samson United Company, featured a decorated porcelain china insert in the lid. The Dominion Electric waffle iron of 1971 has Florentine designed grids.

Middle, courtesy the Smithsonian Institute.

and even a small dessert-size waffle maker. Numerous sandwich toasters were designed with reversible or replaceable griddles that became waffle irons.

As manufacturing technology improved, waffle irons—and sandwich grills—became more sophisticated in operation as well as appearance. Even Teflon found a place on these appliances. Nevertheless, whether America's tastes have changed or for whatever reason, the sale of these two appliances has leveled off at around the one million units a year mark and has remained there for the past decade.

Expansion by Acquisition: McGraw-Edison Company

Growth through merger and acquisition had almost become a way of life for business by the 1960s and early 1970s. And one of the biggest firms in the electric housewares field, the McGraw-Edison Company, is the product of such a policy.

Today the organization manufactures an enormously varied group of electrical products ranging from industrial and commercial equipment of all types of electric housewares. It represents at least seventy-five or more acquisitions over the years, which now comprise twenty-three divisions and five subsidiaries of the corporation whose 1971 sales reached a peak of $663.4 million. Of that total $247.9 million was in consumer goods.

The company's founder Max McGraw decided at an early age he would never be satisfied with average success. Born in Clear Lake, Iowa February 1, 1883, Max McGraw began his business career by covering a fifteen-mile route on horseback delivering newspapers. He had a boyhood interest in that emerging marvel, electricity. He made friends with electricians, subscribed to a correspondence course and at the age of seventeen with $500 he had saved from his paper route, founded the McGraw Electric Company in a basement at 401 Fourth Street, Sioux City, Iowa. One of his first big jobs was installing electric lights in the Sioux City Opera House at a cost of $10,000.

McGraw's first acquisition was in 1912, when he purchased The Joseph R. Lehmer Company of Omaha.

During the next few years he continued to expand his operations (see accompanying chart). In 1926 he met Alfred Bersted, head of a small but enterprising appliance firm, the Bersted Manufacturing Company. The two men took an immediate liking to each other. When McGraw bought the Bersted Company he acquired the close friendship and services of Al Bersted who would play a major role in McGraw's future. Some of the complexities of McGraw-Edison and its policy of expansion by acquisition can be seen in the interesting off-and-on again relationship of Bersted Manufacturing and McGraw-Edison.

The bright-looking future for business that existed when Max McGraw bought Al Bersted's business was far from bright by 1930 after the crash of the stock market. One gloomy day, so the story goes, McGraw is reported to have said to Bersted that it might be best to dispose of the appliance operation.

"I think that's a good idea," Bersted replied. "How much do you want to sell it for?" He named a figure and Bersted bought his company back.

Conditions were different in 1948. Bersted Manufacturing Company had both prospered and acquired several other appliance companies. McGraw had done very well, too; so well McGraw approached Bersted about buying his company—again.

"I made a nice deal with him," Al Bersted related in July 1970 (he was chairman of the board of directors of McGraw-Edison at that time). "Max paid me with 155,000 shares of McGraw stock. Subsequently it was split three times and I ended up with 1,240,000 shares."

There was nothing boastful in the way Bersted said it, but a kind of mischievous twinkle lit his smile. For all his success he was extremely modest, his manner as plain and comfortable as an old shoe.

Al Bersted was born in Chicago in 1898 and began his career as a tool maker there. These random recollections of this business were expressed by him during a luncheon visit:

> I think the introduction of the thermostat probably had more to do with popularizing electric appliances than anything else. Without them we couldn't control the heat. Before the automatic there was one effort I know of to have a variable speed iron. It was made by Waage in Chicago in the 1920s, I think; they made a three-heat iron. But it never really got off the ground.
>
> In the early days manufacturers didn't deliberately make poor products, but there was almost no such thing as quality control as it is known today. In one sense it wasn't really necessary because a manufacturer who undertook to make a fairly good appliance had reasonably good expectations of being paid properly for it. But then, as the market grew, more people got into it, competition became increasingly severe and in order to meet a certain price manufacturers began taking short cuts and quality suffered.
>
> Since the start of the portable appliance business I would guess that at least two hundred fifty or three hundred manufacturers have come and gone in it. There must have been fifty different people that once made electric irons.

The McGraw-Edison annual report for 1971 noted with regret that "Alfred Bersted, formerly president and chairman of the board ...died on February 28, 1972. He had been director since 1949. During Mr. Bersted's long career with the company, his contributions to its success and growth, particularly in the consumer products area, were outstanding and formed the basis for the excellent record that was achieved during tenure."

He outlived his life-long associate Max McGraw by eight years. When McGraw died in 1964 at the age of 81, he left an electrical empire far beyond anything he could have imagined when he opened his little shop in Sioux City in 1900. "Max McGraw had a very definite

An unusual old American waffle iron of the early nineteenth century, from Pennsylvania Dutch country.

Courtesy Philadelphia Museum of Art.

philosophy when it came to buying other companies,'' Nolen McCleary, a retired Chicago associate of Al Bersted recalled in 1972. "I heard it mentioned many times. 'Never buy a company unless it's making money—or seems about to go broke.' "

Major Chronological Developments of McGraw-Edison Company

1900—Max McGraw establishes McGraw Electric Company, Sioux City, Iowa.

1903—McGraw Electric reorganized into Interstate Supply Company.

1907—Max McGraw establishes Interstate Electric Manufacturing Company.

1910—Interstate Electric and Manufacturing Company formed. It combined Interstate Supply and Interstate Manufacturing into one company.

1912—Joseph R. Lehmer Company acquired by Interstate Electric and Manufacturing Company. The two companies are combined into a new McGraw Electric Company.

McGraw Electric Company established a utility, Central Electric and Gas Company in South Dakota, which, in turn, established a subsidiary, Central Telephone.

1926—Acquired the Bersted Manufacturing Company, Chicago.

The wholesale operation of McGraw Electric sold to Westinghouse Electric and Manufacturing Company.

1928—Acquired the Clark Water Heater Company.

Acquired the Bussmann Company (fuses).

1929—Acquired Waters Genter Company, Minneapolis (Toastmaster) from Max McGraw who had bought it personally in 1926.

1930—Sold Bersted Manufacturing Company back to Alfred Bersted.

1939—Acquired the "Focolipse" heater from Pitt Corporation.

1948—Re-purchased the Bersted Manufacturing Company from Al Bersted. Bersted, meanwhile, had acquired United Electrical Manufacturing Company, Adrian, Michigan, ("Eskimo" fans); Swartzbaugh Manufacturing Company, Toledo, ("Everhot" appliances); and Manning-Bowman & Company, Meriden, Connecticut (appliances).

Acquired the "Tip-Toe" iron from Yale & Towne Manufacturing Company.

Acquired Edison of Canada Limited.

1949—Acquired Line Material Company, Canada (power line equipment).

1951—Acquired Tropic-Aire Incorporated (bus air conditioning).

1952—Established McGraw Electric Pan American Corporation to engage in operations in Western Hemisphere.

1954—Acquired the appliance business of General Mills.

1956—Acquired W. E. Moore & Company (industrial dryers).

Acquired Speed Queen Corporation (home laundry equipment manufacturer).

Acquired Lectromelt Furnace Corporation.

1957—Acquired Thomas A. Edison Incorporated.

Corporate name changed to McGraw-Edison Company.

Acquired Griswold Manufacturing Company, part of which it sold to Acquired Vermont Division of Fairchild Camera and Instrument Corporation (portable electric tools).

Acquired Sancor Instrument Corporation, Neptune, New Jersey (precision gears).

Acquired All-Over Manufacturing Company, Racine (hair clippers for home use).

1958—Acquired Heatube Company (heating elements).

Acquired National Electric Coil Company.

Sold Griswold to Wagner.

1959—Merged Canadian Line Materials Limited and Thomas A. Edison (Canada) into McGraw-Edison (Canada) Limited.

1960—Acquired American Laundry Machinery Company (commercial laundry equipment).

1961—Acquired Canadian Laundry Machinery Company Limited and Huebsch Canada Limited, and merged them into McGraw-Edison (Canada) Limited.

1962—Acquired certain product lines from Federal Pacific Electric Company (utility equipment).

Acquired W. F. Meyer & Son.

1963—Acquired the Daven Division of General Mills Incorporated (electric components).

1965—Established Prestige Edison Limited, a joint venture with Prestige Limited, subsidiary of Ekco Products Company, England.

Acquired Village Blacksmith Company, Watertown, Wisconsin (garden goods).

Liquidated Thomas A. Edison (United Kingdom), and Pohatcong R.R. Also sold Medical Gas Division of Thomas A. Edison Company, Wood Products Division and Elgin Real Estate.

Formed joint venture between Line Materials Industries Division and Secode Corporation, subsidiary of Magnetic Controls Company to produce electric utility control equipment.

1966—Acquired lifting magnet business of Cutler Hammer Incorporated.

1967—Acquired Halo Lighting Incorporated (lighting fixtures).

Sold the Lectromelt Furnace Division.

Acquired Ingraham Company (clocks).

1968—Acquired Toledo Kitchen Machines Division of Reliance Electric and Engineering Company.

1969—Acquired the fibre pipe business of the Brown Company.

Acquired Simplicity Products Limited (Canada) (home laundry appliances).

Acquired General Electric's power tool business.

1970—Acquired Fairgrieve & Son Limited (Canada) (home laundry appliances).

Acquired some appliances from Landers, Frary & Clark (Canada).

1971—Acquired Comar Electric Company (relays and switches).

1972—Acquired Brevel Products Corporation (small electric motors).

Acquired the power tool line of G. W. Murphy Company, Houston, Texas.

Manning-Bowman

The name of one of the oldest firms in the housewares business survives in the Manning-Bowman Division of the McGraw-Edison Company of Booneville, Missouri, purchased by Max McGraw in 1948.

Manning-Bowman was founded in Cromwell, Connecticut, in 1849 as Thomas Manning and Son. In 1859 it was changed by Thaddeus Manning and Robert Bowman to Manning-Bowman and Company, and it was incorporated in 1864. Primarily, the company manufactured Britannia ware, planished (toughened and polished) tinware, and, later, mounted porcelain enamelware.

Manning-Bowman and Company did well; but by 1872 it found itself in need of more working capital. Word of the situation promptly reached three shrewd Yankee businessmen, Horace C. Wilcox, Isaac C. Lewis, and George R. Curtis, all deeply involved in the nearby Meriden Britannia Company. In short order they had refinanced Manning-Bowman and Company, moved it to Meriden, and installed Edward B. Manning as president and Robert Bowman as secretary-treasurer.

The character of the company's products would change many times in the ensuing years. By the time it had moved to Meriden, for example, silver-plated ware had largely replaced Britannia ware.

The company also went extensively into "mounted enamelware." This consisted of bowls, pitchers, coffeepots, and teapots of porcelain enamelware embellished by metal bands, handles, or ornamentation, usually of Britannia metal. Manning-Bowman's trademark for this ware reads: "Patent Perfection Granite Iron Ware Girdles the Globe." It also had a line called "Pearl Agate Ware."

Manning-Bowman and Company sought out the hotel and restaurant business, and one of the areas in which they were strong was that of tea and coffee urns—and with good reason. Thaddeus Manning had long been interested in coffee brewing although he did not, as some believe, receive the first patent for the percolator.

A 1946 Manning-Bowman trade advertisement directed to the post war market.

Courtesy House Furnishing Review.

The Manning-Bowman factory in 1872. The company was founded in 1849 in Cromwell, Connecticut, and moved to Meriden in 1872.
Courtesy Curtis Memorial Library, Meriden, Connecticut.

However, in 1873 Manning obtained the first of a number of patents on coffee-brewing devices. The company promoted "Good Morning!" coffee percolators and "Good Evening!" teapots and emphasized the excellence of their coffee and tea-brewing capabilities in a discourse entitled "The Art of Preparing Tea and Coffee" prefacing their 1885 catalog. Lauding Perfection Granite Ironware and Decorated Pearl Agateware, the article concluded modestly: "Even our competitors will not dispute...that in style, quality, and workmanship, these goods stand without a rival in the market."

The company prospered and soon after the turn of the century took electrical household appliances in its stride. Manning-Bowman and Company, along with two other New England firms, Landers, Frary & Clark and the Robeson Rochester Company, came to be known as the leading manufacturers of fine-quality appliances.

Memorable innovations of Manning-Bowman were: "the iron that wags its tail"—a laundry iron with a swivel connection for the cord so that it would readily swing out of the way during ironing, and a "turnover" waffle iron designed to bake two waffles at once.

Possibly the conservatively inclined, old-line management was more "product and production"-oriented than promotion-oriented. With the changes in the once rather easygoing, gentlemanly marketplace, Manning-Bowman sold out shortly after the close of World War II to the Bersted Manufacturing Company, Chicago.

From Beaters to Mixers

Is it more than mere coincidence that the electric mixer and Horlick's Malted Milk both originated in Racine, Wisconsin, around the turn of the century?

Manning-Bowman's decorative "logo" for their Good Morning coffee maker.

All the details may never be known. But it is known that about 1887 William Horlick developed his new milk shake drink, while in 1910 a promotion-minded entrepreneur in Racine named Fred Osius founded the Hamilton Beach Manufacturing Company there.

In 1904 Osius and a man named George Schmidt were forming a company to make vibrators in that city. That appliance had only recently been introduced but had become quite popular. Osius and Schmidt decided to call their new firm the Arnold Electric Company, and no sooner had they opened a small shop when a lanky young farm boy named Chester A. Beach asked for a job. What he lacked in formal training, he more than made up with a natural mechanical genius. At about the same time a cashier on the nearby Barry Steamship Line by the name of L. H. Hamilton applied for and got the job of advertising manager for the new company.

That purely circumstantial association of Hamilton and Beach proved to be an extremely important one for the appliance industry. At that time, it must be remembered, generating plants around the country produced either a.c. or d.c. electricity, which greatly complicated the marketing of motor-driven devices. But these two men perfected a high-speed lightweight "universal" motor which, for the first time, would operate on either type of current. While the theory of such a motor was well known, they transformed it into a reality.

It was also these two untrained individuals who developed a small motor that ran at 7,200 r.p.m.... and eventually at 10,000 r.p.m. (This was not long after Westinghouse had told a new manufacturer of vacuum cleaners named Hoover that it would be unsafe to attempt a motor with a greater speed of 1,700 r.p.m.) Naturally these new high-speed, lightweight motors had many applications in addition to vibrators, such applications as drink mixers and vacuum cleaners. Arnold Electric, incidentally, also started a vacuum cleaner business which it later sold for $300,000.

By 1910 Osius, Hamilton and Beach decided they could do better with an entirely new set up, and so they founded the Hamilton Beach Manufacturing Company. Apparently they reasoned that if the fad for vibrators had made that business so good, a drink-mixing machine would profit from the popular new-fangled "malteds" and "milk shakes." At the start practically all of the mixers the new Hamilton Beach firm made were designed for the commercial field.

However, the household market wasn't being overlooked. As an old company memorandum puts it, "In 1846 Elias Howe released the American woman's fingers from slavery to the needle by inventing the sewing machine. But until 1912 her foot was still chained to its treadle....In that year adaption of the Hamilton Beach 'HOME' motor to drive sewing machines eased the sewing burden for millions of women and revolutionized the industry....As advertisements of that era said, it was 'the easiest-selling electrical household utility ever placed on the market.' "

What made the "Home" motor something of a minor sensation

Forerunner of the household mixer was Hamilton Beach's soda fountain mixer for malteds and milkshakes. This No. 1 "cyclone" model was manufactured in 1924.

265

The first combination base-mounted and/or portable mixer—the Whip-All in 1923.

Courtesy House Furnishing Review.

Good Housekeeping—September—1 column

THE FINE, FAST, EASY-TO-USE LABOR SAVER—*there's only ONE*

Sunbeam ★

MIXMASTER

Trade Name Reg. U. S. Pat. Office

Just like having some one come in to help you get the meals!

NOW ONLY
$18.25
AS SHOWN

Denver and West $18.95

Patented   Built to last, **Does MORE things BETTER**

ENJOY COOKING, BAKING GET MARVELOUS RESULTS

You'll never know how **easy** cooking can be—how much **better** and **faster**—until you've used the Mixmaster. Then you'll discover how quickly and how well this marvel does just about every cooking job that takes arm-work, time and care. Mixmaster is the food mixer with all the CORRECT MIXING speeds—the perfect *low* for folding angel food cakes, the powerful *high* for heavier jobs, etc. That's one reason why Mixmaster is nationally preferred by women. It's scientifically RIGHT. It is rugged, substantial, beautifully finished—truly the great kitchen labor-saver.

MIXES
cakes, cookies, meat loaf, etc.

MASHES
the creamiest potatoes, turnips, squash, etc.

WHIPS
cream, mayonnaise, dressings, etc.

BEATS
icings, eggs, to the finer perfection.

CREAMS
butter and sugar, sauces, shortening, etc.

STIRS
drinks—or anything, slow or fast.

FOLDS
egg whites into batter, etc., etc.

BLENDS
Mayonnaise, salad dressings, etc., etc.

No hand work at all to make feather-light cakes, creamy, mashed potatoes, etc., this easy, better way.

Does everything electrically
But you must have the **Mixmaster** to get the full advantages because there's only ONE Mixmaster. **Women themselves** have made Mixmaster the National food mixer preference. They prefer it because it is the powerful, rugged, easy to use food mixer. Because its beaters are scientifically positioned for perfect mixing, and it has the complete line of attachments. Because it is built to last and has a motor that won't overheat in long runs which assures longer life.

You can get these fine, practical, SAFE attachments as you need them.

Mixmaster is the COMPLETE food mixer. It has the splendid inexpensive attachments that can be added as you need them. Each one performs an every day home task faster, better, easier than it ever could be done by hand. They are well built, useful attachments and Mixmaster attachments are safe to use. A whole staff of servants. See Mixmaster at your light company, department store or dealer's. If not there write Chicago Flexible Shaft Co., 5543 Roosevelt Rd., Chicago. Canada factory, 349 Carlaw Av., Toronto. Mixmaster is one of

Attachments that:

Extract and strain fruit juice

Chop Food-Grind Meat

Slice, shred, grate

Peel Potatoes

Sharpen knives

Polish, buff

Open cans

Mix drinks

Grind coffee

Sunbeam
44 YEARS MAKING QUALITY PRODUCTS
BEST ELECTRIC APPLIANCES MADE

M-15B

In 1930 Sunbeam's Mixmaster lead the way to widespread acceptance of the electric mixer.

were the attachments available with it. Besides running the sewing machine one could attach a grinder to sharpen knives, a buffer to polish silver—and even a cake batter mixer!

The exciting potential of the alluring new electrical appliance business had, of course, begun to attract other manufacturers elsewhere in the country. Insofar as is known, however, Hamilton Beach with its remarkable and unprecedented attachments for the "Home" sewing machine motor was the first to market a cake batter mixer. Its understandable short-comings and inefficiencies, as judged by modern standards, would frustrate today's homemakers. But it helped to point out an important direction the emerging electrical housewares business could and should follow.

It must be remembered too that something like an electrical household mixer, as with all the upcoming motor driven appliances, was then dependent upon and limited by the concurrent development of fractional horsepower motors. In the next few years the increasing knowledge of that new magic called electricity, along with new materials and manufacturing technologies and experience, all contributed to the development of fractional horsepower motors that were not only smaller and lighter, but much more powerful. World War I doubtless did much to speed up the progress in this area.

Meanwhile, the accomplishments of the Hamilton Beach Company had attracted the attention and interest of the Scovill Manufacturing Company in Waterbury, Connecticut, and in 1920 Osius sold them a 51 percent interest in his venture, a move that was followed four years later by selling them the remaining 49 percent.

It was soon after the end of that war, in 1923, that an interesting early version of the household mixer was introduced by Air-O-Mix Incorporated, of Wilmington, Delaware—the "Whip All." As its ads pointed out, it could "be used on a stand or in the hand," thus probably qualifying it as the first combination base-mounted and/or portable mixer. But apparently it failed to stir up sufficient interest to survive very long.

In 1927, however, a new "Dormeyer" electric "household beater" did make a considerable impression on the emerging retail appliance scene. Developed by A. F. Dormeyer it was manufactured originally by the MacLeod Manufacturing Company, Chicago, and was designed so the motor could be readily detached from the bracket holding the beater blades—the idea of simply detaching the beaters didn't come until later.

In the early 1930s the name of the company was changed to the A. F. Dormeyer Manufacturing Company, and it continued to develop and promote mixers—now no longer called "beaters"—intensively.

No account of the early mixer business would be complete without mention of the A. C. Gilbert Company, New Haven, Connecticut. Once probably best known for its famous "Erector" construction set for boys (and their fathers) and now long out of business, Gilbert was an innovative manufacturer and aggressive merchandiser who stressed volume sales of popular priced electrical appliances that often also sold in large quantities as premiums.

In 1929, for example, it produced a "Polar Cub" hand mixer that could be used apart from its stand, especially for the Wesson Oil-Snowdrift people with a list price of $11.95. "Smaller models with glass bowl at $4.95 and $7.50." As related elsewhere, Gilbert also produced a special orange juicer for the California Fruit Growers Exchange.

The developing household mixer business received what was probably the most powerful and sustained support it would have for some time when in 1931, the Chicago Flexible Shaft Company, Chicago, now the Sunbeam Corporation, introduced its "Mixmaster." This was a mixer mounted on a heavy cast metal base, equipped with a juicer attachment and two stainless steel mixing bowls for which there was a ball-bearing turntable. While it was not the first mixer with a substantial cast rather than a stamped or wire base, it was the first to be offered under twenty dollars. (Hobart's household model KitchenAid, which also had a cast base, had been introduced around 1920, but was priced considerably higher.)

Advertised extensively and consistently and promoted at every opportunity with demonstrations in key department stores, the "Mixmaster" quickly gained public acceptance and, for a time at least, became something of a mixer standard in women's minds. The first year, according to Sunbeam, sixty thousand units were sold. By 1936 "Mixmaster" sales reached to more than three hundred thousand units. By then, too, a whole assortment of "Mixmaster" attachments—meat grinder, salad shredder and slicer, can opener, potato peeler, etc.—were also being offered.

Many changes have taken place in the mixer business since production resumed after World War II. Motors have continued to become smaller, lighter, and more powerful. "Solid state" or transistorized controls now make possible a broader or so-called "infinite" range of speeds. A check of the market in 1971 revealed that there were about sixteen manufacturers of household mixers in this country making over fifty different models.

From an engineering as well as appearance standpoint the design of mixers has improved enormously and, as with housewares generally, one finds them in an array of colors. The widespread use of plastics has not only helped eliminate unnecessary weight but has permitted the creation of streamlined forms and shapes previously impossible.

Most significant and far-reaching of all the changes, however, has been the complete reversal of the popularity of the stand mixer and the hand mixer. Whereas before, stand mixers accounted for the biggest share of total annual sales, now it is the hand mixers that dominate.

What brought about the change? A number of factors. In the

From top: This early Hamilton Beach model was designed so the motor unit could be slipped off its base and used as a hand mixer. First mixer to be mounted on its own stand was this 1920 KitchenAid model.

This lightweight, contemporary Panasonic hand mixer features "solid state," eight-speed control.

"PRESS-OR"
(U. S. Pat. Re 17,891)
FRUIT JUICE EXTRACTOR

Hammacher Schlemmer
Sole Distributors, U. S. A.
4th Ave. at 13th St., New York

From top: The beautifully designed Ronson juicer. From an earlier period, Hammacher Schlemmer advertised the manual Press-Or juice extractor.

past, meal preparation for the family was more of an "occasion," certainly it was a much more time and energy consuming task; the stand mixer, along with its various attachments, helped enormously to lighten the burden. Now not only our eating habits and ideas of diet have changed, but even the foodstuffs are often different. The tremendous increase in prepared cake mixes, for example, now makes it unnecessary for the homemaker to mix a cake batter from the basic ingredients as was formerly the case. Then, too, there is the matter of closet space; the large mixers require a lot of shelf space while the small ones can be hung conveniently on the wall.

And finally, there is that slow-starting but now extremely popular Johnny-come-lately in the appliance business, the blender, which has come to earn the room in many homes that was once accorded the stand mixer.

The Orange Juicer

"In no nation are the fruits of accomplishment more secure," President-elect Herbert Hoover assured a prospering nation in his inaugural address in January 1929.

Just how insecure they really were would be tragically demonstrated seven months later when the stock market crashed the nation into its worst economic depression. But one particular fruit which Americans had just begun to enjoy was the orange, and it would become important in the housewares business.

From the start, Americans seem to have preferred their oranges as juice. As oranges became a significant fruit crop in California—and later Florida—juice was extracted by a simple reamer, generally made of glass, china or aluminum. Then various crank-turned reamers appeared to minimize the effort needed for extraction.

Just who first re-introduced the old lever-type lemon juicer redesigned for oranges isn't known. But one of the early juicers was the "Press-or." Hammacher Schlemmer—then a hardware store on Fourth Avenue & 13th Street, New York—was the exclusive distributor and introduced it early in 1931 to retail for $6.85. A year later they were advertising a warning against infringing competitors that had appeared and announced a price reduction to $4.95.

A pioneer in the early promotion of orange juicers was Henry J. Talge, formerly president of the Rival Manufacturing Company which he founded in 1932 in Kansas City. Now chairman of Dazey Products Company, he recalled some of his early experiences in a 1971 letter from Kansas City:

Fred Bryant, one of the housewares buyers for the Famous Barr Co. in St. Louis…during a visit I made to the store in 1932…showed [me] a new orange juicer, a lever-type affair. The lever connected to a flat pressure plate which, when pressed down into the bowl, squeezed half an orange against it. In the process the flat pressure plate also crushed the skin of the orange, but that didn't seem to make any difference then.

Fred was pleased that his ad had sold a third of his juicers. "How many did you buy?" I asked. He replied "six," so I bought another third and when I got home we promptly began working on a juicer of our own. We came up with one made of cast aluminum that we mounted on a small wooden base to provide greater stability. Then we took it across town to the Jones Store Company to show it to George Charlton, the buyer and Vickers, his merchandise manager.

After we talked a while Vickers said, "This would be a great item at $1.29." When I asked what he'd be willing to pay and how many he would buy, he said $9 a dozen and 5,000 juicers. I said "Okay, give me an order"—which he did then and there.

With the help of three demonstrations at the Jones Store, the Talge juicer sold 6,310 units in ten days. Talge continued: "Our new Rival juicer was off and running; that was the beginning of similar promotions...around the country."

Henry Talge recalled he paid a visit to the California Fruit Growers Exchange. "I asked them why they kept advertising the little glass reamer type of juicer rather than one like the lever-type which was so much easier to use, since they were trying to get people to drink more juice?" Talge learned that the lever type devices broke the orange rind and gave juice of an oily, inferior flavor.

"So I returned to Kansas City, determined to design a juicer that wouldn't break the skin of the oranges. After a while Joe Majewski, who was working with me at the time, and I developed an entirely different juicer." Instead of a flat pressure plate it consisted basically of two hemisphere-shaped components, one of which came down upon the other with half an orange in between. But each part was so designed that all direct pressure on the rind was eliminated, thus one got only the juice—the rind wouldn't break and there couldn't be any oil.

The three major juicer competitors Rival had at the time were National Die Casting Company, Landers, Frary & Clark ("Universal"), and the Aluminum Cooking Utensil Company ("Wear-Ever"). To give his newly designed model added distinction, Talge wrote, he decided to bring it out in a choice of colors, probably a first for such items. "The tops were chrome plated, the bases colored, so that when stores displayed juicers they would have five of mine, each of the colors, but only one of my competition's. At one time I think we had something like 100 demonstrations on those 'Juice-O-Mats' going in stores from coast to coast. This eventually got to be big business and we were selling about half a million dollars worth of juicers a month when frozen orange juice made its appearance and the boom faded out."

From top: Henry Talge, founder of the Rival Manufacturing Company (now chairman of Dazey Products) who introduced the Rival juicer. The first orange juicer introduced by the Rival Manufacturing Company was in the early 1930s. In the late 1920s, the California Fruit Growers Exchange of New Haven cooperated to produce the Sunkist Jr.

269

Rival was not only one of the first to bring out an electric juicer but has since become the largest producer of that item.

A Cooperative Effort for Juicers

In the late 1920s, a get-together of the A. C. Gilbert Company of New Haven and the California Fruit Growers Exchange which promoted

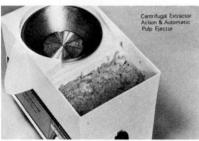

Centrifugal Extractor Action & Automatic Pulp Ejector

270

From top: The juicer attachment on a Magic Maid mixer introduced in the 1920s by Fitzgerald Manufacturing Company (now Son-Chief Electric). Contrast it with today's Panasonic juicer-blender, in solid state.

Sales Volume of BLENDERS			
Year	Units	$ Volume (Retail)	Price
1948*	215,000	8,170,000	$38
1950	225,000	8,437,000	37
1960	455,000	16,357,000	36
1965	1,800,000	45,000,000	25
1970	5,100,000	127,500,000	25
1971	4,200,000	88,200,000	21
*first record of sales			

"Sunkist" oranges probably did more than anything else to not only popularize that golden fruit juice, but at the same time help to educate homemakers concerning the convenience of motor driven home appliances.

Gilbert was already dabbling in the appliance business as witness his "Polar Cub" fan—along with toys and probably some kind of a juicer. But by the time the fruit growers had finished with their specifications (and assurances of support, no doubt!), he had an impressive looking new household model electric juicer, "Sunkist Jr.," to retail for $14.95.

The fruit growers launched a powerful advertising campaign using full-page space, often in color, in magazines, newspapers and at the trade level. "We tell—you sell," their ads told housewares buyers. Indeed the market was ready and waiting: "Irksome hand squeezing...couldn't last," proclaimed the "Sunkist" ads.

By 1932 the Chicago Electric Company had also begun to manufacture a "Juicit" model, influenced no doubt by the success of the "Sunkist" promotion. It proved to be a rather propitious move because by 1935 the fruit growers switched from Gilbert to Chicago Electric, according to Stanley M. Ford, then president of the Appliance Division of Proctor-Silex Incorporated, and formerly with Chicago Electric.

"At some point—I don't have any fix on the date—Sunkist also designed and produced a commercial version of their juicer which they assembled from purchased parts in a small plant in Chicago," he recalled prior to his death in 1972. "Chicago Electric and later Silex continued to produce the 'Juicit' until the mid-fifties, adding the oscillating strainer model in 1940. Prior to World War II, the Growers Exchange purchased the 'Sunkist' juicers from Chicago Electric and handled their distribution and sale. After the war Chicago Electric took over and paid them a small royalty for promotional support."

In the mid-fifties the growers withdrew the right to use the name "Sunkist," fearing possible loss of their trade name through generic use. Thereafter the Silex "juicit" carried the words, "Approved by Sunkist." This continued until about 1961 when, for various reasons, the tie-up was ended. According to Stan Ford, surveys showed that in homes where a "juicit" was being used 50 percent more fresh fruit was consumed.

The Development of Blenders

Ask "who is responsible for the blender" and the answer is likely to be "Waring" or "Fred Waring, the band leader."

Although not correct, it's an undeniable fact that the leader of "The Pennsylvanians" financed the development and marketing of such a device, the "Waring Blendor"—always spelled with an "o." And it is certain that the promotional efforts of his Waring Mixer Corporation (now the Waring Products Division of the Dynamics

Corporation of America) did more than anything else in the early years to acquaint the public with the concept of such a unique device. Its inventor was Stephen J. Poplawski of Racine, Wisconsin. Since about 1915, Stephen J. Poplawski was engaged for over half a century in the design and manufacture of beverage mixers of various types.

In 1922 he applied for a patent, his affidavit (prepared in connection with a 1953 patent litigation) relates, "for the first mixer of my design having an agitating element mounted in the bottom of a cup and a driving motor mounted in a base and adapted to be drivingly connected with the agitator in the cup when the cup was placed in a recess in the top of the base."

He was awarded a patent, but at the time, he declares, "I did not think of using the mixer (based on) this patent, for the maceration of fruits and vegetables." Nor did anyone else in the Arnold Electric Company in Racine where he worked. Racine, it will be recalled, was the location of the Horlick Corporation, makers of the malted milk drink, served at soda fountains. Preparing the malteds with an electric mixer was the commercial market Steve Poplawski wanted to tap.

In 1932 Poplawski joined the Greene Manufacturing Company of Racine, which then took over the production of his latest mixers (patents Nos. 1,937,184 and 1,937,445). Sometime that year, he says, "the mixer was used as a blender in the macerating of fruits and vegetables so as to reduce them to a fluid state."

Obviously the mixer was well on the way toward emerging as a blender—at least in the commercial soda fountain world—and Steven Poplawski made this unequivocal statement in his affidavit: "I am convinced that the John Oster Manufacturing Company, as the successor to the mixer business of the Greene Manufacturing Company, is justified in asserting that its blender is the 'original' blender...."

Meanwhile, Fred Osius, who in 1926 had moved to Florida and then back North during the depression, launched his own version of the blender. An acquaintance who saw a lot of him describes him as "an aggressive optimist who seemed to smell risk money in an endless variety of unorthodox ways."

One of those whom he had already sold on investing money in his new venture was Ronnie Ames, a brother-in-law of Fred Waring's publicity man at the time. Why not approach Waring himself?

The band leader and his Pennsylvanians had just concluded one of their Ford radio broadcasts in Manhattan's Vanderbilt Theater one afternoon in the summer of 1936, when a Waring assistant informed him that "A Mr. Fred Osius is waiting for you backstage; he says he has an appointment."

"Appointment" was stretching the word considerably. But then Fred Osius was never one to accept things at face value if he felt the prospects warranted it. In fact, just to look at him, recalls one who happened to be there that day, revealed that he was "different."

271

From top: This late nineteenth century fly wheel food chopper might be called the ancestor of the blender. The first electric blender; developed for soda fountains by Stephen Poplawski.

Top, courtesy Folk and Country Museum, Cambridge, England; bottom, courtesy Oster Corporation.

From top: A 1956 Hamilton Beach blender, model 6 BL. Typical of the trend toward multi-button models is this 1972 Waring blendor 94-1, featuring a "sixty second timer/blend control, all-in-one-switch."

On this particular occasion, Osius was wearing striped trousers, a cutaway coat and a dark blue woolen shirt touched off by a bright, lemon-yellow tie. On someone else it might have looked ridiculous, but on him it just seemed to belong.

He had brought with him a prototype of his brainchild and although it failed to function, his persuasive power did. By the time he had explained how it would revolutionize people's eating habits, he had sparked Waring's interest in backing it.

Six months and $25,000 later it was evident that, despite continued assurances to the contrary, Osius couldn't produce the working model he had promised. So in September 1936 Waring asked his associate, Ed Lee, to take it over. (Incidentally, he is the same Ed Lee who later became general manager of Chicago's McCormick Place.)

Lee found that three basic engineering problems had to be solved: One involved the manufacture of the uniquely shaped glass container; second was the development of a leak-proof bearing in the base of the container; lastly, a flexible coupling between the motor drive shaft and the blending-comminuting device in the container had to be perfected. All of them were solved in time to permit a presentation of this new "Miracle Mixer" the following September 1937, at the National Restaurant Show in Chicago's Furniture Mart. Featured as a new method for making frozen daiquiris and similar drinks, it attracted tremendous interest and sold for $29.75.

Enthusiastic receptions for the newcomer followed at other trade shows and a national promotion program with Ron Rico Rum involving a coast-to-coast tour to popularize the drinks it could make proved to be "spectacular." By now, it was being called the "Waring Blendor"—"spelled with an 'o' to distinguish it," Ed Lee explained.

The new "Blendor" was promptly considered the "in" thing for bars and restaurants, and the Waring organization began eyeing the consumer market. Its reputation had already reached a point where it didn't take long to place it with the key department and specialty stores in leading cities.

So well had the new "Blendor" been sold—and accepted—as a daiquiri device that it would take a while to educate consumers that it was equally good in the kitchen as well as the bar. It received unexpected and welcome support from a West Coast health food authority and lecturer, Martin Pretorius, who seized upon the new "liquifier" as a nutritional boon. He sold hundreds of them in the course of his lectures.

During the next few years a number of significant changes took place in the corporate activities of Waring which are simplified in the following summary:

1938—The Waring Corporation was incorporated in Delaware on May 27 and used for the early exploitation of the Blendor.

It contracted with the Airway Electric Appliance Corporation, a Toledo vacuum cleaner manufacturer, to produce the Blendor. A contract had also been made with the General Electric Company, Bridgeport, under which it was licensed to produce the Waring steam iron for Waring and under the GE name.

1944—Another corporation, Electrical Appliances Incorporated, was formed in Delaware, October 24. On November 1 The Waring Corporation sold to Electrical Appliances Incorporated all the tools and dies, etc., needed to manufacture the Blendor and the steam iron.

December 5—Electrical Appliances Incorporated entered into an agreement with the Reeves Sound Laboratories for the manufacture of the Blendor and the steam iron.

1945—Dave and Fred Sanford of Los Angeles acquired a 50 percent interest in the Reeves Sound Laboratories; the remaining 50 percent was owned by Hazard Reeves. Reeves Sound Laboratories owned all the stock of Electrical Appliances Incorporated. The D. E. Sanford Company, a sales agency with fourteen branches throughout the country, had the exclusive sales representation of Waring products, among others.

1947—The fact that neither the Sanfords nor Reeves had control in the operations of Reeves Sound Laboratories proved unsatisfactory and the Sanfords sold their interest to Reeves.

1949—By August of that year the Reeves Sound Laboratories was succeeded by the Reeves-Ely Laboratories Incorporated, which also became the owner of 100 percent of the stock of Waring Products Corporation.

Earlier in 1945 and 1946—Claude Neon Incorporated, a New York corporation organized in 1924, had acquired 98 percent of the stock of Reeves-Ely Laboratories. One of its subsidiaries is the Winsted Hardware Company, Winsted, Connecticut, manufacturers of "Durabilt" travel irons. It took over the production of the Blendor for Waring Products Corporation.

1956—On January 20th Reeves-Ely Laboratories Incorporated was consolidated with Dynamics Corporation of America.

Diversifying Use

The stir the Waring Blendor created attracted the attention of other manufacturers, but World War II soon brought blender production to a stop. When it was resumed after the war the manufacturers discovered a curious thing: its image as a drink mixer had become so firmly established in the public's mind it was difficult to get people to consider the blender for other uses. As a result, sales of this still unappreciated device continued to coast along unimpressively.

Waring led the way with some interesting innovations: colored blenders in 1955; an ice crusher attachment in 1956; a coffee grinder attachment in 1957; a timing control in 1964; and the following year the first model with solid state controls.

It was the introduction of the multiple push button switches that probably set off the greatest competition. What was once a simple "Low" and "High" situation presently evolved into the "Battle of the Buttons."

Whether Landers, Frary & Clark in the late 1950s were first to use a button-type switch on the Universal "Mixablend" blender or whether it was not until about 1963 when Dormeyer did so is unresolved. But in 1964 Oster doubled the ante with four buttons, "Low," "Medium," "High," and "Off." Waring introduced the first solid state model in 1965, and Oster followed with eight buttons the next year, to be topped in 1967 by Waring with a nine-button machine. By then dual control circuitry had appeared and a mere six buttons could be featured as a twelve-speed feature.

Meanwhile, Waring had introduced its "Blend Control" timer and at last report in 1972 was in the lead with no less than fourteen

273

From top: The Ronson Cook 'n Stir, first blender to cook and stir simultaneously, was introduced in 1965. Van Wyck International's Giant 8 is said to be 60% smaller than standard sized blenders.

From top: Oster's 1970 blender featured ten continuous speeds. A 1972 innovation is this Ronson power-base model equipped with a variety of attachments.

separate operating buttons plus an "Off" button. While there are those who are inclined to be critical of "all that unnecessary gadgetry" on the blender, industry people are quick to defend it. They admit that such an advanced piece of equipment does not belong in the hands of a beginner. However, they add, the present sophistication of blender cookery not only invites but practically necessitates the kind of operational versatility the multi-speed models provide.

While most manufacturers of blenders included some kind of recipe booklet with their product to help educate consumers to its potential as a food-preparation appliance (Waring's were quite impressive cook books), Oster probably has done the most along those lines. In the mid-fifties G. W. Orr, now president of Oster, launched an intensive program on "a new form of cooking—Spin Cookery," developed entirely around the blender. The program, still in operation in 1972, includes not only "Spin Cookery" schools in retail stores, utility companies and other places, but also a continuing series of mailings to all registered purchasers of "Osterizers" in a program called the Joan Oster Recipe Mailing Series.

By the late 1960s—when industry blender sales were at their peak—Waring, according to informed sources, was reportedly doing about $35 million (including commercial products), but in 1970 it lost $1.5 million. That, explained Andres Lozyniak, president of the Dynamic Corporation of America, according to *Home Furnishings Daily,* was due to the fact that the production-oriented firm had failed to institute financial controls. When sales dropped, inventory piled up. Volume of the Dynamic Corporation in 1970 was $121,060,545. Blenders, it said, account for three-quarters of Waring's volume, the rest from a limited line of mixers, can openers, hair dryers, and lightweight vacuum cleaners. In January 1972 a new president, Milton R. Stohl, moved into the saddle at Waring and promptly revealed that, at a time when firms like Westinghouse and General Electric were cutting down on their lines, he has launched a product diversification program with which he expects to achieve an increase of at least 400 percent in sales by 1980. In the summer of 1972 the Dynamic Corporation of America filed for reorganization under Chapter XI of the federal bankruptcy law, giving as the reason its inability to obtain an extension of certain bank loans. The Waring operation, it was said, was unaffected by the move.

"The blender business, red hot a couple of years ago, is cooling and solidifying in 1971," Bob Okell, housewares editor of *Home Furnishings Daily,* wrote in its August 16, 1971 issue. "With sales continuing to slide this year from peak levels in 1969 when 6.1 million units were sold, the industry is moving through a shakeout period." He goes on to cite some of those who have dropped out of the business since its peak (when about sixty-seven firms made blenders), among them Westinghouse, Presto, Farber, Vornado, and Hamilton Cosco. In 1972 General Electric also bowed out.

He reports that the Trendex figures for the first half of 1971 show that Oster had 29.3 percent of the total industry volume, Waring had 21.2 percent and Hamilton Beach 11.8 percent. Market saturation for blenders at the time was said to be still only around 40 percent "so blenders still have a strong potential among first-time buyers."

The "Battle of the Buttons" seems to have about run its course as manufacturers devote increasing attention to developing this appliance still further as an important if not essential food preparation device.

Betty Crocker's Appliance Venture

In the fall of 1945 the author, who at the time was the housewares editor of *Home Furnishings Daily,* (then called *Retailing Home Furnishings*), was having lunch in New York with Roscoe Imhoff, sales manager of electric housewares for Westinghouse. In those days industry's postwar plans were a major topic of trade conversation, and during the lunch the editor remarked, "You know, Roscoe, some of the stories one hears about the postwar plans of big companies seem almost ludicrous. Why only yesterday I heard a rumor that General Mills is going into the small appliance business. Imagine— a flour milling company making appliances!"

For a long minute Imhoff stared silently at his luncheon partner, a slow smile gradually emerging on his face. "That may not be quite as ludicrous as you might think," he said with satisfying deliberation. "You see, Earl, I've just been hired as general manager of that company's postwar plan."

Just why General Mills, Incorporated, ever decided to venture into such a highly competitive, far-removed business in the first place or, for that matter why they elected to get out of it when they did, are questions that will long be a matter of debate. But for a while it seemed that the electric housewares business had attracted an impressive and formidable new competitor.

Long before World War II General Mills' machinery repair shop had developed through several stages into a highly competent mechanical division, which had achieved substantial expertise in producing high-speed packaging and processing equipment.

Just before the war the company found itself making various types of precision equipment for the armed forces, an activity that mushroomed as America became involved. Later, management was faced with the decision of what do we do with this facility after the war ends? Two possibilities were suggested: develop the high-speed packaging machinery further, or go into the electric housewares business.

One of the company's wartime consultants was Maurice H. Graham, a local inventor who held some patents to the revolutionary "Toastmaster" toaster that had been introduced in 1927, as well as to some other appliances with unique concepts. He convinced General Mills that this business would be successful. All were agreed that the only way the company could really succeed in such an in-

After World War II General Mills attempted to capture a share of the enormous appliance market with a line of Betty Crocker appliances, widely advertised nationally.

General Mills gave its Betty Crocker appliance a brilliant send-off in 1946— but by 1954 the whole venture ended.

tensely competitive and foreign field would be to introduce unusual new products that offered consumers distinct advantages in form and function. Very definitely they would not be "me too" appliances.

An important consideration was that General Mills could enter the appliance business with a powerful equity in its well-known "Betty Crocker" image, a figure that had symbolized its products to homemakers for a quarter of a century. Each appliance would carry a tag line "Sponsored by Betty Crocker." In addition there would be a close tie-in with the Betty Crocker Kitchens to provide recipes and other promotional aids.

Roscoe Imhoff headed a hand-picked staff that included John Sullivan, marketing director; William McDonough, promotion and training manager; James Logan, production manager; and Marion Yerigan, service manager. James S. Fish, serving in the navy at the time and previously in the food division of the company, was named advertising manager upon his return from service. In 1971, he was vice-president for advertising and marketing services for General Mills and the sole survivor of the appliance venture.

With all the careful planning and the unique products, the Betty Crocker appliance program proved to have a brilliant beginning— but despite all this, an unexpectedly quick demise.

"Our line of home appliances strengthened its competitive position," reports the company's 1949-50 financial statement. "The two-millionth Tru-Heat iron came off the assembly line in November, 1949, placing this appliance among the best-selling irons in the nation. The steam ironing attachment...proved increasingly popular. The new General Mills automatic toaster joined the company's appliance family."

And the 1952-53 financial report stated: "[We] completed the development of four new members of the home appliance family. Scheduled for sale in the Fall of 1953 are...[the] food mixer...all-purpose grill-waffle baker...automatic coffee maker...and the automatic fryer-cooker. With the iron, steam ironing attachment and automatic toaster, they will give the company a line of seven top-quality appliances."

But circumstances began to intervene and disrupt. In 1946, right after a new pressure cooker was introduced, the plant in which it was being made burned to the ground. The Korean War suddenly imposed priorities for military needs on civilian production. As competent observers have pointed out, it is virtually impossible to run a high-precision, low-production manufacturing enterprise successfully alongside a low-precision, high-production activity. War work and appliances, it turned out, were just not compatible, especially with the same management structure being applied to both such disparate tasks.

Furthermore, to be successful, an unlikely new entrant in the appliance business like General Mills would have to offer products with recognizable advantages in performance and price over veteran competitors. Initially all this seemed possible. But when this ambitious program developed complications that conflicted with traditional long-term commitments, General Mills decided to bring its appliance venture to a halt, and the business was sold to the McGraw Electric Company in 1954.

The Lady Casco Line

The history of the electric housewares business like many others, is strewn with the record of firms that started out with ambitious plans and high hopes of success and ended up in failure. Somewhere, somehow, either their merchandise, their merchandising, their money or management missed out and everything came to a stop.

One of the best-remembered of such ventures is "Lady Casco," a seemingly sophisticated operation that looked like the personification of success—for a time.

In 1949 an industrial products firm in Bridgeport, Connecticut, Casco Products Corporation, fired with the contagious enthusiasm of that era for the great post war potential in consumer goods, went into the appliance business. It began by producing and marketing an automatic steam and dry iron with considerable success. A few years later the line was expanded to include griddles and electric blankets.

Then in 1960 Casco was acquired by Standard Kollsman Industries, Incorporated; Joseph H. Cone, Casco's president, sold his interest and Leonard F. Cramer was named as his successor. Cramer, a veteran merchandiser who had been with the Dumont television operation, had very definite ideas about the appliance business and proceeded to formulate the "ideal plan" for marketing and merchandising electric housewares.

It was based on a full line of ten "match-mate" appliances—the "Lady Casco" line—the chief item of which was the "Chef-Mate." This was a unique motor-driven power base with a series of attachments, including a mixer, a blender, and others.

Cramer proposed to place the line only in selected stores on a franchise arrangement covered by the "Lady Casco Reciprocal Trade Treaty."

The program offered national advertising, prepaid freight, protected inventory prices, incentive programs, sales training—everything to make the franchise irresistible to a good dealer. The appliances even carried an exclusive five-year warranty backed by a Lloyd's of London insurance policy. All this of course was to replace the existing Casco marketing plan.

If management approved his proposal, Cramer told them, and the projected sales figures are achieved, "Lady Casco will add in excess of $7 million...to its existing volume of Casco products... for approximately ten months of operation in 1961. More important ...we will be well on our way to establishing a consumer distribution system...which will be the envy of the industry."

The Chef Mate topped the short-lived Lady Casco line of appliances.

The Chef Mate power base had a full complement of accessories.

278

The projected profit potential—9.3 percent of net sales before taxes—would also have been the envy of the industry. But Casco was not in a position to produce all the items for its new line and had to buy them from other producers.

By the end of 1961 over two thousand "Lady Casco" retailers had been franchised as planned. Cramer's "ideal" merchandising program seemed to be getting off the ground to fulfill its high expectations. But it didn't. For reasons that have never been revealed, the Kollsman management elected to bring its ambitious venture to an end. In January 1962 Leonard Cramer resigned and Lloyd F. Taylor was named vice-president and general manager of the Casco operation. The "Lady Casco" program was promptly discontinued and its former, traditional method of distribution was resumed.

Valiant efforts to reestablish the former Casco image were made during the following months by introducing a toothbrush, warming trays, and other new items, but with little success. And so this once hope-filled story, caught up in the realities of the marketplace, came to an end in November 1963 when the entire appliance line was sold to the Hamilton Beach Division of the Scovill Manufacturing Company in Waterbury, Connecticut.

The Farberware Story

There is no longer anything extraordinary about the typical American success story: the ambitious and determined young man, often an immigrant youth who, amidst difficulties and lowly surroundings, embarks upon a career which, eventually, leads him and his company to the pinnacle of success; it is a familiar story and the housewares industry is replete with its share of examples.

But occasionally one comes upon a record which is notable not merely for the success it chronicles, but for the number of significant and lasting innovations it has contributed over the years.

S. W. Farber Incorporated, now subsidiary of the LCA Corporation (an affiliate of Walter Kidde & Company, Incorporated, Belleville, New Jersey), is such a company. In 1975 it will celebrate its seventy-fifth anniversary, yet long ago it had already established an important place for itself in the electric and non-electric categories of the housewares industry.

The story starts in 1899 when a twenty-one-year-old youth named Simon W. Farber from the little town of Antipol, Russia (now part of Poland), passed through that famous immigrant gateway of Ellis Island and landed in New York.

The oldest boy in a family of eight children, he was barely twelve when a serious crop failure in Russia made things desperate on the small family farm. So he left to become apprenticed to a tinsmith. Having a keen, mechanical aptitude, he learned fast. By the time he was sixteen he found himself a foreman of a traveling crew of tinsmiths whose sole duty was to maintain the various distilleries of the Czar's liquor monopoly.

Two years later the widow of the owner of a small copper cook-ware factory in Antipol persuaded him to take it over. Simon agreed, but the legendary stories about what a man could do in that land called America were too much to resist. Thus, in 1899 he finally found himself here, not knowing a word of English. He had planned for that, a plan which took him to an uncle in Hartford, Connecticut with whom he would live until he could speak the language. And much of the year he spent going from house to house, often by bicycle, selling women's garments of one kind or another—frustrating days for a good mechanic!

The year 1900 meant much more than the start of a new century for Simon Farber; it was the start of a whole new life. It began in Manhattan's Lower East Side at 66 Norfolk Street, where, in a dingy downstairs basement shop he had his name lettered on the window. Soon he had five men working there, pounding sheets of copper and brass against steel anvils into jardiniers, bowls, and vases, just as they did back home. For ten or more long hours every day the noise in the small, cramped, gas-lit quarters was deafening. But to young Farber it was music, and to make certain thieves didn't break in during the night, he slept there too.

America offered an immediate market for this hand-hammered copper and brass ware. Heretofore such merchandise was almost all imported from Russia and England. In 1905 the prospering venture moved to larger quarters at Broadway and Grand Streets where the whirr of spinning lathes and other new equipment replaced the pounding of hammers.

But 1905 was a momentous year for Simon Farber in another way. On his visits to relatives in Connecticut he had met and fallen in love with a teacher at the Norwich Business College named Ella Sachs. They were married and he acquired a partner who became as important to him in his business as in his personal life. Until his death in 1947, Ella Farber was constantly at his side and played a significant role in the development of the business. She died in 1956.

The couple had two sons, Isidor, who served as president from 1947 to 1970 when he retired, and Milton who became president at that time. Two sons-in-law are also officers of the company. Harvey M. Harrison is a vice-president and Hyman Shanok is secretary.

Highlights of the company's major housewares developments over the years consist of the following:

Samuel and Ella Farber, founders
of S. W. Farber, Inc.

279

1910—Introduced the first line of "Farberware" serving accessories and gift-ware novelties. They were silver-plated and nickel-plated.

1914—Introduced a line of nickel-plated casserole frames holding earthen-ware and Pyrex inserts.

1919—Introduced the "Adjusto-Lite," a portable reading lamp fitted with a clamp—"The Lamp that Clamps"—so that it could readily be used anywhere for reading or other purposes. It sold for five dollars and proved extremely popular.

1925—Began the use of chrome plating on serving accessories, casserole frames, etc.; one of the very first to go in for chrome plating in a big way at that early date. Casserole frames had become such a big item that Farber was Corning Glass Works' biggest customer for inserts.

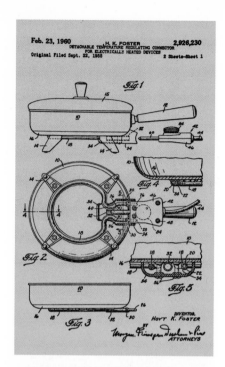

Feb. 23, 1960   H. K. FOSTER   2,926,230
DETACHABLE TEMPERATURE REGULATING CONNECTOR
FOR ELECTRICALLY HEATED DEVICES
Original Filed Sept. 22, 1955   2 Sheets-Sheet 1

1930—Introduced first Farberware percolator. It featured a patented "8 in 1" fuse developed by the company. By means of a revolving disc in the base of the percolator, a blown fuse in it could be instantly replaced up to eight times.

1937—Introduced the Farberware "Coffee Robot." After making the coffee its pre-set thermostat kept it warm for hours.

1938—Introduced the "Broiler Robot." A domed table broiler was equipped with an indicator telling when it was ready for use.

1949—Introduced Farberware aluminum-clad stainless steel cookware. By means of a company-developed process a ⅛-inch thick layer of aluminum is bonded to the bottom of stainless steel utensils.

1954—Introduced a stainless steel, aluminum-clad electric fry pan, only such item made. Also, jointly with Presto Industries Incorporated, introduced the "Probe" removable heat control unit, thus permitting for the first time electric cooking utensils to be fully submerged in water for cleaning.

1962—Introduced the Farber "Open Hearth" smokeless broiler in which the heating element is below rather than above the food to be broiled, marking a milestone in the development of this appliance.

1966—The company was acquired by Walter Kidde & Company, Incorporated, Belleville, New Jersey. At the time of the purchase the Farber business was reliably reported to have been doing an annual volume of about $15 million. It is now a subsidiary of the LCA Corporation, an affiliate of Kidde.

Frying Pans

Like the tail of the tadpole which, in time, disappears, so too has the handle of the frying pan.

In colonial times when cooking was done at the fireplace, frying pans had to have extra long handles to keep the cook from being fried along with the meat. When stoves came into use this requirement also began to change.

As the materials of which cooking utensils were made changed from cast iron on through to stainless steel, the frying pan was always one of the first items to be made of the newer metal. But the most significant changes of all in the frying pan began to take place with the introduction of electrical housewares. And, far from being final, changes and improvements in this basic utensil appear to be greater now than ever before.

The first electric fry pan was introduced by Westinghouse in September 1911. Made of sheet steel, it was six inches in diameter and had the heating element built into its base. When turned upside down on its separate, cast iron stand it also served as a hotplate.

In the early 1900s no one referred to the "in" thing to do. But its equivalent in terms of the height of sophistication was to serve one's guests at the table from a chafing dish. These once popular utensils were always heated by a small alcohol lamp—until Westinghouse introduced its electric model...a forerunner of today's common electric fry pans.

But nearly half a century, forty-two years to be exact, would elapse before anything more would be done about an electric fry pan. Such an enormous time-lag seems strange in retrospect, especially because it was during those years that the appliance industry grew so tremendously and made great strides in product development. There is, however, a very simple explanation why the fry pan failed to share in that development: no one had as yet come up with a practical method for providing positive heat control, and without

From top: Farber's "detachable temperature regulating connector." Sunbeam is in this business (middle photo), as well as Presto with this 1956 model.

280

such control an electric fry pan has no advantage over an ordinary frying pan.

Then in 1953 the industry rather suddenly began turning its attention to this long-neglected appliance. National Presto Industries Incorporated announced a round, electrified fry pan, somewhat deeper than usual. But it lacked positive heat control and had a further disadvantage since it was not submersible for cleaning.

At about the same time the Sunbeam Corporation introduced an unusual square, cast aluminum "Automatic Frypan" that featured controlled heat. "Now," declared their consumer advertising, "... you can fry and cook at the correct, controlled heat every time.... The Fryguide, right in the handle, gives correct temperature. No guesswork...."

Almost at once sales of electric frying pans began to sizzle in housewares departments; America's homemakers eagerly began going for something that had been forty-two years in reaching them.

"When we introduced our fry pan late in 1953 only a few thousand were available," explained a Sunbeam spokesman, adding: "But the following year we sold more than 800,000 and in 1955 2 million were sold. Our volume went even higher in 1956 when we sold 2.5 million of those pans."

Meanwhile, in New York in 1954, H. K. Foster, chief engineer for S. W. Farber Incorporated, developed and patented an entirely new concept in heat controls for appliances. It was a detachable device —later generally referred to as a "probe"—and was ideally suited to fry pans.

Farber promptly moved into that market. But whereas most other pans were square and made of aluminum, theirs was round and made of stainless steel. The aluminum pans sold for about $19.95; the stainless steel for $29.95 in a 12-inch pan, $26.95 in a 10½-inch size. "Thanks to this original Farberware feature [the probe]," declared their advertising, "you can immerse your fry pan *completely* in water."

Apparently Presto had also been working on a version of the "probe" and as a result both companies announced that a "cross-licensing" arrangement had been agreed upon whereby Presto would thereafter also use it.

As with so many other housewares items, there seems to be almost no limit to how far the once overlooked electric fry pan may go or what producers might do next to speed it on its sizzling way. Fry pans keep getting larger, capable of doing more things more conveniently and efficiently and get better looking all the time.

Broiling: Traditional and Popular

Broiling earns a place in the record on two counts: it is probably the oldest form of cooking; and today, certainly in America, one of the most popular. There's a distinctive quality to broiled food that never seems to lose its appeal whether it's done over the embers of a camp

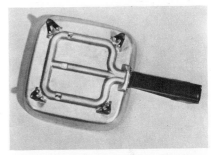

From top: The first electric frying pan ever marketed was introduced in 1911 by Westinghouse. Turned upside down it also served as a hotplate. Not until 1955 did Westinghouse come out with this frying pan showing its underside "across the bottom" heat control. This multi-use modern electric chafing dish was introduced in 1972 by West Bend.

fire or in the superbly equipped kitchen of a gourmet restaurant. Over the years housewares manufacturers have gone far in catering to that appeal.

Broilers of various kinds were used regularly in the fireplaces of the early colonists. About 1890 the first gas range with a broiler burner appeared. In the interim, presumably, broiling indoors was largely confined to restaurants or wealthy homes specially equipped for it.

The broiler burners as well as all other parts of gas ranges were continually being improved and in the early 1900s the electric range appeared. But from all indications, broiled food was not nearly as popular as roasted or fried.

In the late 1920s or early 1930s the picture began to change; people began to be more food conscious and concerned with the kind and the quantity of food they ate. Nutritional values and calories became prime topics of conversation. Rightly or wrongly, fried foods were blamed for many ills and fell into disfavor.

Probably the first table appliance to be specifically designed for broiling—among other things—was the ingenious table stove Charles C. Armstrong invented and marketed in 1916. Advertised as "the stove that cooks three things at once" (steamed eggs, broiled bacon and toast) it retailed for $12.50. It was made in Marysville, Ohio, by Armstrong's Standard Stamping Company which later became the Armstrong Electric & Manufacturing Company of Huntington, West Virginia, and is still in business there (its electric appliance operation, however, has since been discontinued).

The first table broiler of the type now generally in use is believed to have been introduced by the International Appliance Company, Brooklyn, New York. The company is now a subsidiary of Curtis Electro Corporation, both family-owned businesses until Curtis went public in 1965. Curtis, whose headquarters are in Mesquite, Texas, had total sales in 1969 of $10.7 million, but no break-down of subsidiary operations is given. International is generally considered to be the largest producer of household broilers in the country while the balance of Curtis' sales are derived primarily from the manufacture of industrial and commercial lighting fixtures and equipment. (Incidentally, it supplied the lighting for the old as well as the new McCormick Place.)

"My father, William, and his brother started business in a little shop in Brooklyn in 1921 making reflectors for lighting fixtures," Paul H. Litner, executive vice-president of the company related in 1972.

In 1935 the company moved to larger quarters on Metropolitan Avenue in Brooklyn, and in 1937 someone decided it ought to make household broilers and slicing machines. I don't know all the details in connection with it because I was still in school. The "Silver King" slicing machines didn't sell and were soon discontinued. But there was evidently a real need for a broiler and the "Broil King" was an

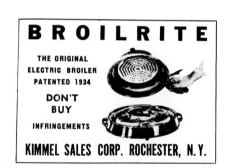

BROILRITE

THE ORIGINAL
ELECTRIC BROILER
PATENTED 1934

DON'T
BUY

INFRINGEMENTS

KIMMEL SALES CORP. ROCHESTER, N. Y.

282

From top: According to the claim in this ad, the Broilrite was patented in 1934 and was "the original electric broiler." The bottom picture shows the first Broil-King—a round model introduced by International in 1937.

immediate success. The International Appliance Corporation was formed to handle the broiler business and has specialized in it ever since.

We have been responsible for a number of innovations in broilers. For example, we pioneered the use of removable, tubular heating elements to simplify cleaning. We were the first to incorporate the "No-turn" broiling feature whereby both sides of the food are broiled at the same time. (A non-electric broiler introduced in 1910 also had that feature.) And most recently, in 1970, we introduced the first self-cleaning or "continuous clean" table broiler.

The first Broil-King broiler was of the type virtually all the early broilers were patterned after. Basically they consisted of a stamped, chrome-plated circular base or tray unit about twelve inches in diameter, fitted with a wire grid to hold the meat and a porcelain enamel pan to catch the drippings; a separate, dome-shaped cover went on top of this and rested on the base. In some models the heating element was in the base, in others it was inside the hood.

Among the early entrants in this field was Manning-Bowman and Company who, about 1937, introduced a table broiler which it claimed would not smoke the way others did. It was designed with a high, rounded dome lid suggestive of a bee-hive, which contained the heating element. It had three small vent holes in the top and the lid rested rather snugly on the tray. That, as it turned out, was something of a performance design deficiency common to most early broilers as broiling requires much greater circulation of air.

Another pioneer in this field was Henry Talge, who, after he started the Puritan Aluminum Company in 1927, went on to found the Rival Manufacturing Company and is now chairman of the Dazey Products Company. In February 1938, he introduced an "electric steak platter," a cast aluminum platter with a well-and-tree recess, a chrome-plated rim around it and an electric heating element underneath. He promoted it very successfully as a $6.95 retail item. Later he developed a broiler.

The first table broiler equipped with a motor permitting the use of a revolving spit to convert it into a "rotisserie" appeared in 1946 when Robert Kemelhor and Charles Green started the Rotissimat Corporation in Long Island City, New York.

"It wasn't exactly a cheap appliance—it sold for fifty dollars," Bob Kemelhor related in a conversation in 1972. "In order to promote it we set up demonstrations in poultry stores where we roasted chickens with the idea of getting sales leads for our dealers. However, instead of buying our Rotissimat the women only wanted to buy the roasted chickens! Incidentally that was the beginning of the commercial chicken roasting concept now found in supermarkets."

His company was doing about $1½ million annually when, in 1954, it was liquidated. "We had gotten off to a nice start," he said, "but competition in those years got so bad, I mean not only intense but so dirty with the fly-by-night operators, we called it quits." He is now a vice-president of International Appliance Corporation.

283

From top: In 1963 Sunbeam introduced the Carousel broiler, an unusual, vertically mounted revolving unit. In 1938 Farber moved into the broiler market with two round models like this and a deluxe oval-shaped one. In 1938 Westinghouse brought out this broiler with a "see-through" lid.

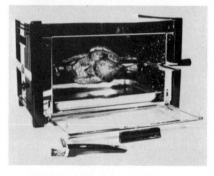

From top: Probably the first broiler to cook both sides of the meat at the same time was introduced in 1910. In 1970, modern broilers hit a new high in performance when International Appliance brought out this self-cleaning Broil-King, the first broiler to have such a feature.

In 1961 the Dominion Electric Corporation, a Scovill subsidiary, came out with an innovative oven-broiler. Used in one position it broils and toasts; turned completely up-side-down it bakes and roasts.

The following year, nearly twenty-five years after its initial entry into the broiler business, S. W. Farber Incorporated announced its revolutionary "Open Hearth" broiler/rotisserie which for the first time made it possible to broil at the table without a hood over the food. Rectangular in shape and made almost entirely of stainless steel, it can be quickly disassembled for cleaning. A simple motor attachment converts it at once into a rotisserie. Unlike the prior conventional broilers, this one has the heating element below the food and, to quote the advertising, "It's the 'cool zone' cooking method which prevents the dripping fat from spattering or smoking." In 1971 *Home Furnishings Daily* commented: "While Farber is the acknowledged leader in the open-hearth type of broiler, it is being challenged by such firms as Mirro Aluminum Company with its 'Mirro-Matic' rotisserie-broiler and Son Chief Electrics Incorporated with its 'Black Angus' broiler."

Table broilers took a giant step forward in 1970 when the technology that had made self-cleaning ovens such a great feature on ranges was finally adapted to this appliance by International Appliance Corporation. It immediately set a new high standard in the industry and it wasn't long before a number of other manufacturers like Son-Chief Electrics Incorporated and Udico Electric Company also had self-cleaning models.

The most ambitious entry into the broiler field came early in 1972 when the Ronson Corporation announced its "Quintisserie" model. As its name implies, it does five forms of cooking: it broils, fries, grills and can be used as a rotisserie as well as a griddle. It retails around one hundred dollars.

Salton's Workable Concept

A newly married man can become very annoyed if, when he happens to be carrying on an interesting conversation with his bride at dinner, he finds it repeatedly interrupted because she has to keep stepping into the kitchen. And if he also happens to be an electronics engineer like Lewis L. Salton, he proceeds to do something to correct the situation—which is exactly what happened.

The story begins in Poland in 1939 when Hitler's armies have Warsaw under siege. Everyone—including Lew Salton—was desperate. As he puts it, "I just barely managed to squeeze through the back door at the very last minute." After escaping from his homeland he journeyed for a year...across Siberia, Japan, Central America, and finally reached the United States.

In New York Lew Salton took a job in the engineering department of the Radio Corporation of America (now RCA Corporation). He decided that in this modern, electrical age it should be possible for hot food to be brought into the dining room on an electrically heated tray where it would be conveniently at hand. Thus trips to the kitchen would be unnecessary.

Lew Salton considered the idea good enough to develop a model. But after he did he couldn't find anyone except his wife who thought it had enough merit to bother with. The concept wasn't given a first, much less a second thought.

But to every action there is a reaction. In this instance the reaction was direct and unequivocal. The following year, 1948, with $10,000 in borrowed capital, he formed Salton Incorporated and proceeded to manufacture the Salton Hotray himself. The new corporation was located on the third floor of an old walk-up loft building in New York City's downtown show district. The rent: twenty-five dollars a month.

At the end of the first year the sales of Salton electronic warming trays came to $12,500. Three years later the operation needed four times as much space and employed twenty-five people; three years later those figures were again doubled.

By 1959 sales passed the $1 million mark and Salton Hotray had become nationally established with increasing consumer acceptance. In that year too the company moved into a multi-story loft building on 72nd Street and the East River—one of the most expensive sections of New York.

By that time the Hotray line had been expanded to seventeen different models. Sales doubled every three years. The company opened an office in London and by 1962 Salton's warming tray was the biggest seller of its kind in England.

In 1965 the warming idea was incorporated in a unique new bun warmer that was added to the line and proved an immediate success. It was the first of a series of other additions that included the introduction of an egg-cooker/poacher brought out in 1968, and a citrus juicer, coffee grinder, and "Filtercup" coffee maker that were added in 1969. The latest entrant is the Salton yogurt maker.

In 1972 production demands reached the point where the factory had to be moved into a 150,000-square-foot plant in the Bronx where over three hundred people are now employed. There is now also a factory in England as well as licensees in Australia and South Africa.

Salton Incorporated became a wholly owned subsidiary of the Corning Glass Works, Corning, New York, in 1970. Lewis Salton continues as president of his entire organization.

New markets—Salton Hotray bun warmers, 1965, followed the success of the Hotray. And, a few years later, catering to a health food market, the Salton yogurt maker.

285

Marshall Hanks of Indianapolis developed the first electric egg cooker using the electric cord from a hotel room floor lamp, attaching it to lead disks. Dropped into water, the device succeeded in boiling the water. In 1920 the Hankscraft Company began to market the electric egg cooker. Pictured is the first employee hired by Hanks.

From CASTLE TO COTTAGE

The **Sweeper-Vac**
ORIGINAL VACUUM CARPET SWEEPER

REMOVES EVERY PARTICLE OF DIRT THREAD AND LINT

3 Machines in one :
(1) Carpet sweeper used alone. (2) Vacuum Cleaner used alone, or (3) In combination, as picture shows.

EIGHT REASONS WHY EVERY STORE WILL EVENTUALLY SELL THE

Sweeper-Vac.

(1) The only sweeper in the world combining a **complete carpet sweeper**—not simply an attachment—with a **complete vacuum cleaner.**
(2) Nationally advertised. Profitable. No cut prices.
(3) Sells easily because it gathers all threads, lint, dust and dirt.
(4) Has perfect mechanical construction.
(5) Does remove from a cupful to a quart of solid dirt from a rug, even after it is beaten.
(6) Light running. No electricity.
(7) Saves beating, laying and tearing of rugs.
(8) Reaches the highest notch attainable in the carpet sweeper development.

The word "SWEEPER-VAC" is stencilled in gold on the top of every original machine. No others are Sweeper-Vacs, nor are they protected by United States basic patent No. 996,810.

SWEEPER-VAC—the vacuum carpet sweeper with an unimpeachable reputation. Manufactured by

PNEUVAC COMPANY, BLAKE BLDG. BOSTON, MASS.

In 1913 this Sweeper-Vac ad offered the housewares retailer eight reasons why every good householder would beat a path to his door. The Sweeper-Vac was "three machines in one," and included the function of a non-electric vacuum cleaner. Note the wide market appeal from cottage to castle as illustrated.

Courtesy House Furnishing Review.

From Brooms to Vacuum Cleaners

Until 1850 the brooms used in America, as in Europe, were quite primitive affairs, usually little more than a bundle of thin twigs tied to a handle. In that year, however, some unsung farmer realized how effectively a tuft of the corn plant could be used as a brush and he inadvertently swept a whole new industry into being.

"The first factory for the manufacture of brooms from corn was founded in 1859 by Ebenezer Howard, at Fort Hunter, Montgomery County, New York," relates the authoritative *One Hundred Years of American Commerce 1795-1895*.

> Before that time the industry was carried on in a desultory way. He subsequently took his son in partnership and the firm became E. Howard & Son....Other broom factories were soon started there.... All...have since become absorbed by the American Broom and Brush Company....The industry is now carried on in the Eastern states almost entirely by [it]. The business in the Western states is in the hands of the Cupples Woodenware Company of St. Louis, and Roseboom & Co., Chicago.
>
> All of the brooms are now turned out by machinery which is entirely of American invention, and which enables the manufacturers to produce 3 million dozen brooms annually, supplying the home market and exporting $250,000 as well. There are now $2.5 million invested in the industry, while 25 years ago there were only $100,000 and 50 years ago none whatever.
>
> Many brooms are made by hand in various penitentiaries throughout the country...[and] in blind asylums as the work is especially adapted to blind men.[1]

FOR WINTER EVENINGS

"The winter evening's work of many farmers throughout the country was the making of brooms," writes Rolla Milton Tryon in *Household Manufacturers in The United States 1640-1890*.

> In New England they were made principally of birch and ash; in other parts of the country hickory answered the purpose as well. To make an ordinary Indian or splint broom, a birch or other tree about five inches in diameter where it was cut off, was used. A stick about six feet long was cut from this tree. Twelve or fourteen inches from the big end of the stick a ring was cut and the bark removed from this end.
>
> The maker then began to sliver with a sharp jackknife little flat slivers up the ring. This was continued until the heart was reached. ...When all this was done, there only remained to whittle off the part above to the size of a handle.[2]

The broom salesman in eighteenth-century London had a counterpart in colonial America.

The Bettmann Archive.

In 1918 the Amsterdam Broom Company, then the largest in the world, acquired its first automotive delivery equipment.

The Amsterdam Broom Company

When, in the mid 1800s, it was found that corn tufts made an excellent broom, it wasn't long before farmers in upstate New York's Mohawk Valley began devoting considerable acreage to the cultivation of broom corn. And, to be close to the source of their raw material, broom factories sprang up throughout the area.

In Amsterdam, New York, Julius Wasserman founded the Amsterdam Broom Company in 1884 in a small three-story brick building. He handled production while his son David took care of sales. Eventually it became the largest broom factory in the world. They and their few original employees worked sixty hours a week, customary for the times.

In April 1907, a disastrous fire destroyed the plant with great loss, but production was soon resumed in temporary quarters in the old Globe mill building. By year end the company was in a much larger new building but soon had to be expanded. The company was incorporated in 1909 with Julius Wasserman as president, a post he held until his death in 1916, when David took over.

The Amsterdam Broom Company made an extensive line of all types of brooms and the descriptions it used for some of its household numbers like the "Gold Bond" broom, speak eloquently for themselves: "A thousand words could not do justice to this remarkable broom. Here we utilize the best quality corn and we allow only hand-picked operators to work on its construction. Our long years of broom making experience have enabled us to uphold the quality of this broom in regard to both the material used and the fine workmanship employed. The Gold Bond broom is 15 inches long, has four rows of stitching and a finely polished yellow handle...it is made in one size only with individual covers on each broom."

Probably the most celebrated sales agent the company had was Max Lowenstein, a manufacturers representative in New York who took the line when it first appeared in 1884 and sold it continuously until his death in 1939. By then he had long been "dean" of the sales agents. His other important line was Magic Silver Polish. He had exhibited both lines at the first housewares show in Madison Square Garden in 1906 and never missed a show.

"I can remember when there were at least four major broom factories in Amsterdam, each employing more than 250 people," Charles Rink, former plant manager of the Amsterdam Broom Company, said in an interview in 1956 in the Amsterdam *Recorder*. He had been with the firm thirty-eight years. "There was a time when there were so many broom makers in Amsterdam that union regulations restricted the number of persons allowed to enter the field each year."

But the broom—even one as fine as Mr. Wasserman's Gold Bond broom—was no match for that remarkable newcomer, the vacuum cleaner, and as cleaner sales increased, broom sales declined. By 1957 the once bustling, largest broom factory in the world had only

Max Lowenstein, New York, "dean of housewares sales reps" represented the Amsterdam Broom Company for fifty-five years.

Courtesy House Furnishing Review.

about thirty employees and the Wasserman heirs sold the factory to the Edy Brush Company, New York. It is now operated as the Amsterdam Brush Company.

"SWEEP AND STILL BE SWEET"!

"For the past half century broom manufacturers have stood by supinely while their industry has been libelled," an article by H. R. Kelso in the July 1919 issue of *House Furnishing Review* declares.

They have let go, unchallenged, that sweeping is drudgery, until the present generation thinks and talks of sweeping as menial labor, unpleasant and to be performed with reluctance. What a misconception! The medical profession in numerous instances, advises women to take up housework, especially sweeping, to offset their ills. Sweeping is exercise of a highly beneficial nature, and therein lies a fertile field for the writer of advertising to correct this false opinion of long standing....

Of late, magazine articles have been particularly brazen in relegating the broom to the ash heap, but warm in their praise of vacuum cleaners. A certain company, engaged in manufacturing carpet sweepers, has for several years in its advertising derided the broom, holding it up to scorn with its cleaning device....

What have the broom manufacturers done to combat such slander? Nothing. Absolutely nothing. So far as they were concerned, if the people wished to accept the harmful statements, the broom manufacturers were willing....But now their attitude has changed. Out of their old docility has come spirited action, and by educational copy the home maker will have the opportunity of knowing that she can "Sweep and still be sweet." The plan for the cooperative advertising of the broom is simple, logical and bars virtually no one in the industry from participating. Promotion work is being carried on by the Broom Advertising Bureau, Chicago. A three year campaign is planned in which national magazines will be used extensively...with other forms of advertising.

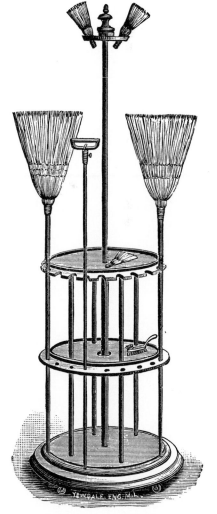

289

STEEL-EDGE DUST-PANS.

The Edges Warranted the best of Tempered Steel. The edge, always straight and close-fitting to the floor, being the best of steel, CANNOT BECOME BENT or distorted at the edge; therefore, all dirt and dust can at once be brushed on the Pan. Will outwear a dozen of the common style. ALWAYS READY FOR USE.

FOR SALE BY

GEO. H. MASON & CO.

WHOLESALE DEALERS IN TIN WARE,

152 Blackstone St., Boston.

	PER DOZEN.
No. 1, Common style, solid steel edge, enameled,	*$4.00*
No. 2, " " " " " ex. heavy, enam'd & decorated,	*5.00*
No. 3, Half covered, " " " hand-painted, fancy,	*6.00*

LIBERAL DISCOUNT TO THE TRADE.

The steel-edge dust pan was considered an important improvement over the ordinary tin dust pan when it was introduced around the turn of the century. For two dollars more a dozen such pans could be had "hand-painted, fancy."

Courtesy The Society for the Preservation of New England Antiquities.

Every well appointed household had a good-size rack for its many brooms, circa 1890.

The Bettmann Achive.

WHISK BROOMS
ALL KINDS
Prices Always   the Lowest

We sell the largest dealers, and can sell you if price and quality are any inducement.

ONONDAGA WHISK
BROOM WORKS
W. A. SHEPARD, Proprietor

SAMPLE ROOMS
150 Nassau St., New York City

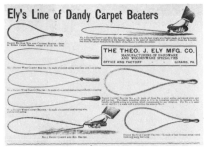

Ely's Line of Dandy Carpet Beaters

THE THEO. J. ELY MFG. CO.
MANUFACTURERS OF HARDWARE
AND WOODENWARE SPECIALTIES
OFFICE AND FACTORY   GIRARD, PA.

290

THE GREAT SCRUB RACE
FIRST QUARTER CO.

LAST

Throw away your old Mop: get a Eureka
J. R. DRAKE & CO. Manufacturers.
Hollister Building. BUFFALO, N. Y.

From top: W. A. Shepard is surrounded by his Onondaga whisk brooms in 1904. Before vacuum cleaners, the Dandy carpet beater had its day. In 1870 "Eureka" was a mop not a vacuum cleaner.

Top and middle, courtesy House Furnishing Review. Bottom, courtesy Library of Congress.

The Evolution of Carpet Sweepers

The creative mind of man never ceases to invent new and better ways to accomplish old tasks. As far back as 1699 a patent was issued in England to Edmund Heming for "a new machine for sweeping the streets of London or any city or town." It consisted of a large circular brush, mounted on a horsedrawn cart, which rotated when the cart moved by means of gears connected to its wheels. According to reports, the clouds of dust it raised were exceeded only by the clouds of protest from residents of the streets it "cleaned." The basic concept of the carpet sweeper had been established although it was not until 1811 that James Hume, also in England, patented the first machine designed to sweep floors. It consisted of a box equipped with a brush which was turned by means of a pulley and string mounted on the broomstick handle of the box.

"Lucius Bigelow invented an even more improved model in 1858," according to the February 1926 issue of *House Furnishing Review.*

> It possessed substantially all the elements of the modern carpet sweeper and was the most popular in Great Britain. Three years before the Civil War, H. H. Herrick brought out a sweeper in Boston.... This device, almost exactly like the English Bigelow sweeper, marked the beginning of the industry in this country....At first the New England metropolis had a monopoly on the patents, so manufacture naturally centered there. One New York merchant placed an order for 30,000...but the war broke out...and they were never delivered. Gradually the business spread. Distinctive names were employed by various manufacturers. The "Weed," "Boston," "Welcome," "Whirlwind," "Lady's Friend," were all popular for a time.

Despite the big head start the eastern manufacturers enjoyed, it would be a "westerner" who would end up with practically all the carpet sweeper business not only in America but in many other countries as well.

In the 1870s Melville R. Bissell and his wife Anna ran a crockery and glassware shop at 22 Monroe Avenue in downtown Grand Rapids, Michigan. Such products were always packed in crates and barrels of loose straw and Mel Bissell soon developed an allergy to the straw dust. The dust problem prompted him to make a bare floor sweeper—an idea which was promptly turned into a carpet sweeper.

Most existing sweepers were not only somewhat fragile but far from efficient; they stirred up more dust than they managed to collect. Bissell's version, though bulky and crude, looked something like present-day sweepers. Its essential feature was a knob for adjusting the brushes to the surface to be swept and in 1876 he was granted a patent on it. The Bissell Carpet Sweeper Company was born.

"Castings and cases were made in small manufacturing plants in the city," relates a company historical memorandum.

In their homes, girls wound tufts of hog bristles with string, dipped them in hot pitch and inserted them in brush rollers and trimmed them with scissors, all by hand. Mrs. Bissell collected the parts in clothes baskets and hauled them by horse and buggy to the store where they were assembled in a shop above it.

Bissell, who was then thirty-three and sported a walrus mustache, demonstrated his new sweeper by picking up a handful of dirt from the dusty street and throwing it on the floor. Prospective customers watched pop-eyed as the dirt dramatically disappeared into the sweeper....Nearly every demonstration resulted in a sale.

Their first big order came on a selling trip to New York. "Anna!" Mel exclaimed, "I sold Wanamaker's five dozen—we're made now!" His words proved true. The company prospered and before many years had passed was known all over the world.

Mrs. Bissell shares the credit with her husband for the remarkable success they achieved with their carpet sweeper in the face of widespread competition. Mel, naturally, was the guiding spirit in the beginning. But when he died in 1888, only twelve years after they launched this venture, his wife took over as president. Later she became chairman of the board, a position she held until her death in 1934.

The wisdom of hindsight always makes it relatively easy to explain someone's success. Many things doubtless contributed to the success of the Bissell sweeper. But when all else has been said, it may well have been due to the fact that, as the economists might put it, the Bissells were primarily promotion rather than production minded. In fact, there are probably few firms in the housewares business during those early years that devoted as much time, effort and money to advertising and promotion as Bissell; it's a record that many present-day firms could be proud of.

The Bissell archives contain a prodigious assortment of special promotions and dealer sales helps of every description. There were promotions for Christmas, for Easter, and all points between. There were special tie-ins for state and county fairs. There were special floor display stands for the merchandise and advertising electros (before the time of newspaper mats) of suggested dealer ads. Apparently one special deal cascaded over a dozen earlier ones without end; there is a special letterhead for a "Confidential Proposition to Exclusive Jobbers" and a form letter dated October 1890, addressed "To The Editor" offering him a carpet sweeper for only one dollar "If you wish to give some lady as handsome and lasting and useful a Christmas present as can be thought of...."—providing he also agrees "to insert an electrotype of the Bissell Carpet Sweeper Co.'s single column advertisement" in his paper for the issues just preceding Christmas...and, of course, submit checking copies too!

There was a special booklet for dealers, "Dust—a carrier of disease," "...to warn against the danger of using the old-fashioned corn broom." And, of course, a continuous barrage of trade and

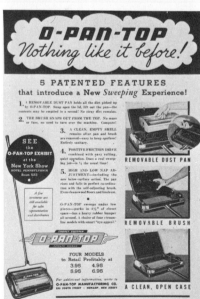

From top: A carpet sweeper of the past with "side whiskers" for cleaning baseboards. The O-Pan-Top: Nothing like it before...a new sweeping experience or a sweeping new experience?

Top, courtesy Bissell Museum. Bottom, courtesy House Furnishing Review.

From top: The original Bissell carpet sweeper. Melville R. and Anna Bissell, founders. An early electric "suction" or vacuum cleaner. The "Positive" claimed to be portable and perfect. From catalogues of the period, 1900-1910.

consumer advertising. It constitutes a most impressive array and goes far to explain why and how the company outdistanced its competition so effectively.

The promotional build-up reached something of a peak in 1917 when, typically, Bissell launched a "Household Labor Saving Devices Week" in which other manufacturers of such housewares were invited to participate. It offered a complete assortment of posters, banners and other material free to dealers and was so well received that it was repeated the following year.

Although exact figures are not available, it has long been conceded in the trade that Bissell has had at least 85 percent of the total carpet sweeper business. Over the years a host of competitors have given up trying to compete. (One notable exception is the Wagner Products Corporation of Hustisford, Wisconsin, which now makes outdoor as well as indoor sweepers.)

The traditional Bissell picture underwent what has been called "a mighty transformation" when in 1953 Melville R. Bissell III became president of the then eighty-four-year-old company. On a forty-two acre tract on the outskirts of Grand Rapids, he built a new, completely modernized factory. Not only was the carpet sweeper re-engineered and re-designed, but a rug shampooer, an electric vacuum cleaner and a whole group of specialty home cleaning and related items were added, totaling over fifty different products.

Since it is not a public corporation, official sales figures are not available. But it is known that sales in 1953 were $4 million and by 1959, following the reorganization, they had reached $14 million. In 1971, according to well-informed sources, sales nearly hit the $35 million mark.

Today the twenty-two, odd-shaped structures that the Bissell Carpet Sweeper Company once called its factory are only a memory and Bissell Incorporated can point not only to its modern plant in Grand Rapids, but plants also in Niagara Falls, Canada, England, Germany, and Australia, making it one of the world's largest producers of home care products.

The Early Years

It seems incredible today, but until around 1900 compressed air, widely used in factories and railroad passenger cars for blowing away dust, was often used in homes for the same purpose, although all it ever accomplished was a redistribution of the dust elsewhere in the house.

Two men and a woman of that era—located an ocean apart—concluded, at almost the same time, that it was pretty pointless to simply blow dust around. In England in 1901 Herbert Booth, so the story goes, suddenly got an idea while sitting in a restaurant that the way to get rid of dust and dirt was to suck it into a container of some kind. To try his theory he put his mouth tightly against the plush upholstery back of his chair and drew his breath in sharply. Instantly he was coughing and choking; Booth was elated—he'd proved his point.

In America a mechanical-minded woman in Savannah, Georgia, and a plumber in New Jersey, each used a different approach with the same principle. The woman, Corrine Dufour, invented an "Electric Sweeper and Dust Gatherer." It consisted of a pair of brush cylinders rotated by a rubber roller that made frictional contact with the carpet, and an electric motor within the cleaner hood operating a fan. The fan created suction which picked up dust and dirt and drove it against a sponge saturated with water. When the sponge became coated with dust the operator simply lifted the cover of the sweeper, removed the sponge to clean it, then replaced it. It's hardly surprising that it wasn't very successful.

The plumber, David E. Kenney, did much better. He devised a "renovator" or nozzle with a slot about twelve inches long and 3/16 inch wide, attached to a metal tube which served as a handle. A ¾-inch hose then connected the metal tube handle to a larger pipe that led to a vacuum pump and separating or filtering devices. He proceeded to patent his idea so thoroughly that thereafter and for many years no vacuum cleaner could be made in this country except under a Kenney license.

Who should actually be credited with the invention of the vacuum cleaner has always been a difficult question and invariably generates controversy. The strength of Kenney's claims lay in the fact that he obtained patents on his developments; he applied for them in 1901 and they were granted in 1907, continuing until they expired in 1923. It has since been pointed out that had someone searched the records of the Patent Office more thoroughly his claim might not have held.

Prior to the time the Kenney patents were issued and the formation of his Suction Cleaner Company in New York, all sorts of ideas had been tried to clean carpets mechanically. The ingenuity of inventors knew no bounds. Basically, of course, the vacuum cleaner is really an advanced development of the "mechanical broom" or carpet sweeper. But that development was, in turn, dependent upon the development of the fractional horsepower electric motor.

Even after the idea of using suction had been pretty well established as the best approach to cleaning rugs and carpets, the available methods for creating really adequate suction in a portable device that could easily be moved over the floor left a great deal to be desired. Everything was being tried from a hand—or foot—operated bellows to an electric motor driven fan.

Obviously the motor seemed to be the most promising. But motors and fans were big and heavy and the so-called portable cleaners on which they were used were clumsy, awkward monsters which, to tell the truth, were usually far better at emitting an impressive roar and clatter than at actually cleaning a carpet. They required so much effort to operate that more often than not it was a job for a man rather than a woman. It would be several years before a

All around the house the early Vortex vacuum did its "easily wheeled" clean-up job.

293

Early vacuum sometimes got out of hand; or is it many, many hands make light work? This not very portable machine was nevertheless moved from place to place to do a complete cleaning job. A 1903 print.
The Bettmann Archive.

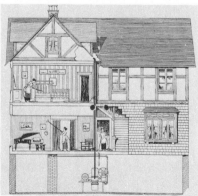

From top: This ad offered auto-vacuum dealerships. The equipment was either motor-driven or horse-drawn. Blaisdell was among the first to suggest built-in central vacuum systems.

reasonably powerful, lightweight fractional horsepower electric motor was developed.

Creating adequate suction was no problem with stationary equipment. And so all sorts of cleaning systems began to appear based on having a suction power plant in the basement of a home or building and connecting it with pipelines to conveniently located outlets on each floor to which a hose with a cleaning nozzle could be attached. Some systems went so far as to have the discharge pipe connected to the sewer line "so that instead of the dirt, dust and germs being deposited in bags it's all carried off and you never see it again." Many of the systems employed a water filtering device to remove the impurities from the air sucked into the machine, a principle later used on some portable cleaners.

"In the introduction of the piston-type pump and air compressor system," states a General Electric report on early vacuum cleaner equipment, "was seen the first sanitary device to be introduced into the field of mechanical cleaning. By it the dust and germ-laden air was removed entirely from the house or apartment and purified by means of separators before being discharged into the outside atmosphere. The effectiveness of this system in removing impurities from the air was clearly indicated by the foulness of the water in the separators or filters." Later some of the portable cleaners would also use water filters.

Often these stationary plants would be mounted on a wagon— later a truck—which would call at a home periodically when a cleaning crew would enter the house and drag a long hose inside to clean the carpets and rugs.

Yet despite the temporary superiority and popularity of the built-in systems, it was the portable vacuum cleaner which eventually triumphed and captured the consumer market. Just how many different models of vacuum cleaners were introduced by hopeful new companies from about 1900 to 1930 is unknown. But there were a great many, and the Hoover Company's famous museum in North Canton, Ohio, contains actual models of hundreds of fascinating ancient cleaners as evidence of the extent of the activity.

The Regina Story

Ever since the first "suction" or "pneumatic" cleaner made its appearance over a century ago, inventors have continued to demonstrate a wide range of truly remarkable ingenuity in the development of vacuum cleaners, although their creations were not always very practical. However, one of the most unique and, as it turned out, extremely practical and popular devices to appear is the "Electrikbroom" introduced in 1945 by the Regina Corporation, Rahway, New Jersey.

Weighing only a third as much as the ordinary cleaner and as easy to handle and hang up as a broom, it was the creation of an engineer named Ward Leathers. In 1934 his Quadrex Company had asked Regina to produce some of these new type cleaners for a market test. But engineering and financial problems developed, and in 1944 Regina acquired an exclusive license to make and market the "Electrikbroom." Its success since then has prompted a number of competitive imitations.

Regina, of course, is one of the oldest companies in the business, although its beginning was far removed from vacuum cleaners. It was in 1892 that a youthful German manufacturer of music boxes named Gustave Brachhausen, eager to make good in the America about which he had heard so much, established The Regina Music Box Company in Rahway. The company prospered; at its peak it employed 175 people and its annual sales occasionally hit $2 million. Regina practically had a monopoly on the American music box market and even began exporting to Europe!

But the future wasn't nearly as bright as it seemed. Only five miles from Rahway a man named Thomas A. Edison had discovered a way to reproduce the human voice and it would just be a matter of time before his new "gramophone" replaced the music box in the nation's homes.

"Because of Regina, Rahway had become a sort of Mecca to every inventor or pseudo-inventor who had anything to do with mechanical music," writes John E. Cann in his history of the company.

Brachhausen was continually accosted by someone trying to sell him an idea for a new way of canning music. According to one persistent but unconfirmed story, around 1900 a caller showed Brachhausen a new machine he had invented which, instead of playing music from cylinders as Edison's machine did, played from flat wax discs. What-

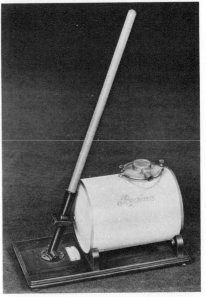

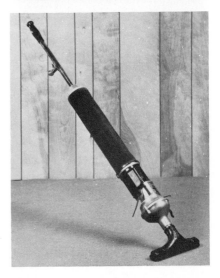

From top: The Regina Corporation began as a maker of music boxes. Then, Regina's 1910 model. Thirty-six years later, Regina introduced its first "Electrikbroom."

From top: Two contemporary Regina vacuum innovations: the "air pulse nozzle" that creates dirt loosening vibrations by means of pulsating air; and a "shag rake" for cleaning deep pile rugs.

ever it played, Brachhausen thought it sounded terrible and sent the fellow on his way. His way happened to be in the direction of Camden, New Jersey—where he became one of the founders of the Victor Talking Machine Co.

It was almost too late to save the company which had overstayed its market, but in 1909 it began to make a pneumatically operated vacuum cleaner, a cumbersome device requiring two people to operate it. Then an electric model was added. In a frantic effort to survive, the company made player pianos in 1911, printing presses in 1912 and phonographs in 1914. The last music box was made in 1919 and in 1922 the Regina Music Box Company was bankrupt.

A new management continued the reorganized business and among the newcomers was Lannon F. Mead who subsequently became president and chairman of the board. In 1929 the company entered the floor polisher field and was the first to produce a twin-brush model. Following its introduction of the "Electrikbroom," Regina expanded its line of canister, upright and other types of cleaners.

From 1922 to 1941 all of the company's sales of cleaners were made exclusively through its own house-to-house sales organization. But after World War II distribution was gradually changed over entirely to regular trade channels. In 1960 Regina was acquired by the General Signal Corporation.

The Hoover Company

In the year 1907 a genial, aging inventor named Murray Spangler in Canton, Ohio, was especially down on his luck. He had taken a "temporary" job as janitor of the Folwell Building there, occupied largely by a department store with endless rugs and carpeting to be cleaned. That meant he was obliged for hours to breathe dust-laden air stirred up by the big carpet sweeper he had to use each night, and as the "temporary" job dragged on for several years he developed a cough that was sapping his strength. If he didn't need the job so desperately he would have given it up. Instead he began to apply his mechanical ingenuity to the problem of making the big sweeper easier and less tiring to push.

He found an electric fan motor no one was using, mounted it on the sweeper brush so that the sweeper practically propelled itself. Now the power-driven brush moved so vigorously it raised even more dust and aggravated his cough further. Finally he developed something that seemed to work.

"It worked, but only well enough to indicate to Murray Spangler that it might be possible to build a machine that would enable him to hold his job," Frank Garfield Hoover relates in *Fabulous Dustpan*, a history of the Hoover Company he wrote in 1955.

He worked on it during the day when his time was his own. He started with an old soap box, sealed the cracks with adhesive tape; he made a roller brush, they say, by stapling goat bristles to a piece of broom handle. And he cut out a better fan from an old stovepipe. The fan

There seemed to be, almost literally, no limit to the ingenuity used for creating suction—either manually or electrically —in the early vacuum cleaners as many tried to get into the business.

Courtesy Hoover Company Museum.

motor provided the power and a pillow case served as the bag. The new machine worked so well that Murray ceased to worry about his job and began thinking his old thoughts...breaking the machine down into production operations....Many times he rebuilt it. The Folwell Building and its acres of rugs became a huge laboratory to Murray Spangler. Gradually his machine became simpler and its efficiency increased. Finally he knew how he wanted to build it....[3]

Finally too, on June 2, 1908, Spangler received a U.S. patent for his latest invention. Then, with the support of a friend who invested $5,000 he formed the Electric Suction Sweeper Company. But it wasn't long before its finances were in a critical state.

Spangler went to New Berlin where he succeeded in selling one of his cleaners to his cousin—who happened to be Mrs. William H. Hoover. The Hoover family had long been in the leather and saddlery business, hardly something with a promising future as those new motor cars began displacing horses. And so, after seeing what his wife's new appliance could accomplish, William Hoover decided to acquire it. On August 8, 1908 the company was reorganized with William as president; his son Herbert became secretary and general manager and Murray Spangler was superintendent. What would become a great, world-wide appliance organization had been born and The Hoover Company was on its way.

Its well-known slogan for its cleaner, "It Beats As It Sweeps As It Cleans," was created in 1919 and immediately developed a lot of competitive reaction that generated derogatory rumors that "The Hoover damages rugs." The beater bar on which the slogan was based had taken three years and about four hundred different designs to perfect. The company was convinced it was good and finally squelched the rumors with a full page ad in the *Saturday Evening Post*. It showed a tall, thin Mr. Tutt sort of character wearing a silk high hat and walking along the far side of a board fence. Some boys were throwing snowballs at him. "It's the plug hat that gets the snowballs!" read the headline, with the copy explaining humorously

By 1909 the Hoover Company had grown to where it could afford full page ads in the *Saturday Evening Post*, of which this is the first.

From top: The 1913 Hoover "Old Baby" model. The head of the Hoover Company, Herbert W. Hoover. At right, another industry pioneer, Andrew S. Knapp, who established the Knapp-Monarch Company, later acquired by Hoover. Contemporary vacuums include many features, this model with "dial-a-matic."

that "the cleaner was drawing a lot of snowballs because it is a standout."

In 1958 Hoover adopted a major policy change—it decided to expand its line to include all types of portable appliances. First item to be introduced was an electric iron. During the next few years it added a can opener, hair dryer, coffee maker, fry pan, hand mixer, and a number of others to round out a complete line. Then in 1969 it took another giant step in the direction of electric housewares when it acquired the long-established Knapp-Monarch Company of St. Louis, one of the best known firms in this business.

The Knapp-Monarch Company was founded in 1925 by Andrew S. Knapp, although originally it was strictly a selling organization— A. S. Knapp and Company—handling the "Knapp Cap," used to train boys' hair to stay back in the pompadour style, a great craze at the time. Later he added an insulated water jug used in the field by farm laborers which he modernized and promoted as a "Thermo Jug" for picnics. In 1928 he merged with the manufacturer, the Monarch Company in Webster City, Iowa, resulting in the name, Knapp-Monarch Company. Manufacturing facilities were set up in Belleville, Illinois.

The new firm went into the electric housewares business in a big way in the early 1930s, despite the growing depression, and by 1933 had an almost complete line of such items. The following year it moved to St. Louis and began a series of acquisitions and expansions that made it a leading producer of popular price appliances:

1934 Acquired the Galvin Electric Company, manufacturer of electric motors for fans and other items.
1936 Acquired the Dover Manufacturing Company, Dover, Ohio, pioneer producer of irons.
1938 Acquired the American branch of the Sparklet Company in Ironton, New Jersey, from the British Oxygen Company, makers of soda syphons. The addition of the Andrews Altofer Company in 1952 and Aeromarine Manufacturing Company in 1964 resulted in the company having the most complete line of inflatable lifesaving equipment.
1955 Acquired tools and dies and the well-known "Nesco" trademark of the long-established National Enameling and Stamping Company, Jackson, Illinois.
1956 Acquired tools and dies of the "Hollywood" rotisserie broiler from the Finders Manufacturing Company.
1964 Acquired the portable tabletop washer from Proctor-Silex Company.

Andrew Knapp died in 1961. His son Robert S. Knapp, now heads the Knapp-Monarch Division of Hoover. Private brand merchandise for Sears, Roebuck and Company, Penney's, and others account for a large portion of Knapp-Monarch's business. Not counting its private brand business, it sells over one hundred different products and models under the name of Knapp-Monarch, Nesco and Sparklet.

The Electrolux

Although the vacuum cleaner in its present form is largely an American development, early in its history a cleaner from overseas began to invade this market—and remained to become an important, "naturalized" product that had far-reaching impact.

SPECIALTY SELLING WAS THE ANSWER

By the time the early, clumsy "suction sweeper" had begun to develop into an important new home appliance that came to be known as a "vacuum cleaner," most manufacturers had also come to realize that it could only be sold successfully by a specialty salesman competent to demonstrate it properly. House-to-house selling thus became established as a major form of distribution in the industry for many years.

"My great good luck," explained W. H. Hoover when he was president of that company, "consisted in finding out the right way to sell vacuum cleaners, rather than the cleaner itself. I would stock up a hardware store with cleaners, go out two months later and find none of them moved. I would get busy and demonstrate them to housewives and move the stock. Quite unwittingly, I stumbled on to the fact that specialty demonstrations were the correct way to sell vacuum cleaners."

Hoover, like others, developed a big direct sales organization, but after World War II when vacuum cleaners had become an over-the-counter appliance in retail stores, most of the house-to-house sales organizations were discontinued. One notable exception is the Electrolux Corporation (now a subsidiary of Consolidated Foods Corporation) which has never sold in any other manner.

A classic. The original "Model O" marked Hoover's entry into the vacuum cleaner business in 1908.

In 1924 Gustaf Sahlin arrived in New York from Stockholm, Sweden. He brought with him what was then considered to be a strange-looking vacuum cleaner made by Aktiebolaget Elektrolux, one of the companies owned by a well-known Swedish industrialist of that era, Axel L. Wenner-Gren. He also brought along the exclusive rights to the use of the name "Electrolux" in the United States, where he soon began to sell those cleaners.

The new machine looked like a small cylinder or tank mounted on gliders—wheels wouldn't appear until later—and a flexible hose attached to a nozzle was used to do the cleaning. Radically different from the standard upright type cleaners then being sold here, it had already been introduced and well received in various countries in Europe.

What prompted the new arrivals to sell their machine on a house-to-house basis rather than through retail channels isn't entirely clear. At any rate Electrolux began doing so right at the start and for many years has had one of the biggest and most successful direct selling organizations in the country. Exact figures have never been revealed, but it is said to have had over ten thousand salesmen—and quite a few women.

By 1931 the company was doing so well that it decided to make the machines here rather than import them, and arrangements for this were concluded with the White Sewing Machine Company in Cleveland. It soon became evident, however, that Electrolux should do its own manufacturing and in 1932 a plant was acquired in Old Greenwich, Connecticut.

In 1924 Electrolux offered the model No. 5, another classic, the first tank or cylinder type cleaner to be sold in this country.

The traditional upright vacuum cleaner had been touted for its floor-cleaning ability; now this new tank-type machine added another dimension to the cleaning story—it could clean above the floors as well, furniture, draperies, etc. And its sales organization made the most of that fact.

During World War II when its factory was devoted entirely to war work, Electrolux launched one of the most unusual and successful merchandising campaigns of any company in the business. For a deposit of twenty-five dollars, it offered homemakers a Preferential Post-War Sales Contract for a new cleaner to be delivered when civilian production could be resumed. This campaign continued for many months and provided a big backlog of business as well as hundreds of thousands of dollars of interest-free working capital.

Early in the 1950s it introduced "the vacuum cleaner with a brain" that never needed emptying; a machine that stopped automatically whenever the dust bag was so full that it impaired cleaning efficiency. It was also equipped with a unique self-sealing dust bag. Soon after Electrolux introduced a "power nozzle" equipped with a motor-driven revolving brush to provide cleaning ability equivalent to upright models with such a feature.

Electrolux probably holds most of the important patents in the industry. Not long after starting its own manufacturing operation in this country, Electrolux became a publicly held American stock corporation and in 1968 it was acquired by Consolidated Foods Corporation. Separate sales figures are no longer issued, but Electrolux, it was authoritatively learned, did a volume of over $125 million in 1971.

In December 1945, promptly capitalizing on a post-war market, Eureka offered a complete "home cleaning" system to housewares dealers.

Courtesy House Furnishing Review.

Specialty Selling of Eureka

A former real estate auctioneer, Fred Wardell, launched the Eureka vacuum cleaner in Detroit in 1910. Today, as a product of the Eureka Williams Company, a division of the National Union Electric Corporation, it continues to be one of the important lines in this business.

Wardell had friends in the Stecher Electric and Machine Company, producing an electric vibrator (a national fad at the time and one of the first of what today are called "personal care" items).

In 1909 Stecher, sensing the potential of the vacuum cleaner, began manufacturing one with Wardell as national sales agent. He named it the "Eureka" cleaner.

"We were lucky," Wardell related in an interview in 1946 in *Electrical Merchandising* (now *Merchandising Week*). "We stumbled onto specialty selling. When we became aware of how intensively one had to work to sell cleaners, we changed our way of doing business and opened branches. At the peak we had 400 (and, reported an associate, 5,000 salesmen). We were selling on installments as was done with the automobile and that in itself opened up vast further reaches of possibilities."[4]

The association with Stecher continued until 1920 by which time, due to other products it was making, it could no longer keep up with the demand for cleaners, and Wardell built a plant of his own. He didn't act too soon. From sales of $42,000 in 1910, Eureka's volume zoomed to over $12 million in 1927 when production for the year came to 270,563 units.

In 1939 Henry W. Burritt came from the Nash Kelvinator Company to assume the presidency of the company. He had visions of developing it into a full-line company but World War II froze all plans. In 1945, however, the Eureka cordless electric iron was introduced; like other such irons it met with limited success, and apparently ended further efforts in that direction.

Burritt, meanwhile, believed the time had come to switch the company's merchandising approach so he brought an end to the house-to-house program and ever since distribution has been primarily through retailers.

In 1954 the company merged with the Williams Oil-O-Matic heating Corporation and became the Eureka Williams Company. Operations were consolidated in the Williams plant in Bloomington, Illinois. Six years later the company merged with the National Union Electric Corporation at which time all heating items were moved to NUE's Armstrong Division, enabling Eureka to concentrate on floor care products.

By 1971 the line had expanded to over sixty-five different models covering all types of floor care products including cannister, upright, lightweight and hand cleaners as well as commercial models and polisher-scrubbers. Special cleaners are made for the direct selling operators.

Some Innovations

Around the turn of the century a young man in Cleveland named James Kirby, who operated a motor repair shop, was destined to leave a lasting mark on the vacuum cleaner business.

"One day a strange looking wagon backed up to the house next door to the Kirby mansion," reported *Electrical Merchandising* (now *Merchandising Week*) in its February 1, 1946 issue,

> a hose was run inside and the place was given a going-over with a giant vacuum cleaner.
>
> "Shucks," said Jim, "I can make a machine to do that without all that apparatus."
>
> His cleaner employed two buckets of water, the water being employed to take the dirt out of the air. It worked, but it was a backbreaking job to carry around two pails of water and it had to be changed pretty often. One party would have to pump the handle while the other cleaned the rugs. The Domestic Vacuum Cleaner Company put this water vacuum cleaner on the market, selling it for twenty-five dollars without a motor and eighty-five dollars with one.[5]

Subsequently Kirby sold his shop and concentrated on developing a so-called broomstick model cleaner he felt was much better. Afterwards he added something more to it—a cut-off arrangement

From top: Fred Wardell, founder of the Eureka Vacuum Cleaner Company and James B. Kirby, an early developer of vacuum cleaners, including the famous "Kirby" model. Two Eureka vacuums from different periods: the 1910 Model 1; and the 1933 easy-to-carry Model H.

From top: Edward L. Frantz and Clarence G. Frantz, innovaters in the vacuum cleaner industry, founded the Frantz Premier Company in 1911. In 1914 the Frantz Premier Models sold for twenty-five dollars as advertised in *Cosmopolitan* magazine.

that permitted attachments to be connected to the cleaner, a great innovation in 1910.

Just at this time three brothers named Frantz were living in Cleveland. The two eldest, Edward L. and Clarence G., were in the building materials business; Walter was a mechanic. Kirby's and their paths would often cross in the years ahead.

In 1971, in the course of an interview in St. Petersburg, Florida, Clarence Frantz, still fully active with his company despite his eighty-four years, recalled a bit of the past:

In 1910 my brother Ed—who died in 1971—was building what were known as "four suite" apartment houses and when Jim Kirby bought one, he and Ed got to know each other.

Kirby was really the pioneer in developing the concept of a very light weight, nozzle-type vacuum cleaner, radically different from the heavy, cumbersome box-like machines such as Hoover was making. Ed was so impressed by what Kirby had done, that he obtained the rights to produce such a cleaner and formed a new company for the purpose called the Premier Vacuum Cleaner Company.

Thanks to the help of a patternmaker named A. P. Schroener a working production model was ready in six weeks time. Ed, of course, financed the venture and my brother Walter handled the manufacturing, which started in 1911. The goal was to produce one hundred machines a week. It's difficult today to realize that one of the problems that faced us then was figuring out to whom we should or could sell. The market sixty years ago was still only in a very formative stage.

Ed suggested the electrical and hardware jobbers as our best bet. There were less than five hundred in the whole country and he sent them a six-page folder. We got an unheard of 52 percent return, which convinced us we were on the right track. The cleaner used a GE 3000 rpm motor and retailed for twenty-five dollars. A Philadelphia jobber named L. D. Berger agreed to take all we could produce.

Not long after, Clarence related, the advertising agency handling the Premier account suggested that the appeal of the ads would be much more effective if the company's image could be personalized in some manner. As a result, he said, its name was changed to Frantz Premier Vacuum Cleaner Company. In 1915 the company was purchased by General Electric who changed its name to Electric Vacuum Cleaner Company. Julius Teuter was named president. This was the basis on which GE entered the cleaner business.

In 1912 Clarence and Walter Frantz decided to start a new company, the Apex Electric Manufacturing Company to make not only vacuum cleaners but washing machines as well. William Orr, who later went with General Electric, designed the first cleaner under the Apex name, and although it employed cast iron bearings, they are said to have stood up remarkably well.

World War I had brought Kirby in contact with the Scott & Fetzer Company which was making armaments and when the war ended they started making a new improved model of the "Kirby cleaner" which, ever since, it has sold exclusively on a house-to-house basis. Kirby meanwhile divided his time working for Scott & Fetzer exclusively on cleaners and for Apex on washers.

The Frantz brothers left an indelible mark on the vacuum cleaner industry, a mark of significant progress. In addition to what has already been mentioned, there were such other important innovations as the divided nozzle in 1913; the first use of a motor driven brush in 1926; and use of a two-speed, vertical motor in 1933. It was in 1933 too that Clarence Frantz, far ahead of the times, retained a prominent industrial designer, George Walker, to style an Apex vacuum cleaner, first one to have a professional styling touch.

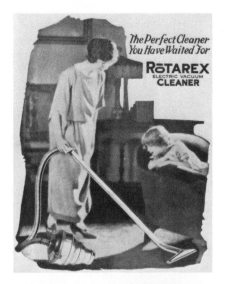

The Brief Life of the Apex Rotorex

Among the unusual vacuum cleaners that have come and gone from the marketplace over the years, one of the most remarkable was the cleaner which looked like a giant-sized version of a child's metal spinning top. It was sold in the United States under the names of "Renovator" and "Rotorex"; in Germany it was called "Rotarex."

Clarence G. Frantz who with his brother, Edward, founded the Apex Electric Manufacturing Company in Cleveland, and is a pioneer of the cleaner business, recalled in 1972 that he had been approached in the early 1920s by an inventor named Stanley McClachie. "He had designed a cone-shaped vacuum cleaner which lay on the floor and rolled around easily to accommodate any position the user might assume with the hose to which it was attached. McClachie was convinced it could be tooled up much cheaper in Germany since he had originally developed it there and could also be sold in that country. So we agreed to go ahead with it.

"He set up a German operation to make and sell it, in Stuttgart, I believe, under the name 'Rotarex' with considerable success," Frantz continued. "Meanwhile we had started to produce it in Cleveland where we were also making the 'Frantz Premier' and 'Apex' cleaners." It was named the "Apex Rotorex."

"However, most of those cleaners were sold under the name of 'The Renovator.' A man named Martin V. Kelley, with whom we were in contact in New York, was so impressed with what he later called 'a new European type electrical purifying machine' that he organized a company called Renovator Incorporated to sell it on a house-to-house basis. Of course, we supplied the cleaners. He managed to survive the depression of the 1930s reasonably well, but then World War II came along and the company was dissolved. The cleaner was never produced after that," Mr. Frantz concluded.

From top: The unusual Rotarex vacuum cleaner, from a circular about 1920. From an earlier period, Skinner Manufacturing offered this model of the "Electric Renovator."

303

Post War Transition

Among the contractors engaged in making special military equipment for the government during World War II was a not-so-small sixty-year-old Brooklyn manufacturer of industrial components called the Lewyt Corporation. Alex Lewyt had assumed the presidency of the family business fifteen years earlier and, like most farsighted manufacturers at the time, was already thinking in post war terms.

Floor care also means rug care. This Bissell Electro-Foam Carpet Shampooer is a big improvement over the manual method. Liquid and dry rug cleaners achieve the desired results.

The potential for home appliances after the war had often crossed his mind but not too seriously since the company had never made any consumer products. Among the items it was producing for the Navy was a cleaning device. One day while inspecting the assembly line he happened to overhear one of the girls working on it say, "Wouldn't it be nice to have a cleaner like this around the house." That decided him, and in 1947 he acted.

In its first year of operation, August 1947 to August 1948, Lewyt sold 100,000 cleaners and moved into an enviable position among the more than twenty cleaner-producing companies.

But first, Lewyt needed to build public recognition for the cleaner and its name. Before there was a single cleaner in the field he launched full-page color advertising in leading national magazines, radio and television, and even billboards.

Another step in his program was to help dealers sell more vacuum cleaners on the floor. Vacuum cleaners must be demonstrated to be sold. "We found that the appliance men were not selling them—they were handling them." To correct the situation for Lewyt cleaners a demonstration-display unit called "The Market Place" was designed. Well-illuminated, with carpeting on the floor, it was equipped with a shelf to display attachments and synthetic dirt for demonstration use.

After making this impressive record, Lewyt decided that other interests were more to his liking and in 1960 he sold his business—not the plant—to the Shetland Floor Polisher Company, Lynn, Massachusetts.

Shetland...Lewyt...SCM

In 1949 a small offshoot of the Signal Manufacturing Company in Lynn, Massachusetts called the Shetland Company Incorporated, and headed by Robert Lappin, was doing nicely marketing a small, all-purpose polisher which could be used for floors or as a hand polisher, drill or sander. It was promoted especially to polish cars but by 1952 the appearance of silicone finishes killed the appeal of that market, so Lappin switched to producing a twin-brush floor polisher. Subsequently a dispenser was added for wax, said to be the first one ever offered. That was followed in 1956 by the "Floorsmith," a combination twin-brush floor polisher and rug shampooer. It retailed for $59.95.

In 1960 Shetland entered the vacuum cleaner field with an innovation consisting of a lightweight "stick type" cleaner equipped with a hard surface floor washing device that also dried the floor. This was followed in 1961 by a similar model without the washing feature. At $29.95 it quickly became a best seller.

In 1961 Robert Lappin entered the vacuum cleaner business. Alex Lewyt rather abruptly decided to end his vacuum cleaner operation and sold it to Lappin, whereupon the Shetland-Lewyt combination came into being.

After acquiring Lewyt, Shetland expanded its line of "stick-type" cleaners with the addition of a cannister cleaner, and although it carried the Lewyt (as well as the Shetland) name, it was completely re-designed. In 1966 under the name "The Fashionables," this model was brought out in a series of eight decorated cleaners, each strikingly different in color and design.

By 1967 Robert Lappin's company was said to be the largest producer of electric shampooers in the country. In addition it had become a factor in the lightweight cleaner and low end cannister type cleaner business, all of which added up to an annual volume said to be around $20 million. It was then bought by the SCM Corporation, operating as the Shetland-Lewyt Division of that company. In addition to its floor care products, this division added a number of table appliances made by the Proctor-Silex Division of SCM, but bearing the Shetland label.

Five years later, however, the Shetland-Lewyt operation came to an abrupt halt when, in July 1972, SCM announced it was being discontinued and put it up for sale.

A Postscript

Three important manufacturers dropped out of the vacuum cleaner industry in 1972, lending further credence to the oft-repeated observation that basically, it is really a specialty business.

In January the General Electric Company's housewares division announced suddenly that, "After a thorough review we have concluded that there are opportunities...which provide a greater return than exists with floor care products," and brought to an abrupt end a business that started in 1910 when Edward and Clarence Frantz founded the Premier Vacuum Cleaner Company in Cleveland.

But the old name has been revived. In June 1972 it was revealed that GE had sold its operation to a group headed by Raymond Finberg, former vice-president of Shetland-Lewyt.

General Electric Company's departure from the cleaner business had barely ceased to be news when the Westinghouse Electric Corporation, conceding that its electric housewares operation—including vacuum cleaners—had lost some $7 million the previous year, announced it was ending the operation completely and put it up for sale. Since then it has been acquired by Scovill Manufacturing Company, presumably for its Dominion and Hamilton Beach operations, but whether cleaners will be produced remains to be seen. Some years ago the Hamilton Beach Division of Scovill ended its cleaner production.

Finally, just prior to the July 1972 NHMA Housewares Exposition, the SCM Corporation gave up also on the cleaner business. "A study indicates that the future of the Shetland-Lewyt floor care operation does not appear promising even if we instituted major changes," company officials declared. When current commitments are fulfilled the operation will be phased out and possibly sold, it was said.

From top: Shetland's first product was this "all purpose" polisher introduced in 1949. With the broomstrick handle detached, it could also be used as a drill, sander, and hand polisher. In the area of floor care products Shetland also offered the Electra Sponge, as seen in this 1969 advertisement.

305

cutlery, can openers and gadgets

Knives, forks, and spoons have for so long been a part of daily life that it is difficult to imagine a time without them—but there was one. The knife was the first to appear.

"When the knife progressed from a blade of flint...to one of metal in the Bronze Age, it also marked the first step forward in elemental eating culture," writes Helen Sprackling in *A Brief History of the Knife, Fork and Spoon.* "Man could now cut meat from the bone and...convey it to his mouth with the point of his knife."[1]

The knife also was a weapon.

Not until the fourteenth century does a knife designed solely for the purpose of eating begin to appear on the table. It became a valued gift ...usually consisting of a pair of knives—one to hold the meat, the other with which to cut and eat....

The spoon was born of its own need....Very ancient spoons have been found crudely formed of clay, hollowed from bone or horn or fashioned from a shell with a slender stick for a handle. Early Egyptians used spoons of considerable sophistication....The spoon was an individual and highly prized possession....It was a treasured piece, and if the owner could afford it, beautifully made of gold or silver-gilt or perhaps carved from ivory....No two were ever alike.

Although the fork had an ancient history of use in the field and kitchen, it was not an important accessory for dining until the Renaissance in Italy, when the upper-class became consciously fastidious. ...The actual precursor of the table fork seems to have been the skewer....From Italy...the fork found its way into France and other continental countries, finally reaching England about the mid-sixteenth century. It was a whole century later, however, before it took the place of one of the knives of the pair which hitherto had been considered necessary for well-mannered eating. Once this alliance was established, the sharp point of the knife was no longer necessary for the spearing of meat. Its point became blunt....

Predominantly two-tined for a period of two centuries, forks were always experimental and sometimes appeared with three or four tines. Not until the French permanently established for themselves a generous, four-tined fork in the middle of the eighteenth century did it slowly come into standard use. The knife, fork and spoon joined forces in the latter part of the seventeenth century.[2]

Miss Sprackling goes on to relate that when royalty entertained, it became customary to make up a set of a knife, fork, and spoon packed in a case for easy carrying.

307

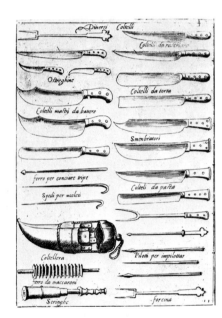

Opposite page: An ancient Roman bas-relief shows merchants selling cutlery from an open stall. The language was Latin; it said "caveat emptor." *This page:* An array of cutlery as shown in Scappi's cookbook published in Venice in 1643. Presumably what every well-equipped Rennaissance chef should have.

Opposite page, courtesy Vatican Museum, Rome. This page, courtesy New York Public Library Rare Book Division, Astor, Lenox and Tilden Foundations.

During the colonial era hand-carved wooden spoons were in common use. Forks were almost unknown and usually only the wealthy traders and English Crown representatives had silver or pewter utensils.

Courtesy Minnesota Historical Museum.

An early nineteenth-century strainer made of wood, used in Europe and America.

Courtesy Index of American Design, National Gallery of Art.

"Letters, books, and inventories show that certain of our American colonists were also alert to this new fashion.... By the beginning of the Georgian era it was quite customary for affluent households to place knife, fork and spoon by the plate on the table much as we do today,"[3] she adds.

For a long time the New World would be dependent upon Europe, and especially on Sheffield in England, for its cutlery and tools. Why the domestic manufacture of these items lagged is not clear. But in the 1830s David Ropes began to manufacture table cutlery at Saccarappa, Maine. Custom dictated the use of ivory for handles, and so Ropes was obliged to go all the way to Meriden, Connecticut, where Julius Pratt and Company, manufacturers of ivory combs, could furnish them. Eventually Ropes decided it would be better for him to move to Meriden, and in 1846 he did so, forming Pratt, Ropes, Webb and Company. In 1855 the company became the Meriden Cutlery Company, with offices in New York City. The early sixties were especially prosperous because the firm patented a new type of hard-rubber handle for cutlery.

The company continued to use other materials as well. "When the company was first started," wrote C. Bancroft Gillespie in *A Century of Meriden,* "Production was limited to ivory-handled knives and forks...[but it now embraces all] table cutlery."[4]

An Acquisition

In 1866 Meriden Cutlery was acquired by Landers, Frary and Clark of New Britain, Connecticut, to round out its rapidly expanding "Universal" line of housewares. It had great plans, for it would now be one of the largest manufacturers in the cutlery business.

An entirely new plant, the Aetna Works, was built and took over all cutlery production. Its completion was celebrated with a ball on the night of March 15, 1867. Six years later it burned to the ground, but was rebuilt on an even larger scale and dominated the market for decades. By 1950 conditions had changed to such an extent that

Landers—to the astonishment of the marketplace—discontinued its cutlery operations. Lander's entire operation, of course, ceased in 1965, at which time its assets were acquired by General Electric.

Some sources date the start of the Meriden Cutlery Company as 1834 or 1835, which, if correct, would challenge its claim to being the first manufacturer of cutlery in America. J. B. Himsworth, in *The Story of Cutlery,* asserts that the John Russell Company in Greenfield, Massachusetts, started in 1834,[5] and *Kanes First Facts* dates that start as even earlier, in 1833.

Other pioneers, according to Himsworth, include Empire Knife Company, Miller Brothers, Southington Cutlery Company, and William Rogers Manufacturing Company, all of Connecticut. Pocketknives and razors were among the most important products of the early factories. In Toledo the Clauss Shear Company specialized in bread knives and scissors, and by 1890 South Milwaukee had an important producer, the Hatch Cutlery Company.

"Cutlery made in North America...closely resembled that produced in England," writes Himsworth, himself a Sheffield Englishman. "One notable exception was the Bowie knife, the only nineteenth-century knife of a truly American origin....

"Sheffield's great influence upon the trend of American cutlery is evidenced by the fact that manufacturers in Connecticut found it worthwhile, as early as 1849, to employ craftsmen from Sheffield who specialized in different processes."[6] He relates the experiences of a Sheffield man named Roberts, employed at the Waterville Company in Waterbury, Connecticut, who had written to England in 1849. Roberts mentioned that his son James, working with him, had re-

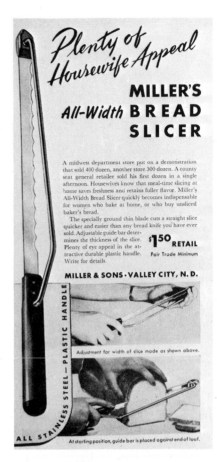

Plenty of Housewife Appeal

MILLER'S All-Width BREAD SLICER

A midwest department store put on a demonstration that sold 400 dozen, another store 300 dozen. A county seat general retailer sold his first dozen in a single afternoon. Housewives know that meal-time slicing at home saves freshness and retains fuller flavor. Miller's All-Width Bread Slicer quickly becomes indispensable for women who bake at home, or who buy unsliced baker's bread.

The specially ground thin blade cuts a straight slice quicker and easier than any bread knife you have ever sold. Adjustable guide bar determines the thickness of the slice. Plenty of eye appeal in the attractive durable plastic handle. Write for details.

$1.50 RETAIL Fair Trade Minimum

MILLER & SONS · VALLEY CITY, N. D.

ALL STAINLESS STEEL — PLASTIC HANDLE

Adjustment for width of slice made as shown above.

At starting position, guide bar is placed against end of loaf.

309

In 1946 Miller's bread slicer delivered all widths with "plenty of housewife appeal."

Courtesy House Furnishing Review.

Throughout history open air vendors sold a variety of "bargains" in stalls or from carts. This picture shows a lower East Side New York cutlery vendor preparing his display. Note the price: seven cents each. The photo dates from the 1930s.

The Bettmann Archive.

cently injured his hand under a stamp, or mechanical hammer, that cut pocket knife springs at one stroke. It is noteworthy that American cutlers used the drop hammer in the middle of the nineteenth century, although their industry had only been established for a few years. This early use of machinery was probably much in advance of the general practice in Sheffield. In his letter Roberts noted that although wages had not improved in England, in Connecticut he was earning seven dollars a week, and that if his daughter could obtain work whetting knives she would get about four dollars a week.

But things changed in February 1852, Roberts later wrote, when "the firm told the Sheffield workpeople that they must supply all their own files and tools or 'go about their business.' " [7] As a result sixteen of them decided to form a new firm, the New York Knife Company of Walden, in Orange County, New York. It lasted into the 1920s.

Ontario Knife Company

Meanwhile, far upstate New York in the little town of Naples (Ontario county), the Ontario Knife Company had been founded in 1889. Although the founder is not known, three men, William B. Ensworth, William Maudsley, and Charles Albert Brace, all related by marriage, were in the picture right from the start. Production depended upon a grindstone operated by waterpower; and when a supply of knives had been built up, the makers would take off through the countryside and sell them. They prospered and seven years later acquired a larger building—an old sawmill—near Franklinville, to which they moved.

In 1900 two Franklinville men, Royal S. Litchfield, a banker, and Will N. Sill, a business leader, joined the company. In 1902 the Ontario Knife Company was incorporated.

The words "Ontario" and "Empire" have been curiously tied to this cutlery firm. A company history relates:

> The Empire State Cutlery Company had started operations twenty-five miles away in Allegany; and in 1904, Walter L. Burritt, head of Empire, and his father, J. L. Burritt, purchased the interests of the original Ontario Knife Company stockholders, combining the two operations in Franklinville in 1905, still under the Ontario Knife Company name. The Burritts remained in control until 1923...In the Fall of 1905 they undertook a substantial building program under a two-way community arrangement....

Increased use of mechanical equipment in the industry had been replacing costlier hand labor and that fact along with the serious impact of the depression, loosed a flood of cheap cutlery in the industry. James A. Chrestensen, then president of the company and the man who initiated its well-known "Old Hickory" brand, "instituted a firm policy of 'quality or else.' Nobody liked to think what 'else' might be, but clearly it could not be good....Ontario worked out a strict policy with quality manufacturing as its aim...It was a

Royal Brand's "jeweltone" tableware handles were made of Catalin, one of the very first plastic materials to be used for cutlery handles. It was introduced in the late 1920s by Sta-Brite Cutlery Company.

Courtesy House Furnishing Review.

daring step…but the policy held…and before long its beneficial results were apparent."

Commenting on developments in the industry, W. J. Hunter, sales vice-president of Ontario, noted: "The age of specialization probably came to the cutlery industry later than to most industries. With the passing…of old time forgers, cutlers, grinders, etc., machinery was developed not only to cut costs, but also to do the jobs no young fellows wanted…." Mr. Hunter went on to say that cutlery firms would have to continue the trend toward specialization to remain in business.

Since 1966 Ontario has specialized in supplying machetes and knives used in service kitchens to the United States government as well as catering to large rack jobbers and hardware wholesalers. In 1967 the company was purchased by Servotronics Incorporated, Buffalo, New York, which has since also acquired the Queen Cutlery, Company, Titusville, Pennsylvania.

Kaylan cutlery offered the "art and skill" of the old masters with its saber-ground edge and other features.

Courtesy House Furnishing Review.

311

ATTRACTING ATTENTION ABROAD

"American hardware and tools had evolved patterns possessing the lightness, grace and handiness that characterized our agricultural implements and they were produced by similar methods," writer Victor S. Clark in his notable *History of Manufactures in the United States* (volume two, dealing with the period from 1860 to 1914). He continues,

these qualities created a demand for them abroad…as they had even before the Civil War….

Although a prejudice existed in favor of English steel for cutlery and the higher grade of tools, American makers shipped sufficient goods of this kind to Great Britain to attract attention there. The British Commissioner at the Centennial Exhibition in 1876, rated American edge tools and miscellaneous hand tools above those exhibited by any other country. He spoke highly of American cutlery….

In 1878 a British authority ascribed the growing demand for American cutlery in foreign markets where British makers previously had a monopoly, not to its cheapness, for it was dearer than Sheffield goods, but to its superior shape and finish. Improvements in machinery and processes steadily reduced the cost of manufacturing in the United States. Solid-handled steel table knives which sold for $5 a dozen in 1867, were priced at one-fourth that sum five years later. Machinery was used for many processes in the manufacture of such articles where hand work was still employed in Great Britain.

At this time American makers manufactured very cheap goods as well as those of better quality, competing successfully in the field that later was occupied largely by German manufacturers. Cast-iron scissors and cast-iron razors were made in this country and served their purpose excellently—at least for a time. Some Connecticut establishments reckoned this cast-iron cutlery among their most important products. These were not combined cast-iron and steel articles which were considered superior to forged steel goods and which had the steel inner-blade cemented on each plate—a pair of scissors, for instance—by the fusion of the iron when it was poured into the mould; but the tools were made entirely of cast iron similar to that used in malleable castings….American pocket-knife manufactories remained throughout this period small village industries, located on water powers and, for the most part, organized on a cooperative basis.[8]

Why close the door
TO THE KITCHEN?

Consider the cook. She's a customer at your counters every day. She is Mrs. Average, at heart a good housekeeper. It's easy to sell her "Stainless."

Why be satisfied with a single sale, when this same woman who demands the enduring beauty of "Stainless" for her dining room is required to work out recipes with ugly, corroded pots and rusted tools... utensils which she rubs and rubs and can't get clean?... Suggest a "Stainless" kitchen and she'll replace this equipment.

Stainless Steel means leisure for the cook. Its market is measured by the number of your customers' kitchens... Write for our booklet "Stainless in the Home"... It points the way to profit.

Genuine Stainless Steel is manufactured only under the *patents* of AMERICAN STAINLESS STEEL COMPANY, Commonwealth Building, Pittsburgh, Penna.

STAINLESS
STEEL

Stainless steel first introduced about 1921 emancipated homemakers from the tedious cleaning of carbon steel knives and forks. It was initially used in the hotel and restaurant field.

Courtesy House Furnishing Review.

There was a period around the turn of the century when tin-plated knives, forks, and spoons were an important item in the flatware business, especially in New York City. The thousands of European immigrants pouring in could afford little better. Lalance and Grosjean, the cookware manufacturer, and R. Wallace and Son were major producers of such flatware. The slightly more affluent bought silver-plated tin flatware.

Another type of flatware, now all but forgotten but sold in quantity both in Europe and America, was known colloquially as "bareback," and in the industry as "alpacca." Also called German silver or nickel silver, this ware, which was unplated, consisted of an alloy containing 18 percent nickel, 63 percent copper, and 19 percent zinc.

The Advent of Stainless Steel

For years all knives had been made of carbon steel. Such steel (except much later when chrome was added) had to have at least sixty points of carbon to give it the necessary hardening and tempering qualities. (World War II technology produced steels containing as much as 120 points of carbon that gave edge-holding qualities and toughness never before available. The higher percentage of carbon in steel improved its wearing qualities but made it more difficult to fabricate.)

But against the advantages of carbon steel stood the inescapable disadvantage of discoloring and rusting. Cleaning carbon steel knives and forks was once an endless chore for homemakers, who spent hours rubbing the blades with a cork and scouring powder or steel wool in the hope of restoring some semblance of brightness.

Then came the great emancipation—the development of stainless steel. As early as 1820 a Frenchman named Berthier had noted the rust resistance of such an alloy during his experiments. But it was nearly one hundred years until, before World War I, the Brearley process, which combined thirty-five-point carbon steel with chromium, was patented and stainless steel cutlery was born.

"It would be difficult to say just who should be credited with being the first manufacturer of stainless flatware in this country," John B. Stevens, president of International Silver Company of Meriden, Connecticut, wrote in 1971.

"I believe our company was first, but this might be disputed. [In 1921 knives with stainless steel blades were introduced in the Ambassador pattern in the "1847" Rogers Brothers silverplate line.] As far as I know the United States was well ahead of Europe in producing it first. Initially the hotel and restaurant field offered the most promising market. Certainly we were the first to market stainless steel on any significant basis."

International very early played an important technological role in developing stainless steel. It had supplied one of the country's largest hotels with a complete new silverplate service, whose knives had stainless steel blades of a formula supplied by the hotel, but

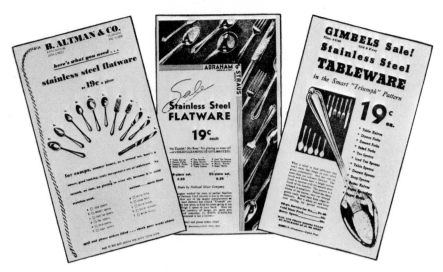

"No tarnish! No rust! No plating to wear off—it's solid gleaming stainless steel." By 1939 these newspaper advertisements for Altman, Abraham & Strauss, and Gimbel's in New York were promoting stainless steel flatware at nineteen cents each.
Courtesy House Furnishing Review.

which soon broke in service. Thereupon International's chief metallurgist, Dr. Birger Egeberg, who had earlier questioned the hotel's specifications, developed a new formula trademarked "Hold Edge," which solved the problem and was soon used, with permission, by other manufacturers.

On another occasion International pioneered a process for hardening stainless steel at such high temperatures that veterans in the business insisted it would not work; they were certain that the continuous belt and other moving parts of the manufacturing equipment would disintegrate. Yet two decades after the first furnace in International's cutlery factory in Florence, Massachusetts, was put into use, thousands of others were in operation around the country.

As stainless steels were improved and manufacturing techniques were perfected, this flatware would become a formidable contender for silver's long-held position of prestige in the field.

Business for Housewares Departments

Housewares departments had long enjoyed a share of the cutlery and flatware business, but they seldom garnered much of the silver or silver-plated flatware sales, since such merchandise was usually confined to the jewelry or silverware department. The arrival of stainless steel flatware suddenly opened up new business for housewares departments—and also for the traditional silver flatware manufacturers when they finally "discovered" these departments.

Typical is the experience of Oneida, Limited. Oneida and International Silver Company are the two largest manufacturers of stainless steel flatware. Established in Oneida, New York, in 1848, these silversmiths had long distributed their merchandise entirely through jewelry stores and silverware departments. By the mid 1950s, how-

From top: In the early 1930s, American Stainless Steel Company ran advertisements like these to help develop trade acceptance for the new metal. Waterproof and crackproof handles in the bottom photo were an important selling point for Samson Cutlery in 1929.
Courtesy House Furnishing Review.

313

Samuel E. Bernstein,
founder of the
National Silver Company.

ever, as the popularity of stainless steel began to mushroom, Oneida and others came to recognize that the housewares rather than the silverware department was the logical place for this new flatware.

"Our stainless flatware sales were initially successful because of our long-established position and merchandising knowhow," Harold E. Johnston, manager of Oneida's new market development, explained in 1971. "But our real success came when we realized the traffic potential of housewares stores and departments."

Having always sold only through distributors, Oneida thereupon set up housewares distributors for its stainless lines. "This association between us and the distributors proved to be a happy marriage," Johnston said. "We had a lot to offer including a national advertising campaign....In return, the housewares distributors taught Oneida a whole new approach to selling. We not only accepted it, we improved on it by investing hundreds of thousands of dollars in the Tabletop Fashion Shop displays, creating a shop-within-a-shop concept."

Although Oneida had made numerous additions to its stainless steel production facilities, Johnston explained, for the most part they were devoted to its high-quality lines. Meanwhile the company, realizing its weakness in the less-expensive and promotional type of stainless flatware, turned in 1968 to Japan, where it contracted for "a large share" of the available production facilities. Oneida has a successful import program, although the company's name is not used on the lower-quality imports.

The National Silver Story

One firm that had long been in the cutlery business and that played a significant role in helping housewares departments develop a large share of the stainless steel flatware volume is the National Silver Company of New York. It traces its beginning to 1890 when a young immigrant, Samuel E. Bernstein, landed in New York and soon became engaged in a small retail house furnishings business. By 1900 he had become a jobber specializing in cutlery, mostly of the tin-plated variety, but including imported pocketknives—something every man then carried—and straight razors.

As the business grew he imported steak knives with white celluloid handles from England, Sabatier-type cutlery from France, and various types of lead-bolstered kitchen cutlery from Solingen, Germany.

By 1912 two of his sons, Morton and Milton, were active in the business, and Morton was placed in charge of a small plant on Broome Street in New York, which began making carving sets with the popular staghorn, bone, horn, and pearl handles as well as other items. Obviously influenced by the name of the silverware giant, the newcomer became the National Silver Company.

Meanwhile Samuel Bernstein—by now the company was Samuel E. Bernstein, Incorporated—was also buying cutlery from various

314

Oneida offered stainless steel "beauty in the early American tradition," and utility in the tradition of modern American technology. A 1959 consumer advertisement.

domestic sources to promote under his own trademark, "Royal Brand Cutlery." It included a wide range of products bought from other firms, such as the American Cutlery Company of Chicago, the Cuba Knife Company of upstate New York, the Knickerbocker Cutlery Company—now United States Cutlery Company—of Belleville, New Jersey, the Ontario Knife Company of Franklinville, New York, and also the Goodell Company of Antrim, New Hampshire.

By the end of World War I Samuel E. Bernstein, Incorporated, was probably the largest wholesaler of cutlery and flatware in the country. Its closest competitor, the J. Busch Federal Cutlery Company, was acquired by Bernstein in 1938.

In 1971 Milton Bernstein, president of the National Silver Company, with which the wholesale operation was merged in 1928, related further details of the company's growth during an interview in New York City:

From 1915 to 1925 my father purchased all our silver-plated flatware from International Silver Company, W. A. Rogers, Oneida Silversmiths, and R. Wallace and Son. For a period of years the entire output of the Robinson Knife Company of Springville, New York, was made for us under the "Royal Brand Cutlery" trademark. Washington Forge, Incorporated, of Englishtown, New Jersey, was formerly Englishtown Cutlery, and from its inception was financed by Samuel E. Bernstein, Incorporated.

In Muncie, Indiana, in the early 1920s the Ontario Manufacturing Company produced flatware for just three customers—Sears, Roebuck and Company, J. Busch, and Samuel E. Bernstein, Incorporated. Later, when Ontario lost the Sears business, we became the sole customer. [Ontario Manufacturing at this time was characterized by *Fortune* as being a formidable rival of International in the inexpensive silverware field.] Our relationship continued for many years, and in 1948 we acquired control of Ontario by buying an 85 percent stock interest.

In 1925 a cousin of Samuel Bernstein, Dr. Samuel Rubin, a metallurgist and inventor, perfected a process for chrome-plating nickel silver flatware. By that time, of course, stainless steel flatware had begun to appear on the market. But it was relatively costly, still pro-

The impact of mass merchandising in marketing cutlery is clearly reflected in the growing use of the attractively card-mounted pieces featured in pegboard displays like these Oneida blister-pack units of stainless flatware.

315

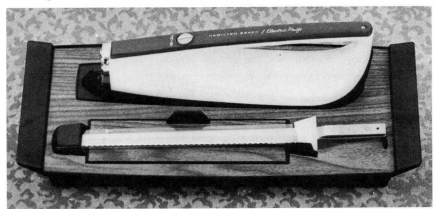

In 1964 Hamilton Beach decided to cut itself a slice of the exploding electric slicer market and introduced a distinctively designed "knife with the hole in the handle." It was directed to the male gift market.

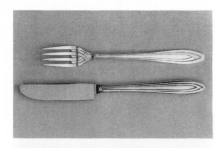

From top: The so-called "Viande"—French for meat—knife, was the very appropriate name given by its designer, the architect Eliel Saarinen. He designed it for a 1929 exhibition of contemporary American design, and it was produced by the International Silver Company. His design achieved great popularity. Graham Kerr, "the Galloping Gourmet," introduced this group of cutlery (in the lower photo) in 1969, "each item of which is designed to do a specific job, and which it does particularly well." The eleven-piece set retailed for $114.

duced only in limited quantities, and the public had not yet learned to appreciate it. However, by then chrome-plating was already well known and accepted. As a result the new flatware was an immediate and tremendous success. Millions of pieces were sold at ten cents to nineteen cents each in the variety chains and housewares departments. But within a few years stainless steel flatware overtook it and the era of chrome-plated flatware came to an end.

In 1931 the company severed its relations with the Englishtown Cutlery Company and began a flatware assembling operation of its own in Brooklyn. Production was devoted mainly to Catalin-handled flatware. Catalin, one of the very first plastics to be used for cutlery handles, had a lovely jewel-like luster and translucency when new. But with use it soon dulled, and hot water often caused it to crack. Nevertheless, its color and novelty gave it great appeal, and for several years it enjoyed wide popularity.

The Sta-Brite Cutlery Company of New Haven, Connecticut, later acquired by Ekco Housewares, Incorporated, is generally credited with being the first to introduce Catalin. Federal Cutlery also used it early. But at this time Sta-Brite and Federal Cutlery both discontinued it, and Bernstein's Royal Brand Cutlery dominated. Meanwhile the new Brooklyn operation had expanded until it employed over five hundred persons.

At this time the company, working in collaboration with the plastics molding division of the Bakelite Company in Bound Brook, New Jersey, introduced cutlery with bakelite handles. For the first time customers could have a choice of handles in pastel colors, two-tone combinations of opaque and transparent colors, and other novelties. Even a simulated staghorn handle was developed, and is still in use by some companies.

By 1935 the National Silver Company was also producing stainless steel flatware in its Brooklyn operation and in the Ontario Manufacturing Company plant in Indiana, which at the time employed nearly six hundred persons. Meanwhile it acquired the F. B. Rogers Silver Company in Taunton, Massachusetts, which had been established in 1883, and in 1945 it bought the Santa Anita Potteries in Los Angeles, which it operated until 1958.

In 1954 the Brooklyn flatware and cutlery manufacturing operations were moved into a single modern plant in New Bedford, Massachusetts. Beset with labor difficulties, it closed after one year. The company had already been experimenting with having flatware made in Japan, and from then on it discontinued all manufacturing operations in the United States. National contributed significantly to the postwar development of Japan's flatware industry and became one of the largest importers of this merchandise from the Far East and Europe.

National Silver, as well as other cutlery firms, found much to be gained by importing high-quality, low-cost items. But, as was to be expected with any large-unit import, problems started to develop.

Flatware Imports

While America has always imported cutlery in some quantity, no previous importations had the same impact or cut more deeply into its own market than did the imports from Japan of stainless steel flatware starting after World War II.

Sensing the potential for developing a new source for this merchandise, American flatware importers were quick to start placing orders in Japan as it began its postwar recovery. Morton Bernstein, chairman of the National Silver Company, is said to have been the first American importer to arrive in Tsubame City, center of Japan's flatware industry, after World War II in 1950.

But besides opening a new flatware source, American importers and manufacturers opened a Pandora's Box of problems which, in 1972, are still not fully resolved, if indeed they ever will be. They found that Japan was not only able to provide stainless steel flatware at remarkably low prices, but also merchandise of exceptional quality at those prices. As in the case of other industries, Japan learned early that quality was the key to its future success in the world's marketplace.

United States imports of Japanese stainless steel flatware soared and in 1957 reached the then unprecedented peak of 10.9 million dozen pieces; yet that figure was dwarfed in 1968 when imports were over 14 million dozen pieces.

In 1959 the Stainless Steel Flatware Manufacturers Association of the United States appealed to the government for relief, and President Eisenhower imposed increased duties on imports in excess of the quota of 5.75 million dozen pieces. Those restrictions expired in 1967, whereupon Japanese flatware imports again zoomed upwards.

In the three years after January 1, 1967, American manufacturers, prompted by the growing market potential, invested more in production facilities than they had done in all previous seven years. But as imports increased their sales of flatware decreased; moreover wage and other costs were going up and serious excess capacity developed. In 1967 profits of American flatware production were at an all time high of about 10.7 percent of sales; but by 1969 they were down to 4.4 percent.

Additionally, retailers and buying groups were now importing flatware directly from the Far East. And by 1969 at least ten United States manufacturers were also buying some of their merchandise there. Several—like International Silver Company in Taiwan—were readying to start overseas production.

In April 1969 the Stainless Steel Flatware Manufacturers Association petitioned President Nixon to reimpose the tariff rate quota on stainless flatware that had expired in October 1967, on the basis of Article 28 of GATT (General Agreement on Tariffs and Trade). This provides that any signatory nation may notify other signatories regarding a specific product on which it wishes to renegotiate a previously agreed tariff. This action may be exercised every three years and 1969 was an "open season" year.

The seventy-seven signatories were apprised in September 1969 of our desire to renegotiate tariff agreements on all stainless steel flatware valued at three dollars and less per dozen and not exceeding 10.3 inches in length. By proclamation decree on August 21, 1971, a new tariff-rate quota, effective for five years, was imposed, effective on October 1, 1971.

The new ruling provides that a total of 16.2 million dozens of stainless flatware can enter this country annually at the GATT concession rate. Each of the supplying countries are allocated a pro rata share based on the average of their 1968-1969 participation. The annual quota is to be controlled by a quarterly tabulation in order to more evenly distribute the quantities over a twelve-month period.

Under that arrangement, quota-type merchandise could enter the United States in any quarter in excess of the allocated quota amounts; but if and when that occurs, the duty rate is automatically increased not to exceed the statutory or 1930 tariff rates.

The fourth quarter of 1971 was the first full quota period experience the industry had under the revised rules. During that period merchandise from Japan, Taiwan, and Korea exceeded the agreed quota limits. But none of the other countries, including Hong Kong, filled its quota.

Kitchen Tools

Kitchen tools, kitchen cutlery, call them what you will, trace their origin back to the most simple items, many of which were often made of wood. For years wooden spoon sets, often hand-carved, along with potato mashers, were imported from Europe by the thousands. Gradually, makers of the basic kitchen or paring knife began to add other items in metal: a pancake turner, a spoon, a fork, a spatula, an egg beater, and so on.

It was a relatively simple business to get into and many small, local manufacturers were attracted to it. Some of them, such as the A & J Manufacturing Company in Binghampton, New York, which started in 1909, eventually developed a sizeable national business, especially with the chain stores. By 1929 A & J had become so successful that it was acquired by Ekco Housewares Company of Chicago, now one of the largest producers of kitchen tools.

At first kitchen tools were made of tin plate. Later they were nickel-plated, then chrome-plated and eventually made of stainless steel. As in the case of flatware, handles of kitchen tools have always been important. Originally of enameled wood, it was a common deficiency for the paint to peel and wear off and the handles to crack. In 1929 the Samson Cutlery Company of Rochester, now out of business, introduced "waterproof and crackproof handles" on a line of stainless steel kitchen tools. Soon, plastic handles began to appear

NEW DREAM CREAM WHIP

THE FASTEST SELLING CREAM WHIP

EVERY ONE SOLD SELLS ANOTHER

The DREAM Cream Whip with the UTILITY Glass Bowl makes a wonderful combination. Whips in half a minute—cannot get out of order. REAL PROFIT for the dealer on this BEST SELLING Whip. Fully Guaranteed.

KOHLER DIE & SPECIALTY CO.
Box B B   DE KALB, ILLINOIS

PATENT LEMON SQUEEZERS AND EGG BEATERS.

Patent "Standard" Egg Beater.

Two basic kitchen tools, the dream cream whip of 1926, and the classic "Standard" egg beater of an earlier period. Both are still very much with us.

Top, courtesy House Furnishing Review.

and while the early ones left something to be desired, they later became extremely practical and colorful and decorative as well.

By the 1950s the all-plastic kitchen tool began to appear. Now such tools, primarily of nylon, have been developed in design and color to an extent once never imagined.

Ekco Kitchen Cutlery

No one has contributed more to the development of kitchen cutlery or is more important in that business than the Ekco Housewares Company, although it didn't start out that way. It all began in October 1881, when a serious-minded, ambitious young man of eighteen named Edward Katzinger arrived at the port of New York from his Austrian homeland.

Already a competent journeyman tinsmith who had learned his trade in Budapest while attending a night school of technology, he soon landed a job. Seven years later, by then a master mechanic and already earning twenty-five dollars a week—important money in those days—he decided his future lay in Chicago. And so, on December 15, 1888, this twenty-five-year-old entrepreneur leased half a store at the corner of Des Plaines and Van Buren Streets and founded the Edward Katzinger Company. Its business: tin pans for commercial bakeries. The Ekco Housewares Company, a name derived from the initials of its founder, was on its way to becoming the largest manufacturer of non-electric housewares anywhere.

Edward Katzinger, who founded Ekco in 1888, and Arthur Keating, his son and former board chairman of Ekco products.

319

In 1946, Ekco introduced the first top quality stainless steel kitchen tools with bakelite handles called the Flint 1900 line. This particular set is popular with school home economics departments.

Today it is a subsidiary of the American Home Products Corporation, which acquired it in 1965. In that year, the last for which separate figures are available, Ekco's sales were $130 million. And it had always pointed with pride to the fact that every year since its founding in 1889 it had operated at a profit. While that may still be the case, there is no way of knowing since the parent company does not reveal figures of its subsidiaries. But well-informed trade sources in 1971 estimated that by then the company's sales were "well above $160 million."

The history of Ekco falls broadly in two parts. Until the 1920s its operations were devoted almost exclusively to producing baking pans for commercial bakeries.

Starting in the middle twenties, when Edward Katzinger's twenty-nine-year-old son Arthur was already actively associated in the business, the company began to turn its attention to housewares. Acquisition of the A and J Manufacturing Company of Binghamton, New York, then the largest producer of kitchen tools, put Ekco in that business in 1929.

From then on, as the accompanying chronology shows, expansion was constant and rapid, and is believed to constitute something of a record for corporate acquisitions in the housewares field.

The elder Katzinger died in 1939, and his son, who meanwhile had changed his name to Keating, became president. Before his death in 1967 he negotiated the sale of Ekco to American Home Products Company.

320

Important Events in the History of the Ekco Housewares Company

1888—Edward Katzinger founded a company to produce commercial baking pans in Chicago, on December 15, in a store at Des Plaines and Van Buren streets.

1892—Moved to larger quarters at 369 South Halsted Street.

1899—Moved to larger quarters again on Washington Boulevard between Union and Halsted streets.

1903—Became Edward Katzinger Company, Incorporated.

1906—Built a five-story building at 120 North Peoria Street.

1913—Built a seven-story concrete building directly behind the Peoria Street building.

1916—Arthur, Edward Katzinger's son, joined the company. He later changed his name to Arthur Keating and eventually became chairman of the corporation. He died December 12, 1967.

1923—Built a large, two-story factory with latest modern equipment on a seventeen-acre site at Cicero and Armitage avenues, Chicago. Began first production and sale of consumer products—a line of bread and cake pans.

1927—Aquired August Maag Company of Baltimore, a producer of commercial baking ware, established before the Katzinger business. Plant replaced with a duplicate of the new Chicago factory in Baltimore. Operations later moved to Chicago; plant and property sold.

1929—Acquired A and J Manufacturing Company of Binghamton, New York, manufacturer of kitchen tools. In 1931 it was moved into an addition to the Chicago plant.

1934—Acquired Geneva Cutlery Company of Geneva, New York, through a company-formed subsidiary, Geneva Forge, Incorporated. In 1958 production was moved to the Canton, Ohio, plant and the old facilities were leased out.

1937—Formed a subsidiary in England under the British Companies Act called Platers and Stampers, Limited. Subsequently, P and S acquired R. E. Collingwood and Sons, Limited (now called Colly Products, Limited), and Champion, Limited. These companies manufacture the same general type of housewares made by Ekco Housewares Company, Incorporated.

Opposite page: A gallimaufry of kitchen items, accessories, and gadgets lend bright color as well as utility to the contemporary American kitchen. From can openers and juicers to special purpose knives, measuring cups, and spatulas, the range is wide in its consumer appeal.

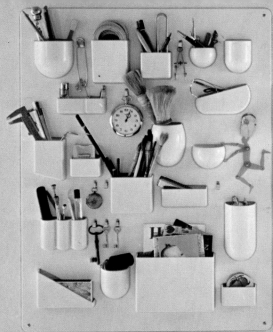

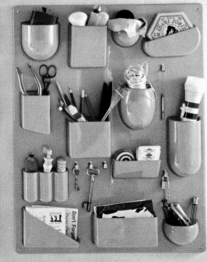

CARRIER COOK KNIFE
BY BUTLER OF SHEFFIELD

CARRIER COOK KNIFE
BY BUTLER OF SHEFFIELD

From top: An Ekco celebration of cutlery...a variety of lines, knives for every purpose. Also, Ekco's famous "Best" food mixer. Standing in the rear is Ekco's contemporary "Extra Sturdy" model.

1939—Edward Katzinger died.

1943—Acquired Sta-Brite Products Corporation of New Haven, Connecticut, manufacturers of stainless steel flatware. Sta-Brite was dissolved; its equipment and property were moved to a Maryland subsidiary, then were moved to the company's Byesville, Ohio, plant in 1948.

1945—Changed name to Ekco Products Company.

Acquired the E. L. Tebbets Spool Company, Incorporated, of Locke Mills, Maine, to produce wooden handles and rolling pins. Now Ekco Wood Products Company. Original plant was destroyed by fire in 1950, but was rebuilt the following year.

Acquired Massillon Aluminum Company of Massillon, Ohio, manufacturers of cooking utensils. Massillon was dissolved in 1948 and is now a division of the company, producing aluminum, stainless steel, and copper-bottomed cookware and tin-coated bakeware.

1946—Acquired the physical assets of Murdock Metal Products, Incorporated, of Chicago, manufacturers of kitchen utensil specialties, in 1947 and transferred operations to Ekco's Chicago plant.

1947—Acquired Byesville Products Company of Byesville, Ohio. It now produces stamped stainless steel tableware, die-cast bathroom fixtures, and other items.

Ekco Products Company, Limited, established in 1947 in Toronto, to produce some of the products made by the parent company in the United States.

Organized a house-to-house selling organization called Prudential Housewares, Incorporated, known today as Ekco Home Products and located in Milwaukee. It sells high-quality cookware, cutlery, and fine china.

1948—Acquired controlling interest in Alumino Ekco S. A., which was Mexico's largest manufacturer of cookware and aluminum utensils. An outright purchase of remaining stock was made in 1954. Today this company is the largest housewares manufacturer in Mexico.

Acquired Bergen Forge Company of Bergen, New Jersey, manufacturer of one-piece flatware knives. This plant burned down and production was switched to the Diamond Silversmith plant, which was acquired later.

1949—Acquired Diamond Silver Company, Lambertville, New Jersey, manufacturers of stainless steel, silverplate, and sterling silver flatware. Its name was changed to Diamond Silversmiths, Limited, and operations were moved to the Geneva, New York, plant. Later they were moved to Byesville, Ohio, plant.

Organized National Glaco Chemical Corporation of Chicago as a subsidiary company. The "Glazon" process is a technical development for treating and coating commercial baking pans to eliminate the need for greasing them. It has fifteen such plants around the country and in Chicago.

1951—Acquired the Minute Mop Company of Chicago, along with its Canadian subsidiary, a pioneer in the development of cellulose sponge mops. Discontinued this line and transferred the production to the English plant.

1952—Purchased Republic Stamping and Enameling Company of Canton, Ohio, manufacturers of enamelware. Line was discontinued and Ovenex Bakeware production was shifted to Chicago plant.

1954—Acquired Adams Plastics Company, Incorporated, of Holyoke, Massachusetts, makers of plastic handles, laminated wood handles, and the exclusive Ekco "Pakkawood" handle.

Acquired the Autoyre Company of Oakville, Connecticut, world's largest manufacturer of stamped and polished bathroom fittings. Operation was moved to the Chicago plant in 1956.

Purchased McClintock Manufacturing Company Division of Whittier, California, manufacturers of aluminum food-handling equipment for meat and supermarkets as well as baking pans and aluminum foil containers.

1955—Acquired Plastics Division of Kilgore Manufacturing Company, which made plastic housewares under the trade name of "Shel-Glo." Transferred operations to Adams Plastic Company in Holyoke, Massachusetts.

Acquired Shore Machine Corporation of New York City, manufacturers of ice cream scoops and paddles for the hotel and restaurant trade. Transferred the operation to Ekco's Byesville, Ohio, plant.

1956—Purchased the Kennetrack Corporation, Elkhart, Incorporated, manufacturers of aluminum and steel gliding door hardware and frames, now in Canton, Ohio.

Acquired Ruby Light Company of Los Angeles, California, and Dallas, Texas, makers of industrial fluorescent lighting fixtures. The Los Angeles operation was moved to the Whittier, California plant.

Purchased the Plasteel division of P. R. Mallory Plastic Incorporated, of Chicago, which made plastic bathroom accessories. Production was turned over to Ekco's Autoyre Company.

Formed Ekco-Alcoa Container, Incorporated, of Wheeling, Illinois, on a fifty-fifty basis with the Aluminum Company of America to roll aluminum foil and produce foil containers for commercial use. The company became a wholly owned Ekco subsidiary in 1962 when it bought Alcoa's shares.

1957—Acquired Felco Lighting Company of Dallas, Texas. The Ruby Company's Texas operation was moved into Felco's plant.

Formed the Ekco Engineering Company to handle the manufacture and sales of Ekco baking pans and baking equipment.

Acquired Emro Manufacturing Company, Incorporated, of St. Louis, Missouri, a leading supplier of can piercers and bottle openers to the beverage industry. Made a division of the Autoyre Company, an Ekco subsidiary. Later it was moved to the Chicago factory and became a division of Ekco.

Acquired Worley and Company, major West Coast manufacturer of steel lockers and shelving for industrial and institutional use.

1959—Acquired Davis Rolling Pin Company of Detroit, Michigan, manufacturers of rolling pins, plastics, aluminum, and wooden, as well as cutting boards. Production was moved to the Locke Mills, Maine, plant.

1960—Acquired Washington Steel Company of Pico, California, manufacturers and wholesalers of cabinet and door hardware.

Acquired Engineered Nylon Products, Incorporated, of Elkhart, Indiana, producers of molded nylon and plastics parts. Moved to the Canton, Ohio, plant to become part of Ekco Building Products.

1961—Acquired the Berkeley Products Company of Jersey City, New Jersey, manufacturers of closet accessories, shoe trees, and garment racks. Operation was moved to the Chicago plant in 1962.

1964—The Ekco Housewares Company was formed when all of the corporation's consumer products operations were separated from its commercial and industrial products operations. Its headquarters were set up in Franklin Park, Illinois.

Formed a new division, Ekco Products Import Company—now called Ekco Products International Company—to specialize in the sale of imported stainless steel flatware and related merchandise.

1965—Acquired by American Home Products Corporation, of which it became a division on September 30.

Ekco Building Products Company formed to give separate identity to the builders' hardware operations. The Kennetrack corporation plant was closed in Elkhart, Indiana, and moved to Ekco's Canton, Ohio, plant.

Can Openers Come of Age

The bayonet, which derives from the town of Bayonne, France, was first designed, it is said, to be used not as a weapon but as a can or bottle opener. At any rate the idea of packaging food, somehow or other, originated in France in 1810. Nicholas Appert, seeking to win the twelve-thousand-franc prize offered by Napoleon for a method to pack food safely so his armies could be fed and fight before they starved to death, asked himself, "Why not pack food in bottles, like wine?"

The idea worked and he won. But in England a man named Peter Durand went Appert one better. He packed food in a tin cannister—later shortened to tin can—and got a patent on it. Ever since the path of civilization has been paved with tin cans...all of which have to be opened!

Perhaps it was Durand's doing that later prompted John Galsworthy to write, "The French cook, but we English open tins." At any rate, an Englishman, William Underwood, established the first cannery in America in New Orleans in 1817.

But it wasn't until 1858 that a Connecticut Yankee from Water-

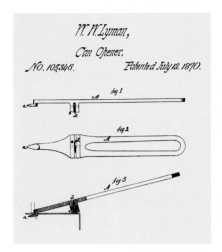

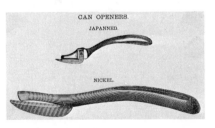

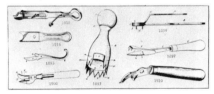

From top: A drawing of the early, classic Lyman can opener of 1870. Next, the Hopper can opener patented in 1896 employed a unique approach. The center pin was used to pierce the center of the can; then the cutting blade, after being adjusted to the edge of the can, was forced around until the top was cut open. Two early eel-like can openers, one "Japanned," the other of nickel. Then, a schematic of basic can openers from 1893 to 1920.

Second from bottom, the Bettmann Archive.

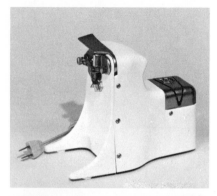

From top: Another classic, the wall-mounted Dazey can opener—"so simple a child can use it." The first electric can opener was made by the Udico Corporation and introduced late in 1956 by Los Angeles department stores. This early model included a knife sharpener. Then, the Klaussen electric can opener, marketed in 1957.

bury named Ezra J. Warner received the first patent to be issued in this country for a can opener. It was a rather forbidding weapon that looked like a combination bayonet and sickle. It was merely the first of a series of even more deadly-looking devices with which Americans would open their cans for the next several decades...or at least try to.

Although there were some exceptions, the design and development of can openers lagged. Then, in 1925, a Swedish-born inventor in Burlington, Vermont, named H. J. Edlund, developed what was said to be "the first practical institutional can opener." It was so successful that he soon introduced a household version, the "Edlund Jr." which the Edlund Company has continued to sell, practically unchanged ever since.

By the mid-fifties buyers were asking can opener manufacturers, "When are you going to bring out an electric can opener?" It seemed a logical and simple transition merely adding a motor to a wall model opener. But many problems were involved.

"As so often happens in developments of this kind, I wonder if it can be said that any one firm 'pioneered' the electric can opener," Bernard F. Sears, executive vice-president of the Rival Manufacturing Company, Kansas City, Missouri (probably the largest producer of electric can openers) said during an interview in 1969.

"I think it would be impossible to credit—or discredit—anyone who might claim to be the pioneer. We, for example, had a so-called 'bread board model' of an electric can opener in 1946. And in 1955 one of our engineers, A. E. Grant, applied for a patent on an electric opener. [It was granted in 1957; No. 2,806,280.]"

As it happened, two manufacturers in California both introduced electric can openers first in 1956. Klassen Enterprises of Centerville introduced a wall-mounted model on which they applied for a patent on March 26 of that year. It was granted the following April.

In Santa Monica, the Udico Corporation (acquired in 1972 by the Cornwall Corporation of Boston), brought out a combination can opener and knife sharpener, on which it applied for a patent December 4, 1956; it was issued August 4, 1959. Little was heard of the Klassen unit and apparently it failed to develop consumer acceptance. On the other hand the Udico was brought out just in time for Christmas selling and met with immediate success. "Bill Woolston, buyer for the May Company, Los Angeles, really got behind it and, I think, was primarily responsible for putting it across," B. Sherman Green, president of Udico recalled.

At the January 1957 Housewares Show in Chicago, both the Rival Manufacturing Company and the Swing-A-Way Manufacturing Company showed electric can openers. The Swing-A-Way, Model 2100, included a knife sharpener and was mounted on four tapered, tubular legs about eight inches long. It was equipped with an automatic shut-off and was priced at $27.95.

Rival decided to make some changes before marketing theirs

and re-introduced it at the July show as Model 757 which, Bernie Sears reported, drew an excellent response.

Before 1957 was over at least eight other manufacturers of can openers had entered the field with rumors of more to come. There were budget models and deluxe models, table and wall types, automatics and semi-automatics, knife sharpeners, scissor sharpeners—and one even included a pencil sharpener. Amidst a profusion of functions and accessories, the electric can opener had finally "arrived."

Major Highlights In The Development of Household Can Openers

1858—First U. S. patent for a can opener, No. 19,063, dated January 5, issued to Ezra J. Warner of Waterbury, Connecticut.

1870—First can opener to use a cutting wheel instead of a spike or knife blade patented by William W. Lyman. The first significant improvement in can opener design, the basic principle continues to be used on modern can openers.

1925—First can opener with a serrated or toothed can "feed wheel" or gear to rotate the can against the cutting wheel, introduced by the Star Can Opener Company, San Francisco. This was another basic development that made can openers easier to operate.

1930—(Est.)—First wall mounted can opener introduced by Dazey Churn & Manufacturing Company, St. Louis, Missouri, later the Dazey Corporation.

1931—First can opener—called the "Bunker"—to use the concept of "a pair of pliers" or pivoted handles with which to hold the can in one hand while a key-type handle geared to a cutting wheel is turned with the other, introduced by the Bunker Clancey Company, Kansas City, Missouri, a firm acquired by Rival Manufacturing Company, also of Kansas City, in 1938.

First portable electric can opener patent issued to Preston C. West, Chicago, No. 1,834,563 dated December 1. Insofar as is known it was never produced.

1935—First can opener—called the "Smoothcut"—designed with the so-called compound-angled cutting wheel principle which shears cans of different diameter and shapes more uniformly; introduced by the Atlas-Ansonia Company, New Haven, Connecticut, and later acquired by the Regina Corporation, Rahway, New Jersey.

1939—First hand-cranked can opener with "positive single-action"—no separate can-piercing lever—introduced by Vaughan Manufacturing Company, Chicago.

1940—First retractable, wall-bracket mounted can opener, the "Swing-A-Way," permitting it to be swung out of the way to the left or the right, introduced by Steel Products Manufacturing Company (renamed the Swing-A-Way Manufacturing Company in 1948).

1942—First can opener, a wall-type, with a gear-driven mechanism introduced by Steel Products (now Swing-A-Way). In 1955 a pliers-type model with that mechanism was introduced.

1946—First hand-cranked "positive single action" can opener to have its mechanism enclosed in an attractive, "streamlined" casing introduced by Rival Manufacturing Company as the "Can-O-Mat."

1948—First can opener with magnetic lid-lifter introduced on its "Swingmaster" Swing-A-Way model by Steel Products (now Swing-A-Way).

1949—First can opener with a cutting wheel that can readily be removed for cleaning and replaced without tools introduced by Rival Manufacturing Company.

1952—First can opener with a vacuum suction cup base, operated by manipulating a cam lever, which could be positioned for use on either a vertical or horizontal surface introduced by Rival Manufacturing Company.

1956—First electric can openers introduced by two California firms. Klassen Enterprises, Centerville, brought out a wall-mounted model for which a patent was applied March 26, 1956 and issued April 23, 1957 under No. 2,789,345. Udico Corporation, Santa Monica, (now owned by Cornwall Corporation), brought out a combination can opener and knife sharpener for which a patent was applied December 4, 1956 and issued August 4, 1959 under No. 2,897,589.

1957—First combination can opener, food grinder, and ice crusher introduced by the John Oster Manufacturing Company, now Oster Corporation, Milwaukee, Wisconsin.

1962—First electric can opener with specialized push-button controls introduced by the Dazey Corporation (a subsidiary at the time of Landers, Frary & Clark, New Britain, Connecticut). Equipped with three buttons, one for each size can, when

From top: In the early 1930s when wall type can openers began to gain popularity, Edlund made a special bracket so its regular table top opener could be fastened to the wall. Next, the first model of the now well-known "Swing-A-Way" can opener originally introduced in 1936. A neat but rather short-lived idea in electric can openers was this push-button model introduced in 1962 by Dazey. Each button was for a different-size can.

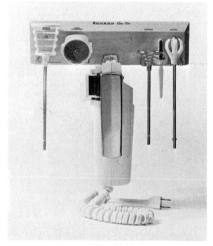

From top: In 1972 the Sunbeam CS 40 was introduced offering an ice crusher. The Ronson Can-Do, the first multipurpose portable electric kitchen appliance. It opens cans, sharpens knives, mixes, blends, mashes, whisks, etc. Looking back from the vantage of today's sophisticated "do-alls" is this selection of 1883 gadgets. Although somewhat primitive in comparison, they attempted to do almost everything that needed doing in that time. Shown are pie sectioners, poppyseed grinders, knife cleaners, and an egg topper.

one of them was pushed the opener started and then stopped automatically when the can top was cut open.

1964—First hand-held, portable electric combination can opener and food mixer, the "Can Do," introduced by the Ronson Corporation, Woodbridge, New Jersey.

1966—First combination can opener and ice crusher combination introduced by Oster.

1968—First combination can opener and juicer introduced by Oster.

1969—First electric can opener with a can-piercing lever that can readily be removed for cleaning and replaced without tools, introduced by Samsonite Corporation (Super Market Division), Denver, Colorado. This patent, No. 3,423,825, later acquired by Rival.

First combination can opener and salad maker introduced by Oster.

1971—First electric can opener designed to cut through the side of a can rather than down through the lid, so that the lid can be re-used as a cover, introduced by Westinghouse Electric Corporation.

(The author acknowledges with thanks the special assistance of Robert L. McLean of the Engineering Department, Rival Manufacturing Company, in this compilation.)

Gadgets: A World of Ingenuity

Scientists, it has been said, are men who prolong life so we will have time to pay for the gadgets they invent. Be that as it may, no other segment of housewares is regarded as more characteristically American or has been the subject of more wisecracks and comments than the never ending parade of products we label as "gadgets."

The word gadget, H. L. Mencken explains in *The American Language,* appears to have come from the French *gachette,* meaning a piece of machinery, in the mid-nineteenth century. The term was long used in England before it became popular in America.

Our American heritage is replete with examples of household devices created by "Yankee ingenuity." This is especially true of New England, where during the latter half of the last century metalworking and mechanical development made remarkable progress on the crest of the industrial revolution.

One man who personified Yankee ingenuity was D. H. Goodell. In 1869 he established the company bearing his name in Antrim, New Hampshire. To this day it is a thriving business, although the nature of its products has changed. Goodell, apparently quite an inventor, was working for the Antrim Shovel Works in 1865 when they decided to sell out to the Oliver Ames Company of Amesbury, Massachusetts. Shortly after the sale, he started making a hand-operated apple peeler he had invented in the old shovel plant.

He soon developed and acquired other items and the business prospered. Before long the original business had expanded to include a wide variety of other devices such as cherry pitters, bean slicers, orange peelers, and seed sowers. A few years later Goodell bought the nearby Woods Cutlery Company, and today commercial and industrial cutlery is the firm's main business.

"The apple peeler and specialty business prospered and remained quite active until about 1950," acording to D. D. Hurlin, current president of the company. "Then the demand diminished until the company was left with just one small household-model apple peeler, of which we still sell about forty thousand a year."

There were other firms, of course, making some sort of "Yankee notions"—as the contraptions of the mechanically minded New Englanders were often called. In fact, for a while most house furnishings other than textiles were called by that name, which today is applied to the "notion department."

Germany, with its long head start in mechanical metalware manufacturing, soon dominated the novelty house furnishings market in America, although it was not until the late 1920s that the term "gadget" was first used for such merchandise. But whether they originated at home or overseas, gadgets of all kinds have always had a particular appeal to Americans—their own intrinsic fascination plus the promise of making homemaking and cooking chores easier. Their attraction is amply shown by their sales success over the years.

"In today's well-managed department-store housewares department, the gadget section usually produces about 6 percent of total sales," according to William F. Mayer, president of the company bearing his name—probably the largest in the gadget business today. Mayer's company took over the G. M. Thurnauer Company in 1968, until then the oldest and largest in the field—and generally credited with being the first to use the term gadget.

"In the old days merchandise of this type was the step-child of the housewares department," Bill Mayer added during an interview. "Small articles of this kind—hand can openers, bottle stoppers, cookie cutters, onion choppers, strainers, and scores of others—were difficult to display and invariably were stored away in drawers and concealed from view. When a customer wanted to buy one of these items she had to ask a salesclerk to find it. The Thurnauer Company helped change all that."

Just what did Thurnauer do? Let's go back to 1881. In that year an industrious young man, Gustav Martin Thurnauer, one of a family of eleven children, arrived in New York from his native Nürnbèrg, Germany. Two years later, at the age of twenty-two, Gustav and one of his brothers opened a small office and loft to launch their business.

"Family friends in New York were already engaged in importing European basketware," recalled Harold Rees during an interview. He became president of Thurnauer's in 1925 and remained in that position until the company was sold to Mayer.

Gustav Thurnauer began by importing toys from Nürnberg, but then he began adding housewares novelties. Gradually, as business increased, he expanded into such things as Viennese and Russian coffeepots, Japanned art candlesticks, baker's tools, molds, and woodenware. Ten years later he had overseas offices not only in Nürnberg but also in Paris and London. He advertised that he had "the most extensive assortment of house furnishing goods at the lowest prices."

Ford Mfg. Co.

Ford's All-in-One-Spoon is a practical combination of twelve useful kitchen utensils, and is the last word in good housekeeping.

It performs twelve different services and does them all perfectly; things that must be done scores of times every day by every housewife, saving her each day many scores of steps that would be wasted in getting and putting back in place the many utensils which this one article so effectively replaces.

The All-In-One-Spoon is made of highly nickel plated one-piece steel and does not corrode, cleans like any spoon and lasts a lifetime.

The manufacturers of this handy and useful device are The Ford Mfg. Co., Inc., of Newark, N. J.

* * * * *

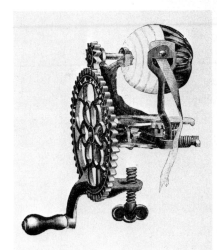

More early American gadgets. From an early Manning-Bowman catalog, a lemon squeezer-nut cracker combination. Next, the Ford All-In-One-Spoon, a "practical combination of twelve useful kitchen utensils...the last word in good housekeeping." In 1914. Then, the Waverly Apple Parer, a standard rural America gadget throughout the late nineteenth century.

Middle, courtesy House Furnishing Review. Bottom, the Bettmann Archive.

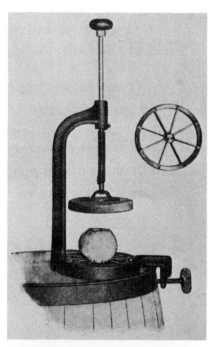

From top: Another rural America stand-by, the Goodell apple slicer dated from the late nineteenth century. The company is still very much in business. American gadgetry called for sales outlets. Michael Barry is shown in one of the Gadget Shops he and his father Myron established. About 1935. A more contemporary gadget outlet, Gimbel's "Gadget World," as seen in their New York store.

Middle, courtesy House Furnishing Review. Bottom, courtesy Gimbel's, New York.

328

In those days, according to Rees, the firm stocked at least one thousand items of housewares, half of which were in the novelty or specialty category—things that later were called gadgets. At the start he catered to restaurants and institutions as well as to all types of retail stores. No other importer in the country could offer the scope and variety of unusual and unheard-of merchandise that fascinated merchants as much as it did their customers.

To cite a few examples: a "pin pick" feather picker to remove feather stubs from poultry; a poppy-seed grinder; a knife cleaner consisting of a can filled with sand and having a slotted lid through which to slide the knives; a match-striking board; an egg topper to remove the tops of boiled eggs; a vegetable quirler for making "Sarah Bernhardt" potatoes; and a beer "shaver" of hard black rubber for scraping the foam off a mug of beer.

After having occupied several downtown locations in 1918 the firm moved to 6 East 20th Street, near the Fifth Avenue Building, an area that was something of a housewares center. After Mr. Thurnauer's death at the age of sixty-three in 1924, the presidency went to Sidney J. Adler, who had started with the company as a three-dollar-a-week errand boy. He was president for twenty-two years. In 1947 his son-in-law, Harold Rees, previously a bond trader on Wall Street, joined the firm, and he became president when Mr. Adler died.

Since the firm specialized to such a great extent in imports, particularly from Germany, France, and other middle European countries, both world wars had serious effects on its business. But by the outbreak of hostilities in 1914, Thurnauer was so well established with its reserve stocks and new sources of supply in this country that it managed to survive fairly well.

During the twenties "gadgets" emerged not only as a trade (and consumer) term but as an important and thriving classification of housewares. Although there is some doubt just who or what launched the gadget business as it is known today, the best available evidence points to the Barry family—Myron M. Barry, his son Michael, and his daughter Lydia—all active participants in the business known as the Barry Importing Company.

Little is known about the Barrys. It is believed that they came from France, where the elder Barry may have been in the giftware business. Sometime in the twenties he started a business at 1150 Broadway, New York City, and soon he was marketing these little kitchen specialties in a unique manner. He ordered hand-painted display cards about ten inches square to illustrate exactly how each gadget was used. For example, he fastened an actual cake cutter to a card showing a layer cake. These cards were mounted on the wall behind a counter of gadgets or simply displayed on the counter.

What these colorful cards did, of course, was not only to intrigue the passerby, but more important, to communicate the point and purpose of the strange-looking devices and encourage sales. Barry also used another device—he often managed to deal directly with the merchandise office, circumventing the buyer. He offered the cards free, but required, it is said, that stores buy from one to three gross of an item, depending on its size and volume.

The originality of the idea made an instant appeal to top management (although the Barrys hardly endeared themselves to the buyers). The "Gadget Shop" had been born. Within a rather short time housewares departments everywhere had some kind of shop or special display with hundreds of gadgets.

The success Barry enjoyed did not go unnoticed. In September 1934 the Thurnauer Company issued a mimeographed thirty-two-page catalog whose cover carried a three-panel display of checkerboard design, with a gadget shown in each square. According to Harold Rees, the catalog, called "The Gadget House," is one of the few remaining bits of the records of the old firm. It doubtless marks one of the earliest uses of the term gadgets by Thurnauer.

During the thirties two new firms were launched that later would become very successful in the gadget field: the William F. Mayer Company of Yonkers, New York, and the H & P House Furnishing Company of Fair Lawn, New Jersey.

After Myron Barry's death (the date is not known), his son and daughter carried on the business to some extent. Rees believes that the last time they exhibited at a show was in Atlantic City in 1952. Not long afterward he was offered the Barry Importing Company's entire inventory at close-out prices.

"It wasn't until after the war that we entered the gadget business seriously," recalled Bill Mayer in an interview.

> At first we supplied hand-painted cards like those used by Barry and Thurnauer. It was easy to get customers. All we had to do was go to an old Barry account and make a deal to relieve the buyer of all the excess stock with which Barry had loaded him. Of course he was delighted. We added one important ingredient: service. Once Barry sold an account, he seldom had anyone go back to the store. We also introduced a stock control catalog.
>
> The use of the individual hand-painted cards was continued until the introduction of pegboards for store display fixtures, a development that gave the gadget business a tremendous boost. Another big improvement was in packaging. In the thirties we mounted items on printed cards or attached labels. Then came individual polyethylene bags with a header containing the necessary product information. Finally, in the late fifties and early sixties we learned how to blister-pack and shrinkpack these items.

But very often it appears that the sales of gadgets really need no help. Americans, male as well as female, even those who don't aspire to become gourmet cooks, seem to have developed an inherent fondness (or weakness!) for gadgets. And so, with the never ending proliferation of new devices the marketplace continues to offer, the gadget shop has earned a spot of real importance in the housewares hierarchy.

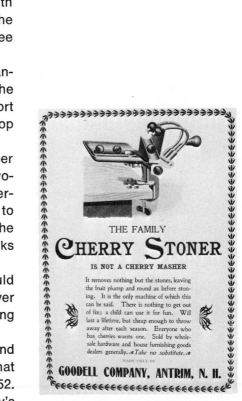

THE FAMILY
CHERRY STONER
IS NOT A CHERRY MASHER

It removes nothing but the stones, leaving the fruit plump and round as before stoning. It is the only machine of which this can be said. There is nothing to get out of fix; a child can use it for fun. Will last a lifetime, but cheap enough to throw away after each season. Everyone who has cherries wants one. Sold by wholesale hardware and house furnishing goods dealers generally. Take no substitute.
MADE ONLY BY
GOODELL COMPANY, ANTRIM, N. H.

329

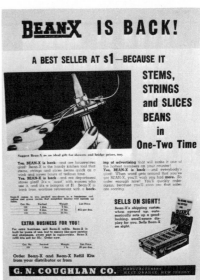

BEAN-X IS BACK!

A BEST SELLER AT $1—BECAUSE IT

STEMS, STRINGS and SLICES BEANS in One-Two Time

EXTRA BUSINESS FOR YOU!

SELLS ON SIGHT!

Order Bean-X and Bean-X Refill Kits from your distributor or from

G. N. COUGHLAN CO. MANUFACTURERS WEST ORANGE, NEW JERSEY

From top: The Goodell Company offered the family "Cherry Stoner" in 1898. (Note: It is not a cherry masher.) As of 1945 this trade advertisement announced that Bean-X is back, from its WW II retirement, and anxious for new markets. About ten million were sold by inventor Gerry N. Coughlan between 1934 and 1967.

Courtesy House Furnishing Review.

The Plastic Parade

No segment of the housewares industry ever got off to such a bad start or tripped over itself so often as plastic housewares. Once an "ugly duckling," plastics have become so important and show such great promise that they are now a darling of the industry. Plastics have been growing at such an unprecedented pace, it's being predicted that by the year 2000 their volume (for all purposes) will exceed that of all other basic materials!

In retrospect it is surprising that the housewares plastics industry performed as well as it did under the circumstances. Few if any new materials were ever so oversold at their inception as plastics. Although the concept of plastics was not new by that time, the developments of the late 1920s and 1930s captured the imagination of many, and presently plastics were being heralded as the wonder material of the century. Moreover, it was freely predicted, not only would virtually everything from clothes to cars soon be made of plastics, but those products would be far superior to anything known.

The glowing publicity allowed people to assume that plastics had the qualities of—or for—almost anything and everything. "Assumptions," it's been said, "are bridges for ignorance." And understandably, the widespread lack of factual knowledge about the early materials—along with the equally widespread lack of experience in molding and using them—afforded endless opportunities for erroneous assumptions to spread.

In the late 1920s and 1930s, as often as not, the raw material producers still didn't know what their materials could—or could not—do, or for what types of end products those materials were best suited. The molders usually knew even less. They were still learning to use plastics.

In such circumstances, it's not surprising the marketplace was flooded with inferior plastic products—sink strainers that curled up when washed in hot water; refrigerator storage boxes that cracked when exposed to cold; trays and containers from which the plasticizer would "migrate" or ooze, leaving them brittle. These were only a few of the problems.

As a result, while plastics may not have been exactly a "dirty word" in the consumer goods marketplace, most of those products had more critics than defenders. It would be an exaggeration to report that every buyer's reaction to the new product was: "Plastics? It's just a bunch of ersatz—and the hell with it!" But the sentiment was there.

"Only the confidence and enthusiasm of the molders—mainly young men in new companies—plus the promotional support of the raw material producers, overcame this early resistance and made plastic housewares the dynamic industry it has come to be," Joseph

331

Opposite page: The twentieth century technology of plastics has created a parade of products in every color used in every room of the home. *This page.* This colonial tin lantern shows the use of one of the earliest forms of plastic in its windows. It was called keratin, or delaminated natural horn.

Above, courtesy Smithsonian Institution.

Opposite page: From a modest beginning and with a mixed history of commercial success, plastics today have met with enthusiastic consumer approval—they not only function well but they decorate beautifully. The opposite page shows an array of contemporary plastics in a variety of colors and materials, from table appointments, highly styled dishes, and attractive storage compartments, to serving pieces. Even champagne is graced by a plastic bucket.

L. Sholkin, president of Beacon Plastics Corporation recalled in 1972. "It is interesting to note that at a housewares show held in 1946 in Atlantic City, there were only two exhibitors in the plastics business, Tupper Plastics Incorporated and us—a far cry from 150 plastic ware exhibitors at the 1972 Chicago show."

While the early problems still seem relatively recent, plastics in the technical sense are easily one hundred or more years old. The industry's first magazine, *Plastics,* in its first issue, March 1926, defined plastics as "any material that by its nature or in its process of manufacture, is at some stage, either through heat or by the presence of a solvent, sufficiently pliable and flowable, in other words, plastic, so that it can be given its final shape by the operation of molding or pressing."

"The earliest [natural] commercial plastics used in this country appears to be albuminoid, called keratin," says DuBois.

> Human hair, fingernails, horses' hoofs and animal horn are composed largely of keratin. Horses' and cows' hoofs, animal horn and tortoiseshell were the principal raw material sources for these first plastics....Although horn was used as a fabricating material from the earliest days of man, there is no record to show when it was first used commercially in this country. Horners and hornsmiths fabricated these natural plastics. Horn windows for lanterns (often dialetically called "lanthorns") were replaced by glass soon after 1740, so that it is obvious that horn plastics were fabricated in the early part of the eighteenth century.[1]

Horn buttons and especially women's combs were among the most important of these early "plastic" products, and Leominster, Massachusetts, became such a center of that industry it came to be called "comb city." Later other materials, especially rubber and gutta-percha, a tree gum imported from the Malay peninsula, came to be used in many plastic formulations and applications.

The first known plastic molder in the United States, says DuBois, was Samuel Peck. He began working with the shellac plastics in 1852 and received his first patent in 1854. He entered into a partnership with Scovill Manufacturing Company, Waterbury, Connecticut, in 1855 under the name of S. Peck & Company, and was bought out by Scovill in 1857.

The history of American plastics as they are known today began in 1868 when a serious shortage of ivory prompted a manufacturer of billiard balls to offer a $10,000 prize for a suitable substitute. A young printer in Albany, New York, named John Wesley Hyatt, succeeded in developing a formula (cellulose nitrate softened with camphor) that did it. He named it "Celluloid" which he registered as a trademark in 1872.

Thereupon he began a small operation called the Hyatt Manufacturing Company to produce billiard balls himself but found his invention suitable for so many other things that eventually the name was changed to the Celluloid Manufacturing Company. A large new plant was established in Newark, New Jersey, in 1873 and by 1890

John Wesley Hyatt, whose invention of celluloid in 1868 is generally regarded as the start of America's plastics industry. At right, Dr. Leo Hendrik Baekeland, the discoverer of bakelite in 1909.

334

From top: An early view of the Celluloid Manufacturing Company in the late 1880s. The first use of plastics for electrical housewares was this General Electric iron in 1925 with a bakelite thumb rest and control knob. The handle was made of wood.

Bottom, courtesy J. H. DuBois.

it had grown to become the American Celluloid and Chemical Corporation. By then, too, "Celluloid" had become a household word in America, and retail counters were well stocked not merely with billiard balls, but with wipe-clean high collars, cuffs, and shirt-fronts for men; combs, hand mirrors, and jewelry for women; as well as dental plates, toys, the first photographic film, and a variety of other things.

In housewares its greatest use was for cutlery handles and millions of knives and forks were produced with Celluloid handles. Celluloid is actually highly flammable, but its utility compared to other materials available during those years was evidently so appealing that the fire hazard was swept aside.

John Hyatt and his brother Isaiah, who had joined him, patented the first injection molding machine in 1872 and the first multi-cavity mold in 1878, equipment that continues to play a vital part in the plastics industry. The American Celluloid and Chemical Corporation was acquired by the Celanese Corporation in 1927.

The Development of Bakelite

The next industry milestone came sixty-eight years later when in 1909, Dr. Leo Hendrick Baekeland in Yonkers, New York, discovered phenolic plastics. He was an eminent research chemist who at thirty-five already had a number of achievements to his credit. He named his new invention "bakelite."

"Dr. Baekeland reported that his hardest job was teaching people to use his new product correctly, avoiding previous habits with shellac and rubber," says DuBois.

> He expected that anyone who understood molding would be able to make a success of Bakelite. He learned the hard way that it is difficult to teach an old dog new tricks. The knowledge of how to mold rubber, shellac or Celluloid in many cases was a block to progress. The older materials were thermoplastic. Bakelite was hardened by heat in the mold and needed high temperatures and high pressures to produce the desired properties...older molders...got bad results... some of the most successful molders of Bakelite were those who had never molded the older plastics. It is interesting to note that the plastics industry repeated this unfortunate stubbornness again when the thermoplastics and injection molding revolution started.[2]

Soon after the development of bakelite in 1909 cold molded plastics appeared. As the name implies, no heat was required to mold them, and they have since been expanded in a variety of formulations for many applications. Among the early ones was the use of cold molded "spacers" between the body of a pan or pot and the handle to minimize heat transference. This was followed by top knobs and side handles on cookware, since cold molded plastics could withstand heat.

During the next three decades, from about 1910 until America entered World War II, plastics technology, especially in the discovery of new types of plastics, developed enormously. A list of plastics published by the Society of the Plastics Industry contains no less than seventeen different types from casein (1919) to polyethylene (1942). Only a few of them proved to be of significance to the housewares field.

Plastics in Housewares

By 1972 there were about forty "essential types" of plastics with no end in sight. It is noteworthy that, unlike the very early days when individual inventors were primarily responsible for developments in the plastics industry, the contributions over the years have more and more been the result of team effort—groups of scientists working together in the laboratories of large industrial firms, supported by millions of dollars of research funds.

Prior to World War II the plastic housewares business was largely in its infancy. Although such important materials as cellulose acetate and polyvinyl chloride appeared on the market in the late 1920s, there were few fabricators or molders sufficiently knowledgeable or interested in the manufacture of plastic housewares. The depression of the early 1930s did nothing to encourage entries into this still strange and unchartered field. But by the late 1930s newcomers like Columbus Plastic Products and Beacon Plastics Corporation had launched their hopeful new businesses. Gebhard W. Keny, retired founder of Columbus Plastic Products, recently recalled some of the developments during that period:

> The relatively few plastic housewares on the market prior to the 1930s and during the early and middle thirties consisted mainly of items compression molded of thermo-setting materials. Typical were bowls, measuring cups, spoons, tumblers as well as housewares components like knobs, handles, housings, etc.
>
> During the middle and late thirties some products of this type were being injection molded of cellulose acetate. The novel properties of this material—its superior impact strength, and its wide color range from opaques and translucents to colorless clear—soon resulted in other products molded of it appearing on the market. Cellulose acetate in sheets, rods, tubes, etc., was also easy to fabricate by drilling, sawing, and sanding as well as solvent-cementing with acetone. Moreover, decorating could be achieved easily and permanently by means of hot stamping, silk screening, and other methods.

In 1938 the introduction of polystyrene opened up a big new market for plastic housewares because this material not only had all the advantages of cellulose acetate, but also greater dimensional stability, could be molded faster, had greater clarity, and, due to its lower specific gravity, was cheaper. "It was with the advent of this material that plastic housewares for the first time really began to sell in volume," Gebhard Keny said.

One of the most important and, from the standpoint of housewares, one of the most useful plastics to be developed was polyethylene which appeared in 1942. The soft, flexible, but extremely durable, character of this material made it ideal for such items as

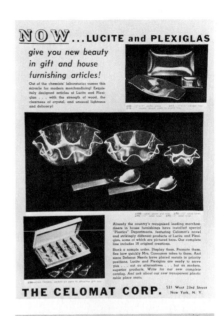

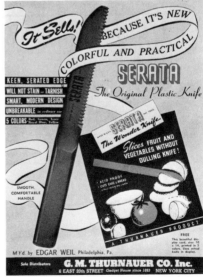

From top: In 1941 acrylics like DuPont's "Lucite" and Rohm & Haas's "Plexiglas" were featured as specialty gift ware items as advertised by the Cellomat Corporation, New York. In the same year the lower ad appeared, and many thought that the future of plastic housewares might be in items that were "unbreakable in ordinary use."

Both courtesy House Furnishing Review.

335

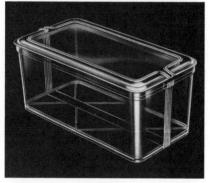

From top: A post World War II advertisement demonstrating the various functions of plastic as well as a mix of plastic materials. The plastic container (lower) made of polystyrene, made by Tri-State Plastic Molding Company, was a prototype of today's plastic refrigerator bowls.

Top, courtesy House Furnishing Review.

bowls and other food storage units. One of the earliest molders to specialize in this material was Earl S. Tupper, founder of Tupper Plastics Incorporated, Farnumsville, Massachusetts. Later the development of high density polyethylene made possible the molding of large items like the twenty-gallon trash barrel brought out by Loma Corporation.

After World War II ended, the plastic housewares business rather quickly resumed its earlier momentum. One of the most important and widely used materials at the time was styrene. It happened to be one of the essentials required for the nation's synthetic rubber program, so production capacity had been greatly expanded and it was readily available. The marketplace saw a flood of such items as soap dishes, tumbler holders, robe hooks, towel bar racks, refrigerator storage containers, egg trays, measuring cups, and spoons, knife racks, clothes hangers, serving trays, and table cutlery trays. Incidentally, these trays rapidly replaced the wooden trays long used for that purpose.

These products sold by the million. Stores whose shelves had been bare while production was directed toward winning the war now eagerly filled their shelves with all available merchandise—and customers kept emptying them almost as fast.

Meanwhile, similar developments were taking place with other materials, notably polyethylene and melamine, especially for plastic dinnerware.

The exploding market for plastics understandably attracted many inexperienced or opportunistic newcomers to the molding field, resulting in widespread misapplications of materials. As mentioned earlier, this sort of technical ignorance did much for a while to harm and hinder the development of all plastic products.

After World War II, to help correct this situation, a number of the leading resin producers as well as the Society of the Plastics Industry launched extensive training and education programs at both the trade and consumer level. They did much to help get this industry properly headed to the important place it commands today.

The housewares historian, seeking to properly record all facets of the industry, finds himself frustrated by the proliferation of products and companies. In plastics, this handicap is especially true. So much has and continues to happen in this fast-moving, innovative business and so many firms are contributing to the action that one can barely mention a few additional random examples. Like Republic Molding Corporation, Chicago, a pioneer in polyethylene and originator of the stacking vegetable bin. Or the highly realistic, simulated wood wastebaskets and hampers in the Brentwood line of Globe Superior, Philadelphia; Heller Designs, Mamaroneck, New York, and their dramatic stackable dinnerware; the Tri-State Plastic Molding Company, Henderson, Kentucky, which since 1941 has developed one of the biggest stocks of packaging boxes and polystyrene food containers anywhere; Arnoldware Rogers, Panama

City, Florida, who introduced the first decorated plastic tumblers in 1958 (and sold over eighty-two thousand dozen at that housewares show); the remarkable plastic "cut glass" ware brought out by Fesco Operations, Cities Service Company, Pittsburgh, and their unique two-tone, appliqued design technique. Then there's the Milano collection of Lucite table accessories by the Eagle Affiliates Division of A P L Corporation, Brooklyn, or the true-to-life stoneware look of the dinnerware patterns of Allied Chemical Company, New York. And the beauty of the multi-colored designs of Alladinware of Lenox Plastics of Los Angeles.

And so it goes. The record is long and impressive and never ending.

The Dow Program

One of the most ambitious efforts made to overcome sales resistance and criticism of plastic products after World War II was launched in 1947 by the Dow Chemical Company, Midland, Michigan, for its own "Styron" brand of styrene.

Dow set up a program that included a Plastic Technical Service Committee, composed of experts on its staff with a backlog of experience and information, whose services were made available without charge to molders and fabricators for an evaluation of their products. These were then rated on four counts: "1—General material application (should the item really be made of plastic—or some other material); 2—Specific (plastic) material application (is Styron best—or some other plastic); 3—Design (from a functional standpoint); and 4—Workmanship." Molders whose products were approved by the committee were given a free supply of "Made of Styron" labels to use on their product so as to tie in with an extensive national advertising program promoting the Styron label.

Dow supplemented its program with a number of conferences of editors of trade and consumer publications. One of the topics discussed was the possibility of establishing quality standards for plastic housewares. But because of the enormous variations not only in products but materials, it was felt the creation of satisfactory standards was impractical.

Tupperware

Among the pioneers in plastic housewares was Earl S. Tupper who in 1938 began business in Farnumsville, Massachusetts, as a custom molder. In 1945 he produced his first polyethylene item, a seven-ounce tumbler. A good merchant and a believer in advertising, he soon began to distinguish his products by promoting them as being made of "Poly-T" rather than ordinary polyethylene. A July 1946 trade ad announced these tumblers "in frosted pastel shades of lime, crystal, raspberry, lemon, plum and orange, also ruby and amber," and goes on: "Here, indeed, is another Tupper masterpiece, one of the most sensational products in modern plastics...."

From top: In 1957 Loma produced the first twenty-gallon trash container. A completely stackable twenty-five piece plastic contemporary dinnerware set by Heller Designs Inc. Then, a selection of contemporary plastic serving and storage pieces by Tupperware.

From top: Gebhard W. Keny, founder of Columbus Plastic Products, Inc. Next, an array of Tupperware bowls and refrigerator storage containers. This plastic cutlery tray, introduced by Columbus Plastic Products soon after World War II, was one of its biggest selling items and eventually replaced the long established wooden cutlery tray completely.

Later he developed the now well-known "Tupperware Seal": by slightly flexing the snug-fitting lid of a polyethylene bowl so as to expel the air inside, outside air pressure thereupon "seals" the lid even more tightly. His multi-use bowls, made in various sizes, were not only unusually functional—such flexible bowls had never before been available to homemakers—but so pleasing in appearance that in its October 1947 issue *House Beautiful* magazine devoted a full page in color to them along with a feature story entitled "Fine Art for 39¢."

Earl Tupper lost little time in taking advantage of this windfall national publicity and his trade ads that month declared that these "Poly-T wonder bowls are part of the Tupper Millionaire Line carried by your jobber." But his marketing through retail stores was rather short-lived. In 1946 he first tried selling his then expanded line of Tupperware on the home party plan with such gratifying results that it soon far outdistanced retail store sales.

By 1951 the operation had become a multi-million dollar business and Tupperware Home Parties Incorporated was formed to sell the line through distributors and dealers on the party plan. Retail store sales were discontinued.

In 1958 the Tupper Corporation (the manufacturing organization) and Tupperware Home Parties Incorporated (the sales organization) were acquired by the Rexall Drug and Chemical Company, for an estimated $9 million, according to *The New York Times*. In April 1969 the Rexall name was changed to Dart Industries Incorporated.

Columbus Molded Plastics Company

In June 1938 a Harvard graduate named Gebhard W. Keny, who had just completed a year of supplemental studies at its Graduate School of Business Administration, took what he thought would be just a summer job with the Paul A. Norris Company, a small plastics fabricating plant in Wellston, Ohio.

By the fall, however, everything changed. The Norris firm was going out of business and Keny, instead of heading back to Cambridge, decided to establish a small custom injection molding plant of his own in Columbus. He was joined by another young man from Norris, W. J. Braley, who became secretary-treasurer and later vice-president of the new enterprise. It was named Columbus Plastic Products, Incorporated, and began with four employees and two second-hand injection molding machines.

At the start the firm produced only plastic components to order and specification for other manufacturers. But at that time injection molded thermoplastic housewares were just beginning to make their appearance and within a couple of years it was decided that the development, production, and marketing of its own line of plastic products should have top priority within the company itself.

By 1946 the custom-molding operations were largely phased out and the original "Zippo" and "Columbus" brand names discontinued in favor of "Lustro-Ware."

Meanwhile, sales soared and by the late 1940s the company was recognized as having the most complete line of thermoplastic housewares in the country. One reason for this is that it always placed great emphasis on the development of new products and for the purpose established its own product design staff as early as 1939. It was headed by Nathan W. Roop until his retirement in 1962. Thereafter, his assistant, Eugene Snyder, took over and the services of outside design firms were utilized to supplement the company's own staff. As a result of this aggressive attitude toward the creation of new products, Columbus was responsible for many "firsts" in the molded thermoplastic housewares field. It pioneered blow molding of plastic housewares items such as waste baskets and watering cans, and was one of the first to make use of injection equipment with pre-plasticizing cylinders, screw injection machines, the in-plant dry coloring of molding materials among numerous other technological developments that helped make better, less costly plastic products a reality.

Columbus was also responsible for a number of significant innovations in the engineering and production of plastic items, many of which were the "brain children" of George W. Kelly who held key positions with the company from 1939 until his retirement twenty-five years later. One of the most important was a contribution to injection molding tool design, his patented valve gating of molds (also called pre-compressed molding). This development, permitting the pre-compression of the raw plastic material prior to injection into the mold, not only resulted in a faster molding cycle, but made possible the molding of certain deep parts or those of unusually large area as well as thin or lacey forms which previously could not be practically molded. Furthermore, strains within the parts were reduced, resulting in greater strength, and since by this molding method there were no "sprues" or "gates" to trim off, economies in finishing were effected too.

The patent rights to this process were sold in January 1959 to the W. R. Grace Company, with Columbus Plastic Products retaining royalty free rights to its use. Kelly also engineered many improvements in the design of injection molding presses, one of the most important of which is a unique, carbon ball bearing non-return valve, vital to the efficient operation of screw-injection molding machines.

In 1966 Columbus Plastic was acquired by the Borden Company. At that time its line consisted of over three hundred items; it employed seven hundred people, and included in the equipment spread over 9½-acres of plants and warehouses were over seventy injection molding presses. Sales had reached $14 million annually. Today as the Lustro-Ware Division of Borden Chemicals, Borden Incorporated, it continues to be a dominant producer in the plastic housewares industry.

339

From top: Some post-war pioneer plastic products by Columbus: a Lustro-Ware bathroom hamper; in 1949, a cannister set; a real "first"—stackable refrigerator egg storage trays made of styrene. Introduced in 1947, they sold in the millions.

From top: When the Korean War created a shortage of polystyrene, Beacon Plastics turned to polyethylene and developed the first round plastic dishpan. A deep rolled rim provided the flexible material with just the right rigidity. Even though Beacon retained the late, famed Dionne Lucas to assist in the promotion of this "shell server" set in 1949, it failed to get public acceptance—once a frequent problem with plastics. A forty-seven piece set of dinnerware in a contemporary design by Artisan is compactly packaged.

Plastic Dinnerware

Melamine, the raw base material used for nearly all plastic dinnerware, was discovered in Europe in 1834. It was a chemical oddity and for the next one hundred years no one gave it a second thought.

In the mid 1930s the American Cyanamid Company, a resin producer in Wallingford, Connecticut, developed a urea formaldehyde resin, a light-colored formulation which, it was believed, held considerable potential for molding plates and bowls for table use. To develop a market for it, they contracted with the Hemco Division of Bryant Electric Company, a subsidiary of the Westinghouse Electric Corporation in Bridgeport, to start producing such items since Hemco had extensive molding facilities.

The new line was marketed under the name "Beetleware." It was molded in gay translucent solid colors and promoted primarily for outdoor and picnic use. But while it seemed to stand up beautifully in the laboratory, in actual use it proved to be far from satisfactory and eventually was discontinued.

Meanwhile, researchers at American Cyanamid "re-discovered" melamine. Tests revealed that it was unique in its resistance to breakage and wear, had a hard, scratch-resistant surface, absorbed little water and was odorless and tasteless. For dinnerware it was obviously far superior to urea and was given a brand name—"Melmac."

By that time (it was the late thirties) the United States Army and Navy had issued an urgent call for crash programs to develop two vital items of a plastic material: a liner for the inside of steel helmets, and dinnerware that could withstand the rough handling to which it would be subjected on shipboard.

As it happened, two molders entered into a joint venture with and for the Navy to develop such dinnerware. One was the Hemco Division of Bryant Electric; the other was the Boonton Molding Company, Boonton, New Jersey. Much of the program, especially the expensive tooling for dies, was financed by the Navy.

By today's standards, the drab-looking, grayish colored dinnerware that resulted from those intensive efforts, was pretty crude, unattractive stuff. But what is important, however, is that the program found a solution to the problem and, along with it, a key with which to launch the production of plastic dinnerware for household use.

After the war the molds were freed for civilian use and both Boonton ("Boontonware") and Hemco ("Hemcoware") began producing plastic dinnerware. Because of the nature of the product at the time, it was promoted primarily to restaurants, hospitals, and other institutions.

Some idea of how fast the plastic dinnerware business expanded can be gleaned from the fact that whereas in 1946 only two molders were in the business, less than ten years later there were sixteen firms engaged in making it.

Meanwhile, American Cyanamid, to help develop a market for

its "Melmac" melamine, retained the noted industrial designer, Russel Wright, to create a new line for restaurant use. "It was first used in the Bickford restaurant chain in New York," Wright recalled in a telephone interview in 1972 from his home in Garrison, New York.

> I received a call from William Bell, then president of American Cyanamid. He told me his wife greatly admired my design of the then very popular dinnerware I had done for Steubenville Potteries and thought something equally successful could be developed in plastics for home use. After the experience his company had had with Beetleware, I don't think he was overly enthusiastic about the idea. But he was willing to try it, so we went ahead....Within a year American Cyanamid was able to interest thirteen plastic molders in the production of Melmac dinnerware. Plastic dinnerware was finally beginning to get off the ground.

It is worth noting that often the molders of this new dinnerware would first offer their line to the china and glass department buyer in department stores, sometimes with rather humiliating results. To these departments, plastic dinnerware was an "ersatz" upstart, which, they didn't hesitate to declare, might be appropriate for institutions and cheap restaurants, but had no place with fine china and glass. Thus the molders turned to the housewares departments which, in most stores, became the recognized headquarters for plastic dinnerware.

Meanwhile, the producers of melamine, mindful of the demands of the market, began to improve it. Originally dull and drab, this basic resin now started coming through in bright attractive colors. Also scratch and stain resistance were continually improved. As volume grew costs began to drop and the scope of promotions increased. The supermarkets, which were then beginning to hit their full stride, seemed a logical place to sell this plastic newcomer. Presently big promotions of place settings were helping to popularize it. One of the most notable of those, many still recall, was the

The original plastic dinnerware designed by Russel Wright for the American Cyanamid Company.

341

THERMO-SERV COMPANY

From a quite unrelated beginning as the producer of the first plastic beverage dispensing faucet for the brewing industry in 1950, the Thermo-Serv Company, Anoka, Minnesota, a division of the West Bend Company (now a part of Dart Industries Incorporated, formerly Rexall) has since come to be a leading manufacturer of vacuum sealed plastic serving ware and accessories in the housewares field.

Its first housewares item was a 32-ounce, double-walled, insulated, vacuum sealed serving pitcher which, in black and gold, has become a familiar sight in restaurants throughout the country and the popularity of which seems undiminished. Thermo-Serv pioneered the concept of vacuum assembly of components and is said to be the first to perfect it. It is now the largest line of such plastic ware. Thermo-Serv also developed the silk screening of tapered plastic forms and was one of the first to use color-printed paper see-through inserts between the double walls of its products.

From top: Fesco's Mayfair accessories are attractive and colorful additions to the home. Then, a selection of flexible plastic housewares from Republic Molding. Another example of bright modern design on plastic dinnerware is the Stoneflower pattern by Artisan.

342

A & P promotion of Westinghouse "Hemcoware." (Westinghouse went out of this business in 1961, at which time it sold its molds to Boonton Molding Company.)

In the mid 1950s the introduction of decals or "inlays" made decorated plastic dinnerware possible for the first time. Since then a wide range of patterns, colors, and shapes has been developed in this field.

For a long time the plastic dinnerware business had been gradually evolving into the higher and the lower price brackets. And in both categories it had also encountered very intensive competition, to which various factors contributed. For example, the production and promotion of so-called "Ironstone" pottery dinnerware reached a point where it began to be directly competitive with popular price plastics and, despite the widespread acceptance of plastic dinnerware, "Ironstone" sets began taking much of the business away.

Meanwhile, another quite unrelated development appears to be having even more of an impact on the sale of the top price bracket plastic dinnerware. In 1971 the Corning Glass Works began marketing a very unusual new line of dinnerware—they call it "Living Ware" —named Corelle. With many of the qualities of china, it is also highly break resistant, in fact guaranteed against breakage, as well as being low in price. Moreover, it is sold primarily in housewares departments. Backed by an intensive promotional program, Corelle sold to the tune of 40 million pieces in the first eighteen months of its appearance. The brunt of its impact has been on plastic dinnerware. Where and how these various competitive factors will level off remain unanswered questions of the market place in 1972.

THE PLASTIC PARADE OF PROGRESS

(Note: Although the dates below indicate the year in which the particular material was first developed, there was often an interval of several years before it was used to a significant extent commercially.)

1868 Celluloid—The first synthetic plastic, invented by John Hyatt, especially to make billiard balls. Widely used for novelties (but not housewares).

1909 Bakelite—Used mostly for industrial purposes; limited use, mostly for parts on consumer goods.

Cold Molded Plastics—Used primarily for industrial purposes and also for handles, knobs, etc. (But not until 1931 was the first molded handle for an iron made by the Mack Molding Company for the C. D. Wood Electric Company.)

1919 Casein—One of the earliest thermoset plastics made of skimmed milk and formaldehyde. Strong and rigid, it can be brightly polished in a wide range of colors and was used for some of the first, simple housewares items like measuring cups and spoons, and small bowls, etc. But heat and moisture, particularly hot water, adversely affects this material and it proved unsuitable in most cases for such use.

1927 Cellulose Acetate—The properties of this material made it of considerable interest to the housewares field. Besides its ability to withstand moisture and moderate heat, it is strong, tough, colorful, and resistant to most household chemicals. Originally available only in sheets, rods, tubes, etc., it was easy to fabricate by drilling, sawing, etc., and lent itself to assembling by solvent cementing with acetone. It could be easily and permanently decorated in many ways such as silk screening, hot stamping, etc. But these were all relatively costly, hand operations, and production was necessarily limited to novelties and specialties that could justify such costs.

It was not until about 1936 that items of injection molded cellulose acetate began to appear such as bathroom tumblers, trays, hand mixers, soap dishes, etc. Lack of experience and knowledge in the use of this material (as with others at the start) often resulted in misapplications with unfortunate results. It had low heat resistance, warped readily, and the plasticizers had a tendency to migrate, leaving the plastic rigid. It was largely replaced later by styrene.

Polyvinyl Chloride (vinyl film)—The most important vinyl polymer. This became the most important material for shower curtains, but it was not until 1937 that it was first used for that purpose. Also widely used for such items as bowl covers, garment bags, etc.

1936 Acrylics—Called one of the most beautiful of the thermoplastics, this crystal clear material has the unique property of being able to carry light unseen from one edge to another, even around curves. Used primarily for higher priced specialty housewares in the giftware category, it was not until well after World War II that any appreciable number of such products appeared.

1938 Styrene (or Polystyrene)—The advent of World War II cut off access of the U. S. to natural rubber, so a number of American chemical companies combined their efforts to produce styrene monomer which was combined with butadiene to make synthetic rubber. Some of this styrene was also converted to the moldable plastic material, polystyrene, in order to provide a substitute for scarce metals and even glass.

With the introduction of styrene and later high impact styrene, housewares for the first time really began to sell in significant volume in the late 1940s and early 1950s. Styrene not only had all the good qualities of cellulose acetate, but also had greater dimensional stability, could be molded faster and, due to its specific gravity, was considerably cheaper. It also had much more clarity.

Polystyrene dominated the application of plastics to housewares right through the 1950s and even to the 1970s continues to be one of the most important plastics in this field.

1938 Melamine-Formaldehyde—The base material for nearly all plastic dinnerware was a chemical oddity when first discovered in 1834. For one hundred years no one gave it a second thought until 1933 when researchers at the American Cyanamid Company in Wallingford, Connecticut, realized its potentials and initiated production of the first melamine formaldehyde molding material. It opened up the field of "Melmac" dinnerware.

Tests revealed that it was unique in its resistance to breakage and wear, had a hard, scratch-resistant surface, absorbed little or no water and was odorless and tasteless. It could be molded in almost any desired shape or color. During World War II all developmental efforts were directed toward supplying the Navy, which was urgently in need of dinnerware that could withstand the rough handling to which it would be subjected on shipboard.

After the war the civilian market for plastic dinnerware zoomed. In 1946 two producers were making such dinnerware, but by 1955 there were sixteen companies in the business.

Nylon—This is the generic name for a family of polyamide resins that include many types of this plastic material. It is strong and stiff, long wearing and has high impact as well as flexural strength. Its use in the housewares field has largely been for specialty items such as salad fork and spoon sets; spoons and spatulas (especially for use in connection with non-stick coated cookware to minimize scratching).

1942 Polyethylene—This material has proved to be ideal for many applications in the housewares field and is widely used. It is extremely tough and resistant to breakage; can be made rigid or flexible, and is virtually unaffected by almost all foodstuffs.

However, it was not until the early 1950s that items made of polyethylene began to appear to an appreciable extent. For the first time it made possible a wide assortment of items ranging from ice cube trays and dishpans to pails and wash baskets. Originally available only in a translucent, frosted-glass shade, it soon could be had in practically any color.

Subsequently, the development of high density polyethylene with its greater heat resistance and rigidity—along with the development of bigger, more sophisticated molding equipment—not only greatly enhanced the utility of many housewares items, but made possible the production of much larger items such as twenty- and twenty-four-gallon trash containers.

1948 Acrylonitrile—An extremely tough and versatile thermoplastic that is resistant to abuse, scuffing and flex-fatiguing. It provides better heat resistance, greater impact strength, and is one of the few plastics that can be successfully chrome plated. In the housewares field acrylonitrile has been used in considerable volume by a number of companies for producing all kinds and sizes of high quality, heavy duty drinking cups and glasses.

343

From top: "Brentwood" by Globe Superior was introduced in the mid-sixties. Made of high impact polypropylene, it successfully simulated wood finishing. The unique versatility and design potential of plastics is seen in this "Fold 'n Pour" dust pan offered by Foley Manufacturing Company in 1966.

1957 Polypropylene—One of the lightest weight plastics, it has many of the virtues of polyethylene plus some of its own. One of its exceptional properties is its superior ability to be flexed or bent indefinitely without breaking. (On one test a specimen was flexed 1½ million times before it broke.) This has made possible self-hinged boxes of various kinds, wall-mounted paper towel holders, and other items.

Engineering Type Plastics—This is a broad term applied to those specialized plastics used for such purposes as housings for vacuum cleaners, mixers, air conditioners, etc., and which are generally formulated to meet specific requirements. One of the earliest of these was polycarbonate which, though introduced in 1957, was really not used until the mid 1960s. Another is polysulfone, originally introduced in 1965, but not used appreciably until 1972.

"Con-Tact"

One leisurely Sunday morning in 1950, David Silman, co-head of the Comark Plastics Division, United Merchants and Manufacturers Incorporated, New York, had occasion to use some cellophane tape to mend a box when a thought struck him: Why wouldn't it be a good idea if such tape were made much wider, say with a colorful design on it?

It wasn't just a good idea—it was a great idea, as it turned out. Next morning he discussed it with Irwin Nathanson, the other co-head of the division who, incidentally, had left the Monsanto Chemical Company to take his joint post with Silman in 1947. That was when the division was formed and United entered the plastics field with vinyl draperies. Nathanson immediately sparked to the suggestion. After the inevitable trials and errors in trying to develop a method for applying a pressure-sensitive adhesive backing to colorfully printed vinyl film eighteen inches wide and then covering the adhesive with an easily-removable paper backing, they finally succeeded four years later. They then named their new creation "Con-Tact."

In 1954 a full-page newspaper ad of Gimbel's, New York, housewares department, announced this unique new product to the public. By the time the store had opened the department was thronged. The remarkable new material became an instant best seller. Its uses are almost endless. There are nearly one hundred patterns, many simulating natural wood and other materials. More recently several "luxury" lines such as Flock, Polished Patent, and now Chrome have been added. It is now sold in over ninety thousand retail outlets all over the world.

Plastics and Rubbermaid

"Just before World War II, when Rubbermaid was really getting started, the only material available to us for our products was natural rubber," explained Jim Caldwell, retired board chairman of Rubbermaid, Incorporated, in relating the beginnings of plastic housewares in this country.

In the late 1930s the production of plastics and synthetic rubber was still extremely limited. The B. F. Goodrich Company had made a beginning marketing their new plastic, "Koroseal," for consumer use, but it was primarily a vinyl film. The first synthetic rubber was put on the market by the DuPont Company and was named "Neoprene." It was much superior to natural rubber in various ways that made it particularly well-suited to Rubbermaid products for the kitchen and bathroom. It was much more impervious to soap, oil, and grease, and so on, and also had greater heat resistance than natural rubber. Incidentally, rubber may be said to be the first plastic—a material that can be molded. In fact the Indians are known to have made rubber balls by moulding rubber from the tree with their hands and squeezing it until all the moisture had evaporated and the mass congealed into a solid state.

We did a lot of experimental work with Neoprene when it was introduced. The product we made of it didn't look any different than if it had been made of natural rubber, but it was ten times as expensive. Neoprene cost three dollars a pound, rubber thirty cents.

Plastics, of course, now compose one of the most important categories of the housewares industry. But few know that it was the chance interaction of two widely separated events, long after they had occurred, that proved to be not only one of the very first but also one of the most significant developments in putting housewares into plastics—and vice versa.

The first of these events was a statement made in 1919 by Arthur Vining Davis, the Napoleonic former chairman of the Aluminum Company of America. At a sales meeting of its Wear-Ever subsidiary, the Aluminum Cooking Utensil Company, in Pittsburgh, that tycoon blandly announced that "none of the managers or superintendents in this company are worth more than $10,000 a year"—or, for that matter, could ever expect to get more.

Two young employees were particularly shocked at this. They were Errett M. Grable, then manager of Wear-Ever's Chicago district, and Horatio B. Ebert, manager of the firm's Kansas City district, based in St. Louis. Grable was later named president of Wear-Ever. Horatio Ebert was national sales manager for Wear-Ever when he retired.

"Errett and I had sold Wear-Ever house-to-house when we were in college and had been lifelong friends," Ebert recalled during a recent interview. At eighty-three, he was in excellent health, and his remarkable vigor and energy were matched by an astonishing memory.

"Both of us started working for the company in 1911. We were approaching forty at the time of that meeting and, naturally, were concerned about our futures. But after hearing that statement we decided that an opportunity just didn't exist for us in the aluminum business and we had better start looking around for something else."

During the next few years, while they kept looking for the desired opportunity, they entrusted spare funds to Grable's father, a retired minister who had become a successful investor in second mortgages. It was in 1926 while on a visit to his parents, then living in Wooster, Ohio, that Ebert first heard of the Wooster Rubber Company and its problems. Founded in 1920 to make novelties and toy balloons, it had been mismanaged and was up for sale.

Three pioneers of Rubbermaid Inc.: Horatio Ebert, one of the Rubbermaid founders; J. R. Caldwell, president of Rubbermaid and later Chairman of the Board; Errett M. Grable, Chairman until 1959.

"I immediately told Errett that this seemed like something for us to consider seriously," Horatio Ebert continued. "By this time, through reinvestments by his father, we each had about $50,000—quite a sum in those days. At any rate, we bought the rubber company—its business equipment but not the building—for $16,000. We promptly reorganized things there and by the end of the first year that we owned it we made $8,000 profit! Besides balloons we made gloves and nipples. That gave us enough confidence in the possibilities to erect our own factory building." All this time both partners continued in their jobs with Wear-Ever.

Meanwhile, about seven hundred miles northeast of Wooster, the second event mentioned earlier was beginning to take place. James R. Caldwell, the youthful (twenty-seven years old) and ambitious vice-president of the Seamless Rubber Company in New Haven, Connecticut, was eager to get his company started making specialty items for the home. It was during the late 1920s, when the synthetic dye industry was making bright new colors which for the first time could be utilized in rubber products.

"My whole background and training was in rubber chemistry, manufacturing, and management, and after seeing these new color ingredients I was convinced that there was an opportunity to market a whole group of attractive, colorful molded rubber items for kitchen, bathroom, and general home use," Jim Caldwell related during an interview at his home in Boca Raton, Florida.

"Every evening my wife Madeleine and I would spend hours discussing possible new varieties and colors of items for the home —things which, made of molded rubber, could be much more desirable than if made of some other material. Eventually we had a list of twenty-nine items, all of which we felt sure could be best sellers."

It was now 1932, and factories everywhere had shut down and were for sale at almost any price. Used rubber manufacturing equipment prices were at rock bottom. "Things reached the point in our company where, about every three months, all employees and management were asked to take a 25 percent salary cut in order to try to keep the business going," Caldwell explained.

After the fourth cut my wife and I decided that if we were going to starve to death it would be better to do so working for ourselves on our ideas. It was obvious that if anything was ever to come of all our hopes and plans we would have to do it or it would never be done. And there would probably never be another time when it would require so little capital to go into business. So I resigned from Seamless and we moved to Norton, Massachussetts, near Providence, where I hoped to get started.

The couple decided that their first item would be a molded rubber dustpan on which they later got a patent. They located a toolmaker to make the molds for a 10 percent down payment and the balance "when." The enthusiasm and high hopes with which he took the dustpan to Joe Bason, then housewares buyer for the Outlet

The first Rubbermaid product, the original molded rubber dust pan of the early 1930s. It came in several colors.

346

Company in Providence, were quickly demolished. "The only kind of dustpan that will sell today is a 39¢ pan—not one for $1 like yours," Caldwell remembers the buyer telling him. Again he went over his well-rehearsed, convincing sales story: it was rubber and flexible enough to adjust to uneven floors; the legs in back always kept it tilted at the right angle; it wouldn't chip holes when hung on a plaster wall—and it could be had in various beautiful colors. But the buyer was adamant. "Even if it were made of solid gold, it's still a dustpan," Bason told him, "unless I can sell it for 39¢ I'm not interested."

To Caldwell's amazement he got the same story everywhere, even from Al Porcelain in Jordan Marsh and Company of Boston, then one of the most important housewares buyers in the country.

"Driving home from Boston that afternoon I wondered what to try next," he continued. "I kept asking myself, 'How can all those buyers claim to be so sure about a rubber dustpan when they've never even *tried* to sell one?' Then I remembered how the Fuller Brush man did very well selling directly to women house-to-house. Why not try the same approach? Since every penny we had in the world had been invested in our dustpan mold, I didn't have much choice."

At that point he found himself in Attleboro, Massachusetts. He drove up a side street lined with neat, two-family houses, stopped and rang the first convenient doorbell. He continued his story:

> "My heavens! What have you there?" asked the pleasant woman who answered, pointing to the five colored dustpans under my arm. When I told her they were made of rubber she wanted to know why; so I told her that if I could come into her kitchen and use her broom I could explain better, and she invited me in.
>
> I showed her all its features, even sweeping up the plaster on her closet floor caused by the chipping of the wall from her tin dustpan. "I've been after my husband for months to fix those holes," she confided. Then she asked me the price. "Only one dollar," I replied bravely. Then she said, "Can I have the red one?"—and the very first Rubbermaid sale had been made!

From then on for nearly a year all efforts were directed toward direct selling to the homemaker. Within a day after he returned from Attleboro, twenty-five salesmen had been engaged to sell house-to-house; getting salesmen then was no problem. "I hired only the ones I thought I could trust with samples, offering them 40 percent commission," Jim recalled. "Even so a number of them disappeared, along with the samples."

Within six months sales had begun to build up until it was possible to add some of the other items tucked away in the Caldwell's "hope chest"—a rubber sink strainer, a rubber drainboard mat, and so on. Most gratifying of all was a letter from Al Porcelain saying, "Since we are getting calls from customers for Rubbermaid dustpans and other products, please have a representative call on us."

When Jim called on Porcelain the next day—a day he has never forgotten—he got his first retail store order, a dozen of each of his

A LEADING ITEM NOW SOLD IN OVER 500 HOUSEFURNISHING DEPTS.

Rubbermaid Steel Wool Holder Makes Cleaning Easy and Safe

Protects hands when using all kinds of steel wool. Mounted on individual self-selling display cards.

THE WOOSTER RUBBER CO. WOOSTER, OHIO

347

The Rubbermaid story: A copy of the 1933 rubber dustpan patent issued to the Caldwells. In 1936 the Wooster Rubber Company offered products like this steel wool holder suggested by Rubbermaid founder, Horatio Ebert. Later, of course, Wooster became Rubbermaid. During World War II Rubbermaid's know-how was put to use making leak-proof bullet-seal gas tanks for fighter planes.

items—in assorted colors, of course. But there was a little string attached to it. "Sit down, young man, I'd like to talk to you," he remembers being told. Then followed his first lecture on retail merchandising and advertising.

"You know," began Porcelain, switching his role from buyer to seller as so many skilled buyers readily do, "we could sell a lot more of your new rubber things if we had a demonstrator." The term was one Caldwell had never encountered before, and when Porcelain finished explaining that it was a special salesperson for his merchandise, he promptly agreed. "That's no problem," he replied. "We've got the best demonstrator in the world for Rubbermaid products." And the next morning Madeleine Caldwell was on the selling floor where, for the next several weeks, she served so effectively that reorders began coming through immediately.

By this time—1934—it became increasingly evident that Rubbermaid couldn't continue on a subcontracting basis and that the only practical thing to do was to get its own manufacturing facility. "I felt we would never really be in business for ourselves until we had our own factory where, in particular, my fourteen years of experience in compounding rubber formulas and processes could be used to maximum advantage," Caldwell added.

The time had come when the two events previously referred to would finally merge. The depression had made itself felt in unmistakable terms in Wooster, Ohio, and in the fortunes of the new owners of the Wooster Rubber Company. Although they had recouped their $16,000, the $30,000 debt incurred for their new factory building was proving to be a burden, especially with sales of balloons and gloves down. What the rubber business needed, they decided, was some molded work, which would avoid the fierce competition of the dipped goods they had been making. Both Grable and Ebert had continued their association with the Aluminum Cooking Utensil Company, and they used it to good advantage for all concerned.

Kitchen modernization moved a step further ahead in 1966 when Rubbermaid introduced these storage units with which homemakers could completely organize the contents of their kitchen cabinets: sliding shelves, bins, drawers, turntables—all plastic, of course. Later a group of specially designed under-cabinet units to accommodate rolls of wax paper, foil, etc., as well as foodstuffs, was added, providing further efficiencies.

Their long experience with aluminum cooking utensils often suggested useful related items. For instance, steel wool was recommended for cleaning aluminumware, but women complained that it scratched their fingers. Thereupon Ebert developed a small rubber holder for steel wool to protect the fingers, and began making it in the Wooster plant. Similarly they developed a rubber spatula, still in the line today.

"But what we really needed," Ebert recalled, "was a factory manager who knew the molded rubber business."

One day while playing golf with Tom Stackpole, the then well-known buyer for the May Company of Cleveland, I learned of just such a man. His name was Jim Caldwell, and we met the following Sunday morning for the first time in the Statler Hotel in Cleveland. We talked the situation over nearly all day and then drove to Wooster to look over the factory. Caldwell was delighted; it was just what he had been looking for.

The business didn't have any money with which to pay him a salary; the creditors were already knocking on our door. Jim said that the minimum he could get along on was four hundred dollars a month, so Errett and I agreed that until the business could afford it, we'd pay him out of our own pockets.

In our position with Wear-Ever we were able to provide considerable assistance in getting the new Rubbermaid line started. Naturally we knew all the top buyers. We'd casually mention that there was an interesting new line called Rubbermaid they might want to look at... that was all, but it helped a lot.

Sales for the first fiscal year ending September 30, 1935, were $79,858. Within three years—1938—the struggling new venture was able to show its first profit. At that time it was decided to recapitalize the company. (But the name of the Wooster Rubber Company was not changed to Rubbermaid, Incorporated, until December 12, 1957.) We issued 7 percent preferred stock, most of which we took ourselves. But we also sold some to our friends and others and with each share of preferred stock they bought we gave them one share of common stock free. Later we redeemed all the preferred. We made a lot of millionaires; of course, we did pretty well ourselves.

Jim Caldwell did a magnificent job. I don't believe all this would have been possible without him.

A natural leader with an engaging personality, Caldwell proved to be a unique combination of imaginative technical and manufacturing competence and, along with it, equal ability as a dynamic and creative merchandiser. Year after year new products with great consumer appeal were added to the Rubbermaid line. And year after year the company's policies—predicated primarily on assuring dealers a fair and adequate profit on its products—helped to entrench the line firmly with retailers.

How well those policies have paid off is reflected in the fact that over the years the company's sales have continued to increase and in 1971 passed the $78 million mark, an all-time high. In that year, too, its net profit reached a new peak of over $6 million, solid indication of the success of Rubbermaid.

PENDULUM SHOP

THE MELTING POT

Paradoxically, the greatest strength of the housewares business is also its greatest weakness. The diversity of its merchandise categories is enormous. Each year they keep expanding.

Yet that very condition also constitutes a perpetual problem, especially for the merchant if not always for the manufacturer. It is not merely a matter of keeping track of all the competitive developments; of more immediate urgency is finding enough space on the retail sales floor so as to do justice in the presentation of this seemingly endless array of merchandise. There is never enough room to accommodate *everything,* certainly not as completely as one would wish to. And then, as if the basic space problem wasn't already bad enough in itself, the demands of seasonal goods add even further pressure.

It should come as no surprise, therefore, that a printed record of this industry should also find itself faced with the same problem—insufficient space to present all areas as one would like to. What follows now are reports of a more or less representative group of important product categories not previously covered. Regrettably, they are not always accorded the depth of detail one wishes were possible. But at least they provide some insight into areas of the industry which, otherwise, might have had to be passed over entirely. Life—and the problem of trying to put a big industry into small print—is like that.

Personal Care Housewares

A thing of beauty is a joy forever! But keeping it that way can be a pretty costly matter.

In 1972, Americans spent close to $1 billion for "personal care" housewares products. (Add that to an estimated $4 billion or more they spent in beauty parlors, barber shops, on cosmetics and you have the current cost of vanity!)

Vanity, fashion, or whatever, the traditional housewares outlets continue to share this boom business with drug, toilet goods, and other retailers.

The heritage of personal care items as housewares probably stems from two sources. First, in the pre-electric gas era, curling irons and their appurtenances understandably gravitated to the de-

Opposite page: The housewares industry is truly a melting pot of indoor and outdoor products meant for the home. From lawn and garden goods to department store personal care centers, the range is diverse. *This page:* Some early housewares, including a member of the Pet Shop. Birds and bird cages provided an important category for housewares departments in the early 1900s.

This page, both courtesy House Furnishing Review.

In 1899, Lehman Brothers offered this functional companion to winter travel.

Courtesy House Furnishing Review.

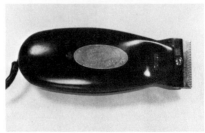

From top: Colonel Jacob Schick's earliest prototype of an electric shaver. It utilized a flexible drive shaft separate from the reciprocating head. This concept never went into production but Schick made several models which he gave to friends. Then, the first commercially produced electric shaver, introduced by Schick in 1931.

partment that carried the hardware type of merchandise. Also, it was the housewares department where the first electrical appliances were sold in department stores. Thus any product, regardless of its end use, equipped with a cord and operated by electricity, belonged in the housewares department. Obviously! It's impossible to peg specific dates and places that other departments especially drugs and/or toilet goods, first timidly began to take over electric items that really might have been theirs from the start. But since it was in the 1920s that drug stores first began handling electric curling irons and heating pads, that's about as close as one can come to marking the transition.

By 1972 the scope and potential of these personal care products had continued to expand to the point where there seems to be no end to what can be included in this category.

Electric Shavers

If for no other reason than to get his beard out of his way and prevent it from interfering with his actions, the human male since earliest days has shortened his whiskers by one means or another. The first shaving instrument there is any record of: a crude flint razor made by the Indians of Peru over four thousand years ago. Throughout later history man has been trying to develop some kind of a mechanical shaving device which would eliminate the need for soap and a blade.

In 1928 the first practical mechanical shaver was patented by Colonel Jacob Schick—the Schick electric shaver. Perhaps he got the idea while serving with the army in Alaska in the early 1900s, where shaving in a cold climate was hardly pleasant. To raise funds to market the invention he sold his interest in the Magazine Repeating Razor (still being manufactured in Milford, Connecticut, by Schick Safety Razor Company). Colonel Schick opened his first plant to produce electric shavers in Stamford, Connecticut.

One of the major hurdles he had to overcome in developing his shaver was the need for a very small motor, powerful enough to drive a shaving head. The impulse motor he perfected for this purpose is said to have been the most powerful of its size in the world at that time. The first Schick shavers went on sale in New York in 1931 at twenty-five dollars each. Total production that first year was three thousand, and while the shaver seemed to be off to a promising start, the Great Depression wasn't the most propitious period in which to launch a high-priced innovation. Nevertheless the intrinsic merit of this remarkable advance in shaving readily commanded recognition and in 1931, ten thousand units were sold. By then the price could be reduced to fifteen dollars. By the end of 1936 one million Schick shavers were in use and the electric shaver was here to stay.

Within a few years after the Schick shaver was introduced, Remington, Sunbeam, and over fifty others entered the business, but of that early group only the first three named had survived in 1972.

The Schick shaver had been on the market almost seven years when, in 1937, the Remington Shaver Division of the Sperry Rand Corporation entered that business. "The first model," a company history recalls, "was a feeble affair indeed. Small and single-headed, it was wistfully christened 'The Remington Close Shaver'....It was in 1939 at the New York World's Fair that Remington got its first big boost toward wide public acceptance."

The following year the company made industry history when it introduced the first two-headed shaver. Called The Dual, it pioneered the trend toward multi-headed shavers that continues to the present. And in 1940 Remington created something of a minor sensation when it brought out an electric shaver designed especially for women. In that year it also added an Auto-Home model that operated from a car cigarette lighter outlet.

Remington achieved a technological as well as a sales breakthrough in 1956, the year it brought out its roller comb innovation in shaver design and was able to gain about 40 percent of the market as a result. Then, three years later, it introduced the first adjustable electric shaver, the Roll-a-matic. It continued its program of innovations the following year, 1960, by announcing the first cordless shaver to be marketed in this country, the Lektronic, which, aided by the development of the rechargeable nickel cadmium battery, helped spark the trend toward cordless appliances. It topped that in 1962 with Lektronic II, for use with or without a cord.

The Sunbeam Corporation also decided to enter the appealing electric shaver field in 1937, with its Shavemaster Razor—a name obviously inspired by the company's then already well-known Mixmaster.

In the following years Schick, Remington, and Sunbeam battled each other for leadership with a succession of product innovations and intensive promotional programs that did much to develop the market for men's shavers (and for women's shavers). By 1954 Sunbeam asserted that over four million men were using its latest model.

Sunbeam terms the new models it brought out in 1972 "a new generation of Shavemaster Shavers," embodying not only models of a radically different design, but various basic improvements as well. The most significant feature is a shaving head development that puts a new slant or bevel and a new degree of sharpness, it is said, on each shaving hole for a smooth fast shave. The newly designed motors are said to produce more than twice the life of previous models. The group includes cordless and corded models and a multi-volt shaver for use almost anywhere in the world.

The Toothbrush Goes Electric

"What! An electric toothbrush?" When he first learned that his housewares division planned to make such an item, no one was more skeptical about its prospects than Fred Borch of General Electric. Borch, who retired as Chairman of General Electric in 1972,

353

From top: Remington entered the electric shaver field in 1937 with its model 60 (left). On the right is a 1972 model, the Mark II, featuring a micro slot shaving head system. Sunbeam (middle photo) calls this 1972 model "a new generation of Shavemaster Shavers." North American Philips introduced its Norelco shaver, featuring a rotary-action round head with six finely ground self-sharpening steel cutters in 1948. It was an improved version of the Philips dry shaver many GIs brought back from Europe.

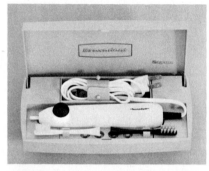

From top: This so-called "electric" toothbrush was "permanently charged with electro-magnetic current." The Broxodent introduced in 1960, was the first successful electric toothbrush in the U.S. John W. Mattingly, an engineer, and Dr. Gerald M. Moyer, a dentist, developed the Water Pik in 1966. This is the first retail model.

recalled not only his skepticism, but his later delight at being proved wrong when GE's toothbrush became an immediate success. "Maybe now we ought to consider making a combination toothbrush and shoe polisher for the man who, whenever he opens his mouth, puts his foot into it," Borch remarked.

Attempts to market a powered toothbrush were made as far back as 1920 but without success. A notable effort was made in 1939 by Julius Schmidt, who had developed a well-made if rather primitive looking unit. But that too was a failure.

After World War II an entirely new concept in a corded electric toothbrush was developed and manufactured in Switzerland. In 1960 the E. R. Squibb and Sons Division of the Olin Mathieson Chemical Corporation acquired a Swiss model, and under the name Broxodent, introduced it nationally in this country. It has an up-and-down brush action, and is endorsed by the American Dental Association.

Meanwhile, General Electric had been researching an electric toothbrush, but elected to make a rechargeable cordless model. "Before completely committing ourselves to a cordless model requiring a recharger," a company memorandum on the project states, "we were faced with the question of how many bathrooms actually have continually energized outlets into which the recharger could be plugged? If most bathrooms were controlled by a light switch or an outside switch, we'd clearly be in trouble. So...we surveyed the situation—and breathed a sigh of collective relief when we found two-thirds of all United States bathrooms were equipped with live outlets."

The memo also notes that "The earliest studies on the toothbrush were conducted on dogs...and the researcher was relieved to find that the dogs actually liked to have their teeth brushed...no other dogs in history so aptly fitted the adage, 'clean as a hound's tooth.' "

General Electric test-marketed its first model, equipped with rechargeable, nickel cadmium batteries, in 1961 and the following year distributed it nationally. It had back-and-forth brush action. In 1966 it introduced a new cordless model with up-and-down brush action to replace the earlier one; and in 1969 its "dual motion" with up-and-down-and-back-and-forth brush action was announced. Then in 1971, to compete directly with Broxodent, a corded model was added. General Electric also received American Dental Association endorsement.

It was in 1963 that the Sunbeam Corporation moved into the growing electric toothbrush market with a rechargeable battery-operated model having up-and-down brush action. It had its own recharging unit and holder for four brushes.

When the electric toothbrush first appeared it was regarded not only as a novelty, but was also subjected to endless cynical comment such as "How lazy can you get?" Despite all, the electric toothbrush was an immediate success. In 1963, for example, within two years of its introduction, 2.2 million units with an estimated retail value of $33 million were sold.

Styling Combs

The use of the heated metal curling device to "iron" or shape the hair of men as well as women is an ancient custom dating to Biblical times. There are many accounts of that practice among people in all parts of the world. Sometimes it was done for religious significance, sometimes for ceremonial occasions and most often as a matter of personal vanity.

Who was first to bring out an electric curling iron is uncertain. But long before there was an electric curling iron, electricity itself was being used to some extent to heat ordinary curling irons. Perhaps the earliest reference is to be found in the August 20, 1887 issue of *Scientific American* magazine: "In Berlin...in certain theaters electric stoves are employed for heating the curling tongs, the use of gas jets and spirit lamps being rigorously forbidden."

In this country a number of the early electric hand iron manufacturers included at least one model, often a "traveling iron," in the heel of which was a deep hole just large enough to insert a curling iron which would be left there until it was sufficiently hot for use. The American Electrical Heater Company, Detroit (makers of the American Beauty iron), made three ornamental electric curling iron heaters. By World War I there were a number of electric curling irons on the market, including Marcel wavers as well as complete hairdressing sets. All of them were predecessors of today's popular electric combs.

In the early 1920s, Beardsley & Wolcott Company, Waterbury, Connecticut, offered a set consisting of "Five separate and distinct units; rod, cord set, curler clamp; Marcel clamp; and drying comb." These attachments slipped into place over the rod which heated them for use. The complete set retailed for $2.50. But those items, good as they might have been for their time, seem almost primitive compared to the elaborate hair grooming appliances of today.

Trying to trace the beginnings of this boom in beauty wares and determine just who in the personal care field was first with what, ends up being something of an exercise in futility. Not only is there a woeful lack of standard terminology, which immediately creates its own confusion, but there is apparently little agreement in the industry about who was first with what. The situation can be explained to some extent by the fact that many of these specialty items now considered standard consumer products were originally made and sold only for professional use. Before long—as long hair grew longer —these items found their way into consumers' hands and heads. From then on it was only a short time until the manufacturers recognized the demand and began to supply it through retail channels.

There appears to be little question that the styling comb (actually a sophisticated development of the basic, hand-held dryer) origi-

355

From top: The electric vibrator can claim to be one of the first electric personal care products. It appeared in the early 1900s. This New Life model by Hamilton Beach was introduced in 1912. Then, the Lindstrom Smith Company vibrator included this warning: "Caution—Do not use vibrator in bath tub, or when body is connected with a water, sewer or gas pipe or standing on wet floor." The Jet Age dryer and styling comb was of Japanese origin. Finally, Remington's Hot Comb, a personal care product designed expressly for men.

North American Philips added something new to hair care devices when it introduced this Norelco untangler in January 1971.

A Pneumatic vacuum cleaner circular in 1906 suggested "using the current of pure, fresh air from the exhaust" for drying milady's hair. Note that the tank type cleaner was connected to a ceiling light outlet.

nated in Europe, probably Switzerland. One of the first such imports is said to have been the Shavex which was promoted in 1965.

Shortly a Japanese version appeared. Called the Jet Set (later the Jet Age Hair Dryer), Macy's New York Drug Centre introduced it in 1967 for $19.95. The term "styling comb" had not yet come into use, but, promised an ad, "this revolutionary concept in hair care... used for years by famous hair professionals. Now you can use it at home...."

But the Jet Age Hair Dryer didn't last very long—at least under that name. It was, the importers discovered to their surprise, a name already registered by the Sunbeam Corporation, which promptly demanded an immediate end to its use. By then these unique imports had unmistakably pointed the path not only to the long-established, familiar, and expected women's hair care market, but rather astonishingly to a totally unexpected new men's market. And these men to a great extent, were hardly the long-haired "hippie" types. The vanguard of the styled, long hair fashions for men had arrived, and the new fashion plate (or pate?) was buying these new types of personal care equipment. Men with thinning hair and balding areas also discovered that these new "dryers" could help make their hair look thicker, look like more than it really was. Barbers and men's hair stylists had been aware of this feature for some time, but now retailers were discovering it.

It is interesting that a shaver manufacturer should have been the first to market a styling comb. In 1969 the Remington Electric Shaver Division of the Sperry Rand Corporation introduced its notable Hot Comb, which is also a registered trade mark. Made to retail for about $24.95, it was an immediate success and promptly generated intense competition.

What has happened since then has become a wattage and velocity race, as one manufacturer after another tried to outdo competition. Schick, for example, introduced models with 330 watts for men and women in the fall of 1970, followed the next year by Clairol's Air Brush boasting 500 watts and a high and low switch, for men and women. In 1971 too, Gillette's MAX moved strongly into this area.

No one seems to doubt that this category of merchandise is in for a long and prosperous run. That seems to be taken for granted. But how long will long hair be next year? Next month?

Hair Dryers

In 1909 the electric hair dryer hadn't yet been developed. But that didn't preclude some women from utilizing the wonderful convenience of electricity to dry their hair via the great new invention, the vacuum cleaner. An early circular for the Pneumatic Cleaner illustrates a lady at her dressing table drying her hair with the hose from a tank type of cleaner and, explains the caption, she can do so "by using the current of pure, fresh air from the exhaust."

The ultimate appearance of the hand held hair dryer, as with other small, motor driven appliances, had to wait upon the development of the fractional horsepower motor. By the 1920s that was well under way and compact dryers like the Race made by the Racine Universal Motor Company and the Cyclone made by the Hamilton Beach Company, both in Racine, Wisconsin, began to appear.

During the next several decades a great many different hair dryers were marketed, some very successfully. As always, new materials and technologies contributed to changes in efficiency and design. Some came equipped with their own pedestal; some had various speeds and/or high, low, and medium heat switches. But basically, they were all hand held.

What may well have been the first variation of the hand held dryer was a model offered by Sears, Roebuck & Company in its fall and winter 1951 catalog. It consists of a hand held dryer equipped with a bracket to fasten it against the wall and a plastic bonnet that connects directly to the blower and fits over the user's head. It operated on 250 watts and sold for $12.95. The same catalog also offered an Ann Barton enameled steel hood hair dryer mounted on an adjustable tripod stand, operating on 400 watts and selling for $19.95. That may have been the first "hard hat" or professional type dryer offered for general use.

In 1956 the Sunbeam Corporation created considerable excitement with a greatly improved concept of its wall-mounted model by introducing a table top blower unit connected by means of a flexible plastic hose to a gaily printed vinyl bonnet or hood. Equipped with a dial temperature regulator the Lady Sunbeam controlled heat dryer was said to be "38 percent faster than other types." Four years later the Handy Hannah division of Landers, Frary and Clark added a neat extra touch by building the whole unit into a compact "hatbox" carrying case so that it could easily be taken along on trips. Called the Bettina hair dryer, it was updated in 1972 by General Electric (which had acquired LF&C in 1965) and marketed as the Bettina Universal.

At about the same time the Dominion Electric Corporation (now a subsidiary of Scovill) introduced a compact, brief-case size travel model dryer. It was the first to be featured on national network television and proved very popular.

By 1963 the popularity of bonnet dryers had begun to wane for various reasons. The Rayette division of Faberge Incorporated in St. Paul, Minnesota, had been studying the trend, and in that year introduced the first hard-hat dryer specially designed for home use. It was called the Rayette portable hair dryer. Several other models followed, notably the Salonette beauty mist hair dryer which included a built-in facial sauna. Rayette's venture into the appliance field prompted competitors to bring out hard hat dryers too, and in 1969 Faberge sold its operation to the Waring Products Division, Dynamics Corporation of America.

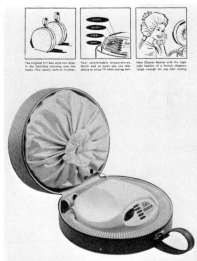

From top: The Race hair dryer was introduced in the early 1920s by the Racine Universal Motor Company, Wisconsin. The Bettina Universal hair dryer in a hatbox traveling case is an updated (1972) version of the original Bettina introduced in 1960 by the Handy Hannah division of Landers, Frary & Clark.

One of the first facial sauna devices to appear was this 1966 model by Standard Products. There are those who feel that skin care items may well prove to be the biggest and most important area of personal care products.

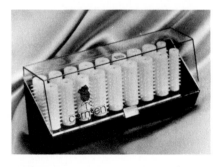

From top: Sun lamps were another of the earliest personal care products. This Norelco sun/heat lamp features a "programmed tanner" offering a choice of tanning schedules for sensitive skin. The Carmen 18 Instant Hairsetter was the original of this now very popular personal care product.

And by that time, the hard hat home model dryer had become a firmly established segment of the personal care products business.

Mirrors

The first version of the electric make-up mirror which has come to be such a popular item in the personal care category today, was probably one called the Facelight, marketed in the early 1930s by a small company in Long Island City, New York.

It wasn't until 1966 that a completely new concept in electric mirrors appeared. The Bercy Manufacturing Company of Hollywood, California, introduced an illuminated make-up mirror in a compact travel bag primarily for the theatrical trade. But it quickly became a best seller with women everywhere. And it just as quickly generated numerous competitors...as well as severe price cutting.

In the fall of 1968 a new and innovative approach to make-up mirrors appeared when Clairol Incorporated introduced its True-to-Light mirror equipped with multiple-light settings that enabled a woman to apply her make-up in the type of illumination in which she expected to be seen—daylight, office lighting, or for evening. Other models followed. Clairol added improved versions as well as a travel True-to-Light model. In 1969 General Electric introduced a make-up mirror with four light settings including fluorescent and home lighting.

The make-up mirror is long past the novelty stage and has become something of a staple in the personal care category with sales leveling off in 1969 and 1970, for example, at around 2.7 million units.

Hair Setters

A number of American manufacturers who visited Denmark in the early 1960s noticed a unique new electric hairsetting device on sale in the stores. It was invented by Aren Bybjerg Pederson who had formed Carmen Hair Curlers of Denmark to market it. The attention the Carmen hair setter commanded from women shoppers didn't escape the overseas visitors. All but one manufacturer though concluded that it "wasn't something for the American market."

In 1965 Clairol Incorporated arranged to become the sole distributor in the United States for Carmen curlers. In the next few years the hairsetter became something of a sensational success for Clairol and for several competitors. The new device eliminated the necessity for women to use old-fashioned hair curlers and sleep with a head of curlers at night. In about ten minutes time, women could set their hair in the morning for the entire day. This type of hairsetter was the "dry" type, and later a "mist" version appeared.

The original Clairol model was called the Carmen 18. It was the first of a complete line of Carmen hairsetters which were fair traded and marketed exclusively in major department stores. In 1967 Clairol manufactured the first of a series of Kindness instant hairsetters for distribution through mass merchandising outlets.

In 1967, when Clairol first introduced the Carmen model, sales totaled 700,000 units. In 1969 they had zoomed to 6.7 million units. Yet in 1972 sales estimates pegged this item at less than 3 million units. Various explanations have been advanced for the drop, but the most plausible seems to be the rapid development of the styling comb and its presumed greater flexibility in meeting the ever-changing whims not only of women but also of men.

Fireplace Goods

Time was when the hearth, glorified through the centuries in song and story, was truly the "heart" of the home.

Today many would assert that the cathode ray tube has long since usurped that position!

The origin of andirons and other fireplace tools is lost in antiquity when man discovered his fire would burn better with the logs up off the ground. In due course, iron replaced the rocks once used for that purpose. But the early devices for the fire, and later, the fireplace, were of necessity conceived as much to facilitate cooking as to aid the fire in generating heat for comfort. Museums here and abroad are filled with ingenious devices developed for those functions. There were even revolving roasting spits driven by a rope connected to a nearby dog-powered treadmill.

During colonial times all sorts of hooks and trammels as well as other ingenious devices were employed for hanging pots and kettles.

With the development and use of stoves for cooking all that eventually changed. And so the role of the fireplace—and its accessories—became largely one of providing heat along with the glow and coziness it contributes to the home.

Meanwhile, the manufacturing of fireplace equipment continued to be important. As with stoves it would long be largely a regional business. For the most part the local blacksmith or nearby iron foundry supplied the needs of the community. Moreover, the heavy weight of the product and poor transportation facilities discouraged shipments to any great distance.

It would be many years before firms with well-established names in the fireplace business emerged. It tended to be a seasonal part of varied manufacturing operations, a sort of "coal and ice" approach. Nor has it developed any really big companies; the nature of the business has not been conducive to concentration and it continues to be primarily a field of relatively small firms.

Nevertheless, progress has been made. Wire mesh spark guard screens of either the rigid or panel type had long been in use when, in 1928, John Turner of the Bennett Ireland Company, Norwich, New York, announced a woven spiral wire mesh screen that could easily be opened or closed like a curtain. Called Flexscreen, it was permanently mounted to the fireplace and proved to be a landmark development since copied by all others.

Then, in 1951, John Lytle, head of the Thermo-Rite Manufactur-

ACCLAIMED AT THE SHOW!
Wayne Fireplace Goods
Andirons — Fire Sets
Portable Grates
Cast Brass, Black & Brass, Burnt Antique Brass, Flemish & Black

NEW YORK SHOWROOM
HARRY LEVITZ
1150 BROADWAY

WAYNE AGRICULTURAL WORKS, INC.
GOLDSBORO   NORTH CAROLINA

359

From top: Tradition endures in fireplace goods. Not only in the design of the classic, colonial brass andirons but now also in a revival of the famous Ben Franklin stove.

Top, courtesy House Furnishing Review.

ing Company, Akron, Ohio, introduced another radically different fire screen. This one, made of heat-treated plate glass, was invented by Gerry Merriweather. Its patent has since expired and others are now making it.

But it took a surprisingly long time until fireplace fixtures and accessories of good, modern design made their appearance. Probably the first manufacturer to specialize in such fixtures was the late Fred Meyer who after World War II started business in San Francisco under the name of Fred Meyer of California. Using contemporary designs and such materials as stainless steel, chrome plating and finishes not usually used in the business, he filled a long-felt need with considerable success. Since then others have added modern designs to their lines. Fred Meyer launched another innovation with a program whereby orders for special custom-made curtain or recess screens from dealers are shipped by his company directly to the consumer, eliminating annoying delays.

"Prior to World War II and quite a while thereafter, fireplace equipment was considered a highly seasonal item," related William P. Sherman, president of Portland Willamette Company, Portland, Oregon, and a veteran of the industry, in a discussion early in 1972. "Stores where a customer might find a good assortment of such merchandise at anytime during the year were very few and far between. The only ones I knew of were a few lighting fixture showrooms and furniture stores—nowhere else." He continued:

> At that time, as nearly as I can reconstruct the business, the principal manufacturers of fixtures and accessories—not built-in fireplaces—were Bennett-Ireland Company, Norwich, New York; Peerless Manufacturing Company, Louisville, and now a division of the Dover Corporation; the Vulcan Manufacturing Company, whose 'Hart' line is now owned by the Anchor Division of Stratton & Terstegge Company in New Albany, Indiana; Logan Fireplace Equipment Company, Louisville; Centre Brass Works Incorporated, New York, operated by Jack Kraft; Sheffield Manufacturing Company, New York; Wilshire Manufacturing Company, Los Angeles; and American Windshield Company, Milford, Connecticut, who sold under the Puritan brand, and which is now owned by the Federal Department Stores Incorporated, Detroit. I suppose one might refer to them as companies with so-called national distribution.

At that time—1946—Bill Sherman was running a one-man operation, the Portland Willamette Company, from a small office in a public warehouse in Portland. The company was the marketing arm of the Modern Firescreens Company, a three-man firm located in the basement of a local house. All sales were made by Portland Willamette under the Modernscreens brand name. In 1964 they acquired the Portland Firescreens Company which originally had been the Packard Malloy Company, a lighting fixture manufacturer which had developed a highly styled, top quality line of fireplace fixtures. In 1970 a new, modern 106,000-square-foot plant was erected and all operations were combined under the Portland Willamette Company. Now

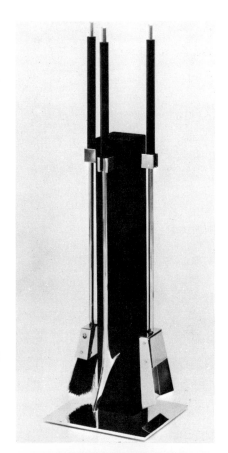

360

From top: This 1968 fireplace tool set by Christen Inc. of St. Louis received a Housewares Design Award. Portland Willamette Company offers heat-treated glass fire screens—contemporary materials and techniques for a very traditional way of heating an area.

in addition to its Modernscreens name it also uses Glassfyre as the brand name for its heat-treated glass fire screens.

After World War II some far-reaching, basic changes took place in the fireplace business which resulted in the start of a whole new era. One of the most important of these developments took place in 1955 when Robert Thulman was granted a patent on a pre-fabricated, non-masonry fireplace and chimney flue. Most important, it met the rigid requirements of the Underwriters Laboratories and became the first such flue to get their approval.

Shortly thereafter the Majestic Company, Huntington, Indiana, a manufacturer of hardware and equipment for flues and fireplaces since 1907, became the exclusive licensee of the Thulman unit and proceeded to develop a whole new line of pre-fabricated fireplaces. There are now units for use with wood, gas or artificial electric firelogs.

Meanwhile other developments were taking place that helped revolutionize the traditional status of the fireplace business. Some architects and several manufacturers showed imaginative and unusual new concepts, especially in free-standing and wall-hung units. In Seattle, for example, the Condon King Company, which had started business in 1954, introduced a dramatic-looking, free-standing fireplace in color called the Fire Hood. It met with instant success, and quickly established itself as a classic design that had far-reaching influence. The Fire Hood was widely copied. In 1970 Condon King became a division of Majestic, which itself had become a division of American Standard.

In Mount Pleasant, Iowa, Vega Industries Incorporated contributed another innovation in 1957 with a wall-hung wood-burning fireplace unit called Heatilator Mark 59. This has since been modified and made in gas-burning and electric units using artificial firelogs, and has also been extensively imitated.

The popularity of the free-standing units, it's interesting to note, also revived considerable interest in reproductions of the old-fashioned, cast iron Ben Franklin stove, since it offered still another decorative variation. To quote Louis Christen, Jr., president of Christen Incorporated, St. Louis, "Robert Thulman provided the means whereby interior designers could exercise their art, but I still consider Ben Franklin to be the basic innovator." Mr. Christen's company traces its start back to 1848 as one of the oldest producers of bellows for blacksmiths and industrial uses. In 1946 it began to make decorative bellows for household fireplaces and has since added specialty accessories such as giant matches, Colorflame Nuggets and other items.

A departure that has generated wide interest is the pre-fabricated, built-in metal fireplace now made by several firms. Who was first with this is in doubt, but numerous styles and types are available.

In the immediate post war period, the low-priced, free-standing mesh fireplace screen proved to be an exceptional best seller. It had

This Heatilator Mark 5900, introduced in 1957 by Vega Industries, is said to have been the first wall-hung, wood-burning fireplace.

361

wide-spread impact on the industry, especially the keen retail competition it generated. In the 1950s, however, the recessed, custom-fitted screen began to replace it as the public's favorite, but the steps involved in handling it created obstacles. As already related, it was at this point that Fred Meyer got an edge on competition by mailing the finished, made-to-measure screen directly to the dealer's customer.

Fireplace screens with panels or doors of tempered glass have also undergone radical development. The basic product, introduced in 1951, had enjoyed modest success in the following ten years. Then, in 1962, the Portland Willamette Company introduced an innovation in the form of a glass screen featuring so-called French-fold doors in decorative metal panels equipped with top and bottom draft controls. They were offered in special sizes, special construction, and a big assortment of finishes.

Special mention should be made too of the progress the industry has made in creating more realism in artificial fire logs, especially gas and to a lesser degree, the electric types. Such logs are not new, but the increasing popularity of free-standing and wall-hung fireplaces has spurred their development.

As one reviews the developments in the fireplace industry, the question comes to mind: will the housewares or the home-building and improvement field distribute the major share of fireplace products in the future? There are no reliable industry statistics, but trade observers agree that the builder is unquestionably garnering an ever-increasing share of this business.

Many believe that the changed character of fireplace merchandise will now require the services of a specialist to be successfully sold, and that this will bring forth a new breed of specialty shop as it has in other merchandise categories. Commenting on the situation, one manufacturer declared: "Such shops have been started from scratch only recently. Generally they evolved in the past from a hardware or furniture store whose owner elected to specialize in fireplace goods and phase out the other merchandise. Those who have undertaken to start a shop without a previous base have had a checkered success pattern. Currently, attempts are being made to franchise such specialty shops in shopping centers throughout the country as well as to install them in department stores. At present the independent dealer specializing in fireplace equipment seems to enjoy the best volume and growth potential."

But at least there is still a lively fireplace business! Its traditional form and accessories keep changing, but the basic appeal of the fireside remains changeless.

Unpainted Furniture

It is a revealing commentary of the times in 1972 that the headline of a retail ad read, "Furniture in the Nude," although what it offers is merely that basic staple of the housewares business, unpainted

362

HERE THEY ARE!

THE EMERSON ELECTRIC MFG. CO.,
ST. LOUIS, MO.   112 Liberty St., NEW YORK.

The first practical fan motor for use on commercial circuits was devised by Dr. Schuyler Skaats Wheeler. He invented the desk fan in 1882. While earlier fans were usually two-bladed affairs, this 1896 Emerson fan looks similar to its modern counterparts. General Electric and Westinghouse were some early manufacturers in this field. Today, electric fans are still a popular housewares item, with almost 10 million sold in 1970.

furniture—a term which, since its introduction, has been embellished to "unfinished" or "ready-to-paint" furniture.

The beginnings of unpainted furniture trace back half a century when, in answer to a growing demand for an extra chair or two, generally for use in the kitchen, a number of woodenware and furniture manufacturers started to supply them.

At first they were as simple as an ordinary straight-back, box-seat chair could be—and as inexpensive. But it wasn't long before customers found quite an assortment of styles to choose from: bow-backs and ladder-backs; Windsor's and fiddle-backs; even arm chairs with rockers to match.

"I remember how we used to get box seat chairs made of clear gum and poplar for $12.25 a dozen from the Liberty Chair Company, Liberty, North Carolina," Sam Salmanson, head of Salmanson & Company, New York, and a veteran in this business, recalled during the January 1972 Housewares Show.

At that time, the early twenties, the firm's name was Salmanson & Baumritter. Subsequently Ted Baumritter left to form the Baumritter Corporation.

"At the start the unpainted business was primarily an item business," Salmanson continued. "No one imagined it would develop the way it did. The chairs soon required tables to go with them...the twenty-four by thirty-six-inch size, then twenty-five by forty followed by drop leaf, butterfly and extension tables—all kinds. In fact it was those unpainted table and chair sets that gave birth to the big breakfast set business which later evolved into the even bigger tubular chrome dinette set business, like Arvin."

The first people in the unpainted furniture business to a significant extent, according to Ted Baumritter, who discussed the subject in Miami Beach in 1971 where he now lives, were William A. Stokes & Company, Pennsburg, Pennsylvania, established in New York City in 1870 making woodenware; Frank & Son Incorporated, New York; and Salmanson & Baumritter Incorporated, in that order.

Frank & Son Incorporated, furniture manufacturers, got into the unpainted business in the early 1920s and Edwin B. Frank, now Chairman of the Board of that company, recalls just how it happened. "It started with Thomas F. Delaney, then the buyer for John Wanamaker in New York," he wrote early in 1970.

> He walked into our showrooms one day and asked if he could buy our furniture without any finish on it whatsoever. It sounded rather odd, but he explained that he thought he could promote it and paint by selling it in conjunction with their well-known paint department.
>
> I recall that he bought four or six standard packages of each of about twenty-five pieces in our line, such a package containing anywhere from one to a dozen individual pieces. It was a great success and, at least as far as we were concerned, marked the start of such business. Other stores around the country immediately began selling unpainted furniture and there was such a demand that in 1927 we got out a special catalog.

FURNITURE IN THE NUDE

SPARTA
THE FINEST NAME IN UNFINISHED Furniture

CORRELATED GROUPS
LETS YOU MIX
MATCH 'N STACK
Select Hardwood Construction

SENSIBLY PRICED
Your Choice of Modern or
Early American

• WALLPAPER

• CARPET SQUARES & TILES • WOOD SPINDLES

LAUDERDALE PAINT
510 SO. ANDREWS, FT. LAUDERDALE

From top: Whether called nude, unpainted or unfinished, this type of do-it-yourself furniture is a basic staple of the housewares industry. The lower photo shows a breakfast set offered by Salmanson & Baumritter in their 1931 catalog.

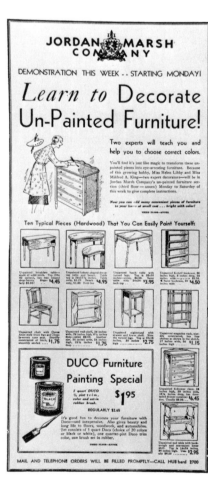

JORDAN MARSH COMPANY

DEMONSTRATION THIS WEEK -- STARTING MONDAY!

Learn to Decorate
Un-Painted Furniture!

Two experts will teach you and help you to choose correct colors.

You'll find it's just like magic to transform these unpainted pieces into eye-arresting furniture. Because of this growing hobby, Miss Helen Libby and Miss Mildred A. King—two expert decorators—will be in Jordan Marsh Company's un-painted furniture section (third floor — annex) Monday to Saturday of this week to give complete instructions.

Now you can add many convenient pieces of furniture to your home at small cost . . . bright with color!

Ten Typical Pieces (Hardwood) That You Can Easily Paint Yourself:

$4.45 $4.95 $3.95 $4.50

$1.75 $1.75 $2.75 $1.15

DUCO Furniture
Painting Special $1.95

REGULARLY $2.65

It's good fun to decorate your furniture with Duco—and inexpensive. Also gives beauty and long life to floors, woodwork, and automobiles. Set consists of 1 quart Duco (choice of 20 colors or black or white), one quarter-pint Duco trim color, one brush set in rubber.

$2.95

MAIL AND TELEPHONE ORDERS WILL BE FILLED PROMPTLY—CALL HUBbard 2700

Department stores often advertised their unpainted furniture department in 1932 and offered how-to demonstrations, an effective strategy for many housewares items.

Courtesy House Furnishing Review.

Frank & Son created quite a stir in the trade about 1927 when they brought out their Skyscraper line of unpainted furniture. It was around that period when the vogue for "art moderne" furniture and furnishings enjoyed great popularity and the Skyscraper pieces were radically straight-line and angular in design.

Another large firm in the unpainted furniture business is S. J. Bailey & Sons Incorporated, Clarks Summit, Pennsylvania, manufacturers of the Master-Craft line. For many years until his death in 1967 John E. Postley in New York was the exclusive and highly successful sales representative of this factory. In fact he was instrumental in putting Bailey into this business. In the 1930s Postley was in business with his father, Charles, a manufacturers sales rep in New York. At the time folding wooden clothes dryers, the kind constructed primarily of wooden dowels, were very popular and the Postleys were looking for a factory that could make them.

"We had been given the name of a man in Nicholson, Pennsylvania who made things of that kind, and in 1927 John and I drove down there to see him," Mrs. Gertrude Postley said in 1972 in recalling the incident. "When we asked about him at a gas station we were told he had gone out of business. But the attendant suggested we try a shop nearby run by Sam Bailey. The business was started in 1910, he told us, making such things as bushel crates and truck slats. When we got there we found him making shipping crates for live chickens. Those are also made primarily of wooden dowels and John made a deal with him. That's how the business started."

Presently Bailey was also making door racks, ironing boards, and unpainted furniture—of sorts. "Chicken crates, of course, can be made of almost any kind of scrap lumber filled with knots," Mrs. Postley went on. "And as we began to get into furniture the preponderance of knots soon got to be something of a standing joke as well as a problem."

In 1972 it was generally agreed in the trade, the unpainted furniture business had become bigger and better than ever. There are no industry statistics, but informed "guestimates" place it at around $100 million at retail. However, the department store no longer enjoys the lion's share of this business as it once did. One hears the usual explanations for the change—mounting costs of warehousing and delivery; lack of display space; inability to get proper help, etc. Certainly the specialized attention customers formerly received in buying unpainted furniture in department stores has all but disappeared.

Since World War II, this vacuum they left was—and continues to be—filled by others. There are now numerous stores—and even chains—that specialize in this merchandise; it is featured by paint stores and in lumber yards; in the do-it-yourself shops and by the mail order chains, to name some. In its current catalog, for example, Sears, Roebuck & Company devotes thirteen pages to ready-to-paint furniture.

Perhaps it's the casualness, the desire for greater self-expression or something in the make-up of the customers, especially the younger ones that makes unpainted furniture so appealing to them. Whatever the reason, it never enjoyed greater popularity.

Soda Syphons

"To many native New Yorkers seltzer is the wonderdrink of the Lower East Side and a source of gastronomic nostalgia comparable only to Marcel Proust's *chocolat madeleine*," wrote Nicholas Pileggi in the *New York World Journal Tribune* some years ago, adding, "It is a carbonated gestalt, an unsurpassed conjurer of half-forgotten ghetto memories, the peptic panacea which helped generations of Middle European immigrants cut through the leaden delights of Jewish cooking. The ubiquitous seltzer syphon…was a kitchen table staple in the boyhood apartments of future governors, senators and merchant millionaires…seltzer was not a luxury. It was the only palatable, non-dyspeptic, poison-free drinking water available…."

It derived its name, he explained, from the naturally carbonated water of Selter Spa near Weisbaden, Germany, where before 1750 it was considered as fashionable a drink as any cupped in Vichy or Perrier, France, or Bath, England. And the old, heavy glass, wire mesh covered syphons—specially made in Czechoslovakia then—withstood the one hundred pounds square inch pressure packed into seltzer and had, it was claimed, a life expectancy with constant rough handling of forty to fifty years.

Today those old seltzer syphons which, many will recall, often played a splashy role in Mack Sennet's comedies, are becoming largely collectors' items.

Taking the old bottles' place in recent years and doing it to an ever-increasing degree, is the modern household soda syphon designed to make its own carbonated water or other beverage. The origin of this modern convenience dates back to 1885 in London. A company known as Sparklets Limited, announced what was then a rather startling invention; it introduced a pint-sized glass bottle, reinforced with a wire mesh outer-covering and which, when filled with water, could carbonate the water by discharging a small cylinder of compressed CO_2 carbon dioxide gas into it.

In 1926 the English company formed a subsidiary in New York called Sparklets U.S.A. and began to manufacture its bottle here with considerable success. By 1929 it had added a syphon bottle with a full quart capacity. Incidentally, it used a cartridge identical with the one that would be used later for the famous Mae West Life Preservers.

Repeal of the Volstead Act in 1933 and the end of "Prohibition" helped to boost Sparklets sales sharply. In fact the market looked so attractive to a fire extinguisher manufacturer in Bloomfield, New Jersey named Walter Kidde & Company that also used CO_2, that through a subsidiary, Old Faithful Corporation, they proceeded to

This original Sparklet soda syphon was introduced by Aerators Limited, London, in 1899. It is actually an aerator bottle rather than a soda syphon as such. While the water was charged as in a syphon, it was not squirted out. Instead the top was removed and the contents poured out.

Courtesy the Hoover Company.

365

go into the soda syphon bottle business too, using the name Soda King. However they copied the Sparklets mesh-covered bottle so closely that in 1935 Sparklets obtained a sweeping injunction which put an end to their operations, at least temporarily. By the end of that year a new and different Soda King syphon appeared; a chrome-plated decorative steel shell replaced the wire mesh covering and Kidde was now in the business to stay.

Just before the outbreak of World War II production facilities had reached a point where the company produced 40 million gas cartridges annually.

It was at that time when Britain was already being threatened by Nazi Germany, that the English company approached the Knapp-Monarch Company, St. Louis, with the idea of selling Sparklets U.S.A. It wanted to convert the dollars it had invested into desperately needed compressed gas cylinders for the military emergency its country faced. Knapp-Monarch bought the American business, all the proceeds being used to buy the cylinders here for shipment to England. Hoover, of course, bought Knapp-Monarch in 1969 and has continued in the soda syphon business.

Household Products from Hamilton Cosco

"Had you been in Clarence Hamilton's room at the Pennsylvania Hotel (now the Statler Hilton) in New York that spring day back in 1945, you would have seen practically every important local housewares buyer drop by," related *Home Furnishings Daily's* column, "If You Ask Me," on May 26, 1969, adding, "They came, eagerly, and with good reason." It went on:

> Clarence, now chairman of the board and chief executive officer of Hamilton Cosco Incorporated of Columbus, Indiana, at that time represented a small firm owned by his family called the Columbus Specialty Company, established in Columbus, Indiana, in 1935. Like all other metal fabricators it was deeply engaged in war work. But Clarence, along with his father and brothers, had been looking ahead to the postwar period and developed some new products certain to make every stock-starved housewares merchandiser practically drool with anticipation....

Outstanding among the new items was a metal kitchen step stool that was shipped knocked down and retailed for one dollar. It was the first of a full line of such stools and related items for which the company would soon become well-known, and the volume of business, Clarence wrote, was beyond anything ever imagined.

By the time the company had reached its twenty-fifth anniversary in 1960 it had also passed the $25 million mark in annual sales. By that time too it had five well-established product lines: it was the leading manufacturer of household stools, utility tables and serving carts, and metal juvenile furniture; one of the two leading makers of folding bridge furniture and had an appreciable share of the office chair market. In that year too the Cosco Business Furniture Division was formed.

366

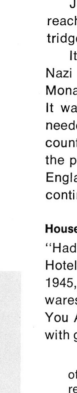

Development of the first all-metal kitchen step stool played an important role in the growth of Hamilton-Cosco Inc. As of 1972, it estimates that it has produced about 22 million household stools since the first in 1945.

In addition to its main plant in Columbus, Indiana, it has a plant in Weirton, West Virginia, and one in Gallatin, Tennessee, built when the Business Furniture Division was formed. The company's policy of expansion and growth through acquisition inaugurated in 1964 has resulted in the following additions:

1964—Acquired the Cal-Dak Company (housewares), of Colton, California, and Little Rock, Arkansas. Moved into the Columbus plant in 1968 and liquidated 1971.

Acquired Norcor Manufacturing Company (business furniture), Green Bay, Wisconsin. Moved to Gallatin plant, 1965.

1967—Acquired Harper J. Ransburg Incorporated (housewares), Indianapolis, Indiana.

Acquired National Blenders Incorporated (electric housewares), Alhambra, California. Liquidated, 1970.

Acquired Tucker Manufacturing Corporation (plastic housewares), Leominster, Massachusetts, and Arlington, Texas.

1968—Acquired Master Metal Products Incorporated (housewares), Buffalo, New York. Moved into Ransburg plant, 1969.

1969—Acquired Tyndale Incorporated (home furnishings), New York City and Philadelphia, Pennsylvania.

Acquired Sunset Lamp Corporation (home furnishings), Los Angeles and Glendale, California.

1970—Acquired Sunlighting Systems Incorporated (home furnishings), Gaithersburg, Maryland.

1971—Acquired Globe-Wernicke Company (business furniture), Toledo, Ohio. Moved into Gallatin plant, 1971 and 1972.

The Gourmet Craze

The Great Depression of the 1930s suddenly changed things for millions of Americans. One of the changes was a big increase in home entertaining, obviously much less costly than going "out on the town" for an evening as so many had become accustomed to doing.

The realization that entertaining at home could really become a special occasion also launched a wonderful merchandising opportunity for the housewares business, one which it has taken full advantage of. Today the marketplace abounds with an almost endless assortment of convenient and colorful—one might even say glamorous—accessories for entertaining at home. Many stores, often even those that have no regular housewares department, have set up special shops or boutiques where such merchandise is featured. And now that the interest in gourmet cooking and sophisticated serving accoutrements are at such a peak, this merchandise category continues to enjoy something of a boom.

If anyone can be said to have started the development of so-called home entertaining items or at least made one of the first most significant contributions to it, one would have to name Russel Wright, the industrial designer. In 1932 he introduced a full line of what he called "stove to table ware" of brushed aluminum supplemented with serving accessories made of the same material but decorated with natural birchwood. It was made and sold under his name and, for several years, was very well received. But eventually the rigors of the depression and intense competition brought this pioneering venture to an end. But Home Entertaining and the Gourmet Craze would become big business.

Of the many paradoxes of the 1960s none is stranger than the fact

From top: Aiding and abetting the gourmet craze, as well as lending their names to housewares products in this category were three kitchen celebrities; Graham Kerr, the Galloping Gourmet, the late Dione Lucas, and Robert Carrier.

that at a time when Americans had become more calorie-conscious than ever before, they simultaneously embarked upon a splurge in "gourmet cooking" and "exotic foods." This craze continues unabated and continues also to nourish the housewares business with a diet of lucrative merchandising.

What generated it was a unique combination of circumstances. First, as soldiers in World War II, millions of young (and not so young) Americans were exposed for the first time to strange and unusual food in foreign lands. Then followed years of prosperity, when we became infected with the "wanderlust."

At home also, Americans began to appreciate more fully their own melting pot of cuisines. A series of World's Fairs on the east and west coasts also implanted the idea of exotic foods and drinks.

Yet other things contributed to the trend. One of the earliest and most influential was the pioneer television cooking school launched in 1947 on CBS by the author and cooking authority Dione Lucas. It ran for years, with a devoted following, and initiated millions of men and women into the mysteries of Cordon Bleu cuisine. In 1969 the Dione Lucas Gourmet Center in New York was opened, featuring her own housewares specialties and a cooking school.

Cooking schools continued to burgeon on television and almost everywhere else as their devotees sought to become gourmet graduates. In 1963 a new culinary star, an outgoing lady named Julia Child, began teaching cooking skills on television. She was a hit, and "Julia Child" promptly became a household word. In housewares departments, "gourmet" was a merchandising glamour word.

Typical of the rise of gastronomical sophistication is the experience of Réné Verdon, the French chef who served in the White House during the Kennedy administration. Resigning in 1966, reputedly because he could not be enthusiastic over President Johnson's predilection for "ranch style" cooking, Verdon was engaged by the Hamilton Beach Division of the Scovill Manufacturing Company as their culinary consultant. Since then he has visited the country's leading housewares departments showing eager-to-learn homemakers how to create such delicacies as crepes suzettes, quiche lorraine, or chocolate mousse with the help of a modern blender or mixer.

In 1969 still another television contender emerged. Graham Kerr, an ebullient Australian who calls himself "the Galloping Gourmet," began broadcasting his show on six United States television stations, after a period on Canadian television.

He is now head of his own network show. He is a competent and serious student of fine cooking—"I was raised in the hotel business"—and an astute merchandiser of housewares specialties under the "Galloping Gourmet" brand name. And Robert Carrier and his Cookshops have also contributed to the gourmet trend.

Meanwhile, everyone—or so it seems—was trying to get into the gourmet housewares act. Time, Incorporated, which published the

Time-Life cookbooks, began to get so many inquiries about specialty items called for by the recipes—the Chinese wok was one—that it began selling them by mail. Columbia House, "a service of CBS," launched an international home dining shopping service catalog. Finally, the American Express Company offered a twelve-piece Revere-made Limited Edition Gourmet Cookware set of solid heavy-gauge copper.

By 1972 the word "gourmet," with all the attention and glory showered upon it during the past decade or more, had developed a rather charismatic quality and was often being used in connection with a great many products which, by any reasonable judgment, simply didn't warrant such distinction.

As far as can be determined, the use of the word "gourmet" in merchandising, aside from foods, was started about 1942 when the Pfaltzgraff Pottery Company of York, Pennsylvania, "Potters since 1811," and now a subsidiary of the Susquehanna Broadcasting Company, began advertising "Gourmet Ovenware by Pfaltzgraff." The term was apt, since the products were excellent reproductions of traditional French brown ovenware, glazed on the inside but unglazed on the outside. At that time World War II had almost ended production of metal cookware, and the demand for pottery was greatly stimulated. The brand name is still in use.

In 1949, one of the housewares tenants in Chicago's Merchandise Mart, Schiller and Asmus, Incorporated, originated an idea to merchandise the gourmet concept more widely. In addition to handling the Pfaltzgraff line, Willard Asmus, the firm's president, related in an interview that they had also begun to import the LeCreuset enameled ironware line, Vincent Savarese's line of Jenzo copper cookware (since discontinued), and George S. Thompson's line of pepper and spice mills.

"We asked ourselves 'Why not package all these things together in a colorful and attractive Gourmet Shop for the housewares departments?'" Asmus said. "We proceeded to do so. The three of us even went a step further. We incorporated a non-profit organization under the name 'International Institute of Gourmet Manufacturers.'" Since then, he estimates, about five hundred such shops have been installed in housewares departments around the country.

Corn Poppers

The "great American favorite," tradition insists, is apple pie, especially a la mode. But there are those who claim that if a survey were made in the early 1970s, the winner would be popcorn, not pie.

If popcorn isn't exactly in first place yet, the booming sales of corn poppers, now in the area of 2½ million units annually, may soon push this movie-munching morsel into first place. What's especially interesting about all this is that popping corn is one of the oldest American customs. It's said that the Pilgrims enjoyed it at the first Thanksgiving.

The Gourmet Shop at Jordan Marsh, North Miami, is a colorful array of basic utensils and esoteric specialty items.

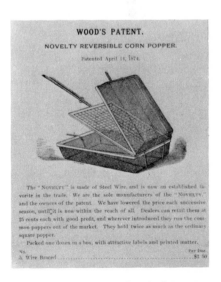

Bromwell Wire Goods Company, Coopersville, Michigan, was founded in 1819 and is the oldest housewares firm continuously in the business. One of its late-1800 catalogs shows this corn popper.

Courtesy Leigh Products.

This Butter-Upper model was introduced in 1971 by Hamilton Beach. As the heat cooks the corn, butter from the lid insert melts and drips down on the popping corn. It also has a kernel separator to sift out those that fail to pop.

The oldest known manufacturer of corn poppers is the Bromwell Products Division of Leigh Products, Incorporated, Coopersville, Michigan. Incidentally, it also has the distinction of being the oldest firm in the housewares industry, having been in business continually since it was founded in 1819 near Cincinnati as the Bromwell Wire Goods Company. A footnote in one of their late 1880s catalogs advises that "Confectioners' Poppers," holding a bushel of corn, sell for ten dollars. One of the models the company makes today is very similar to one offered in that catalog.

The first electric corn popper appeared in 1907. Although it fails to identify the maker, a magazine article that year notes: "Of the host of electrical household utensils, the new corn popper is the daintiest of them all. Attach the connection with the electric light socket, and the children can pop corn on the parlor table all day without the slightest danger or harm....The results are far better than the old way of building a red hot fire in the kitchen range and suffering from the heat while popping corn."

America may still be quite a way from the time when, as Mirro's vice-president Frank Prescott once suggested, popcorn will become a breakfast favorite. ("But omit the salt"!) Yet at the rate corn poppers are increasing in numbers and popularity, such an eventuality would surprise no one.

The Backyard Barbeque

For a great many people, cooking outdoors is, in the words of a once popular song, "Doin' what comes natcherally." For more than a hundred years the early pioneers and travelers cooked that way. In the early 1800s settlers moving west, emulating an old practice found in many parts of the world, broiled a whole beef carcass over a pit of embers on special occasions and bequeathed the barbeque idea to the rest of the nation.

From a merchandising standpoint the barbeque business really took off after World War II. It was a propitious time. The exodus to the suburbs was under way and expanding prosperity made it possible for suburbanites to enjoy their full two-day weekends. Suddenly the backyard barbeque or the patio grill were "in."

Small, folding sheet steel grills, primarily for camping purposes, were available in the 1930s from people like Poloron Products Incorporated of New Rochelle, New York, and Eclipse Metal Products Company of Eden, New York. But during that time people on the West Coast, always avid for the outdoor life, began to develop larger and better grills. Jerome S. Lippe of Leipzig & Lippe Incorporated, and one of the early entrants into the barbeque grill business, recalled in 1970 some of his experiences. During the period to which he refers his firm had represented the Eclipse Company.

In the early 1930s the Ford Motor Company went into the charcoal briquette business, and in order to promote their use it contracted with the Eclipse Metal Products Company to make two small, portable picnic grills of sheet metal embossed with the Ford name, one to retail for one dollar and a slightly larger size for two dollars. They arranged to give a box of briquettes free with the small one and two boxes with the larger one.

Cornwall and Reed, New York City, were named sales agents, but they were in the gift business and in 1935 R. L. Richardson, president of Eclipse, gave the line to Leipzig and Lippe, since we were in the housewares field.

About 1939 we became aware of the fact that out in the Hollywood area of California people were beginning to buy a large, so-called outdoor barbeque grill in place of the little conventional picnic grill. So I flew out to investigate.

What Jerry Lippe learned was that a man named Charlie Robinson was doing a nice little business making wrought iron outdoor grills to order, and that the Huntington Iron Works was marketing a line of aluminum barbeque grills with considerable success. In discussing it with Richardson on his return, the Eclipse president thought it was just a passing fad; but he agreed to design some competitive grills. Then the outbreak of World War II put an end to all such plans.

"Soon after the war the factory finally developed some impressive looking samples of grills," Jerry Lippe continued.

Richardson and I went to Chicago for a meeting with Lou Weiss, then the buyer for picnic and barbeque goods for Sears, Roebuck and Company. Originally our samples had been priced somewhat higher, but after considerable negotiation we finally got the price of one model down close to six dollars which offered the possibility of a $9.98 retail price. Weiss seemed to like the idea but was hesitant. Then Richardson, not really expecting Weiss would agree, said that if he would take ten thousand grills, he could have them for six dollars. Weiss promptly placed such an order and sold many thousand not only of that model but various others. It wasn't long before we were supplying grills to many other retailers and the popular priced barbeque grill was on its way.

Since the barbeque grill was first developed in California, it isn't surprising that the manufacturer of one of the earliest and most elaborate lines also happens to be located there, the Big Boy Manufacturing Company in Burbank. Originally in the roofing supply business, it decided to get into the barbeque grill business after World War II. R. Wade Busby, national sales manager for Big Boy, recalled some of the early days during an interview in 1972.

To the best of my recollection, one of the first people in this business was the Albert Manufacturing Company in Los Angeles. They made a kind of brazier using standard stock tank-ends for the bowl, but they didn't stay in business very long.

We had some quite different ideas about making a barbeque. In 1951 we designed a kind of cart or wagon out of heavy gauge aluminum with a compartment for a couple of jars and accessories. Our first customer was Sears, Roebuck. They sold it for about seventy-nine dollars—the highest priced model then on the market—and did very well with it.

The success of the cart concept, he said encouraged the addi-

371

From top: Marshallan Products brought out this barbeque model in 1962. It retailed for $10.95. Now growing in popularity are gas and electric powered grills, like this model from Lectra-Chef made by Permanent Mold Inc. of Tennessee.

Another Big Boy, No. 600, is said to have been the first barbeque-smoker. Retailing for $300, it was the highest priced grill ever offered and was replete with every known feature including a stainless steel hood.

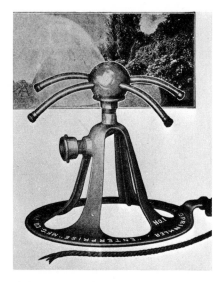

This early Enterprise Lawn Sprinkler, a staple in the lawn and garden goods section of housewares, could sprinkle an area up to twenty feet.

Courtesy House Furnishing Review.

tion of special features like end boards, work surfaces, shelves, electric lights, a motor-driven spit, as well as a stainless steel hood that converted it into a smoker as well as a grill. "I believe we were the first ones to introduce a smoker," Wade Busby added. "The first model we offered in our own line about 1953 retailed for $300."

Meanwhile the idea of rotisserie cooking added something extra. During those years the barbeque business boomed—and so did the competition. The basic item was rather simple to make before the elaborate embellishments were added and at one point, it is estimated, there were at least eighty-five to one hundred manufacturers of barbeques and grills of one kind or another. Bright, gay colored grills were to be seen everywhere, the more expensive models often having a porcelain enamel finish. Popular and imitated was the Japanese Hibachi, the small, cast iron charcoal grill or brazier used for centuries for family cooking in that country. Then there was the Swaniebraai Safari Grill using only a pierced pail and crumpled newspapers with which, it was said, a hamburger could be flash-cooked in three to four minutes.

New concepts in design and pricing abounded as newcomers entered the field and—inevitably—drop outs and mergers changed the make-up of the business.

The shake-out of conventional barbeque manufacturers was hastened by another development—the introduction of gas and electric grills. With their basic appeal of convenience and cleanliness—as compared to charcoal—and backed by intensive promotions, often by local utility companies, these soon managed to establish themselves firmly in the marketplace.

According to the Gas Appliance Manufacturers Association in Arlington, Virginia, the first outdoor gas-fired barbeque was the Char-Glo Broiler introduced in 1957 by the Joseph Del Francia Company, Los Angeles. It has since become part of Waste King Universal, a subsidiary of Norris Industries in that city.

Whether gas and electric models, for all their convenience and cleanliness, will oust charcoal barbeques seems doubtful. These models have helped increase the industry's total annual volume since their relatively higher retail prices tend to offset the constantly decreasing level of promotional grills. While accurate statistics are lacking, informed industry sources place total annual volume close to $50 million. There are now probably less than thirty manufacturers in the business with about a third of them accounting for the major share.

As to the future, some contend that the industry's long-overdue recent "shakedown" era still has a way to go; many think the business is now tending to polarize with the low end grills gravitating toward the mass merchandisers and the upper end products going to the department and specialty stores; yet others predict that constantly increasing freight and other costs may make this a regional business.

AUTOMOBILES AND CHARCOAL BRIQUETTES

How did Ford Motor Company happen to be in the business of selling charcoal briquettes for barbeque grills?

"That goes back to the days when Ford was making the wooden bow supports for the folding tops of his famous Models A and T," W. Wade Busby, national sales manager of the Big Boy Manufacturing Company Incorporated, recalled.

"After they had cut the bows and found they had a lot of hardwood scraps left, they decided it would make fine charcoal, so they developed the charcoal briquettes in order to utilize all the hardwood waste."

But no one doubts that this typically American contraption, the barbeque grill, is here to stay in the back yard…and in the housewares business.

Garden Goods

Ordinary gardening tools have always been a part of housewares. But the important garden goods business that is now part of the housewares industry first began to develop after World War I.

Formerly the average "lawn" might consist more of a luxuriant growth of closely cropped weeds than grass, and only the rich could afford to have something better. Really weed-free grass seed would not be developed for many years. Moreover, horse and other animal manure—replete with weed seeds—was then the most common form of garden fertilizer and the presence of weeds was accepted.

In a lawn, weeds are unsightly. But to the farmer concerned with maximum crops, weeds can take a costly toll. In 1868 a young farmer, Orlando Mumford Scott, returned to his home in Marysville, Ohio, after having served in the Union army in the War Between the States. At first he and his brother operated a hardware and farm supply store. Soon after, however, aware that weed-free farm seed was not available, he decided there was an opportunity for him to process and sell such seeds. The neighboring farmers provided a market.

His business grew far beyond his expectations. O. M. Scott and Sons Incorporated, a now 105-year-old firm, has grown into the largest and best-known company in the world specializing in lawn care products. In 1970 its net sales were over $67 million; its net income over $3.3 million. That is the last year for which sales figures are available because it has since been acquired by the International Telephone and Telegraph Company of which it is now a subsidiary.

In the early 1920s, Charles B. Mills, who had been hired eight years earlier as an office boy, was sent to Germany to buy bentgrass seed for the golf course market. And soon after, Paul C. Williams was hired to sell seed door-to-door. Each subsequently became president and chairman of the company, though both are now retired.

From top: The original Scott seed store in Marysville, Ohio. In 1924, as this window display shows, stores had little more than enamelware with which to promote outdoor cooking. Then, a goat-drawn lawn mower from England in 1888. Finally, what is said to be the first English mower, circa 1825.

Second from top, courtesy House Furnishing Review.

From top: A unique early model of a power lawnmower. Judging from the handles, it was a walk-behind, reel-type mower powered by an old-fashioned steam engine. The reel-type power mower in the lower photo had wooden wheels. The first power mower in this country was developed by Colonel Edwin George, who used the gasoline motor from his washing machine. In 1919 he marketed his development by forming the Moto-Mower Company. After World War II when steel for civilian goods was still in short supply, manufacturers began to produce a rotary blade mower since it required less steel than the reel-type machines shown above.

Courtesy The Outdoor Power Equipment Institute.

374

The lawn seed business had an important turning point in 1924. Oscar Webber, then president of the J. L. Hudson Company department store in Detroit, was so impressed with the lawn grass seed Scott produced he decided that it should be carried in his store. "It sounds strange now," Paul Williams recalled, "but Mr. Scott was reluctant to sell Hudson's because he did not want his business to get into the clutches of those wicked department store people!" At any rate, John Henry, then Hudson's very well-known housewares buyer, was the first retailer to place an order for Scott seed and probably the first to have a full-fledged garden shop in a department store. Hudson's move was soon followed by other big merchants and garden goods or as it was often called, The Garden Goods Shop, really began to flourish.

BASIC DEVELOPMENTS FOR LAWNS BY SCOTT

1927—The publication *Lawn Care* was established in recognition of the widespread, primary consumer need for education about lawns. The first issue was mailed to five thousand homeowners. Published regularly ever since, it is mailed free on request and now goes to over two million home owners.

1928—Turf Builder introduced; the first fertilizer designed specifically to provide the special nutritional requirements of grass.

1930—The Scott Spreader introduced; the first practical spreader permitting home owners to apply fertilizer evenly and accurately.

1937—Scott began research to find a method for eliminating weeds without digging them out. In 1946 it established the first full-time commercial research organization devoted exclusively to grass.

1947—Weed & Feed introduced; it combined for the first time a grass fertilizer with completely selective chemical control for dicot weeds in lawns.

1950—Scutl introduced; the first pre-emergent, dry, lightweight, and easy-to-apply chemical control for crabgrass.

1957—The "Trionized" bonding process of chemicals perfected by Victor Renner, vice-president of Scott's research. A major advance in the new science of surface tension chemistry, it makes controlled growth performance of grass possible.

1958—Halts introduced: the first crab grass preventative completely compatible with seeding lawn grass.

1960—The Silent Scott hand lawn mower introduced; a minimum noisemaker.

1962—Windsor, a superior performance grass seed introduced; the first grass plant of economic importance to be granted a patent: United States Plant Patent No. 2,364, issued February 11, 1964.

The Thermos Bottle

Invention of a vacuum bottle—popularly referred to as a "thermos" —the double glass walls of which retain the hot or cold temperature of its contents intact for several hours, is credited to a British physicist, Sir James Dewar, in 1892. He used it to store the just discovered supercold liquified air, and the idea was given to the world and never patented. What happened next is related in *Fifty Golden Years,* an anniversary brochure published in 1957 by the American Thermos Products Company, Norwich, Connecticut:

> Dewar's German glass blower, Reinhold Burger, was a partner in the firms of Burger and Aschenbrenner, manufacturers of scientific glass apparatus. While making flasks for Dewar, they conceived the idea of a domestic vacuum flask with protective metal casing. They secured a patent in German in 1903. (The name "Thermos," from the Greek word meaning heat, was selected as the result of a contest.)

Burger...Aschenbrenner and a third man, Gustav von Paalen, formed a company known as Thermos Gesellschaft M.B.H. in Berlin for the manufacture of vacuum flasks.... When Burger and an American business man, William B. Walker, met in Berlin in 1906, Walker realized the potential sales value of the vacuum flask...in the United States.... Late in 1906 Walker was importing the "Thermos" bottles from Germany and selling it in the United States. At the same time he was securing the necessary patent rights from Burger and raising capital to manufacture vacuum bottles in this country.... A new company was organized...the American Thermos Bottle Company of New York. Its first president, Patrick F. Murphy of the Mark Cross Company, was succeeded two months later by Walker.

In its early days, the American Thermos Bottle Company used all sorts of publicity gimmicks—including this one.

When the new company started the country was in an economic depression, but it prospered so that after the first fifteen months of operation the retail price of the nickel-plated quart bottle was reduced from $7.50 to $5.75 and the pint from $5 to $3.75. Reports the anniversary booklet: "A 'Thermos' seemed always to be in the hands of men who made history. It was not only used at the White House by President Taft but throughout the world by famous explorers and adventurers of the time. One was carried to 111 miles of the South Pole by Lt. Shackelton; it accompanied Lt. Peary to the top of the world and the Col. Roosevelt expedition to Mombasa...and into the air by the Wright Brothers and Count Zeppelin."

But in the early 1920s the country suffered a serious business recession and "anxiety for the future of the business he had founded and years of vigorous activity caught up with Walker.... He died in December, 1922." His wife decided to sell the business and the Walker stock was purchased by a syndicate formed by Tobey and Kirk, investment bankers. It was reorganized as The American Thermos Bottle Company of Maryland.

The following year, 1924, it introduced its famous No. 24 pint size Blue Bottle to retail for ninety-eight cents. It proved to be something of a merchandising sensation and is said to be the turning point in the company's recovery. In 1925 it acquired the Icy-Hot Bottle Company in Cincinnati, at which time it was again reorganized under the laws of Ohio as The American Thermos Bottle Company; then as the American Thermos Products Company. It acquired the Plastene Corporation of Crawfordsville, Indiana, in 1952 and in 1955 it purchased Hemp and Company, McCoomb, Illinois.

By 1960 sales of the American Thermos Bottle Company had reached $6.8 million and in December of that year it was bought by the King Seeley Company and is now the Thermos Division of the King Seeley Thermos Company. But one thing management had apparently failed to do was to exercise the necessary diligence in protecting its trade name from becoming a generic word. It came to denote vacuum insulated bottles and jugs generally and competitors began using the word freely. So in 1958 the American Thermos Products Company brought suit against one of its most formidable competitors, Aladdin Industries Incorporated, Nashville, Tennessee, for alleged infringement of its "Thermos" trademark.

375

From top: This unique one-hand clock introduced in 1923 by the One Hand Clock Company, Warren, Pennsylvania, may have a place among the world's unusual time pieces. But from a sales standpoint, it lost time right from the start. In 1946, when this Barr digital clock was introduced, the concept had few takers.

Both courtesy House Furnishing Review.

This proved to be a protracted action which, with appeals, resulted in five trials, the latest verdict being issued on July 14, 1970. Basically all of them hold substantially that "There is sufficient evidence in the case...to show that 'thermos' has become and is now a generic term in the English language as used in the United States," so that, except for certain typographical and style stipulations, Aladdin (and others) were free to use the long-litigated word.

Today, thanks to modern plastics, Thermos vacuum bottles have never been better from the standpoint of quality, of attractiveness, or of business!

Clocks

Now, when time as well as space are about to run out, let's close with an all-too-brief glance at the clock, that product which, since its early days as a Delft blue china wall decoration for grandmother's kitchen, has become important throughout the house—and to the housewares business.

Strange as it seems to us now, most clocks in Colonial America operated with a wooden mechanism.

In 1916 Henry Warren of Ashland, Massachusetts, had perfected a synchronous electric motor, designed to "count" the waves of pulsation in alternating current and translate them into time on a clock. But there was one major obstacle. Although most power companies thought they were producing sixty-cycle electricity, actually the currents varied from 25 to 125 cycles. Henry Warren realized that only if and when the power companies adopted the idea of a standard frequency would an electric clock be possible. At that point he turned to the General Electric Company for help and the following year, 1917, GE acquired half-interest in Warren's operation.

Today the clock business, estimated to be about $300 million annually and growing, consists of many long-established firms such as the Seth Thomas and Westclox Divisions of the General Time Corporation; Sunbeam Corporation; Howard Miller Clock Company; Bulova Watch Company; Sessions/United Company; and McGraw Edison's Time Products Division. Now too, the imports have begun to pick up importantly, especially from Japan and have become increasingly important in the marketplace. A dominant share of these imports have been in the digital type clocks. While the Japanese didn't originate them, they continue to develop many interesting variations and models. Heretofore digital clock mechanisms have been of three basic types, drum, leaf and tape. Newest is the solid state, illuminated, computer-type which, as its cost is cut, will be much more widely used.

With the advent of the digital dial the traditional, two-handed clock may be losing "face," so to speak. And one Japanese manufacturer, Panasonic, has introduced an electronic clock which, at the wave of one's hand, actually announces the time. That's a clock that literally tells the time.

376

A contemporary digital, this time by Sunbeam. Traditional or digital, the clock business today represents about $300 million in sales a year for housewares.

Looking Back...and Ahead

What has been chronicled here is largely an overview of the more significant events and continuing developments which have brought the housewares industry to the place of importance it has earned in the nation's economy. Perhaps even more rewarding is the high esteem housewares has earned from the homemakers of America which it so diligently serves.

There is an oft-told tale about an unidentified commissioner of the United States Patent Office who, toward the end of the 1800s, recommended that Congress terminate the Patent Office and close it. His reason: "By now it must be perfectly obvious to all that anything and everything capable of invention has now been invented."

As one glances through the record of these tightly-packed pages and sees the almost unbelievable progress inventive ingenuity has made possible in today's housewares, one may, like the commissioner, sometimes wonder: What else is left? What more can there possibly be? The answer, quite properly, is "Everything!"

It requires no clairvoyance to predict that in only a relatively few years from now the housewares industry will abound with exciting new products not yet conceived. For today the world's technological progress and products are accelerating at an almost fantastic pace. The rate at which they are moving is dramatically—perhaps awesome is a better word—illustrated by what has happened in transportation. As Alvin Toffler reminds us in his compelling book, *Future Shock,* in 6000 B.C. the fastest transportation available over long distances was the camel caravan, averaging eight miles per hour.

Over seven thousand years elapsed before the first horse-drawn mail coach in England in 1784 was capable of an average speed of ten miles an hour. But only one hundred years had to elapse until a steam locomotive traveled one hundred miles an hour in 1880. It took only fifty-eight years more for man to quadruple that record with a four-hundred-mile-an-hour plane in 1938. Yet by the 1960s rocket planes were doing four thousand miles an hour and now space capsules are traveling at eighteen thousand miles per hour and more. "The pattern here and in a thousand other statistical series is absolutely clear and unmistakable. Millennia or centuries go by, and then, in our times, a sudden bursting of the limits, a fantastic spurt forward," he declares.

The housewares industry, being the innovative, dynamic, and competitive force that it is, will unquestionably be in the front ranks of that fantastic spurt forward. As it moves forward, its products will continue to presage and reflect the needs of America's consumers.

New concepts and configurations...new materials and manufacturing methods...changed patterns of distribution...all these things and more portend a fascinating and exciting future in the marketplace. The housewares story will reflect that excitement.

Knives and forks, pots and pans, and a plethora of gadgets and aids for the kitchen. This eighteenth-century engraving shows a cook dressed in the appurtenances of his trade. Today's cook has a much wider variety of utensils and appliances from which to choose. And the needs of tomorrow's homemaker will be even more varied and more challenging for the housewares industry.

The Bettmann Archive

Notes

Changing Patterns of Distribution

1 Hoving, Walter. *The Distribution Revolution.* Ives Washburn Inc. New York, 1960.
2 Tryon, Rolla Milton. *Household Manufacturers in the United States 1640-1860.* University of Chicago Press, Johnson Reprint Corporation. New York, 1917.
3 Tunis, Edwin. *Colonial Craftsmen and the Beginnings of American Industry.* World Publishing Co. Cleveland and New York, 1965.
4 Andrews, Charles M. *The Colonial Period of American History* (Volume I). Second Edition. Yale University Press, 1964.
5 Harrington, Virginia D. *The New York Merchant on the Eve of the Revolution.* Peter Smith. Gloucester, Massachusetts, 1964.
6 Tryon, *Household Manufacturers.*
7 *Tunis, Colonial Craftsmen.*
8 Depew, Chauncey M., editor. *One Hundred Years of American Commerce 1795-1895.* D. O. Haynes & Co. New York, 1915.
9 Dolan, J. R. *The Yankee Peddlers of Early America.* Clarkson N. Potter Inc. New York, 1964.
10 Wright, Richardson. *Hawkers and Walkers in Early America.* Second Edition. Frederick Ungar Publishing Co. New York, 1965.
11 Wright, *Hawkers and Walkers.*
12 Carson, Gerald. *The Old Country Store.* E. P. Dutton & Co. New York, 1965.
13 Carson, *Old Country Store.*
14 Carson, *Old Country Store.*
15 Carson, *Old Country Store.*
16 Mayfield, Frank M. *The Department Store Story.* Fairchild Publications. New York, 1949.
17 Hower, Ralph. *History of Macy's of New York 1858-1919: Chapters in the Evolution of the Department Store (Studies in Business History, Series No. 7).* Harvard University Press. Cambridge, Massachusetts, 1943.
18 Hower, *Macy's.*
19 Resseguie, Harry. *Business History Review.* Autumn, 1965. Harvard Graduate School of Business.
20 Resseguie, *Business History Review.*
21 Hower, *Macy's.*
22 Wendt, Lloyd and Herman Kogan. *Give the Lady What She Wants—the Story of Marshall Field & Co.* Rand McNally. Chicago.
23 Carson, *Old Country Store.*
24 Kurtz, David L. "Historical Development of Professional Selling." *Business and Economic Dimensions.* August 1970.
25 Briggs, Edward P. *Fifty Years on the Road: The Autobiography of a Traveling Salesman.*
26 Briggs, *Fifty Years.*

Evolution of the Kitchen

1 Holloway, Laura C. *The Hearthstone, or Life at Home, a Household Manual.* 1883.
2 Alcott, William A. *The Young Housekeeper, or Thoughts on Food and Cookery.* 1838.
3 Beecher, Catherine E. and Harriet Beecher Stowe. *Principles of Domestic Science as Applied to the Duties and Pleasures of Home.* 1870.
4 Holloway, *The Hearthstone.*
5 Holloway, *The Hearthstone.*
6 Holloway, *The Hearthstone.*
7 Holloway, *The Hearthstone.*
8 Holloway, *The Hearthstone.*
9 Holloway, *The Hearthstone.*
10 Peyser, Ethel R. *Cheating the Junk Pile.* Dutton & Co. New York, 1922.

Pots and Pans Plus

1 Marcosson, Isaac. *Copper Heritage.* Dodd, Mead & Co. New York, 1955.

The Bath Shop

1 (A feature story on *Mechanization Takes Command*) *Life.* August 9, 1948.
2 Wright, Lawrence. *Clean and Decent.* Viking Press. New York, 1960.
3 Giedion, Siegfried. *Mechanization Takes Command.* Oxford University Press. New York, 1948.
4 "The Washtub in the Kitchen." Bill Hennefrund. *Nation's Business.* September 1947.
5 Rosebury, Theodor. *Life on Man.* Berkeley Publications, 1970.
6 Rosebury, *Life on Man.*
7 Quoted in an article in *House Furnishing Review,* July 1933, Page 29.
8 Young, James H. *Medical Messiahs: A Social History of Health Quackery in 20th Century America.* Princeton University Press, 1967.

The Electric Age

1 Silverberg, Robert. *Light for the World! Edison and the Power.* Nann-Rein Press, 1967.
2 Silverberg, *Light.*
3 Silverberg, *Light.*
4 Gould, Mary Earl. *The Early American House.* Charles E. Tuttle Co. Rutland, Vt., 1949 & 1965.
5 Clark, Victor. *History of Manufacturers in the United States from 1607-1828.* Peter Smith.
6 Gould, *Early American House.*

From Brooms to Vacuum Cleaners

1 "Broom and Brushes. Page 667. *One Hundred Years of American Commerce 1795-1895.*
2 Tryon, *Household Manufacturers.*
3 Hoover, Frank Garfield. *Fabulous Dustpan. The story of the Hoover Co.* World Publishing Co. N.Y. & Cleveland, 1955.
4 *Electrical Merchandising,* Apr. 1, 1946.
5 *Electrical Merchandising,* February 1, 1946.

Cutlery, Can Openers and Gadgets

1 Sprackling, Helen. *Setting Your Table.* William Morrow. New York, 1960.
2 Sprackling, *Setting Your Table.*
3 Sprackling, *Setting Your Table.*
4 Curtis, George M. *A Century of Meriden.* Journal Publishing Co. 1906.
5 Himsworth, J. B. *The Story of Cutlery.* Ernest Benn. London, 1953.
6 Himsworth, *Story of Cutlery.*
7 Himsworth, *Story of Cutlery.*
8 Clark, Victor S. *History of Manufacturers.*

The Plastic Parade

1 DuBois, J. Harry. *Plastics History U.S.A.* Cahners Publishing Co. Boston, 1972.
2 DuBois, *Plastics History.*

Index

Numbers in boldface indicate an illustration of the subject mentioned.

379

383

384